T0213566

Lecture Notes in Computer Science 9512

Commenced Publication in 1973
Founding and Former Series Editors:
Gerhard Goos, Juris Hartmanis, and Jan van Leeuwen

Editorial Board

David Hutchison
  Lancaster University, Lancaster, UK
Takeo Kanade
  Carnegie Mellon University, Pittsburgh, PA, USA
Josef Kittler
  University of Surrey, Guildford, UK
Jon M. Kleinberg
  Cornell University, Ithaca, NY, USA
Friedemann Mattern
  ETH Zurich, Zürich, Switzerland
John C. Mitchell
  Stanford University, Stanford, CA, USA
Moni Naor
  Weizmann Institute of Science, Rehovot, Israel
C. Pandu Rangan
  Indian Institute of Technology, Madras, India
Bernhard Steffen
  TU Dortmund University, Dortmund, Germany
Demetri Terzopoulos
  University of California, Los Angeles, CA, USA
Doug Tygar
  University of California, Berkeley, CA, USA
Gerhard Weikum
  Max Planck Institute for Informatics, Saarbrücken, Germany

More information about this series at http://www.springer.com/series/7411

Jörn Altmann · Gheorghe Cosmin Silaghi
Omer F. Rana (Eds.)

Economics of Grids, Clouds, Systems, and Services

12th International Conference, GECON 2015
Cluj-Napoca, Romania, September 15–17, 2015
Revised Selected Papers

 Springer

Editors
Jörn Altmann
Seoul National University
Seoul
Korea (Republic of)

Omer F. Rana
Cardiff University
Cardiff
UK

Gheorghe Cosmin Silaghi
Babeş-Bolyai University
Cluj-Napoca
Romania

ISSN 0302-9743   ISSN 1611-3349 (electronic)
Lecture Notes in Computer Science
ISBN 978-3-319-43176-5   ISBN 978-3-319-43177-2 (eBook)
DOI 10.1007/978-3-319-43177-2

Library of Congress Control Number: 2016945782

LNCS Sublibrary: SL5 – Computer Communication Networks and Telecommunications

© Springer International Publishing Switzerland 2016
This work is subject to copyright. All rights are reserved by the Publisher, whether the whole or part of the material is concerned, specifically the rights of translation, reprinting, reuse of illustrations, recitation, broadcasting, reproduction on microfilms or in any other physical way, and transmission or information storage and retrieval, electronic adaptation, computer software, or by similar or dissimilar methodology now known or hereafter developed.
The use of general descriptive names, registered names, trademarks, service marks, etc. in this publication does not imply, even in the absence of a specific statement, that such names are exempt from the relevant protective laws and regulations and therefore free for general use.
The publisher, the authors and the editors are safe to assume that the advice and information in this book are believed to be true and accurate at the date of publication. Neither the publisher nor the authors or the editors give a warranty, express or implied, with respect to the material contained herein or for any errors or omissions that may have been made.

Printed on acid-free paper

This Springer imprint is published by Springer Nature
The registered company is Springer International Publishing AG Switzerland

Preface

The way in which IT resources and services are being provisioned is currently in flux. Advances in distributed systems technology have allowed for the provisioning of services with increasing flexibility. At the same time, business and academia have started to embrace a model wherein third-party services can be acquired with minimal service provider interaction, replaced, or complemented. Organizations have only started to grasp the economic implications of this evolution.

As a global market for infrastructures, platforms, and software services emerges, the need to understand and deal with these implications is quickly growing. In addition, a multitude of new challenges arise. These are inherently multidisciplinary and relate to aspects such as the operation and structure of the service market, the cost structures, the quality experienced by service consumers or providers, and the creation of innovative business models. These challenges emerge in other service domains as well, for example, in the coordinated operation of the next-generation electricity grids that are characterized by distributed generation facilities and new consumption patterns.

The GECON conference series brings together researchers and practitioners from academia and industry to present and discuss economics-related issues and solutions associated with these developments and challenges. The contributed work comprises successful deployments of technologies, extensions to existing technologies, economic analyses, and theoretical concepts, achieving its objective of building a strong multidisciplinary community in this increasingly important area of the future information economy.

The 12th edition of GECON took place in the city of Cluj-Napoca, Romania, the heart of Transylvania, the land "beyond the forest" and the home of Dracula. Built on the grounds of the ancient Roman city of Napoca, with one of the most vibrant economies, Cluj-Napoca is among the largest cultural and educational cities in the country.

Founded in 1581, Babeş-Bolyai University (UBB) is the oldest university in Romania and has a long history of education, research, and serving the local community. Currently, UBB is the largest university in the country, bringing together more than 38,000 undergraduate, graduate, and doctoral students, enrolled in 516 programs that are offered in Romanian, Hungarian, German, English, and French. The university is evaluated and ranked among the top three universities in Romania for the quality of its programs and research.

For the first time in the conference's 12-year history, we launched the call for papers of the conference around eight specific tracks as follows: Economics of Big Data; Smart Grids; Community Nets and the Sharing Economy; Economically Efficient Resource Allocation and Service Level Agreements; Economics of Software and Services; Economics of Service Composition, Description, and Selection; Economic Models of Networked Systems; Legal Issues, Economic, and Societal Impact.

Each track was led by two chairs and included a specific description for topics of interest, helping the authors to better position their contribution in the conference. GECON 2015 attracted 38 high-quality submissions, and the Program Committee selected 11 long papers and nine work-in-progress papers for presentation at the conference. These 20 papers together with an invited paper submitted by Prof. Dana Petcu and based on a very welcomed keynote lecture form the current proceedings. Each paper received between three and five, reviews. The schedule of the conference was structured to encourage discussions and debates on the presented topics. We hope that we succeeded in boosting an open and informal dialogue between the presenters and the audience, enabling the authors to better position their work and increase the impact on the research community.

We organized the contents of the proceedings according to the thematic topics of the conference sessions as follows:

In the "Resource Allocation" section, the allocation optimality problem is debated from two perspectives: the resource provider and the service user. The paper of Leonardo P. Tizzei et al. attacks the problem of the financial losses incurred by pricing models for IaaS cloud providers when applications release resources earlier than the end of the allocated time slot. The authors present a tool to create and manage resource pools for multi-tenant environments and demonstrate its effectiveness. The paper of Ovidiu-Cristian Marcu et al. handles the problem of scheduling tasks in hybrid clouds for small companies with a fixed restricted budget. The authors propose an architecture that meets the challenges encountered by small business in their systems for task scheduling and discuss the efficiency of the proposed strategy. In their paper, Dmytro Grygorenko et al. discuss cost-aware solutions to manage a virtual machine placement across geographically distributed data centers and to allow providers to decrease the total energy consumption while keeping the customers satisfied with high-quality services. They propose a Bayesian network constructed out of expert knowledge and another two algorithms for VM allocation and consolidation and show the effectiveness of their approach in a novel simulation framework. Ilia Pietri and Rizos Sakellariou tackle the problem of choosing cost-efficient resource configurations in different scenarios, depending on the provider's pricing model and the application characteristics. They analyze two cost-aware resource selection algorithms for running scientific workflow applications on deadline and with a minimum cost. Finally, Pedro Alvarez et al. propose a method to determine the cheapest combination of computing instances to execute bag-of-tasks applications in Amazon EC2, considering the heterogeneity of the resources as well as the deadline and the input workload provided by the user.

The "Service Selection" section includes the well-received keynote lecture delivered by Prof. Dana Petcu. The keynote was centered around the scientific contribution developed in a couple of European FP7 and H2020 projects as well as in a project supported by the Romanian National Authority of Research. The mentioned projects developed support platforms for ensuring a certain quality level when using multiple clouds. The paper analyzes the existing approaches to define, model, evaluate, estimate, and measure the QoS offered to cloud-based applications, with an emphasis on model-driven engineering techniques and for the special case of data-intensive applications. The second contribution to the service selection topic comes from Kyriazis et al., who present an approach for selecting services to meet the end-to-end QoS requirements enhanced with a relevance feedback mechanism regarding the importance of the content and the service. The effectiveness of the approach is demonstrated in a real-world scenario with a computer vision application. The paper of Mathias Slawik et al. presents the Open Service Compendium, a practical, mature, simple, and usable approach to support businesses in cloud service discovery, assessment, and selection. Developed within the H2020 Cyclone project, this information system offers business-pertinent vocabularies, a simple dynamic service description language, and match-making functionality.

One of the major topics of interest at the GECON 2015 conference was "Energy Conservation and Smart Grids." In this section, the team of Prof. Ioan Salomie from the Technical University of Cluj-Napoca, Romania, contributed two papers that address optimization of energy consumption in data centers. The first paper authored by Marcel Antal et al. defines energy flexibility models for hardware in data centers aiming to optimize the energy demand profiles by means of load time shifting, alternative usage of non-electrical cooling devices, or charging/discharging the electrical storage devices. The second paper authored by Cristina Bianca Pop et al. presents a particle swarm optimization method for optimizing the energy consumption in data centers. An additional paper on energy conservation has been contributed by Alberto Merino et al. Their paper deals with requirements of energy management services in short- and long-term processing of data in massively interconnected scenarios. They present a component-based specification language for building trustworthy continuous dataflow applications and illustrate how to model and reason with the proposed language in smart grids. The paper of Baseem Al-athwari and Jorn Altmann considers user preferences when adjusting the energy consumption of smartphones, in order to maximize the user utility. They show how the model can be employed and how the perceived value of energy remaining in the smartphone battery and the user's perceived costs for energy consumption in cloud-based applications and on-device applications vary. Richard Kavanagh et al. present an architecture that focuses on energy monitoring and usage prediction at both PaaS and IaaS layers, delivering energy metrics for applications, VMs, and physical hosts. They present the initial results of the architecture utilizing a generic use case, building the grounds for providers passing on energy consumption costs to end users.

The next section, "Applications: Tools and Protocols," presents three contributions that shows how grids and clouds can enhance various application domains. The paper of Soheil Qanbari et al. introduce the "Diameter of Things," a protocol intended to provide near real-time metering framework for Internet of things (IoT) applications. The authors show how the diameter of things can be deployed to implement real-time metering in IoT services for prepaid subscribers and pay-per-use economic models. Tanwir Ahman et al. present a tool to explore the performance of Web applications and investigate how potential user behavioral patterns affect the performance of the system under testing. The third paper, authored by Mircea Moca et al., introduces E-Fast: a tool for financial markets allowing small investors to leverage the potential of on-line technical analysis. The authors present results obtained with a real service implementation on the CloudPower HPC.

The "Community Networks" section brings together two contributions investigating cloud applications deployed in community networks, as a complement to traditional large-scale public cloud providers. The paper of Amin Khan et al. models the problem of reserving bandwidth for guaranteeing QoS for cloud applications. They evaluate different auction-based pricing mechanisms for ensuring maximal social welfare and eliciting truthful requests from the users. The paper of Roger Baig et al. presents a sustainability model for the guifi.net community network as a basis for a cloud-based infrastructure. The authors assess the current status of the cloud community in guifi.net and discuss the operation of different tools and services.

The section on "Legal and Socio-Economic Aspects" brings the technical models discussed within the conference closer to the business and society. The paper of Cesare Bartolini et al. describes the legal challenges incurred by cloud providers' viability, as the commercial Internet is moving toward a cloud paradigm. Given that the cloud provider can go out of business for various reasons, the authors propose several ways of mitigating the problem from a technical and legal perspective. Kibae Kim explores the ICT innovation systems of various countries with respect to the key drivers for economic growth. Given the world-wide knowledge base of patents, the paper undertakes a network analysis, identifying how the cluster of developing countries is linked with the developed ones and how the structure of the innovation network evolved during its history. The last paper in this topic was contributed by Sebastian Floerecke and Franz Lehner. In their paper, they perform a comparative analysis of the dominating cloud computing ecosystem models, identifying relevant and irrelevant roles of market players acting in the system. They define the Passau Cloud Computing Ecosystem model, a basis for investigating whether each role can be actually covered by real actors and which typical role clusters prevail in practice.

We would like to thank the GECON 2015 Program Committee for completing their reviews on time and for their insightful feedback to the authors. We extend our thanks to the administrative and financial offices of Babeş-Bolyai University and other external suppliers, who assured a smooth running of GECON in Cluj-Napoca. We also acknowledge partial support from UEFISCDI, under project PN-II-PT-PCCA-2013-4-1644. A special thanks goes to Alfred Hofmann for his ongoing support for the GECON conference series.

April 2016

Gheorghe Cosmin Silaghi
Jörn Altmann
Omer Rana

Organization

GECON 2015 was organized by the Department of Business Information Systems, Babeş-Bolyai University of Cluj-Napoca, Romania, the Technology Management, Economics and Policy Program of Seoul National University, South Korea, and the School of Computer Science and Informatics of Cardiff University, UK.

Executive Committee

Conference Chair

Gheorghe Cosmin Silaghi   Babeş-Bolyai University, Romania

Conference Vice-Chairs

Jörn Altmann   Seoul National University, South Korea
Omer Rana   Cardiff University, UK

Publication Chair

Netsanet Haile   Seoul National University, South Korea

Track 1 (Economics of Big Data) Chairs

Dan Ma   Singapore Management University, Singapore
Maurizio Naldi   Università di Roma Tor Vergata, Italy

Track 2 (Smart Grids) Chairs

José Ángel Bañares   Universidad de Zaragoza, Spain
Karim Djemame   University of Leeds, UK

Track 3 (Community Nets and the Sharing Economy) Chairs

Felix Freitag   Universitat Politècnica de Catalunya, Spain
Dražen Lučanin   Vienna University of Technology, Austria

Track 4 (Economically Efficient Resource Allocation and SLAs) Chairs

Gheorghe Cosmin Silaghi   Babeş-Bolyai University, Romania
Gilles Fedak   Inria, University of Lyon, France

Track 5 (Economics of Software and Services) Chairs

Daniel S. Katz   University of Chicago and Argonne National Laboratory, USA
Neil Chue Hong   University of Edinburgh, UK

Track 6 (Economics of Service Composition, Description, and Selection) Chair

Mathias Slawik   Technical University of Berlin, Germany

Track 7 (Economic Models of Networked Systems) Chairs

Frank Pallas   Technical University of Berlin, Germany
Valentin Robu   Heriot-Watt University, Edinburgh, UK

Track 8 (Legal Issues) Chairs

Nikolaus Forgó   University of Hannover, Germany
Eleni Kosta   Tilburg University, The Netherlands

Steering Committee

Jörn Altmann   Seoul National University, South Korea
José Ángel Bañares   Universidad de Zaragoza, Spain
Steven Miller   Singapore Management University, Singapore
Omer Rana   Cardiff University, UK
Gheorghe Cosmin Silaghi   Babeş-Bolyai University, Romania
Kurt Vanmechelen   University of Antwerp, Belgium

Program Committee

Heithem Abbes   UTIC/LIPN Tunisia
Filipe Araujo   Coimbra University, Portugal
Alvaro Arenas   IE University, Madrid, Spain
Costin Bădică   University of Craiova, Romania
Roger Baig   guifi.net Foundation, Spain
Felix Beierle   Technical University of Berlin, Germany
Robert Andrei Buchmann   Babeş-Bolyai University, Romania
Renato Lo Cigno   University of Trento, Italy
Tom Crick   Cardiff Metropolitan University, UK
Bersant Deva   Technical University of Berlin, Germany
Patricio Domingues   Polytechnic of Leiria, Portugal
Tatiana Ermakova   Technical University of Berlin, Germany
Soodeh Farokhi   Vienna University of Technology, Austria
Marc Frincu   University of Southern California, USA
Sebastian Gondor   Technical University of Berlin, Germany
Kai Grunert   Technical University of Berlin, Germany
Netsanet Haile   Seoul National University, South-Korea
Haiwu He   Chinese Academy of Science, Beijing, China
Aleksandar Hiduc   Austrian Institute of Technology, Austria
Kibae Kim   Seoul National University, South Korea
Somayeh   Seoul National University, South Korea
  Koohborfardhaghighi
Ana Kosareva   Technical University of Berlin, Germany

Boris Lorbeer	Technical University of Berlin, Germany
Cristian Litan	Babeş-Bolyai University, Romania
Rodica Lung	Babeş-Bolyai University, Romania
Leonardo Maccari	University of Trento, Italy
Roc Meseguer	UPC Barcelona, Spain
Mircea Moca	Babeş-Bolyai University, Romania
Javier Diaz-Montes	Rutgers University, USA
Syed Naqvi	Birmingham City University, UK
Leandro Navarro	UPC Barcelona, Spain
Virginia Niculescu	Babeş-Bolyai University, Romania
Ipek Ozkaya	Carnegie Mellon Software Engineering Institute, USA
Manish Parashar	Rutgers University, USA
Rubem Pereira	Liverpool John Moores University, UK
Dana Petcu	West University of Timişoara, Romania
Ioan Petri	Cardiff University UK and Babeş-Bolyai University, Romania
Ilia Pietri	University of Manchester, UK
Claudio Pisa	University of Rome tor Vergata, Italy
Florin Pop	University Politehnica of Bucharest, Romania
Radu Prodan	University of Innsbruck, Austria
Ivan Rodero	Rutgers University, USA
Sandro Rodriguez Garzon	Technical University of Berlin, Germany
Peter Ruppel	Technical University of Berlin, Germany
Anthony Simonet	Inria Lyon, France
Rafael Tolosana-Calasanz	Universidad de Zaragoza, Spain
Dirk Thatmann	Technical University of Berlin, Germany
Luís Veiga	Universidade de Lisboa, Portugal
Claudiu Vinţe	Bucharest University of Economic Studies, Romania
Dejun Yang	Colorado School of Mines, USA
Sebastian Zickau	Technical University of Berlin, Germany
İlke Zilci	Technical University of Berlin, Germany

Contents

Applications: Tools and Protocols

Community Networks

Legal and Socio-Economic Aspects

Resource Allocation

Optimizing Multi-tenant Cloud Resource Pools via Allocation of Reusable Time Slots

Leonardo P. Tizzei[1]([⊠]), Marco A.S. Netto[1], and Shu Tao[2]

[1] IBM Research, São Paulo, Brazil
{ltizzei,mstelmar}@br.ibm.com
[2] IBM T. J. Watson Research Center, Yorktown Heights, USA
shutao@us.ibm.com

Abstract. Typical pricing models for IaaS cloud providers are slotted, using hour and month as time units for metering and charging resource usage. Such models lead to financial loss as applications may release resources much earlier than the end of the last allocated time slot, leaving the cost paid for the rest of the time unit wasted. This problem can be minimized for multi-tenant environments by managing resources as pools. This scenario is particularly interesting for universities and companies with various departments and SaaS providers with multiple clients. In this paper we introduce a tool that creates and manages resource pools for multi-tenant environments. Its benefit is the reduction of resource waste by reusing already allocated resources available in the pool. We discuss the architecture of this tool and demonstrate its effectiveness, using a seven-month workload trace obtained from a real multi-tenant SaaS financial risk analysis application. From our experiments, such tool reduced resource costs per day by 13 % on average in comparison to direct allocation of cloud provider resources.

Keywords: Cloud computing · Multi-tenancy · Resource allocation · Elasticity · SaaS · Charging models · Financial cost saving

1 Introduction

Infrastructure as a Service (IaaS) providers usually follow a pricing model where customers are charged based on their utilization of computing resources, storage, and data transfer [7]. Typical pricing models for IaaS providers are slotted, using hour and month as time units for metering and charging the resource usage. For several IaaS providers, the smallest billing unit is one hour [7], which means that if clients utilize cloud resources for only 1 h and 30 min, for example, they have to pay for 2 h and waste 30 min of the remaining time.

Some IaaS providers, such as Amazon, offer a service called *spot instances* [1], which allows clients to bid for instances provided by other clients in auctions. If the bid price is greater than the current spot price for the specified resource, the

© Springer International Publishing Switzerland 2016
J. Altmann et al. (Eds.): GECON 2015, LNCS 9512, pp. 3–17, 2016.
DOI: 10.1007/978-3-319-43177-2_1

request is fulfilled. However, the utilization of these resources might be interrupted if the spot price rises above the bid price. Such interruption is not tolerable for many Software as a Service (SaaS) applications, especially for critical enterprise applications—such as those in financial sector.

For multi-tenant environments, resource waste can be minimized by managing resources as pools. In particular, large organizations can benefit from this resource pool, which would enable their subdivisions (*e.g.*, departments) to share these resources. Similarly, SaaS providers with multiple clients could benefit from such pools. A resource manager can allocate cloud resources released by a tenant for consumption by another tenant thus minimizing resource waste. Furthermore, such allocation avoids the need for provisioning new cloud resources and might accelerate the acquisition time since the allocation of cloud resources is generally faster than their provision.

In this paper we study how the reuse of allocation time slots in a multi-tenant environment can save IT costs. The contributions of the paper are:

- A motivation scenario for reusing resources among multiple tenants based on real data from tenants accessing a financial risk analysis application over a seven-month period (Sect. 2);
- Description of a tool for managing cloud resources as pools for multiple tenants, which can be executed on both simulation (single machine) and real (cloud environment) modes (Sect. 3);
- Evaluation of the tool using a seven-month period workload from multiple tenants (Sect. 4).

2 Motivation and Problem Description

SaaS applications rely on elasticity to offer a service to its clients without underutilization of its cloud resources. Elasticity becomes essential in scenarios such as when a subset of workload tasks of a SaaS application is compute-intensive. Then, the SaaS application scales-out its infrastructure to run this subset of compute-intensive tasks. When their execution ends, the SaaS application scales-in the infrastructure. Thus, the provider of such application scales-out and scales-in its infrastructure, because under-provisioning of resources might cause Service Level Agreement (SLA) violations and over-provisioning of resources causes resource-waste [13] and, consequently, additional costs to SaaS providers.

We define resource-waste as the amount of time a cloud resource is not utilized by a SaaS application after its acquisition. For instance, two clients A and B submit workflows (i.e., in this case, a set of compute-intensive tasks that are executed in a predefined order without human intervention) to the SaaS application, which provisions one cloud resource to execute compute-intensive tasks. The execution of client A workflow tasks lasts 3 h and 40 min and the execution of client B workflow tasks lasts 2 h and 10 min. When both executions end, the SaaS application does not have anything else to do in remaining time for each cloud resource so it cancels both of them and wastes 70 (20 + 50) minutes.

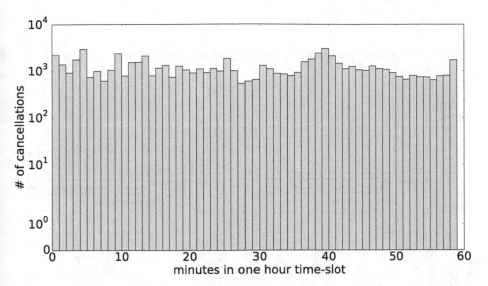

Fig. 1. Histogram of number of executions of compute-intensive tasks that end in each minute of one hour time-slot.

If several of these workflows run in parallel, resource-waste can be reduced by pooling together cloud resources.

We extracted data from a seven-month workload trace of a real cloud-based risk analysis application (further described in Sect. 4.1) to illustrate the problem of resource-waste. Figure 1 depicts when executions of compute-intensive tasks end within one hour time-slot. The closer to the zero minute the greater the resource-waste. For instance, a resource release at minute 10 of the last allocated time slot means that 50 min were wasted. This figure shows a significant number of cloud resources were under-utilized, which might increase operational costs for the SaaS provider.

SaaS applications would only be able to allocate cloud resources from one client to another if several clients submitted workflows constantly. Otherwise, the SaaS application would have to maintain cloud resources between two workflows that are far apart. Furthermore, clients have different profiles for the time they submit their workflows and for the duration of these workflows. The data from the SaaS application contains 32 clients and they submit workflows in different periods of the day and their workflows have different durations. Figure 2 illustrates the profile of four of these 32 clients. Each histogram shows the number of tasks of the workflows that are submitted by clients in each hour of a day. These charts show that, for this SaaS application, clients submit workflows in different periods of the day. Since there are several clients that have heterogeneous profile of utilization, this scenario is suitable for allocating cloud resources from one client to another.

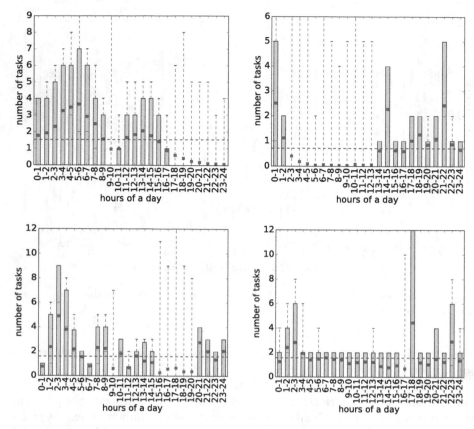

Fig. 2. Boxplots describing the number of tasks executed in each hour of a day over a period of seven months. Each plot shows the profile of one client.

Thus, the research question we address in this paper is: *Can a resource manager reduce resource-waste for multi-tenant cloud-based applications by reusing already allocated resources?*

3   PoolManager: A Cloud Resource Manager Tool

This section describes how we designed the software architecture and developed a tool, called PoolManager, to address the resource-waste problem mentioned in Sect. 2.

3.1   Overview

The PoolManager tool has two goals: (i) to reduce financial cost for SaaS applications by minimizing resource-waste; (ii) to support SaaS applications to meet SLA by minimizing acquisition time. These goals are overlapping because the minimization of resource-waste by allocating resources from one client to another might also reduce provision times of new resources. In order to achieve these goals, we designed PoolManager to lie between SaaS and IaaS providers to control the access to cloud resources. This control is necessary to create a pool of resources aiming to minimize resource-waste. Figure 3 provides an overview of our solution and defines the scope of our contributions inside the dashed square.

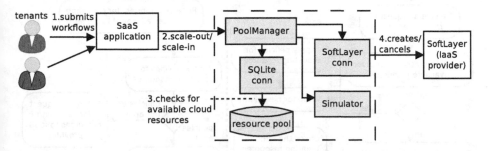

Fig. 3. Overview of the PoolManager architecture.

Tenants submit workflows to the SaaS application provider, which might need to scale-out its infrastructure to meet SLAs. Then, it requests the Pool-Manager for cloud resources, which checks the resource pool to decide whether it is necessary to create new resources. If so, PoolManager submits a request via a cloud connector (*e.g.*, SoftLayer conn)[1] for resources to the IaaS provider. Otherwise, it checks the policy for allocating resources, erases existing data of selected resources, and configures those according to the client. The number of resources available in the pool might be insufficient for the request, thus new resources might be created alongside to the allocation of existing ones.

After expanding its infrastructure, SaaS application provider will probably shrink it to reduce operational costs, which will trigger a similar flow of messages as described above. The Simulator plays the role of an "artificial" cloud connector and it was built for helping developers to explore data and create resource allocation policies, as described in Sect. 4.

3.2 Operations and Software Architecture

PoolManager has two main operations, where SaaS application providers: (i) request for cloud resources; and (ii) request to cancel cloud resources that were used to execute client workflows. Figure 4 describes these two operations using a UML activity diagram notation [15].

In the first operation (Fig. 4a), PoolManager receives a request for creating cloud resources. Then, it checks if there are cloud resources available in the

---

[1] Other cloud connectors could be created to access resources from various other cloud providers, similar to the concept of broker in grid computing.

pool. If so, it allocates available resources to the SaaS application according to allocation policies (policies are further described in Sect. 3.3). It might be the case that the number of available resources is not sufficient to fulfill the request, so it submits a request for creating new cloud resources to the IaaS provider.

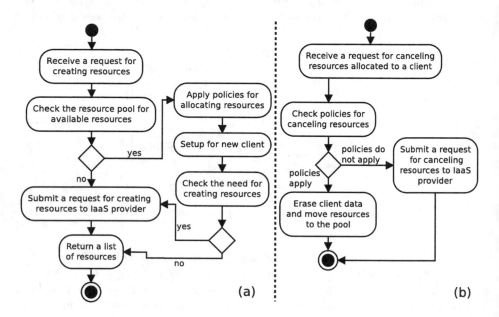

Fig. 4. Two main operations: (a) request for creating cloud resources and (b) request for canceling cloud resources.

For the second operation (Fig. 4b), PoolManager receives a request for canceling cloud resources that were allocated to a client. Then, the PoolManager checks if any policy applies, so it can later be allocated to another client. If policies apply, then all data of the previous client is erased. Otherwise, PoolManager submits a request to the IaaS provider to cancel cloud resources. In some situations, some resources are canceled, whereas others have their data erased and moved to the pool. Note that after receiving a request for canceling resources, they can be either canceled or maintained by PoolManager, but they cannot be allocated directly from one client to another.

The architecture of this solution is similar to the Proxy architectural pattern [5], because the PoolManager plays the role of a placeholder that aims to reduce provisioning time of cloud resources. In such manner, it mediates the access from SaaS applications to the IaaS provider to allocate resources released by one client to another. From our experiments, we observed reductions of 2–10 min of cloud provisioning time to a few seconds for cleaning up the data of an existing instance of a client to deliver it to another client. To perform such a process we rely on the cloud provider, in our case SoftLayer, to refresh a VM. However, additional scripts to delete data could be provided.

PoolManager was implemented using Python2.7, it has around 2.2 KLOC, and uses SQLite3 database and SoftLayer [3] IaaS provider, but other databases and IaaS providers could be used as well.

3.3 Time-Based Allocation and Cancellation Policies

There are several types of resource allocation policies for cloud [9,22,24]. We implemented two policies considering time-slots: one is related to the request for creating resources and the other is related to the request for canceling resources. Exploring the best optimization policies is out of the scope of this paper and we leave it as future work.

Both policies aim to save costs by reusing already allocated resources. In the first policy PoolManager allocates resources that are the closest, in terms of time, to be canceled. For example, if PoolManager receives a request for creating two cloud resources and it has five in the pool, the two cloud resources closest to be canceled will be allocated. We also investigated other allocation policies, including, for instance, offering resources that still have a long time to complete the hour. We observed that the most cost-effective solutions lie when offering resources near the initial of the hour or closer to be canceled. Near the initial hour has the benefit of reusing most of the already allocated hour, whereas close to the cancellation time avoids re-provisioning of machines.

The second policy aims to minimize resource waste. It defines that a resource should not be canceled if it was utilized for less than 50 min or more than 59 min within one hour time-slot. By "one hour time-slot" we mean the last of one hour time-slots of cloud resources that have been already paid. For instance, a cloud resource is created and it is utilized to execute the workflow which lasted 2 h and 45 min. Within the last (*i.e.*, the third) of one hour time-slots, such cloud resource was utilized by 45 min. The rationale behind this policy is to maximize the chances of a client to reuse an existing instance. The 50th min has been chosen empirically, which leaves 10 min before the next billing hour. Our experience has shown that such time is usually enough to cancel cloud resources even in the presence of faults (*e.g.*, temporary lack of network connection). Given that, we believe 50 min is a conservative number, though it can be easily changed in order to enhance the optimization of resources. Note that after the 59th min the resource should not be canceled, because there is a risk it is already too late to cancel it before the next billing hour.

4   Case Study: Financial Risk Analysis in the Cloud

4.1   Goal and Target SaaS Application

The goal of this case study is to assess whether PoolManager can minimize resource-waste. We used Risk Analysis in the Cloud (RAC) as target SaaS application (the application name is fictitious due to the contract between RAC provider and its clients). RAC manages risk and portfolio construction for financial organizations, such as banks and trading desks. We were provided with a real workload that was computed by RAC application. This workload describes the workflow execution of 32 clients, which submitted 74,753 tasks—including 8,933 compute-intensive tasks—over a period of 214 days (seven months). Each compute-intensive task demands the creation of eight cloud resources in order to increase performance thus meeting SLA while non-compute-intensive tasks are executed on on-premise environment.

4.2   Planning and Operation

We defined two metrics: (i) *resource-waste per day*, which is the number of minutes that cloud resources were idle per day; (ii) *financial gain per day*, which is the subtraction of the amount paid to IaaS provider from the amount clients pay to SaaS provider per day.

First, we defined resource-waste per day metric as presented in Eq. 1.

$$W = \sum_{k=1}^{T} 60 - (U_k \bmod 60) \tag{1}$$

where cloud resource-waste is W, utilization of cloud resource in minutes is U and T is the total number of times that any cloud resource was utilized by the SaaS provider. If the same cloud resource was utilized twice, *e.g.*, for executing the task of one client and afterwards of another, it is represented by two k values.

In order to assess how PoolManager influenced resource-waste in terms of time, we compared the PoolManager tool against the direct-access between SaaS and IaaS providers (hereafter called *direct-access* approach, for short). To collect resource-waste per day for the direct-access approach, we implemented a parser for the workload, which identified the beginning and end of compute-intensive tasks that demand the creation of cloud resources. Thus, in the beginning of each of these tasks, eight cloud resources would be created and when these tasks ended, resources would be canceled if we were running the real application. Since we are interested in measuring the resource-waste, the parser computed the utilization of cloud resources as the time between the beginning and the end of a compute-intensive task. Then, for each one of them, it calculated resource-waste per day according to Eq. 1.

To collect resource-waste per day metric for the PoolManager approach, we replaced its connector to a real cloud provider by an artificial one, which simulates the creation and cancellation of cloud resources, because the creation of approximately 9,000 cloud resources for such workload was out of our budget. Furthermore, such simulator enabled us to run faster the workflow (further information about the simulator below). Then, we implemented another parser for the workload that identified compute-intensive tasks and generated a script that simulates clients submitting requests to RAC application. Finally, we executed this script and stored all information related to the creation and cancellation of cloud resources into a database, which was parsed to collect the metric defined by Eq. 1.

The second metric assesses the amount of money that can be saved by pooling cloud resources. SaaS providers, such as RAC provider, must pay per usage of cloud resources that are offered by IaaS providers. Equation 2 represents how can one measure the costs of these cloud resources.

$$C_{IaaS} = \sum_{k=1}^{T} \lceil U_k/60 \rceil \tag{2}$$

where C_{IaaS} is the cost of IaaS in units of money, U represents cloud resource utilization measured in minutes, T represents the number of times cloud resources were utilized. This equation is a simplified version of the real cost, because it does not consider the cost variation according to the type of cloud resource. Only the time aspect is being considered.

In order to measure the financial benefits of pooling cloud resources from the SaaS provider's perspective, it is also necessary to measure its income. However, we did not have access to the real contract between the RAC application and its clients. Thus, we defined that the clients of SaaS application follows the same pay-per-usage model between SaaS and IaaS providers—using time slots. That is, the amount of money each client pays to the SaaS provider is proportional to the duration of workflow execution. Equation 3 defines how it is measured:

$$C_{SaaS} = \sum_{c=1}^{N} \sum_{k=1}^{T} \lceil U_{ck}/60 \rceil \tag{3}$$

where C_{SaaS} is the cost of SaaS in units of money, U_{ck} measures cloud resource utilization k to execute the workflow of a client c. N is the total number of clients and T represents the number of times cloud resources were utilized by a client c. Based on Eqs. 2 and 3, we can define the *financial gain* metric as follows:

$$G = C_{SaaS} - C_{IaaS} \tag{4}$$

Discrete Event Simulator. In order to replicate the execution of a seven-month workload in a feasible manner, we developed a discrete event simulator. When this simulator receives creation or cancellation requests, instead of actually creating or canceling cloud resources, it executes the allocation policies and stores decisions and resource related information into the database exactly the same way that would be stored if the real connector was executed. The idea is to log all request information so it can be later parsed to extract the metrics mentioned in Sect. 4.2. For instance, if a request for creating cloud resources demands a creation of a new cloud resource, then the simulator will 'accelerate' time, instead of waiting for the average provisioning time. Another example: if two requests are apart for more than one hour and there is no request between them, the simulator will cancel all cloud resources that are in the pool, because the PoolManager would not maintain a cloud resource for such a period of time.

4.3 Result Analysis

The results for the comparison between the *direct-access* approach against Pool-Manager are presented in Fig. 5, which shows resource-waste (in minutes) over the days. Results show PoolManager minimized *resource-waste per day* significantly. Both curves in Fig. 5 have an erratic behavior with peaks, which represent work days, and valleys, which represent weekends. Despite this similarity, the curve that represents the direct-access approach has more intense peaks. For all days, PoolManager reduced resource-waste in comparison to direct-access approach and such difference is even higher in the peaks of both curves. For instance, in the day 173, the direct-access approach wasted 22,424 min while PoolManager wasted 2,936 min. This is consequence of the reuse of the VMs among several clients.

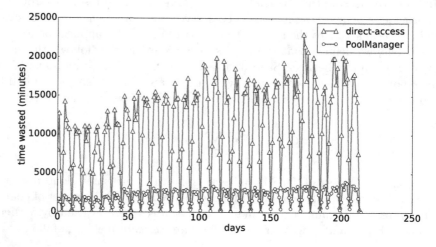

Fig. 5. Resource-waste per day for direct-access approach versus PoolManager.

Figure 6 illustrates why PoolManager minimized resource-waste as it presents a histogram of the number of times cloud resources were canceled in each minute of one hour time-slot. Note that PoolManager did not cancel any cloud resource before the 50th min of one hour time-slot, according to time-based cancellation policy. The figure also shows a peak around 50 min which is a result of the cancellation policy. An administrator having a detailed understanding of the workload and client needs could be more aggressive and move the cancellations to 55 min or even further to obtain further cost reductions, but increasing the risk of delaying the cancellation process and having to allocate another entire hour—this trade-off needs to be carefully analyzed to configure the cancellation policy.

For the *financial gain per day* metric, the results show that PoolManager saved an average of 238 monetary units per day for the SaaS provider (see the

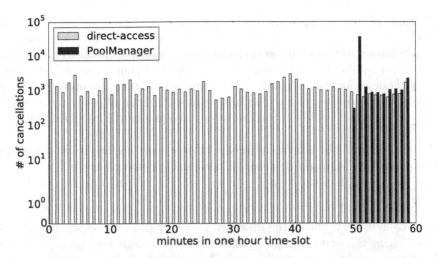

Fig. 6. Comparing resource utilization using direct-access approach and PoolManager.

blue dashed line in Fig. 7). This means that the allocation of cloud resources—according to allocation policy—from one client to another has been effectively performed to minimize cloud resource provisioning. Furthermore, cancellation policy supported cost reduction, because resources that were utilized once to execute the workflow of a client were maintained and often re-utilized to execute the workflow of other clients. From our experiments, PoolManager reduced resource costs per day by 13 % on average in comparison to direct allocation from cloud provider resources: Direct-access cost per day of 545.83 on average $(+/-285.22)$ against PoolManager cost per day of 473.45 on average $(+/-254.92)$.

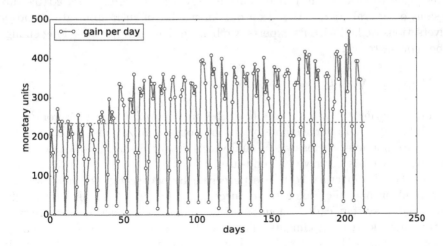

Fig. 7. Gain per day

Pooling resources minimized the need for provisioning cloud resources and, since allocation time is usually shorter than provisioning time, such approach can also contribute to reduce acquisition time thus supporting the SaaS provider to meet SLAs. PoolManager allocated around 49 % of all cloud resources that were utilized. If our assumption that allocation time is shorter than provisioning time is correct (which we observed in our experiments: 2–10 min of provisioning versus seconds for cleaning up VMs), such results can significantly reduce acquisition time.

Therefore, given the aforementioned research question, the results provided evidence that PoolManager succeeds in minimizing resource-waste.

4.4   Threats to Validity

Threats to internal validity are influences that can affect the independent variable, which in this study is the PoolManager tool, with respect to causality, without the researcher's knowledge [23]. One threat to internal validity that we identified is related to the instrumentation of this case study. We implemented two parsers to collect data and they might have bugs, which can cause erroneous results. We minimized this threat by testing both parsers and by manually analyzing parts of their execution.

Threats to external validity are conditions that limit our ability to generalize the results of our experiment to industrial practice [23]. We identified two threats to external validity: (i) RAC application might not be representative of SaaS applications and (ii) the workload sample that was analyzed in this study might not be representative of a typical SaaS application workload. Regarding the first threat to external validity, we cannot totally avoid it, but our target application is a real industry application, which was *not* developed by any of the authors. Regarding the second threat to external validity, the workload sample corresponds to seven-month of execution logs, which were generated by submissions of several clients. Based on our knowledge of such application and on conversations we had with its experts, we believe that such period is long enough to be representative.

5   Related Work

Resource sharing is a concept that became popular in grid computing [4,6,11,12,14], where participants of autonomous organizations shared computing resources among themselves. Usually this resource sharing did not involve any monetary costs perceived by end-users.

With cloud, monetary costs are perceived by end-users and therefore they are careful on how they allocate resources [22]. For instance, Shen et al. [21] introduced a system called CloudScale to manage elasticity of resources for multi-tenant cloud environments. Their work focused on resource and energy savings and explored resource demand predictions and accuracy of those predictions. Gong et al. [13] also used predictions to scale resource capacity according to applications' demands. Other resource efforts [17,24] considered dynamic resource allocation using auctions. In addition projects have been exploring resource sharing in clouds [8, 20] via the use of virtual currency.

Nathani et al. [19] proposed a scheduling algorithm for allocating virtual machines on cloud environments. The multi-tenancy aspect is explored by reorganizing allocation requests according to user deadlines. Lin et al. [18] focused their studies on resource allocation for multiple users considering the application level instead of trying to map physical to virtual resources.

León and Navarro [16] introduced an incentive mechanism for users to report their actual resource requirements inorder to save energy costs and meet QoS demands on multi-tenant clusters. Espadas et al. [10] proposed a resource allocation model for SaaS applications considering multi-tenancy with the aim to avoid under and over resource utilization.

The main difference between these research efforts and ours is that we focused on services that need to manage resources for multiple tenants considering the hourly slotted-time charging model and exclusive use of resources for each tenant. We also show the benefits of managing resource pools instead of having individuals renting resources directly to IaaS providers.

6   Conclusions

Multi-tenant SaaS applications need to meet SLA and provide low prices to be competitive. These applications might benefit from pooling cloud resources together because it enables the allocation of cloud resources from one client to another, thus minimizing cloud provisioning. We developed a tool called Pool-Manager, which manages a pool of cloud resources through configurable policies, aiming to minimize resource waste. We evaluated PoolManager in a case study which involved a real risk analysis application. Based on the seven-month workload of this application, we compared the benefits of using PoolManager against its absence. The main lessons of this case study are the following: (i) it is important to understand how resources are consumed using historical data in order to understand how much resource-time is being wasted before designing any pooling optimization policy; and (ii) clients have different resource demands and arranging the resources as pools can bring great benefits to the entire group of clients and to the SaaS provider managing the resources for these clients.

As cloud providers reduce the billing unit (e.g., Google's GCE by-the-minute billing [2]), resource waste decreases and thus the benefit of using PoolManager is minimized. Even though, PoolManager's policies can be easily adapted to such billing unit aiming to increase reuse of cloud resources in order to minimize the number of fails during their provisioning.

As future work, we will explore how the configuration of existing and new policies affect the results regarding resource waste. In particular, how to use resource demand predictions to determine, in a proactive way, the size of the resource pool.

Acknowledgements. We would like to thank Xin Hu and Miguel Artacho from IBM Analytics team for their valuable help with the application used in this paper. We would like to thank Anshul Gandhi's contribution in initial analysis on the workload, David Wu, Alexei Karve, Chuck Schulz for discussions and environment setup, and the anonymous reviewers for their comments on this paper. This work has been supported and partially funded by FINEP / MCTI, under subcontract no. 03.14.0062.00.

References

1. Amazon elastic compute cloud: How spot instances work. http://docs.aws.amazon.com/AWSEC2/latest/UserGuide/how-spot-instances-work.html. Accessed Ago/ 2015
2. Google cloud platform. Accessed Ago/2015
3. IBM SoftLayer. www.softlayer.com. Accessed Ago/2015
4. Andrade, N., Cirne, W., Brasileiro, F., Roisenberg, P.: OurGrid: an approach to easily assemble grids with equitable resource sharing. In: Feitelson, D.G., Rudolph, L., Schwiegelshohn, U. (eds.) JSSPP 2003. LNCS, vol. 2862, pp. 61–86. Springer, Heidelberg (2003)
5. Buschmann, F., Meunier, R., Rohnert, H., Sommerlad, P., Stal, M.: Pattern-Oriented Software Architecture: A System of Patterns, vol. 1. Wiley, Hoboken (1996)
6. Buyya, R., Abramson, D., Giddy, J., Stockinger, H.: Economic models for resource management and scheduling in grid computing. Concurrency Comput. Pract. Experience **14**(13–15), 1507–1542 (2002)
7. Buyya, R., Broberg, J., Goscinski, A.M.: Cloud Computing: Principles and Paradigms, vol. 87. Wiley, Hoboken (2010)
8. Chard, K., Bubendorfer, K., Caton, S., Rana, O.F.: Social cloud computing: a vision for socially motivated resource sharing. IEEE Trans. Serv. Comput. **5**(4), 551–563 (2012)
9. Endo, P.T., de Almeida Palhares, A.V., Pereira, N.N., Goncalves, G.E., Sadok, D., Kelner, J., Melander, B., Mangs, J.E.: Resource allocation for distributed cloud: concepts and research challenges. IEEE Netw. **25**(4), 42–46 (2011)
10. Espadas, J., Molina, A., Jiménez, G., Molina, M., Ramírez, R., Concha, D.: A tenant-based resource allocation model for scaling software-as-a-service applications over cloud computing infrastructures. Future Gener. Comput. Syst. **29**(1), 273–286 (2013)
11. Foster, I., Kesselman, C.: The Grid 2: Blueprint for a New Computing Infrastructure. Elsevier, Amsterdam (2003)
12. Frey, J., Tannenbaum, T., Livny, M., Foster, I., Tuecke, S.: Condor-g: a computation management agent for multi-institutional grids. Cluster Comput. **5**(3), 237–246 (2002)
13. Gong, Z., Gu, X., Wilkes, J.: Press: predictive elastic resource scaling for cloud systems. In: Proceedings of the International Conference on Network and Service Management. IEEE (2010)
14. Grimshaw, A., Ferrari, A., Knabe, F., Humphrey, M.: Wide area computing: resource sharing on a large scale. Computer **32**(5), 29–37 (1999)
15. Larman, C.: Applying UML and Patterns: An Introduction to Object-Oriented Analysis and Design and Iterative Development, 3rd edn. Pearson Education India, Delhi (2005)
16. León, X., Navarro, L.: Incentives for dynamic and energy-aware capacity allocation for multi-tenant clusters. In: Altmann, J., Vanmechelen, K., Rana, O.F. (eds.) GECON 2013. LNCS, vol. 8193, pp. 106–121. Springer, Heidelberg (2013)

17. Lin, W.Y., Lin, G.Y., Wei, H.Y.: Dynamic auction mechanism for cloud resource allocation. In: Proceedings of the International Conference on Cluster, Cloud and Grid Computing. IEEE (2010)
18. Lin, W., Wang, J.Z., Liang, C., Qi, D.: A threshold-based dynamic resource allocation scheme for cloud computing. Procedia Eng. **23**, 695–703 (2011)
19. Nathani, A., Chaudhary, S., Somani, G.: Policy based resource allocation in IaaS cloud. Future Gener. Comput. Syst. **28**(1), 94–103 (2012)
20. Punceva, M., Rodero, I., Parashar, M., Rana, O., Petri, I.: Incentivising resource sharing in social clouds. Concurrency Comput. Pract. Experience **27**(6), 1483–1497 (2015)
21. Shen, Z., Subbiah, S., Gu, X., Wilkes, J.: Cloudscale: elastic resource scaling for multi-tenant cloud systems. In: Proceedings of the Symposium on Cloud Computing, p. 5. ACM (2011)
22. Vinothina, V.V., Sridaran, R., Ganapathi, P.: A survey on resource allocation strategies in cloud computing. Int. J. Adv. Comput. Sci. Appl. **3**(6), 97–104 (2012)
23. Wohlin, C., Runeson, P., Höst, M., Ohlsson, M.C., Regnell, B., Wesslén, A.: Experimentation in Software Engineering. Springer Science & Business Media, Berlin (2012)
24. Zhang, Q., Zhu, Q., Boutaba, R.: Dynamic resource allocation for spot markets in cloud computing environments. In: Proceedings of the International Conference on Utility and Cloud Computing. IEEE (2011)

Dynamic Scheduling in Real Time with Budget Constraints in Hybrid Clouds

Ovidiu-Cristian Marcu$^{(\boxtimes)}$, Catalin Negru, and Florin Pop

Computer Science and Engineering Department,
University Politehnica of Bucharest, Bucharest, Romania
ovidiu21marcu@gmail.com, {catalin.negru,florin.pop}@cs.pub.ro

Abstract. In this paper we handle the problem of scheduling tasks in hybrid clouds for small companies which can spend only a fixed budget in order to handle specific situations where the demand is high and cannot be predicted. We describe a model with important characteristics for the resource utilization and we design an algorithm for scheduling tasks which are sent continuously for execution, optimizing the schedule for tasks with high priority and short deadline. We propose an architecture that meets the challenges encountered by small business in their systems for tasks scheduling. We describe the main components, Configuration Agent and Task Scheduler, and we analyze different test scenarios, proving the efficiency of the proposed strategy.

Keywords: Hybrid clouds · Dynamic scheduling · Task priority · Deadline · Budget

1 Introduction

Every company wants to offer the best services to its customers. A service is characterized by the execution of a task in an existing IT environment in which there is a limited number of virtual machines of different types. For the most part of the system's life, the applications are responding well during the execution of the tasks. However, at some point in time there can be an increase in demand for these services and in such cases of peak, we need to analyze the internal systems which can manage only a limited bag of tasks.

There are peak situations when a company system must deal with an increased and difficult to predict number of tasks with different priority ranks. The problem becomes complicated when the tasks are continuously sent for execution and the environment is very dynamic. In such a case we are unable to predict what will be the complete image of the entire scheduling system. We acknowledge that in these peak situations the private systems cannot handle all the tasks in order to successfully meet all the tasks' deadline.

With the arrival of the services offered on demand by different Cloud providers we have at our disposal many offers for the adjacent resources we may need in order to handle the extra workload that reaches the system in an

© Springer International Publishing Switzerland 2016
J. Altmann et al. (Eds.): GECON 2015, LNCS 9512, pp. 18–31, 2016.
DOI: 10.1007/978-3-319-43177-2_2

unplanned way. A company generally opts for a cloud provider based on both the feedback received from its internal consultants and the price of the virtual machines offered in the geographical region of the respective business.

In this paper we build an algorithm for dynamic scheduling in real time with budget constraints in hybrid clouds. The main goal is to minimize the number of tasks which exceed the deadline in the context of scheduling in hybrid clouds, having at our disposal a fixed monthly budget and considering that every task has known required characteristics like CPU, memory etc.

The problem of scheduling tasks under budget constraints in hybrid clouds needs to be approached since there are many small companies which do not have the option to invest in costly systems for an optimal scheduling, but they want to develop and do what is necessary in order to address efficiently the problem of scheduling. We need to take into consideration both the capacity of the private resources and the demand for services observed in different time periods in order to optimally schedule tasks in hybrid clouds.

We consider that the private system is composed of a very limited number of virtual machines with different types of resources like CPU, memory etc. Every week their system can handle a limited number of tasks. The problem occurs when the demand for services grows unexpectedly and the IT department does not have enough time to handle the situation properly. Thus, there is a high risk of losing customers due to the fact that the private system is not prepared for such a situation.

Although the recent research puts forward different approaches to solve the problem of scheduling tasks in hybrid clouds, we failed to identify one simple solution apt to provide an advantageous algorithm which can be implemented in several contexts and easily simulated in order to asses its profit. Thus, it is of utmost importance to offer an efficient solution for scheduling tasks in hybrid clouds for small companies having a limited budget.

The paper is structured as follows. Section 2 presentes several strategies for schesuling in Cloud with some limitations. Then, Sect. 3 descriebes our proposed model, while Sect. 4 is presenting in details the scheduling algorithm with budget constraints. Using simulations, Sect. 5 shows that the obtained results sustain the optimality of proposed schesuling algorithm. The paper ends with conclusions.

2   Various Scheduling Algorithms Strategies

The problem of scheduling a bag of tasks in hybrid clouds has been researched on many occasions and different strategies have been proposed in order to make an optimal allocation of new resources when unexpected tasks are arriving to a system which is normally not prepared for additional compute efforts.

An interesting algorithm (BaTS) for scheduling a large bag of tasks under budget constraints is proposed in [1]. BatS learns to estimate task completion time at runtime and offers significant cost savings when compared to Round Robin scheduler, at the expense of compute time. The tasks are independent of each other and can be preempted and rescheduled. BaTS uses an initial sampling phase to build a first VM allocation and after a monitoring interval it refines the results. All this effort is made in order to give the user guidance for choosing between Cloud offerings, using an economic model for resource utilization.

In [2] an extension of the BaTS algorithm is researched to give estimates for budget and makespan for different scenarios and finally the user executes the schedule selected within the given budget. BaTS work is useful when we do not know a-priori task execution time. However many systems are in good knowledge of their tasks average execution time, like in our approach.

Tail-Phase optimization for BaTS is added in [3] with the main idea to use the idle machines in the tail phase and to decide which tasks are to be replicated based on task execution time information saved during the execution. BaTS learns runtime distribution properties of the bag of tasks for the considered cloud offerings. In this paper research it is proven that BaTS gives the user freedom in choosing between optimizing costs or improving execution time for a given bag of tasks, using the total number of tasks and the price of the VMs. It does not considers the machine utilization. The results are enhanced for users who can increase their budget and improvement exists in minimizing the makespan.

Preemptive tasks characterized by memory, CPU and data transmission requirements are considered to be scheduled in hybrid clouds having budget constraints in [4] and a binary integer program is formulated with the goal to deploy a fixed number of applications (having a fixed number of tasks and a specific deadline) while minimizing the total execution cost. The algorithm takes into consideration different VM instance types with parameters like CPU, memory and price. The authors acknowledge that in the hybrid setting the solution given has rather a poor performance and invite the users to develop custom heuristics.

HICCAM (Hybrid Cloud Construction and Management) project is proposed in [5] in order to investigate the design of software applications and algorithms for scheduling in hybrid clouds and it focuses on the optimization problem of allocating resources in both private and public infrastructures. This model is considering non preemptive workloads with a hard deadline with characteristics like CPU, memory and network bandwidth. It takes into consideration data transmission speeds and data locality during the scheduling process.

CAMTH (Cost optimal algorithm for multi-QoS constraints for Task Scheduling in Hybrid Cloud) model and algorithm are proposed in [6], considering three steps: private cloud scheduling, provider selection and public cloud scheduling. It supports security and reliability for QoS (Quality of Service) constraints. This model considers jobs consisting of many tasks; a task has a few characteristics like deadline, workload, data size which impact the data transmission and execution cost, different resource slots with compute power, price, storage cost, input and output data costs, network bandwidth, estimated execution time and estimation of VM finish time. In different experiments CAMTH is compared with FIFO (first in first out), Greedy and an efficient heuristic scheduling algorithms.

A hybrid algorithm for workflow scheduling is proposed in [7] in order to reduce the CPU idle time and to ensure a good load balancing. This raises a general problem of reducing wasted resources when scheduling in hybrid clouds. A technique to ensure the QoS using the reputation of the offered resources is analyzed in [8] and a reputation guided genetic algorithm is build for scheduling independent tasks in inter cloud environments. Cost efficient scheduling heuristics for deadline constraint workloads are proposed in [9], taking into account computational and data transfer costs. There are three components, a public cloud scheduler when given runtime of the VM types are available and given data set size while taking into account the cost for execution and transferring data, a private cloud scheduler and a hybrid cloud scheduler to decide.

A family of heuristics for BoT scheduling are defined in [10] and consists of two phases: task ordering and task mapping. The authors propose an algorithm that implements the Contract Net Protocol, a task sharing protocol where the collection of nodes is the contract net and each node can be a manager or a contractor. The heuristics consider unordered, ordered by size large to small or small to large tasks and a few task mapping policies like Random, maximum expected remaining allocation time, Maximum current remaining, the same with the minimum order. It does not take into consideration neither the budget nor makespan minimization. When dealing with scheduling problems in practice there are a number of general proposed procedures for deterministic scheduling [11]. The following techniques are heuristics so they do not guarantee an optimal solution but rather reasonably good solutions: Dispatching Rules: Service in Random Order, First Come First Served; Composite Dispatching Rules; Local Search: Simulated Annealing and Tabu-Search. There are two types of Heuristics: constructive (starting without a schedule but building one in time) and improvement (starting with a complete schedule and trying to obtain a better one by updating the previous) [11].

Because most of the scheduling problems in the real world are NP-hard, it is difficult to find an optimal solution just using a single VM resource. In practice, most systems have a very high utilization so investing in adjacent resources just for the sake of the scheduling problem is not taken into consideration because of the low budget. Recent research approaches are considering different aspects when trying to solve the BoT scheduling problem when dealing with hybrid clouds. Task characteristics like priority, arrival rate, execution time, deadline or data size input or output constraints are important and mainly considered in the studied papers. In practice we need simple algorithms which can be implemented easily based on different task patterns. Having all of these options in mind when designing a solution for a practical scheduling will give a better chance for modeling the system in order to apply some heuristics based on a possible input of the problem.

3   Model Description of the Problem

We will further present you a mathematical model that will be considered in solving our scheduling problem and we describe the notations that we use in this paper. We define two participants of the hybrid clouds, Tasks (T) and Virtual

Machines (VM), and we describe the most important properties that we consider to be used in the developed algorithm presented in this paper. We acknowledge that in the real systems there may be other properties that can influence the scheduling problem and we specify that such properties are not considered.

A task has the following definition:

$$T_j = (Type_j, TaskReq_j, e_j, d_j, w_j, input_j, output_j) \tag{1}$$

where $Type_j$ is the type of a task, basically an unique name which describes its resources, role and execution time; $TaskReq_j$ are requirements of the task: $TaskReq_j = \{CPU_j, Memory_j\}$; e_j represents the date time when the task execution is completed; d_j represents the deadline of the task expressed as a date time; w_j is a priority index and its value ranges in a scale of 1 to 10, for example it can be LOW=1, MEDIUM=5, HIGH=10; $input_j$ is the size of data input the task needs to process when the execution of the task begins; $output_j$ is the size of the data output that the task produces after its execution.

A Virtual Machine has the following definition:

$$VM_i = (VMType_i, CPU_i, Memory_i, Bandwidth_i, VMPrice_i) \tag{2}$$

where $VMType_i$ is the type of the VM and it is basically a name hiding the resources offered. We assume that the public cloud providers offer similar VMs like those provided by the private data center; $VMPrice_i$ is the price of a VM expressed in units per hour, for example 1 u for one hour.

A task will be mapped only to a VM_i which corresponds to at least its characteristics described by $TaskReq_j$. The private data center offers a limited number of VMs with different characteristics $VMType_i$ and these resources are offered at no extra cost. The budget B is limited for a fixed period (a number of days) and is expressed in units, for example $B = 1000u$ for seven days. We do not have restrictions to retain a part of the budget for a specific task or period of the day. Our goal is to minimize the number of tasks for which the execution time exceeds the deadline, especially those with higher priority, in the given budget, as defined by the Eq. (3).

$$\min \left\{ \sum_{d_j - e_j < 0} j \right\}, \quad B - fixed. \tag{3}$$

4   Scheduling Algorithm with Budget Constraints

The first steps to take before implementing a strategy for a hybrid cloud computing is to understand the current state of our own private data center. After careful analysis we have to determine the following architectural and model elements: describe the current infrastructure in terms of VM types and resources they offer ($VMType$); give each task a priority, a type and check its requirements ($w_j, TaskReq, Type \leftarrow j$); save the average execution time for each task and the

VM type used for scheduling (E_{ji}); create a database to save the current state that will be used later for scheduling. We acknowledge the fact that a task can be executed on different VMs based on its characteristics and this could influence the execution time in some cases.

4.1 Dynamic Scheduling Algorithm

In every moment tasks can arrive in the system and we need to correctly schedule each one so that the number of tasks that exceeds the deadline is minimized. We cannot know how many tasks (and their deadline) will arrive at some point and it is difficult to predict the number of extra resources we need to acquire from the public cloud in order to reach our goal. Scheduling tasks in the hybrid clouds raise two major problems: the first problem is to estimate at some point in time the total number of extra resources needed in order to satisfy each task's deadline, and this is equivalent to the current need for on-demand public cloud VMs we need to acquire; the second problem is to make a good choice for what task to schedule first and to which VM from either private or public cloud and what task characteristics to consider when scheduling. Both problems will be translated into decisions based on the bag of tasks arrived in the task's queue.

To resolve the first problem we propose a Configuration Agent (CA) that will have the role to inspect all the tasks currently scheduled or not, but with their work execution not completed, and to calculate the configuration of necessary public VMs in an optimal estimation. The CA runs based on a configuration time (a few seconds), it calculates the list of extra VMs it needs to acquire from the public cloud and finally it delegates the role of acquiring the VMs to separate services developed to this end. We, therefore, present the pseudo-code of the algorithms executed by the CA. The following notations are used: T is the list of tasks not scheduled or not fully executed; T' is the list of tasks not scheduled; N is the list of available private VMs; M is the list of available public VMs; B is the budget; q is a constant/configuration parameter; m is a map with the estimated execution time for each task type; L is a list of VM types available in the public clouds; L' is a list of required VMs computed at previous configuration.

CA Calculate Configuration Needed

```
Required: T, N, M, B, q, m, L.
begin
  sort T by w=(deadline-currentTime-estimatedExecution)*priority
  initialize private VMs start time with the current time
  sort VMs by CPU, Memory and price
  Run Tasks scheduling simulation algorithm
  Obtain a list of tasks with the deadline exceeded
  Keep the tasks where arrivalTime+estimatedExecution <= deadline
  Every task can be scheduled to a VM from L
  Calculate the number of VMs to acquire for each VMType
  return a List of necessary VMs to allocate from the public cloud
end
```

We can further try to reach a better schedule by giving a second chance to the configuration agent by activating the phase described by the algorithm Check Reconfiguration and Relaunch.

CA Check Reconfiguration and Relaunch

```
Required: L', q.
begin
 calculate c = T/q
 if L' is not empty and c>0
  decrease c by one
  Run Calculate Configuration Needed
  update L'
 return L', a list of extra VMs to allocate from the public cloud
end
```

We further present the Tasks Scheduling Simulation algorithm that is used by the CA.

CA Tasks Scheduling Simulation

```
Required: T, N, M, m, B.
begin
 initialize an empty list of tasks with deadline exceeded, TD
 for each task j in T
  bestStartTime = null
  bestVM = null
  for each VM i in M
   if tasks requirements are covered by VM CPU, Memory, Storage
    vmRule = vmStartTime + taskEstimatedExecution - vmEndTime
    if vmRule < 0
     if bestStartTime is null
       bestStartTime = vmStartTime; bestVM = VM
     else if bestStartTime > vmStartTime
       bestStartTime = vmStartTime; bestVM = VM
  endfor
  for each VM i in N
   if tasks requirements are covered by VM CPU, Memory, Storage
    if bestStartTime is null
      bestStartTime = vmStartTime; bestVM = VM
    else if bestStartTime > vmStartTime
      bestStartTime = vmStartTime; bestVM = VM
  endfor
  if bestVM not null
   save task schedule simulation on bestVM
   update task execution time=bestVmStartTime+taskEstimatedExecution
   update bestVmStartTime = task execution time
   if task execution time > deadline
    add task to TD
```

```
  else
    add task to TD
  endfor
  return TD
end
```

To resolve the second problem we propose a Task Dispatcher Scheduler (TDS) that will have the role to schedule all the tasks arrived but not yet proposed for execution. TDS has two components: the first one is a simple listener for new tasks and has the role of saving and proposing for execution each new task arrived (Dispatcher), while the second one is the Scheduler component and it will run based on a configuration time (few seconds but less than the CA parameter). We, therefore, present the pseudo-code of the algorithm executed by the TDS.

TDS Tasks Scheduling

```
Required: T', N, M, m.
begin
 sort T' by w=(deadline-currentTime-estimatedExecution)*priority
 initialize private VMs start time with current time
 sort VMs by CPU, Memory and price
 for each task j in T'
  scheduled = false
  for each VM i in M
   if tasks requirements are covered by VM CPU, Memory, Storage
    vmRule = currentTime + taskEstimatedExecution - vmEndTime
    if vmRule < 0
     schedule task j on VM i
     update VM i not available
     scheduled = true; break
  endfor
  if scheduled is true
   update M; continue
  for each VM i in N
   if tasks requirements are covered by VM CPU, Memory, Storage
    schedule task j on VM i
    update VM i not available
  endfor
  update M and N
  if M is empty and N is empty
   break
 endfor
end
```

4.2 Scheduling System Architecture

We further illustrate in Fig. 1 the architecture for dynamic scheduling in hybrid clouds, consisting of the following components: the task queue being the input of the system; the TDS component having the role of saving and scheduling each task according to the proposed algorithm; the CA component with its role to calculate the configuration of extra VMs to be acquired from the public cloud; the private and public cloud VMs available for scheduling; the DB database to persist the tasks information and VMs configuration.

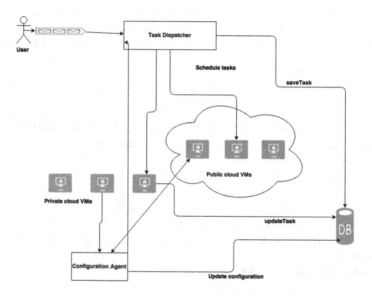

Fig. 1. System components and main events

5   Scheduling Test Scenarios and Analysis of the Results

In order to show the manner in which the algorithm works for the considered architecture we have implemented a set of services, for simulation purpose, based on Java technologies. We have built a database with the following tables:

- *Tasks* table contains information on the scheduled tasks such as type, priority, deadline, resources required, arrival and execution time;
- *Vms* table contains information on the available VMs in the private and public cloud;
- *TasksSched* table contains the schedule information of the tasks such as task identifier, VM name and start time of the execution;
- *TasksEstimates* table contains the average execution time for each task type, initially populated with an estimated execution time values.

Table 1. Private cloud VMs and resources

Name	CPU	Memory	Price	Storage price	Bandwidth price	Instances
Small	1	1024	0	0	0	2
Medium	2	1024	0	0	0	1
High	4	4096	0	0	0	1

We describe the Virtual Machines and the tasks that we have considered in our test scenarios (Table 1).

Every private VM is backed by a similar public VM. We consider that the number of the VMs that can be acquired in the public cloud is unlimited, so this should not influence our tests (Table 2).

Table 2. Public cloud VMs and resources

Name	CPU	Memory	Price	Storage price	Bandwidth price	Instances
Small	1	1024	1	0.01	0.005	∞
Medium	2	1024	2	0.02	0.005	∞
High	4	4096	4	0.02	0.01	∞

We have considered tasks with different priorities and we define multiple types in order to restrict the execution of a task to different VMs based on the task requirements like CPU, Memory (Table 3).

Table 3. Task types and requirements

Type	Priority	CPU	Memory	Execution estimate	Deadline (Random)
1	1	1	1024	5 s	100–150 s
2	1	2	1024	6 s	550–600 s
3	5	1	1024	10 s	250–300 s
4	5	2	1024	12 s	400–500 s
5	10	1	1024	15 s	550–600 s
6	10	2	1024	20 s	350–400 s
7	10	4	4096	25 s	550–600 s

All the tasks can be executed in both private and public cloud VMs. There are tasks having their execution restricted to some VMs, for example the task with the types 2, 4 and 6 can be executed only on *medium* or **high** VMs.

We run multiple tests considering the following distribution of tasks (Table 4):

Table 4. Tasks distribution scenarios

Type \ Count	300	600	900	1200	1500	1800	2400	3000
1	20%	25%	40%	30%	35%	50%	40%	40%
2	20%	25%	20%	25%	20%	5%	20%	20%
3	20%	20%	10%	10%	20%	15%	10%	10%
4	20%	20%	10%	10%	15%	5%	10%	10%
5	10%	5%	10%	20%	5%	20%	10%	10%
6	5%	5%	5%	0%	5%	5%	5%	5%
7	5%	0%	5%	0%	5%	0%	5%	5%

When scheduling, in practice, it is important to understand what is the distribution of tasks that a system normally handles. We have considered different patterns for a total number of tasks from 300 to 3000. We have executed each simulation considering our approach where the CA is sorting the list of tasks T by $w = (deadline - currentTime - averageExecutionTime) * priority$. We have configured CA to run every three seconds and the TDS to run every second. We have configured the parameter q to be equal 20. Every 2 seconds we have calculated the tasks' average execution time that will be used by the CA task scheduling simulation algorithm.

The results are very promising, enabling us to reduce the number of tasks exceeding the deadline to zero. For the considered test cases we present the consumed budget, necessary to obtain the perfect minimization (Table 5).

Table 5. Budget consumed for public VMs

Budget \ Total	300	600	900	1200	1500	1800	2400	3000
500	13	26	43	98	35	56	121	188

Load balancing of tasks is good in every case, being ensured by the algorithm, as we can see from Fig. 2.

We have considered a Special Test with Multiple Peaks and we have chosen a tasks' distribution with multiple peaks as illustrated in Fig. 3. We send three times the same amount of tasks respecting the distribution proposed. The total number of tasks scheduled is 26250 and is executed in a time interval of 1890 seconds The reason for choosing this test configuration is to asses the performance of CA and TDS components in a scenario as realistic as possible.

We repeat the test three times, the first one considering the tasks are ordered by the proposed weight w, the second one considering the tasks are ordered by $w = estimatedExecutionTime$ and arrival date, the third one considering the

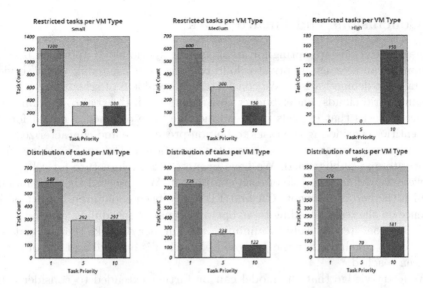

Fig. 2. Load balancing. (Color figure online)

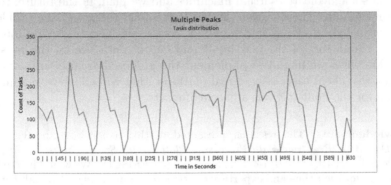

Fig. 3. Large bag of tasks.

tasks are ordered by $w = priority$ and arrival date. The results of the tests, considering the proposed approach, shortest execution first and respectively order by priority, are the following:

- budget consumed is 1513 u, 1998 u and respectively 1597 u;
- total number of tasks with deadline exceeded is 9, 37 and respectively 14;
- the total number of seconds representing the delay in meeting the deadlines is 97, 331 and respectively 127.

We observe the fact that the consumed budget in the executed test scenarios is not always in the same range and we conclude that it depends on the manner in which the tasks are ordered, both for scheduling and for its simulation.

6 Conclusions and Future Work

Many organizations are opting for an attractive hybrid cloud approach because a company can leverage its private cloud resources but use public cloud services when a peak demand arises. We considered the problem of scheduling a bag of tasks in hybrid clouds, under budget constraints, with the goal to minimize the number of tasks that exceeds the deadline. We have outlined a model for the main entities considering the tasks to be non-preemptive and characterized by a type, priority and resource constraints for execution and virtual machines from the private and public cloud. We have proposed an architecture for scheduling and we have defined the role of each component. We observed that the manner in which the two components CA and TDS have been configured has a positive influence on the results leading to an optimal dynamic scheduling. Thus, in view of the our goal, respectively to minimize the number of tasks that exceeds the deadline, we conclude that the proposed algorithm is optimal and the objective has been reached.

We acknowledge that the model can be further extended to consider other characteristics such as tasks that are restricted to run only in the private cloud or only on some dedicated virtual machines and we plan, in the future, to take these elements into consideration. We further intend to extend the problem of scheduling in hybrid clouds under budget constraints also by taking into consideration the impact of the task input and output data size on the consumed budget. Moreover we intend to implement the proposed architecture and algorithm in a real client case, using a real platform, that will allow us to adjust the algorithm for the fault-tolerant adjacent impacts.

Acknowledgements. The research presented in this paper is supported by the project *DataWay: Real-time Data Processing Platform for Smart Cities: Making sense of Big Data*, PN-II-RU-TE-2014-4-2731 founded by UEFISCDI. We would like to thank the reviewers for their time and expertise, constructive comments and valuable insight.

References

1. Oprescu, A.-M., Kielmann, T.: Bag-of-tasks scheduling under budget constraints. In: 2010 IEEE Second International Conference on Cloud Computing Technology and Science (CloudCom), Indianapolis, IN, 30 November–3 December 2010, pp. 351–359. IEEE (2010). Print ISBN: 978-1-4244-9405-7
2. Oprescu, A.-M., Kielmann, T., Leahu, H.: Budget estimation and control for bag-of-tasks scheduling in clouds. Parallel Process. Lett. **21**, 219–243 (2011). doi:10.1142/S0129626411000175
3. Oprescu, A.-M., Kielmann, T., Leahu, H.: Stochastic tail-phase optimization for bag-of-tasks execution in clouds. In: IEEE/ACM Fifth International Conference on Utility and Cloud Computing (2012)
4. Van den Bossche, R., Vanmechelen, K., Broeckhove, J.: Cost-optimal scheduling in hybrid IaaS clouds for deadline constrained workloads. In: 2010 IEEE 3rd International Conference on Cloud Computing, pp. 228–235. IEEE (2010). Print ISBN: 978-1-4244-8207-8

5. Van den Bossche, R., Vanmechelen, K., Broeckhove, J.: Online cost-efficient scheduling of deadline-constrained workloads on hybrid clouds. Future Gener. Comput. Syst. **29**(4), 973–985 (2013)
6. Yanpei, L., Chunlin, L., Zhiyong, Y., Yuxuan, C., Lijun, X.: Research on cost-optimal algorithm of multi-QoS constraints for task scheduling in hybrid-cloud. J. Softw. Eng. 33–49 (2015)
7. Nicolae, A.A., Negru, C., Pop, F., Mocanu, M., Cristea, V.: Hybrid algorithm for workflow scheduling in cloud-based cyberinfrastructures. In: International Conference on Network-Based Information Systems (2014)
8. Pop, F., Cristea, V., Bessis, N., Sotiriadis, S.: Reputation guided genetic scheduling algorithm for independent tasks in inter-clouds environments. In: 27th International Conference on Advanced Information Networking and Applications Workshops (2013)
9. Van den Bossche, R., Vanmechelen, K., Broeckhove, J.: Cost-efficient scheduling heuristics for deadline constrained workloads on hybrid clouds. In: Third IEEE International Conference on Cloud Computing Technology and Science (2011)
10. Gutierrez-Garcia, J.O., Sim, K.M.: A family of heuristics for agent-based cloud bag-of-tasks scheduling. In: International Conference on Cyber-Enabled Distributed Computing and Knowledge Discovery (2011)
11. Pinedo, M.L.: Scheduling Theory, Algorithms and Systems, 4th edn. Springer, Berlin (2012). ISBN 978-1-4614-1986-0

Cost-Aware VM Placement Across Distributed DCs Using Bayesian Networks

Dmytro Grygorenko, Soodeh Farokhi$^{(\boxtimes)}$, and Ivona Brandic

Faculty of Informatics, Vienna University of Technology, Vienna, Austria
{dmytro.grygorenko,soodeh.farokhi,ivona.brandic}@tuwien.ac.at

Abstract. In recent years, cloud computing providers have been working to provide highly available and scalable cloud services to keep themselves alive in the competitive market of various cloud services. The difficulty is that to provide such high quality services, they need to enlarge
data centers (DCs), and consequently, to increase operating costs. Hence,
leveraging cost-aware solutions to manage resources is necessary for cloud
providers to decrease the total energy consumption, while keeping their
customers satisfied with high quality services. In this paper, we consider
the cost-aware virtual machine (VM) placement across geographically
distributed DCs as a multi-criteria decision making problem and propose a novel approach to solve it by utilizing Bayesian Networks and
two algorithms for VM allocation and consolidation. The novelty of our
work lays in building the Bayesian Network according to the extracted
expert knowledge and the probabilistic dependencies among parameters
to make decisions regarding cost-aware VM placement across distributed DCs, which can face power outages. Moreover, to evaluate the proposed approach we design a novel simulation framework that provides
the required features for simulating distributed DCs. The performance
evaluation results reveal that using the proposed approach can reduce
operating costs by up to 45 % in comparison with First-Fit-Decreasing
heuristic method as a baseline algorithm.

Keywords: Cloud computing · Bayesian Networks · MCDA · Simulation

1 Introduction

The emergence of big data centers (DCs) causes power consumption issues for
cloud providers while they usually use energy plans which are not optimal [1].
In other words, how to achieve cost-optimized solutions to run geographically
distributed (geo-distributed) cloud DCs is a major challenge in the era of ris-
ing electricity costs and environmental protection on the one hand, and high
expectation of cloud customers in terms of quality of service (QoS) on the other
hand [2]. From a cloud provider point of view, the designated challenge introduces the necessity of a multi-criteria decision making solution involving several
external factors such as power-outages in DCs, weather conditions, and electricity prices, as well as internal factors, such as resource demands and the usage

© Springer International Publishing Switzerland 2016
J. Altmann et al. (Eds.): GECON 2015, LNCS 9512, pp. 32–48, 2016.
DOI: 10.1007/978-3-319-43177-2_3

of different cooling modes. All of these factors can influence the VM placement decision under some levels of uncertainty.

Although various techniques have been devised for efficient cloud resource management, an effective solution for governing cloud resources in geo-distributed DCs is still an open issue. The current work suffers from short comings such as: ignoring the expert knowledge and thereby loosing important information for building efficient system models; partially addressing cloud management problems, i.e., virtual machines (VM) placement [3,4], temperature-aware energy usage [5], VM migration [6]. In other words, there is a lack of research that tries to model a combination of these problems while taking into consideration their interconnections and dependencies.

In this paper, we propose a new approach to reduce the cloud operating costs taking the cloud provider point of view by proposing a VM placement approach that is applied across distributed DCs. The proposed approach consists of the VM allocation and consolidation algorithms. Each of these algorithms uses a similar Best-Fit-Decreasing (BFD) heuristic that utilizes certain utility function for assessments of the most optimal decision. The proposed approach includes three steps: (i) constructing a Bayesian Network (BN) [7] to represent expert domain knowledge on cloud infrastructure management; (ii) applying Goal Question Metric (GQM) method [8] to define the underlying measures for the chosen criteria based on the BN's output; (iii) applying a method, called multi-criteria decision aid (MCDA) [9], to create the utility function as the final decision making indicator. For the evaluation, we compare our approach with two VM placement baseline algorithms, namely First-Fit-Decreasing heuristic (*FFD*) which supports both allocation and migration, as well as a First-Fit VM allocation approach with no migration strategy, named *NoM*. Evaluation is performed using a proposed cloud simulation framework, named *CloudNet*.

Contributions of the paper are twofold. First, we propose an approach to reduce the cloud operating cost by applying VM placement across geo-distributed DCs. It leverages the cloud expert knowledge and models them in a BN. The outputs of BN reasoning are further utilized in a utility function built based on GQM and MCDA methods and used in the proposed VM allocation and consolidation algorithms. Second, due to the lack of necessary features for evaluating of geo-distributed DCs, we propose and design *CloudNet* as a novel cloud simulation framework.

The remainder of this paper is organized as follows. Section 2 briefly presents the related work, while Sect. 3 brings up the challenges of VM placement across geo-distributed DCs. Section 4 describes formal definition of the VM placement problem and proposes a cost-aware solution for it. *CloudNet* is introduced in Sect. 5. While Sect. 6 includes discussion on the evaluation metrics and results, Sect. 7 concludes the paper.

2   Related Work

In this section we first give an overview of existing approaches on cloud management and then focus on existing cloud simulation frameworks.

Cloud Management Approaches. Beloglazov et al. [10] propose a green cloud solution that allows not only to minimize operating cost but also to reduce environmental impact. Li et al. [2] present a consolidation and forecast-based resource provisioning algorithm that utilizes BNs. Calcavecchia et al. [11] consider dynamic nature of the incoming stream of VM allocation requests and propose a technique called Backward Speculative Placement (BSP) that projects the past demand behaviour of a VM on a candidate target host. Song et al. [12] state that the key improvement of resource utilization and service throughput depends on using an optimized dynamic resource allocation method. They propose a two-tier resource allocation mechanism consisting of local and global resource allocation with feedback to provide capacities of concurrent applications. A recent research by Lučanin et al. [13] introduces the usage of the location- and time-dependent factors to leverage them in distributed DCs to enable flexible energy-efficient cloud management via SLA models. Altmann and Kashef [14] propose a cost model along with a model-based service placement optimization algorithm. Their approach takes into consideration the total cost of all possible service placement options in federated hybrid cloud environments and identifies the optimum placement decision.

Despite the mentioned work, there is not enough research attention on identification of causal relationships hidden in expert knowledge which can enable a more cost-aware VM placement across geo-distributed DCs. This motivated us to work on modeling such relationships using BNs and applied methods such as GQM and MCDA on the designed model.

Cloud Simulation Frameworks. *CloudSim* [15] provides a tool kit for modeling and behaviour simulation of various cloud components such as DCs, physical machines (PMs), and VMs. It includes typical cloud features, i.e., VM allocation, cloud federations, and dynamic workloads. Its main usage is the evaluation of cloud resource provisioning strategies in a controlled simulated environment. *D-Cloud* [16] is a dedicated test environment build upon Eucalyptus. It allows to simulate different regular faults in a cloud environment, and to inject them into host operating systems. *PreFail* [17] is a framework for systematic and efficient failure exploration, and validation of correctness of cloud recovery protocols. However, none of the existing tools provides features for simulating geo-distributed cloud DCs. Hence, we design a cloud simulation framework named *CloudNet* (see Sect. 5) to provide such features.

3   Challenges of VM Placement Across Distributed DCs

The main goal of a cloud provider is to minimize the operating costs of running infrastructure while meeting Service Level Agreements (SLAs) with customers. Cloud providers tend to distribute their DCs all over the world in order to cover specific customer requirements and improve the performance of their services. However, for supporting the VM placement across distributed DCs, cloud providers need to handle several challenges in order to achieve a cost-aware solution: (i) each region has its own electricity market that directly effects energy costs. Global electricity price comparison [18] shows quite big price differences that can dynamically change in various countries. Moreover, due to the different weather in various regions, temperature-aware management of distributed DCs can greatly reduce energy cost, specially the cooling cost. More precisely, DCs in cold regions have smaller partial power usage effectiveness (pPUE) rate [5] or broadly speaking consume less energy to cool their infrastructures (e.g., see Fig. 2a and d); (ii) power outages can lead to big issues for a cloud provider. Statistics of electrical outages [19] reports the countries with frequent power outages in spite of a low energy price, hence, it might be impossible to guarantee some QoS metrics such as availability in such regions; (iii) decision making regarding the live VM migration is directly affected by factors such as VM RAM size, bandwidth of the migration link, and Dirty Page Rate (DPR), which effects the migration period; (iv) the trade-off between reducing the energy cost (including power and cooling) of DCs on the one hand, and keep the customers satisfied in terms of QoS on the other hand, is a multi-criteria decision making problem for cloud provides. For instance, switching on and off VMs, or frequent migration of VMs can lead to SLA violations and consequently penalty costs that can invert the effect of such actions on cost efficiency.

In general, VM placement across distributed DCs with highly dynamic environment injects a lot of uncertainty about various internal and external factors that makes it a challenging multi-criteria decision problem. Therefore, it needs effective solutions to reduce the operating costs without QoS degradation.

4   The VM Placement Approach

In this section, we first formalize the VM placement problem and then present the proposed algorithms for cost-aware solution across distributed DCs by utilizing BNs to deal with uncertainty.

4.1   Problem Formulation

In this section, we introduce a model of the cloud aspects which are used in our proposed solution.

VM States. At each point of time t each VM can operate within two possible sets of states, either already allocated to a PM, $allocated(t)$, or has to be allocated, $waiting(t)$. The set of all VMs is called $all(t)$, where $all(t) = waiting(t) \bigcup allocated(t)$. The set $migrated(t)$ defines a set of VMs that are being migrated to other PMs at time t, where $migrated(t) \subseteq allocated(t)$, i.e., all VMs of this set are currently under migration. At each execution step, a VM placement method should find a target PM for: (i) all VMs in the set $waiting(t)$; (ii) the VMs from the set $allocated(t)$ that their current allocation is not optimal enough based on a calculated utility value.

Resources. In our modeling, a DC consists of M distinct PMs. Each PM m is defined with a certain set of resources R. Each resource r has a known limited capacity C_{mr}, where $m \in \{1..M\}$ and $r \in \{1..R\}$. We define the binary variable $x_{ij}(t)$ that indicates if a VM v_i is allocated to a PM j at time t. Equation 1 states that each VM from the set $allocated(t)$ is allocated exactly to one PM.

$$\sum_{j=1}^{M} x_{ij} = 1, \quad \forall\, v_i \in allocated(t) \tag{1}$$

Each VM v_i has its specifications that define upper bound of each resource $max(vr_{ir}(t))$ required by it at any point of time. During each execution step, a VM requires a certain amount of resources vr_{ir} that is considered during decision making process of the VM placement. Since these resources will not be necessarily provisioned for the VM, we introduce the amount of resources $vp_{ir}(t)$ that are provided for the VM. This value can be less (in case of the VM downtime) or equal to the resources required by the VM $vr_{ir}(t)$. Equation 2 guarantees that the amount of the provisioned resources for all VMs allocated to a PM does not exceed the overall capacity of the PM.

$$\sum_{i\, \in\, allocated(t)} x_{ij}(t) \cdot vp_{ir} \leq C_{jr}, \quad \forall\, j = 1..M,\ r = 1..R \tag{2}$$

Moreover, Eq. 3 states how the utilization U_{jr} of a PM j and certain resource r with allocated VMs can be computed:

$$U_{jr} = \sum_{i \in allocated(t)} x_{ij}(t) \cdot vp_{ir}, \quad \forall\, j = 1..M,\ r = 1..R \tag{3}$$

Note that the resource which we more focus on in this work is CPU.

Live VM Migration. In Eq. 4, we define the binary variable $y_{ij}(t)$ that indicates a VM v_i is under migration to a PM j at time t. This equation states that each VM from the set $migrated(t)$ can be migrated exactly to one PM.

$$\sum_{j=1}^{M} y_{ij} = 1, \quad \forall\, v_i \in migrated(t) \tag{4}$$

In our model, we assume that the migration of a VM will not affect the resources of a target PM until the migration is completed. Equation 5 states how DPR depends on the RAM size of a migrated VM:

$$dpr_i(t) = f(vr_{iram}), \quad \forall\, v_i \in migrated(t) \tag{5}$$

where $dpr_i(t)$ is the DPR of the VM and f is a custom defined functional dependency. For simplicity we assume f is a certain linear function. The amount of migrated RAM of VM i to another PM, $migratedRAM_i(t)$, is computed by

Eq. 6, where $bw(t)$ is a bandwidth speed rate between the source and the target PMs and $\Delta(t)$ is the period when the VM has been under migration.

$$migratedRAM_i(t) = \frac{bw(t) \cdot \Delta(t)}{dpr_i(t)} \tag{6}$$

Energy Consumption and Costs. We utilize a commonly used technique for power saving, namely *Dynamic Voltage and Frequency Scaling* (DVFS) [20]. DVFS allows to adjust the frequency of a microprocessor and thereby to reduce power consumption. In our model, energy consumption of a certain PM j is defined by CPU utilization and is stated in Eq. 7, where f is the power specification of the PM:

$$W_j = f(U_{jCPU}) \cdot \Delta(t) \tag{7}$$

Energy consumption of a DC is the sum of all included PM energy consumptions plus energy consumption for cooling. As originally was modeled in [5], overall DC's energy consumption is defined in Eq. 8:

$$W_{DC} = \sum_{i=1}^{n} W_i \cdot pPUE_{DC}(T) \tag{8}$$

where $pPUE_{DC}(T)$ is the pPUE rate of a DC at temperature T. Energy costs of a DC for a given period of time depend on energy price at that period and the amount of consumption. In our model, energy costs are defined in Eq. 9, where P_{DC} is the energy price at the DC location.

$$C_{DC} = W_{DC} \cdot P_{DC} \tag{9}$$

4.2   Decision Model

Building a decision model is started with the definition of objectives and an appropriate set of actions that allow to achieve the goal. The goal of a cloud provider is to reduce its operating cost while satisfying its customers in terms of QoS. In our model, the set of possible decision actions are *Allocate VM*, *Migrate VM*, *Switch-on PM*, and *Switch-off PM*. Afterwards, we identify a set of criteria which are important to be considered from the cloud provider's point of view during the VM Placement. Each criterion is a function of a certain quantitative measurement of a cloud infrastructure. Table 1 contains the list of criteria used in our model.

There are several assumptions based on which we define the migrated list, $migrated(t)$. We assume that penalty costs are relatively high for all requests (e.g., see Table 4), hence the cloud provider should avoid placement of VMs to PMs where their SLAs can be violated with a high possibility. Therefore we define *VM unavailability* (g_1) that can be computed according to Eq. 10:

$$g_1 = \frac{\sum(downtime\ duration\ v)_i}{billing\ period}, \quad where\ v \in allocated(t) \tag{10}$$

where the numerator is the duration of VM downtime i during the billing period. Higher value of this criterion increases the possibility of SLA violation.

The second criterion, *PM power consumption* (g_2), directly influences energy costs of the cloud provider. Equation 11 states the calculation of g_2 for a certain PM j:

$$g_2 = (W_{max} - W_j \cdot pPUE_{DC}(T))/W_{max} \qquad (11)$$

where W_{max} is a constant that defines the maximal utilized power of a PM by considering of energy consumption for cooling. While W_j is the PM power consumption (Eq. 7), $pPUE_{DC}(T)$, as introduced in Eq. 8, is the pPUE rate of the DC at temperature T. Equation 11 utilizes the pPUE rate of a DC where a certain PM is hosted. Indeed, we define g_2 as a function where values closer to 1 are preferred over the values close to 0.

PM CPU utilization (g_3) is an indicator for efficient energy consumption. Although a cloud provider tends to utilize as less resources as possible, it should consider the risk of higher CPU demands than the PM capacity which may lead to QoS degradation.

Runtime load balancing in the cloud is performed via live VM migration. Since lower *VM migration duration* (g_4) value decreases the period of VM reallocation, it allows more efficient usage of cloud resources.

We define *Energy price* (g_5) as another factor that explicitly impacts energy costs of a cloud provider. Equation 12 defines the calculation of this criterion:

$$g_5 = (P_{max} - P_{target\ PM})/P_{max} \qquad (12)$$

where P_{max} defines the maximal energy price over all geo-distributed DCs managed by a certain cloud provider, and $P_{target\ PM}$ is the energy price of a DC which hosts the target PM where the VM is going to be migrated to.

In summary, while some of these criteria can be directly measured or observed (e.g., g_2, g_3, g_5), others may depend on hidden factors (e.g., g_1, g_4). Since some criteria may depend on hidden factors, this induces a level of uncertainty during the decision making process from the cloud provider's point of view. Therefore utilizing BNs would be a proper way to handle such issues and reason about these levels of uncertainty. In the remaining of this section, BN model and MCDA technique, which are used in decision making process of our approach, will be introduced.

Table 1. The list of criteria used for the VM placement problem in our model.

Criteria	Abbreviation	Related equations
VM unavailability	g_1	Eq. 10
PM power consumption (incl. cooling)	g_2	Eqs. 7, 11
PM CPU utilization	g_3	Eqs. 1, 2, 3
VM migration duration	g_4	Eqs. 4, 5, 6
Energy price	g_5	Eq. 12

Bayesian Network. Bayesian Networks are graphical models that represent variables of interest (e.g., object features, event occurrences) and probabilistic dependencies among them via direct acyclic graph. The main benefit of such models lays in possibility to simulate the mechanism of exploring causal relations between key factors using Bayes theorem. This theorem explains the probability of an event based on the conditions related to the event [21].

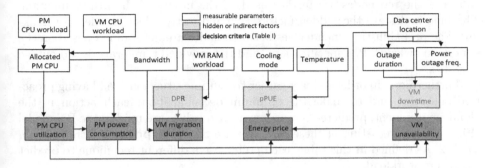

Fig. 1. A snapshot of the designed Bayesian Network. (Color figure online)

MCDA. Although a BN model can be efficiently used to aid decision making by observing the value of uncertainty corresponding to each node, the VM placement problem, which is addressed in this work, is a multi-criteria decision problem, so utilizing the BNs alone is insufficient and using methods such as MCDA is necessary. While deciding about multiple criteria, each alternative can be in conflict with the others, therefore all criteria should be combined simultaneously and be evaluated considering their preferences. More specifically, MCDA is a mean to combine measured results and rank all alternatives. These alternatives are evaluated based on a set of criteria. MCDA allows sophisticated and flexible utilization of BNs in decision making analysis [22].

4.3 Phases

The proposed VM placement approach works in the following three phases which will be explained in this section:

1. designing the BN to represent expert domain knowledge on cloud infrastructure management;
2. using GQM method to define the underlying measures for the chosen criteria based on the BN's output;
3. applying MCDA method to create the utility function as the final decision making indicator.

Phase 1: Designing Bayesian Network. As the first phase of the proposed approach, a BN depicted in Fig. 1 is constructed. This figure represents a simplified snapshot[1] of the BN. The structure of the BN was defined based on the extracted knowledge of cloud management experts. There are three types of nodes in this network. The white nodes define the parameters that can be directly measured at runtime. The red nodes denote the criteria which were presented in Table 1 and influence on the VM placement decision making. The values of the red nodes are further used as the inputs of the utility function. The blue nodes are the hidden factors that indirectly affect the decision making. The probabilistic dependencies between nodes are determined based on the experts knowledge, PM specifications, and the provided temperature and outage statistics.

Furthermore, in order to react earlier to runtime situation (i.e., having proactive behavior) and to make the optimum decision about each action in the cloud environment, predicted resource workload values are used in the BN model (Fig. 1). For forecasting of these data, we use the three **policies** introduced in Table 2. As defined in this table, each policy use a different technique to predict the future workload.

Table 2. The workload prediction policies used in BN as input.

Policy name	Abbrev.	Definition
Last workload	BN-LW	Next workload value equals to the last one
Trend workload	BN-TW	Values follows a certain linear trend
Linear regression workload	BN-LRW	Applying linear regression on historical data

Phase 2: Using GQM Method. While the BN was constructed at the first phase, the second phase is utilizing GQM method to define the underlying measures for the chosen criteria. Table 3 represents the mapping of each criterion value $\in [0, 100]$ to its corresponding utility value $\in [0, 1]$, where 0 denotes the worst value and 1 indicates the best value. The mapping for g_3 was found empirically, while for the other criteria, we consider 10 % increment of their value as 0.1 increment of the corresponding utility value. In case of g_3, if the value exceeds 100 % (i.e., over-usage of CPU), the selected action which leads to this condition will be immediately rejected.

Phase 3: Applying MCDA. As the third phase, once values for each criterion are computed, MCDA is applied in order to combine the values for each possible action, namely allocation or migration to some PM, and rank the results. Each criterion g_i is defined with a weight w_i that represents its relative importance in the context of the given decision problem. Equation 13 defines the utility function $U(a)$ of an action a:

$$U(a) = \sum w_i \cdot g_i(a) \tag{13}$$

---

[1] A complete snapshot of the designed BN: https://goo.gl/Gt4DX6.

Table 3. Mapping the criteria values $\in [0, 100]$ to the utility values $\in [0, 1]$.

g_1,g_2,g_4,g_5 [%]	0-10	10-20	20-30	30-40	40-50	50-60	60-70	70-80	80-90	90-100
utility value	1	0.9	0.8	0.7	0.6	0.5	0.4	0.3	0.2	0.1

g_3 [%]	0-10	10-20	20-30	30-40	40-50	50-60	60-70	70-80	80-90	90-100
utility value	0.125	0.25	0.375	0.5	0.625	0.750	0.875	1	0.66	0.33

The utility function $U(a)$ is used to evaluate the benefits of the possible actions. A VM is either allocated or migrated to a PM with the highest utility value.

4.4   Algorithms

We propose a VM Placement algorithm based on the defined utility function (Eq. 13) to leverage the most important criteria of cloud infrastructures such as energy prices, resources consumption, VM availability, and penalty costs of SLA violation. VM placement algorithm implies the usage of the BN model based on the application of MCDA approach. VM placement can be divided into allocation of incoming VM requests to PMs (i.e., the *Allocate VM* action) and consolidation of the current running VMs (i.e., the *Migrate VM* action). The VM allocation is triggered when a new VM request arrives, while the VM consolidation is applied periodically on running infrastructure at each interval. Both VM allocation and consolidation problems can be reduced to a Bin-Packing problem. In our work, we use a modification of BFD heuristic [23] that will be introduced in this section.

Allocation Algorithm. As presented in Algorithm 1, first VMs $\in waiting(t)$ are sorted in decreasing order by their SLA priorities. In our approach we support three SLA priority levels, namely *Gold*, *Silver*, *Bronze*, which define the priority of resource allocation for a VM. A VM with a *Gold* SLA has the highest priority for the resource allocation and consequently has the highest penalty cost (e.g., see Table 4) in case of SLA violation. Afterwards, based on the computed utility value for each PM according to Eq. 13, a PM with the highest utility value is chosen as the target PM for allocating the VM. If the chosen PM is off, the action *Switch-on PM* is applied (Lines 12–13).

Consolidation Algorithm. The consolidation of the running VMs is performed in two phases. **First**, we detect the VMs that need to be consolidated, based on the calculated utility value for each PM using different prediction workload policies introduced in Table 2. **Second**, we migrate them according to Algorithm 2 similar to the allocation algorithm (Algorithm 1). Migration of a VM to a certain PM is triggered, if the utility value of that PM is higher than the utility value of the PM where the VM is currently allocated in. Algorithm 2 triggers *Switch-off PM* action, if there is no allocated VMs on this PM (Lines 13–15).

Algorithm 1. Allocation algorithm.

input : pmList, vmList: vm ∈ waiting(t)
output: vmAllocationMap

```
1  vmList.sortDecreasingSLAPenalty();
2  foreach vm ∈ vmList do
3  │    maxUtility ← 0 ;
4  │    allocateToPm ← NULL;
5  │    foreach pm ∈ pmList do
6  │    │    utility ← computeUtility(pm,vm);                    ▷ Eq. 13
7  │    │    if utility > maxUtility then
8  │    │    │    allocateToPm ← pm;
9  │    │    └    maxUtility ← utility;
10 │    if allocateToPm ≠ NULL then
11 │    │    vmAllocationMap.put(vm, allocateToPm);
12 │    │    if allocateToPm.isSwitchedOff() then
13 │    │    └    allocateToPm.switchOn();
14 return vmAllocationMap;
```

Algorithm 2. Consolidation algorithm.

input : pmList, vmList: vm ∈ allocated(t) \ migrated(t), vmAllocationMap
output: vmMigrationMap

```
1  vmList.sortDecreasingSLAPenalty();
2  foreach vm ∈ vmList do
3  │    maxUtility ← 0 ;
4  │    migrateToPm ← NULL;
5  │    foreach pm in pmList do
6  │    │    utility ← computeUtility(pm,vm);                    ▷ Eq. 13
7  │    │    if utility ¿ maxUtility then
8  │    │    │    migrateToPm ← pm;
9  │    │    └    maxUtility ← utility;
10 │    currentPm ← vmAllocationMap.get(vm);
11 │    if migrateToPm ≠ currentPm then
12 │    └    vmMigrationMap.put(vm, migrateToPm);
13 foreach pm ∈ pmList do
14 │    if pm.hasNoVMs() then
15 │    └    pm.switchOff();
16 return vmMigrationMap;
```

5   CloudNet, a Novel Simulation Framework

CloudNet is a novel framework, proposed in this work, which allows cloud providers to simulate their infrastructure in a repeatable and controllable way, in order to find the performance bottlenecks, and evaluate the different management scenarios under real world data traces. The most important feature of *CloudNet* that distinguishes it from the other similar frameworks is the ability of simulating distributed DCs while taking into consideration the energy and cooling costs, power outages, weather temperature, and energy prices. It also supports several SLA priority levels with different penalty costs. For the evaluation of our VM placement approach, we designed *CloudNet* to be able to simulate the management of geo-distributed DCs with frequent power outages. To facilitate the reproduction of our research, we released the source code of *CloudNet*[2]. More implementation details can be also found in [25].

To evaluate the proposed algorithms based on the regional electricity prices and temperature differences, we first configured *CloudNet* as summarised in Table 4. In our simulation, we have one VM type (1000MIPS, 768 MB RAM) and one PM type in terms of resource capacity (3000MIPS, 4 GB RAM). Furthermore, each VM has an availability-related SLA metric which is defined as the time of the overall downtime per billing period. Note that the used billing period is one month in our work. As mentioned before, our approach supports three SLA priority levels, namely *Gold*, *Silver*, *Bronze*, with different SLA penalty costs which are shown in Table 4.

For the evaluation, we setup *CloudNet* with five distributed DCs in different time zones. Each location has regional electricity prices and temperature values which are time-dependent. The temperature changes can cause the necessity of using different cooling modes and directly effect the pPUE rate. The geo-temporal input parameters for each DC are shown in Table 5.

Table 4. *CloudNet* general configuration.

#DCs	#PMs	#VMs	Bronze.SLA penalty	Silver.SLA penalty	Gold.SLA penalty
5	25	25	0.05$/% violation	0.1$/% violation	0.2$/% violation

Table 5. *CloudNet* geo-temporal input parameters for each DC.

Data center		Brazil	Canada	Norway	Austria	Japan
Day/night switch hours	(hour)	8–23	8–23	8–23	6–22	8–23
Day energy price	($/kWh)	0.162	0.117	0.159	0.2484	0.24
Night energy price	($/kWh)	0.162	0.117	0.1113	0.1678	0.20
SAIDI	(min/month)	1101.6	220	218	39	6

---

[2] https://github.com/dmitrygrig/CloudNet.

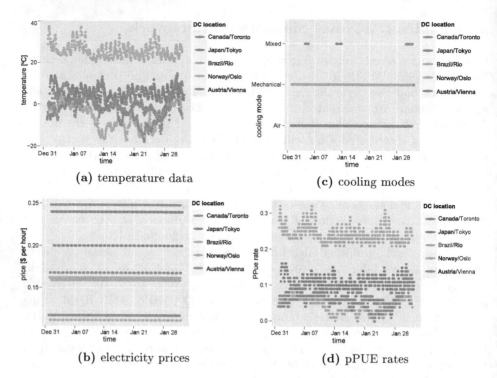

(a) temperature data   (c) cooling modes

(b) electricity prices   (d) pPUE rates

Fig. 2. Real world data traces used as inputs for the chosen DCs and evaluation period. The sources of the exposed data are as follows: a [24], b [18], c and d [5]. (Color figure online)

The chosen locations for DCs allow to evaluate the proposed algorithms considering a combination of various real world input data such as electricity price, power outage statistics, cooling models, and temperature. Conducting the evaluations, we simulate one month (from January 1 till February 1, 2013) operation of running distributed DCs, with management interval of 1 h. We use the following real data traces as the input parameters of *CloudNet*:

- **Temperature data.** We retrieved the real temperature data traces for the chosen period and locations from the public web service, Forecast.IO [24] with the granularity of 1 h (see Fig. 2a).
- **Cooling modes.** We simulated Emerson's DSE™ cooling system, described in [5]. This system has three different cooling modes: *Air*, *Mechanical*, and *Mixed*. One mode is switched to another one when the outside temperature is changed. In our evaluation, we switch *Air* mode to *Mixed* after temperature exceeds 12° C and *Mixed* to *Mechanical* after exceeds 18° C. Figure 2b depicts the switching between various modes of cooling system.
- **Electricity prices.** Electricity prices for the chosen locations are defined using statistics in [18]. Some locations such as Austria have different pricing

models for day and night as shown in Table 5. Figure 2c shows changes of electricity prices for different locations.

- **Power outage statistics.** We obtained the data traces of the power outages corresponding to the chosen locations and period for our simulation from [19]. As shown in Table 5, the electric measure *system average interruption duration index* (SAIDI) is utilized. Note that we used the real values of a year for the simulation period of a month in order to better show the ability of our approach in handling more unreliable DCs in terms of power outage.
- **PM power specification.** We use data traces of *SPECpower benchmark* (HP ML110[3]) to define power specification for each PM in simulated DCs.

Figure 2d shows the values of the pPUE rate of the chosen DCs. In general, as shown in Fig. 2a and d, a lower temperature drastically decreases pPUE and hence is more energy efficient due to the lower cooling cost.

6   Evaluation

In this section the proposed cost-aware VM placement approach is evaluated using the designed BN based on data extracted from the real-world traces in the presented simulated environment (Sect. 5).

6.1   Baseline Algorithms

The proposed VM placement approach under three introduced workload prediction policies (see Table 2) is evaluated in comparison with the two baseline approaches, FFD and an approach named NoM that follows a First-Fit VM allocation strategy, but does not support VM migration. The rationale behind having such a baseline is to show that the migration does not have inverse effect on a cost-aware VM placement algorithm in terms of SLA violation. All approaches have the same input parameters and configurations. The goal of the evaluation is to show the ability of the proposed approach to use the designed BN model which includes the extracted information about the cloud infrastructure in order to perform more efficient decisions concerning placement of VMs across distributed DCs. An approach is said to be better if the total cost including the energy cost and the penalty cost of the SLA violation is minimised. To get comparison results with FFD approach, we used it under two resource allocation policies. The first policy, *First-Fit-Decreasing Agreed* (FFD-A), statistically allocates the amount of resources agreed by the SLA, while the second policy, *First-Fit-Decreasing Requested* (FFD-R), is more dynamic and it allocates the amount of resources which are required by the VM at runtime.

---

[3] https://goo.gl/ZvmK6o.

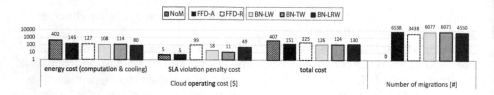

Fig. 3. Aggregated evaluation results throughout one month of simulation. (Color figure online)

6.2 Evaluation Metrics

The following metrics are considered as the evaluation metrics: (i) *energy cost* that presents the total operating costs includes the computation cost and the cooling costs of all DCs; (ii) *SLA Violation penalty cost* that is a penalty cost and has to be paid by the cloud provider in case of SLA violation; (iii) *number of migrations* that represents the migration actions triggered during the simulation whether to avoid the SLA violation due to the power outage or due to the consolidation. In general, the migration action should be applied by a cloud provider if it has appreciable impact on the operating cost.

6.3 Results

Figure 3 shows the aggregated evaluation results obtained during the whole simulation run, one month. The usage of the proposed approach (reddish plots) leads to better results with all the three used policies, while under BN-TW policy it has the best results. BN-TW policy improves costs usage by up to 69% (124$ vs. 407$ total cost) in comparison with NoM approach. This improvement is by up to 45% (225$ vs. 124$ total cost) in comparison with FFD-R which has less number of migrations, and by up to 18% (151$ vs. 124$ total cost) in comparison with FFD-A which has more number of migrations.

The results reveal that the usage of a more enhanced prediction policy, e.g. linear regression (BN-LRW policy) in our approach, increases the cost efficiency in the terms of energy costs (incl. computation and cooling), however it has more SLA violations in comparison with other used policies (i.e., BN-LW, BN-TW).

Moreover, the results in the case of NoM approach in comparison with FFD and the proposed approach indicate the necessity of supporting migration strategy while managing distributed DCs in order to decrease the operating cost. This is because of including the knowledge about the dynamic geo-temporal input parameters and their influence on the energy cost such as temperature, electricity price, etc. Furthermore, since by using *CloudNet* we could simulate DCs with frequent power outages, approaches like NoM even with a high energy cost, still suffer from SLA violation as they cannot handle situations like a power outage.

In comparison with FFD approach (i.e., FFD-A and FFD-R) the proposed VM placement approach gained less energy cost while keeping the penalty cost under control in a way that the total operating cost is less under all used policies. The reason is due to the utilization of the prediction workload policies, using the extracted knowledge about the cloud management (i.e., modeling power outage in cloud DCs) modeled as BN, the effectiveness of MCDA applied on BN reasoning, and supporting different SLA models. In summary, the proposed cost-aware VM placement approach under all workload prediction policies achieved better results in terms of both energy and total costs in comparison with the two baseline approaches.

7   Conclusion and Future Work

In this paper, we proposed a novel approach for cost-aware VM placement across distributed DCs to reduce the energy and penalty costs paid by a cloud provider. This approach creates a decision model using Bayesian Networks, and then applies an MCDA method along with two proposed algorithms for the VM allocation and consolidation. For the evaluation, we focused on geographically distributed DCs where the cloud infrastructure experiences frequent power outages, and the cloud provider aims to decrease the total cloud operating cost (i.e., power, cooling, and violation penalty) while keeping the customers satisfied in terms of less SLA violation. The proposed approach was evaluated in a novel simulation framework, which provides the features of distributed DCs, by comparing the results with two baseline algorithms, namely NoM and FFD. The simulation results showed that the proposed approach decreased the energy cost by up to 69 % in comparison with NoM approach and by up to 45 % compared to the FFD approach.

We plan to extend this work along several directions: (i) enhancing VM placement by using *Kalman Filtering* as a workload prediction technique; (ii) utilizing *hybrid Bayesian Networks* to be able to use the analogous data and make the BNs' parameters more precise. The future extensions will lead to make even more cost-optimized VM placement decisions.

Acknowledgements. This work was partially supported by the adaptive distributed systems doctoral college and the HALEY project at Vienna University of Technology, and the Vienna Science and Technology Fund (WWTF) through the PROSEED grant.

References

1. McKendrick, J.: Cloud Computing's Hidden Green Benefits. http://www.forbes.com/sites/joemckendrick/2011/10/03/cloud-computings-hidden-green-benefits
2. Li, J., Shuang, K., Su, S., et al.: Reducing operational costs through consolidation with resource prediction in the cloud. In: International Symposium on Cluster, Cloud and Grid Computing, pp. 793–798. IEEE (2012)
3. Li, K., Zheng, H., Wu, J.: Migration-based virtual machine placement in cloud systems. In: International Conference on Cloud Networking (CloudNet), pp. 83–90. IEEE (2013)

4. Masoumzadeh, S.S., Hlavacs, H.: Integrating VM selection criteria in distributed dynamic VM consolidation using fuzzy Q-Learning. In: International Conference on Network and Service Management (CNSM), pp. 332–338. IEEE (2013)
5. Xu, H., Feng, C., Li, B.: Temperature aware workload management in Geo-distributed datacenters. In: SIGMETRICS Performance Evaluation Review (PER), vol. 41, pp. 373–374. ACM (2013)
6. Akoush, S., Sohan, R., et al.: Predicting the performance of virtual machine migration. In: International Symposium on Modeling, Analysis and Simulation of Computer and Telecommunication Systems (MASCOTS), pp. 37–46. IEEE (2010)
7. Premchaiswadi, W.: Bayesian Networks. InTech, Rijeka (2012)
8. Basili, V.R., et al.: The goal question metric approach. In: Encyclopedia of Software Engineering. Wiley (1994)
9. Fenton, N., Neil, M.: Making decisions: using Bayesian nets and MCDA. Knowl.-Based Syst. **14**(7), 307–325 (2001)
10. Beloglazov, A., et al.: Energy-aware resource allocation heuristics for efficient management of data centers for cloud computing. Future Gener. Comput. Syst. (FGCS) **28**(5), 755–768 (2012)
11. Calcavecchia, N.M., Biran, O., et al.: VM placement strategies for cloud scenarios. In: International Conference on Cloud Computing (CLOUD), pp. 852–859. IEEE (2012)
12. Song, Y., Sun, Y., Shi, W.: A two-tiered on-demand resource allocation mechanism for VM-based data centers. Trans. Serv. Comput. (TSC) **6**(1), 116–129 (2013)
13. Lučanin, D., Jrad, F., Brandic, I., Streit, A.: Energy-aware cloud management through progressive SLA specification. In: Altmann, J., Vanmechelen, K., Rana, O.F. (eds.) GECON 2014. LNCS, vol. 8914, pp. 83–98. Springer, Heidelberg (2014)
14. Altmann, J., Kashef, M.M.: Cost model based service placement in federated hybrid clouds. Future Gener. Comput. Syst. (FGCS) **41**, 79–90 (2014)
15. Calheiros, R.N., Ranjan, R., et al.: CloudSim: a toolkit for modeling and simulation of cloud computing environments and evaluation of resource provisioning algorithms. Softw.: Pract. Experience **41**(1), 23–50 (2011)
16. Banzai, T., Koizumi, H., et al.: Design of a software testing environment for reliable distributed systems using cloud computing technology. In: International Conference on Cluster, Cloud and Grid Computing, pp. 631–636. IEEE (2010)
17. Joshi, P., Gunawi, H.S., Sen, K.: PreFail: a programmable tool for multiple-failure injection. In: SIGPLAN Notices, vol. 46, pp. 171–188. ACM (2011)
18. E-Pricing. http://en.wikipedia.org/wiki/Electricity_pricing
19. World Electrical Outages Statistics. http://www.nationmaster.com/country-info/stats/Energy/Electrical-outages/Days
20. Kim, W., Gupta, M.S., et al.: System level analysis of fast, per-core DVFS using on-chip switching regulators. In: International Symposium on High Performance Computer Architecture (HPCA), pp. 123–134. IEEE (2008)
21. Pollino, C., Henderson, C.: Bayesian Networks: a guide for their application in natural resource management and policy. Technical report (2010)
22. Vincke, P.: Multicriteria decision-aid. Multi-Criteria Decis. Anal. (MCDA) **3**(2), 131 (1994)
23. Yue, M.: A simple proof of the inequality FFD (L)<11/9 OPT (L)+ 1, for all l for the FFD Bin-packing Algorithm. Acta Math. Appl. Sin. (AMAS) **7**(4), 321–331 (1991)
24. Online: Forecast Weather Web Service. http://www.forecast.io
25. Grygorenko, D.: Cost-based decision making in cloud environments using bayesian networks. Master thesis, Vienna University of Technology, Austria (2014)

Cost-Efficient CPU Provisioning for Scientific Workflows on Clouds

Ilia Pietri[⊠] and Rizos Sakellariou

School of Computer Science, University of Manchester, Manchester, UK
{pietrii,rizos}@cs.man.ac.uk

Abstract. Cloud providers now offer resources as combinations of CPU frequencies and prices, with faster resources (which operate at higher frequencies) charged at a higher monetary cost. With the emergence of this new pricing scheme, the problem of choosing cost-efficient configurations is becoming even more challenging for users. The frequencies required to achieve cost-efficient configurations may vary in different scenarios, depending on both the provider's pricing model and the application characteristics. In this paper, two cost-aware algorithms that select low-cost CPU frequencies for each resource to complete a scientific workflow application within a deadline and at a minimum cost are presented. The proposed approaches are evaluated and compared through simulation using different pricing models that charge resource provisioning also based on the CPU frequency.

Keywords: Cost · Workflows · Cloud computing

1 Introduction

Cloud providers now offer users a large number of configurations, charging CPU provisioning based on the selected frequency of each resource. For example, ElasticHosts [1] and CloudSigma [2] offer users the flexibility of choosing the computing capacity from a wide range of options with more powerful and faster resources (which operate at higher frequencies) costing more. In their pricing model, even 1 MHz of CPU frequency more may still incur a small but still higher monetary cost. As users can choose between configurations with different cost and execution time performance, a challenge that arises is selecting the CPU frequency per resource so that cost-efficient configurations that meet the user's application needs are achieved.

Although providers may charge a lower price for the provisioning of resources that operate at a lower frequency, the reduction in frequency may adversely affect the overall cost incurred by the user. This is because frequency reduction may impact application performance in different ways, depending on the application characteristics. For example, CPU-bound applications that are more sensitive to the allocated frequency show significantly poorer performance when executed at lower frequencies. As a result, a CPU-intensive application may need to run on

© Springer International Publishing Switzerland 2016
J. Altmann et al. (Eds.): GECON 2015, LNCS 9512, pp. 49–64, 2016.
DOI: 10.1007/978-3-319-43177-2_4

fast resources to meet a specified deadline or incur a lower cost, as execution time may be greatly affected when a lower frequency is used. In other scenarios, running the resources at a lower speed sometimes with a slightly longer execution time, may be more cost-efficient, motivating users to choose configurations with lower speed performance. This problem may be more profound in applications such as scientific workflows [3], which consist of collections of tasks with a different behaviour (some of them may be CPU-bound, some of them may be I/O-bound). The execution schedule of such applications may also include gaps (idle time) as a result of task dependencies that need to be satisfied. This gives further scope to take advantage of such gaps by choosing and provisioning CPU resources at different frequencies that minimize the cost, yet achieve a reasonable makespan within a deadline.

Assuming that users are interested in completing a workflow within a specified deadline, this paper contributes two algorithms that can be used to obtain cost-efficient resource provisioning for scientific workflows by choosing appropriate CPU frequencies. Cost-efficient provisioning is understood as provisioning that results in a low overall cost for the user. Typically a low overall cost is not achieved by choosing either high-frequency resources alone or low-frequency resources alone. Instead, cost-efficient provisioning is typically achieved by a combination of resources in between high and low frequencies. The two algorithms start with an initial allocation where all CPU resources are chosen at either high-frequency or low-frequency. The algorithm starting with highest frequencies (Cost-based Stepwise Frequency Selection from Maximum Frequency, CSFS-Max) is iteratively trying to reduce CPU frequencies for as long as the cost is minimized and prioritizing the biggest cost savings at the time (building on an idea suggested in an earlier poster in [4]). Conversely, the algorithm starting with lowest frequencies (Cost-based Stepwise Frequency Selection from Minimum Frequency, CSFS-Min) is iteratively trying to increase CPU frequencies by prioritizing the best makespan savings subject to an overall cost saving. The two algorithms are comprehensively evaluated using three different scientific workflow applications and three different pricing models for CPU frequency. These pricing models include a linear, a sublinear, and a superlinear pricing model, which capture three different ways of varying the price of resources based on CPU frequency. By appropriately choosing CPU frequencies, the two proposed algorithms achieve cost savings that allow users to meet their deadlines at a low cost.

The rest of the paper is organized as follows. Related work is described in Sect. 2. The model and assumptions made follow in Sect. 3. The algorithms developed are presented in Sect. 4. Finally, the evaluation and results are explained in Sect. 5, while Sect. 6 concludes the paper.

2   Related Work

Existing work on task scheduling and resource provisioning addresses various optimization goals in different computing systems such as grids [5–8] and clouds

[9–11]. Execution time and cost optimization is the focus in many studies [12–14]. The Heterogeneous Earliest Finish Time (HEFT) algorithm in [14] is a well known heuristic that deals with workflow scheduling on heterogeneous systems. HEFT schedules each task by selecting the slot with the earliest finish time from a number of available resources, also taking into account communication costs. In [12], HEFT is extended by introducing a cost-conscious factor to select slots with a balance between execution time and cost. In that way, cost-efficient schedules with an acceptable penalty on execution time are developed. The work in [13] considers different combinations of Virtual Machine (VM) capacities and prices to reduce the monetary cost, while achieving good performance in terms of makespan. Their algorithm initially allocates tasks to the cheapest VMs and then reassigns non-critical tasks (tasks that are not in the critical path) to less expensive VMs stretching their execution time without impacting overall makespan.

A lot of work focuses on workflows with deadline constraints [9,10,15–17]. The work in [9] tries to determine the minimum resource capacity required to minimize the workflow cost within a deadline constraint to achieve elastic resource provisioning. This is done by dividing the execution of the workflow into time intervals, set equal to the time unit used in the pricing, and estimating the resource capacity required at each period. The algorithm in [17] schedules tasks to the cloud resources using Particle Swarm Optimization so that both execution time and cost are minimized. The algorithm also considers a budget constraint for the workflow. Similarly, in [16], a scalable environment to the user is provided by choosing proper VM instance types to dynamically schedule and execute the jobs within the deadline while reducing the cost.

In contrast to all related work, the two algorithms presented in this paper determine CPU frequencies of the resources to be provisioned in order to lead to cost-efficient execution within a specified deadline, taking also into account different pricing models to charge for the use of such CPU frequencies.

3   Problem Description and Assumptions

In the problem considered, the user submits a workflow for execution to be completed within a specified deadline on a number of available resources. The aim is to determine the CPU frequencies of the resources in order to achieve cost-efficient configurations. Each resource is provisioned from the time the workflow execution starts until the whole workflow finishes. CPU capacity is charged according to the CPU frequency selected for each resource, while the cost of other characteristics, such as disk and storage, is considered to be fixed, as this paper investigates only issues related to the selection of CPU frequencies.

Application Model. The paper considers scientific workflows modelled as a Directed Acyclic Graph (DAG) assuming that information on task runtimes, when resources operate at maximum CPU frequency, and data transfer times is provided. Task runtimes, when running at a frequency lower than the maximum, can be estimated based on the task's CPU-boundedness [18,19]. Hence, the runtime of a task t at a frequency f is given by:

$$runtime_{t_f} = (\beta \cdot (\frac{f_{max}}{f} - 1) + 1) \cdot runtime_{t_{f_{max}}}, \qquad (1)$$

where $runtime_{t_{f_{max}}}$ is the task runtime when running at maximum frequency, f_{max} and the parameter β captures the impact of the CPU frequency on job runtime, ranging between 0 and 1 for jobs with low or high CPU activity, respectively [19].

Cloud Resources Model. Homogeneous resources which can work on different CPU frequencies, regularly distributed between a minimum and maximum frequency, f_{min} and f_{max} respectively, with step $freqStep$ are assumed. Each resource is charged for the time provisioned according to the allocated frequency with each workflow task having exclusive control on the resource slot where it runs. The curve of the pricing model may be tuned according to the provider's needs and goals [20]. For example, the cost of resources may increase superlinearly for more capable (faster) resources [21], or it may increase sublinearly with the performance level as in [20,21]. Similarly, in [12] the price increases exponentially with the speed of the VMs.

Hence, three different pricing models are investigated in this paper: *linear*, *sublinear* and *superlinear*; these are shown in Fig. 1.

In the case of the linear model, when the frequency is reduced, the price of provisioning a resource decreases at the same rate for each pair of successive frequencies. In the case of the superlinear model, the reduction in price is significant while the frequencies are still high, but gets smaller while approaching low frequencies. In contrast to superlinear pricing, when using a sublinear model the increase in price is significant while moving from low to higher frequencies and reduces while approaching high frequencies.

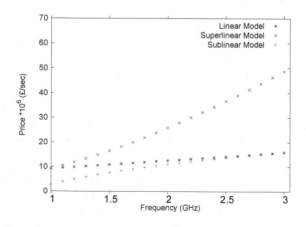

Fig. 1. Pricing models used.

To compute the price charged for each frequency three different functions are used, one for each different pricing model. For linear pricing, the per unit of time cost, C_{f_r}, of resource r operating at frequency f_r is computed by

$$C_{f_r} = C_{min} + C_{dif} * (\frac{f_r - f_{min}}{f_{min}}), \tag{2}$$

where C_{min} is the price of the resource operating at minimum frequency, f_{min}, and C_{dif} is a coefficient used to generate the charge at each frequency. The per unit of time resource cost under superlinear pricing is given by:

$$C_{f_r} = C_{min} + C_{dif} * ((1 + \frac{f_r - f_{min}}{f_{min}}) * \log(1 + \frac{f_r - f_{min}}{f_{min}})), \tag{3}$$

while the cost under sublinear pricing is computed as:

$$C_{f_r} = C_{min} + C_{dif} * \log(1 + \frac{f_r - f_{min}}{f_{min}}). \tag{4}$$

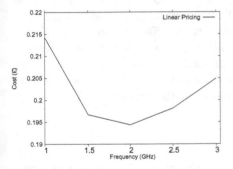

Fig. 2. Cost of CPU provisioning for 4 resources at the same frequency.

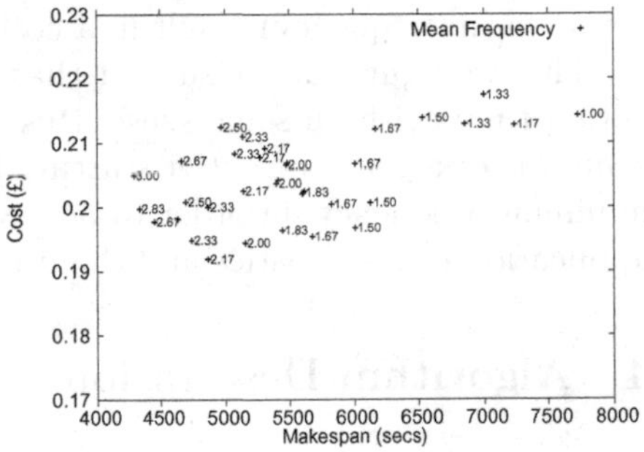

Fig. 3. Cost for different combinations of CPU frequencies (3 resources).

The overall cost required to run the workflow is computed by Eq. 5:

$$userCost = \sum_{\forall r \in plan} Cost_r, \tag{5}$$

where $Cost_r = C_{f_r} \cdot makespan_{plan}$ is the cost of running each resource r in the schedule ($plan$) at its assigned frequency f_r for the whole scheduling period, $makespan_{plan}$.

Motivation. Using the lowest possible frequencies to run a workflow within the specified deadline may not always lead to cost savings, as application performance degradation may be significant. This observation is an important aspect to help appreciate the contribution of the paper. To illustrate this, Fig. 2 shows the cost to execute the LIGO workflow [22] with 50 tasks on 4 resources. All resources run at the same CPU frequency but five different CPU frequencies are considered from low to high; the price charged for each resource changes linearly with the reduction in frequency. It can be seen that while moving from high to low frequencies the cost decreases until 2 GHz is reached but then it increases as it approaches the lowest frequency (1 GHz). This suggests that although the overall workflow execution time increases when moving from high to low frequencies, there is a point until which the cost can be minimized due to a more efficient resource utilization.

We also investigated the performance of the same workflow in terms of execution time (makespan) and cost for all the possible combinations of CPU frequencies in the range of 1–3 GHz with a step of 0.5 GHz. Figure 3 shows the results when the workflow runs using 3 resources. The label shows the mean frequency for the three resources used in each run. Varying CPU frequencies results in different execution time and cost, even if the mean CPU frequency is still the same. For example, for a mean frequency of 2.17 GHz, the best cost (£0.192) and makespan (4869.7 s) is achieved with resources running at 2.5 GHz, 2 GHz and 2 GHz. At the same time, resources running at 2.5 GHz, 2.5 GHz, and 1.5 GHz (same mean frequency) result in a cost of £0.209 and makespan of 5308.9 s.

The two figures above suggest that different trade-offs between cost and execution time exist. In some sense, this work attempts to explore feasible nearby solutions of a Pareto frontier starting from an extreme point, e.g. maximum or minimum frequency, in order to achieve locally optimal solutions based on the application characteristics and the pricing model of the provider.

4   Algorithm Description

In this section two cost-aware algorithms to determine the frequencies per resource to be provisioned to execute a workflow at a minimum cost within a deadline are described. The algorithms can work for different pricing models with the per unit of time cost decreasing when a lower CPU frequency is used. The output of the two algorithms is an execution plan (or simply plan) that schedules tasks onto resources and determines an appropriate frequency for each resource.

Cost-Based Stepwise Frequency Selection from Maximum Frequency (CSFS-Max). Initially, a schedule (plan) of the workflow tasks onto a number of resources is built, assuming that the resources operate at maximum frequency. This initial schedule is built using HEFT [14]. It is noted that the use of HEFT to build an initial schedule is not an intrinsic requirement of the proposed algorithm. In fact, such an initial schedule can be built by any DAG scheduling algorithm such as HBMCT [23] or any of the heuristics compared in [24].

The algorithm (shown in Algorithm 1) iteratively lowers the frequencies of the resources following the range of the available frequencies to determine in each step whether cost savings can be achieved for each resource by provisioning a lower frequency. At the end of each iteration (for each available frequency) the impact on overall workflow cost from using the lower selected frequencies than the currently assigned frequencies to the resources is assessed to determine if the new plan will be accepted (lines 15–17).

To do so, in each iteration the next available frequency, $freq$, is used to lower the frequency of each resource when the cost for the resource decreases with the reduction in frequency, prioritizing resources with higher cost savings. The detailed steps repeated for each iteration (available frequency) are the following: The cost savings of each resource r from the transition to a lower frequency f are computed as:

$$costSavings_r = curCost_{f_r} - newCost_f, \qquad (6)$$

where $curCost_{f_r}$ is the cost of running the resource at its currently assigned frequency, f_r, and $newCost_f$ is the cost of the resource at the resulted schedule where a lower frequency $f \in [freq, f_r)$ which allows the workflow execution within the deadline is used. Note that only resources where the reduction in frequency leads to cost savings without exceeding the deadline are considered to be candidate resources to adjust their frequency (line 11). Starting with the

---

Algorithm 1. Cost-based Stepwise Frequency Selection from Maximum Frequency.

Require: w: workflow, $curPlan$: HEFT plan at maximum frequency, $deadline$: user deadline

1: **procedure** FREQUENCYSELECTIONMAX(w, $curPlan$)
2:     **while** $freq > f_{min}$ **do**   ▷ Starting with $freq = f_{max}$
3:         $currentCost$: cost of $curPlan$ ▷ Eq. 5 for all resources and time
4:         $freq- = freqStep$ ▷ next available lower frequency
5:         $newPlan = curPlan$
6:         $candResources = \forall r \in newPlan$ ▷ candidate resources
7:         **while** $candResources$ not empty **do**
8:             **for** $\forall r \in newPlan$ **do**
9:                 Compute $costSavings_r$ ▷ 0 when deadline is exceeded
10:            **end for**
11:            $candResources = \forall r \in newPlan: costSavings_r > 0$
12:            Remove $r \in candResources$ with largest $costSavings_r$
                Update task runtimes for each task $t \in r$ using Eq. 1
                Update start and finish times for each task $t \in w$ in the plan ($newPlan$)

13:        **end while**
14:        $newCost$: cost of $newPlan$
15:        **if** $newCost >= currentCost$ **then** Reject $newPlan$ and break
16:        **end if**
17:        Accept plan ($curPlan = newPlan$)
18:    **end while**
19: **end procedure**

---

most cost-efficient resource (line 12), the runtime of each task assigned to this resource is updated for the new selected frequency, f, and the slots of all the workflow tasks are adjusted to build a new plan. The same procedure (lines 8–12) is repeated until there is no other candidate resource to adjust its configuration based on the current available frequency $freq$. After each iteration (when there are no other candidate resources) the cost of the new plan is computed to determine if reducing the frequency further also leads to overall cost savings. When the overall cost is reduced the algorithm continues to the next iteration, repeating the same procedure until either the minimum frequency is reached or no cost savings are achieved for any resource by lowering the frequency further. When the overall cost does not decrease, the new plan is rejected and the algorithm terminates.

Cost-Based Stepwise Frequency Selection from Minimum Frequency (CSFS-Min). Same as with CSFS-Max, the CSFS-Min algorithm (Algorithm 2) also works in two phases to initially produce a schedule of the workflow tasks onto the resources and then determine the frequencies to be used per resource. The algorithm initially maps the workflow tasks onto the resources using HEFT again, but, in contrast to CSFS-Max, assuming that resources operate at minimum frequency. Then, the algorithm iteratively increases the frequencies of the resources following the range of the available frequencies for as long as the deadline is not met or cost savings are achieved. The idea of the algorithm is that as resources operating at lower frequencies are charged less, using lower frequencies may lead to less expensive configurations. However, using the lowest possible frequency may not always be cost-efficient due to the impact of frequency reduction on execution time. Thus, gradually higher frequencies are used in an attempt to reduce the overall workflow cost.

The algorithm tries the next higher available frequency in each iteration as long as the deadline is not met or the overall workflow cost is reduced. Thus, a higher frequency is assigned to each resource when the provisioning time for the resource (which is equal to the workflow makespan), is reduced. The makespan savings of each resource (the decrease in makespan when assigning the higher frequency to the resource) are computed as:

$$makespanSavings_r = makespanCur - makespanNew, \qquad (7)$$

where $makespanCur$ is the makespan resulting from operating the resource at the currently assigned frequency and $makespanNew$ the makespan achieved by increasing the frequency to the higher possible frequency in the current iteration. Starting from the resource with the highest makespan savings, the runtimes of its assigned tasks are updated for the higher selected frequency f and the slots of all the workflow tasks in the new plan are adjusted. The same procedure (lines 9–12) to find the next candidate resource and increase its assigned frequency is repeated until there is no other candidate resource to adjust its configuration based on the current available frequency $freq$. Candidate resources (line 11) include only those for which the increase in frequency results in a

---

Algorithm 2. Cost-based Stepwise Frequency Selection from Minimum Frequency.

Require: w: workflow, $curPlan$: HEFT plan at minimum frequency, $deadline$: user deadline

  1: **procedure** FREQUENCYSELECTIONMIN(w, $curPlan$)
  2:　　**while** $freq < f_{max}$ **do**　　　　　　　　▷ Starting with $freq = f_{min}$
  3:　　　　$currentCost, currentMakespan$: overall cost, makespan of $curPlan$
  4:　　　　$freq+ = freqStep$　　　　　　　　　　▷ next avail. frequency
  5:　　　　$newPlan = curPlan$
  6:　　　　$candResources = \forall r \in newPlan$　　　　　▷ candidate resources
  7:　　　　**while** $candResources$ not empty **do**
  8:　　　　　　**for** $r \in newPlan$ **do**
  9:　　　　　　　　Compute $makespanSavings_r$
 10:　　　　　　**end for**
 11:　　　　　　$candResources = \forall r \in newPlan{:}makespanSavings_r > 0$
 12:　　　　　　Remove $r \in candResources$ with largest $makespanSavings_r$
　　　　　　　　Update task runtimes for each task $t \in r$ for the new frequency
　　　　　　　　Update start and finish times for each task $t \in w$ in the plan ($newPlan$)

 13:　　　　**end while**
 14:　　　　$newCost, newMakespan$: overall cost and makespan of $newPlan$
 15:　　　　**if** $newCost >= currentCost$ && $currentMakespan < deadline$ **then**
　　　　　　　Reject $newPlan$ and break
 16:　　　　**end if**　　　　▷ deadline already met in $curplan$, cost increases in $newplan$
 17:　　　　Accept plan ($curPlan = newPlan$)
 18:　　**end while**
 19:　　**if** $newMakespan > deadline$ **then** $curPlan$ =generate HEFT plan at f_{max}
 20:　　**end if**
 21: **end procedure**

---

smaller makespan ($makespanSavings_r$). This is because when no reduction in makespan is achieved, lower frequencies which are charged less are preferred. At the end of each iteration, the makespan and cost of the new plan are computed to determine if increasing the frequency further is possible. If the new plan exceeds the deadline or it results in no cost savings then it is rejected and the algorithm terminates (lines 15–18). In some cases with strict deadlines the algorithm may not generate a plan that allows the workflow to be completed within the deadline, as the initial conditions start with a plan that exceeds the deadline; this may require successive frequency adjustments to make the schedule meet the deadline. If the algorithm does not succeed, it reverts to computing a schedule at maximum frequency using HEFT (lines 19–20).

5　Experimental Evaluation and Results

In this section the performance of the two proposed algorithms is evaluated and compared using three different pricing models and three workflows with the system and application characteristics described below.

Methodology. The simulator in [25], originally developed in [11], was used to implement and evaluate the two proposed cost-aware algorithms. Resources that operate at a range of frequencies between a minimum and maximum frequency, $f_{min}=1000\,\text{MHz}$ and $f_{max}=3000\,\text{MHz}$, with a frequency step (f_{step}) of 100 MHz are assumed. Each resource corresponds to one-core VM while task runtimes when using maximum frequency are considered to be known. In order to compute the price charged for the provisioning of each resource, the parameters C_{min} and C_{dif} for each pricing model – the linear, superlinear and sublinear pricing models of Eqs. 2, 3 and 4, respectively – are the following:

$$C_{min} = £9.24 * 10^{-6}, £9.24 * 10^{-6}, £2.78 * 10^{-6},$$
$$C_{dif} = £3.33 * 10^{-6}, £4.44 * 10^{-6}, £1.2 * 10^{-5}.$$

The values were chosen to approximate roughly the monthly charges of ElasticHosts for the provisioning of VMs, assuming time units in seconds. A network of 1 Gbps was assumed to compute the communication costs between tasks assigned to different resources.

Synthetic data of three real scientific workflows, namely LIGO [22], SIPHT [26] and Montage [27], were used by the workflow generator in [28] to generate a workflow of 1000 tasks for each application and investigate the performance of the algorithms for applications with different characteristics. LIGO, a scientific workflow for the detection of gravitational waves in the universe, can be characterized as a data-intensive application with many CPU-intensive parallel jobs processing large amounts of data. SIPHT, a workflow that searches for sRNA encoding genes for bacterial replicons mainly consists of CPU-intensive jobs with low I/O utilization and can be characterized as a CPU-intensive application. Montage, a workflow that generates image mosaics of the sky, can be characterized as I/O-intensive with low CPU utilization for most jobs. The average CPU utilization of the jobs was computed for each application based on the workflow profiling data in [29] and was used to compute the slowdown from the reduction in frequency for each application setting the parameter β (see Eq. 1) equal to 0.4, 0.8 and 0.36 for LIGO, SIPHT and Montage, respectively.

Results. In the evaluation, HEFT [14] was used as a baseline algorithm to generate schedules with CPU resources running at maximum frequency, which are compared with the performance of our two algorithms. In order to assess the performance of the algorithms with reasonable deadlines that would allow to stretch the execution of the workflow tasks using low CPU frequencies, the user deadline was set equal to $1.05 * M_{f_{min}}$ (where $M_{f_{min}}$ is the makespan obtained by HEFT when all resources operate at minimum CPU frequency). This allows the evaluation of the two algorithms with a wide range of different CPU frequencies as opposed to what would be the case if strict deadlines were chosen where mostly high CPU frequencies would be feasible. The results obtained are presented in Figs. 4–12, and include plots for each pricing model (linear, superlinear and sublinear model) and workflow used (LIGO, SIPHT and Montage).

The performance of the algorithms is compared in terms of the cost (given in £) and time (given in *secs*) required for the workflow execution. The plots of the workflow makespan also show the deadline used in each scenario on top of the HEFT bar. The number of provisioned resources ranged between 5 to 35, as shown on the x-axis in the results, to create scenarios with a varied resource utilization.

With *linear pricing*, where the provisioning cost of each resource changes at the same rate between each pair of subsequent frequencies, when using LIGO and Montage, CSFS-Max and CSFS-Min achieve similar performance in terms of execution time and user cost (Figs. 4 and 6). However, in the case of the CPU-intensive SIPHT (Fig. 5), overall high frequencies are more cost-efficient, as the penalty in workflow execution time is significant when using lower frequencies exceeding the reduction in price. More specifically, CSFS-Max achieves performance similar to HEFT in terms of cost and execution time as using high frequencies is more cost-efficient, while CSFS-Min leads to increased execution time resulting in higher cost, due to the different assignment of the tasks to the resources and the lower frequencies used.

With *superlinear pricing* (Figs. 7–9), price reduction from high-frequencies to subsequently lower frequencies is significant and gets smaller while moving to lower frequencies. This means that CSFS-Max will iterate and reach low frequencies where the cost savings exceed the penalty on execution time. Also, CSFS-Min increases the frequency of a resource when the reduction in execution time exceeds the increase in price. As overall cost does not decrease while approaching high frequencies, low frequencies are chosen. As a result, both algorithms achieve similar performance for all three workflows, stretching the workflow execution time compared with the baseline HEFT algorithm to achieve cost-efficient configurations. Still, the benefits are less profound with SIPHT, which is CPU-intensive.

Finally, with *sublinear pricing* (Figs. 10–12) scaling the frequencies iteratively starting from maximum frequency may lead to more expensive configurations, such as the case of SIPHT. This is because the provisioning cost of each resource does not decrease greatly with a small reduction in frequency while the frequencies are high. As a result, CSFS-Max fails to reach lower frequencies where the cost savings become significant exceeding the penalty in execution time.

Overall, the results show that both algorithms may explore cost-efficient frequencies in most scenarios of different pricing and workflow characteristics. As their initial conditions and iterative procedure differ, the two algorithms complement each other. Starting from maximum frequency ensures that execution time is stretched only if makespan increases lead to satisfactory cost savings. On the other hand, starting from minimum frequency may lead to difficulties to reduce execution time and obtain sufficient cost savings. This is visible with SIPHT, a CPU-intensive application, where high frequencies are more suitable to use to achieve a low cost for linear or superlinear pricing. However, starting from the minimum frequency appears to be more suitable for scenarios under sublinear pricing where low frequencies may be preferred. Sublinear pricing is the case where the two algorithms result in the most significant cost savings.

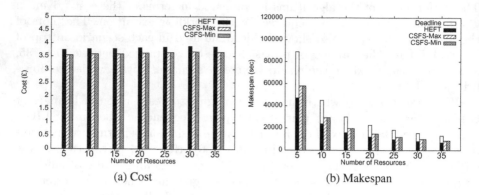

Fig. 4. LIGO of 1000 tasks under linear pricing.

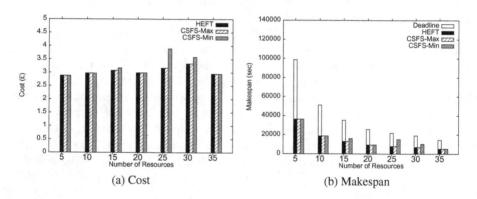

Fig. 5. SIPHT of 1000 tasks under linear pricing.

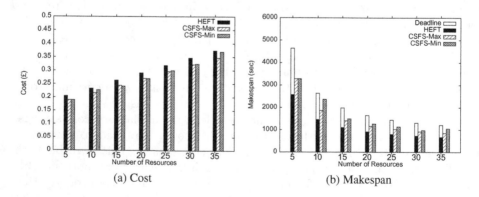

Fig. 6. MONTAGE of 1000 tasks under linear pricing.

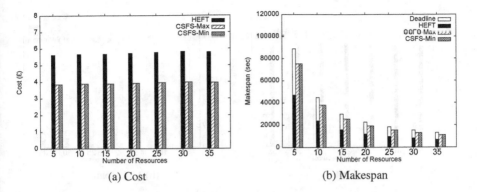

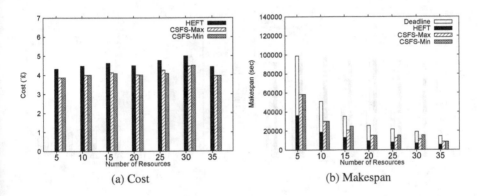

Fig. 7. LIGO of 1000 tasks under superlinear pricing.

(a) Cost

(b) Makespan

Fig. 8. SIPHT of 1000 tasks under superlinear pricing.

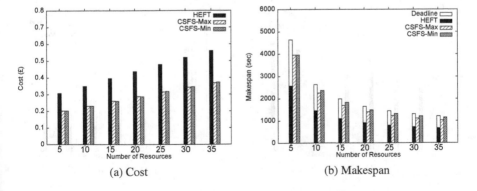

(a) Cost

(b) Makespan

Fig. 9. MONTAGE of 1000 tasks under superlinear pricing.

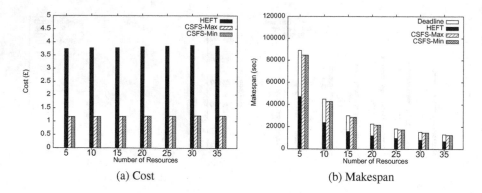

(a) Cost

(b) Makespan

Fig. 10. LIGO of 1000 tasks under sublinear pricing.

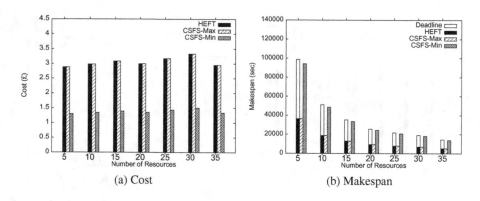

(a) Cost

(b) Makespan

Fig. 11. SIPHT of 1000 tasks under sublinear pricing.

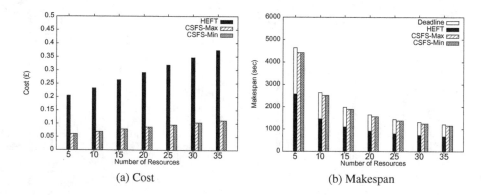

(a) Cost

(b) Makespan

Fig. 12. MONTAGE of 1000 tasks under sublinear pricing.

6   Conclusion

This work considered the problem of cost-aware resource provisioning for the
execution of deadline-constrained scientific workflows, proposing algorithms that
select a separate CPU frequency for each provisioned resource to reduce the
overall user cost. The evaluation of the algorithms suggests that the algorithms
can be beneficial under different circumstances, particularly in the case of a
sublinear pricing model. Also, the workflows that appear to benefit more are
data-intensive workflows as execution time is affected less when using lower CPU
frequencies. Future work could try to develop and assess different algorithms (not
necessarily iterative) to solve the problem. One issue to investigate could be how
to combine the strengths of both proposed algorithms in order to decide what
a good initial schedule is. Finally, the performance of the proposed algorithms
could be evaluated through real experiments.

References

1. ElasticHosts. http://www.elastichosts.co.uk/
2. CloudSigma. https://www.cloudsigma.com/
3. Taylor, I.J., Deelman, E., Gannon, D., Shields, M.: Workflows for e-Science.
   Springer, London (2007)
4. Pietri, I., Sakellariou, R.: Cost-efficient provisioning of cloud resources priced by
   CPU frequency. In: Proceedings of the 7th IEEE/ACM International Conference
   on Utility and Cloud Computing, pp. 483–484. IEEE (2014)
5. Abrishami, S., Naghibzadeh, M., Epema, D.: Cost-driven scheduling of grid workflows using partial critical paths. IEEE Trans. Parallel Distrib. Syst. **23**(8), 1400–
   1414 (2012)
6. Fard, H.M., Prodan, R., Barrionuevo, J.J.D., Fahringer, T.: A multi-objective approach for workflow scheduling in heterogeneous environments. In: Proceedings of
   the 12th IEEE/ACM International Symposium on Cluster, Cloud and Grid Computing, pp. 300–309. IEEE (2012)
7. Prodan, R., Wieczorek, M.: Bi-criteria scheduling of scientific grid workflows. IEEE
   Trans. Autom. Sci. Eng. **7**(2), 364–376 (2010)
8. Sakellariou, R., Zhao, H., Tsiakkouri, E., Dikaiakos, M.D.: Scheduling workflows
   with budget constraints. In: Gorlatch, S., Danelutto, M. (eds.) Integrated Research
   in GRID Computing, pp. 189–202. Springer, New York (2007)
9. Byun, E.K., Kee, Y.S., Kim, J.S., Maeng, S.: Cost optimized provisioning of elastic
   resources for application workflows. Future Gener. Comput. Syst. **27**(8), 1011–1026
   (2011)
10. Huu, T.T., Montagnat, J.: Virtual resources allocation for workflow-based applica-
    tions distribution on a cloud infrastructure. In: Proceedings of the 10th IEEE/ACM
    International Conference on Cluster, Cloud and Grid Computing, pp. 612–617.
    IEEE (2010)
11. Malawski, M., Juve, G., Deelman, E., Nabrzyski, J.: Cost- and deadline-constrained
    provisioning for scientific workflow ensembles in IaaS clouds. In: Proceedings of the
    International Conference on Supercomputing, pp. 10–16. IEEE (2012)
12. Li, J., Su, S., Cheng, X., Huang, Q., Zhang, Z.: Cost-conscious scheduling for
    large graph processing in the cloud. In: Proceedings of the IEEE International
    Conference on High Performance Computing and Communications, pp. 808–813.
    IEEE (2011)

13. Su, S., Li, J., Huang, Q., Huang, X., Shuang, K., Wang, J.: Cost-efficient task scheduling for executing large programs in the cloud. Parallel Comput. **39**, 177–188 (2013)
14. Topcuoglu, H., Hariri, S., Wu, M.Y.: Performance-effective and low-complexity task scheduling for heterogeneous computing. IEEE Trans. Parallel Distrib. Syst. **13**(3), 260–274 (2002)
15. Byun, E.K., Kee, Y.S., Kim, J.S., Deelman, E., Maeng, S.: BTS: resource capacity estimate for time-targeted science workflows. J. Parallel Distrib. Comput. **71**(6), 848–862 (2011)
16. Mao, M., Li, J., Humphrey, M.: Cloud auto-scaling with deadline and budget constraints. In: Proceedings of the 11th IEEE/ACM International Conference on Grid Computing, pp. 41–48. IEEE (2010)
17. Verma, A., Kaushal, S.: Bi-criteria priority based particle swarm optimization workflow scheduling algorithm for cloud. In: Recent Advances in Engineering and Computational Sciences (RAECS), pp. 1–6. IEEE (2014)
18. Hsu, C.H., Kremer, U.: The design, implementation, and evaluation of a compiler algorithm for CPU energy reduction. ACM SIGPLAN Notices **38**(5), 38–48 (2003)
19. Etinski, M., Corbalan, J., Labarta, J., Valero, M.: Optimizing job performance under a given power constraint in HPC centers. In: Proceedings of the IGCC, pp. 257–267. IEEE (2010)
20. Shi, W., Hong, B.: Towards profitable virtual machine placement in the data center. In: Proceedings of the 4th IEEE International Conference on Utility and Cloud Computing, pp. 138–145. IEEE (2011)
21. Sharma, U., Shenoy, P., Sahu, S., Shaikh, A.: A cost-aware elasticity provisioning system for the cloud. In: 31st International Conference on Distributed Computing Systems (ICDCS), pp. 559–570, IEEE (2011)
22. LIGO project, L.i.g.w.o. http://www.ligo.caltech.edu/
23. Sakellariou, R., Zhao, H.: A hybrid heuristic for dag scheduling on heterogeneous systems. In: Proceedings of the 18th International Parallel and Distributed Processing Symposium, p. 111. IEEE (2004)
24. Canon, L.C., Jeannot, E., Sakellariou, R., Zheng, W.: Comparative evaluation of the robustness of dag scheduling heuristics. In: Gorlatch, S., Fragopoulou, P., Priol, T. (eds.) Grid Computing, pp. 73–84. Springer, New York (2008)
25. Cloud Workflow Simulator. https://github.com/malawski/cloudworkflowsimulator
26. Livny, J., Teonadi, H., Livny, M., Waldor, M.K.: High-throughput, kingdom-wide prediction and annotation of bacterial non-coding RNAs. PloS One **3**(9), e3197 (2008)
27. Katz, D.S., Jacob, J.C., Deelman, E., Kesselman, C., Singh, G., Su, M.H., Berriman, G., Good, J., Laity, A., Prince, T.A.: A comparison of two methods for building astronomical image mosaicson a grid. In: Proceedings of the IEEE International Conference on Parallel Processing Workshops (ICPPW), pp. 85–94. IEEE (2005)
28. Workflow Generator. https://confluence.pegasus.isi.edu/display/pegasus/Workflow Generator
29. Juve, G., Chervenak, A., Deelman, E., Bharathi, S., Mehta, G., Vahi, K.: Characterizing and profiling scientific workflows. Future Gener. Comput. Syst. **29**(3), 682–692 (2013)

Cost Estimation for the Provisioning of Computing Resources to Execute Bag-of-Tasks Applications in the Amazon Cloud

Pedro Álvarez[1,2]([⊠]), Sergio Hernández[1,2], Javier Fabra[1,2], and Joaquín Ezpeleta[1,2]

[1] Aragón Institute of Engineering Research (I3A), Zaragoza, Spain
[2] Department of Computer Science and Systems Engineering, University of Zaragoza, Zaragoza, Spain
{alvaper,shernandez,jfabra,ezpeleta}@unizar.es

Abstract. The economic cost is a decisive factor that influences the migration of an application to a cloud infrastructure. Once the migration has been decided, the cost of cloud resources that will be hired to run the application must be minimized considering the application and user constraints. In this paper, we propose a method to determine the cheapest combination of computing instances to execute bag-of tasks applications in the Amazon Elastic Compute Cloud (EC2) infrastructure. The method considers the heterogeneity of the resources (types of computing instances, regions and availability zones, or purchasing and payment options) as well as the deadline and the input workload provided by the user. The paper also shows how the proposed method improves provisioning decisions previously adopted by the authors to execute a linked-data application.

Keywords: Cloud computing · Resource provisioning · Cost minimization · Parallel applications · Amazon EC2

1 Introduction

Cloud computing offers several advantages for the deployment and execution of applications. However, the decision of migrating a system or an application to a cloud-based environment is complex [1,2]. Even when the migration has been decided, the multiple alternatives in which an application might be deployed using the services offered by the cloud providers must be evaluated. The economic cost represents a decisive factor that influences how these decisions are adopted from the customer's point of view.

The first stage when planning the execution of an application in a cloud environment is to determine the resources (number and type) needed to execute the tasks. Nowadays, cloud service providers offer a big variety of computing and storage resources as Infrastructure-as-a-Service (IaaS). From an economic perspective, finding the best combination of resources for a given system is a

© Springer International Publishing Switzerland 2016
J. Altmann et al. (Eds.): GECON 2015, LNCS 9512, pp. 65–77, 2016.
DOI: 10.1007/978-3-319-43177-2_5

challenge that fits on the field of cloud resources provisioning. The price and performance of cloud resources, the application requirements and the customer constraints (budget and time constraints, mainly) are critical issues for determining a well suited provisioning. Some researchers [3–5] have calculated the cost of provisioned resources once the application has been executed, or define models to estimate the cost of resources according to an specific provisioning policy. However, our interest focuses on determining the cheapest provisioning of resources for a considered bag-of-tasks problem.

Different methods for minimizing the cost of executing an application in a cloud environment are presented can be found in [6–9]. Most of those methods are proposed for certain types of cloud-based applications, ignoring the wide heterogeneous catalogue of cloud resources offered by the providers.

In this paper we present a method to get the cheapest resource provisioning in a cloud provider in order to execute a *bag-of-tasks* application. Our interest in the cost-driven provisioning arose from a research paper that we published previously in this conference [10]. We had developed a parallel application to semantically annotate a large-scale repository composed of more than 15 million of educational resources. Initially, the application was executed in both cluster and grid computing environments, and the annotation process was completed in about 178 days. In [10] we estimated the cost of migrating the programmed application to the Amazon cloud. First, the ratio performance/cost of the different computing instances offered by Amazon Elastic Compute Cloud (EC2) was obtained through experimentation. This helped us in choosing the most suitable computing instances required for the execution of the application. In order to solve the problem in the same time as the cluster/grid approach (178 days), we concluded that 95 on-demand *m1.xlarge* instances would be necessary, being the estimated cost about $158,457.46€$. However, is this solution the best one?

The method in this paper will help us to answer this question and, in general, to determine the cheapest provisioning of cloud resources needed for executing any bag-of-tasks application. The contributions of our solution with respect to the existing approaches are the following: first, the method is independent of the selected IaaS cloud provider and uncoupled of any concrete scheduling or scaling mechanism; second, the method does not only consider the heterogeneity of cloud resources, but also the different purchasing and payment options offered by providers as well as the geographical distribution of available resources. Similar solutions for workflow or Map-Reduce based applications [11] have been proposed. However, they do not consider the case of bag-of-tasks applications (in [3] the need of defining a different cost estimation model for each type of application is discussed), which is the third contribution of this paper.

The remainder of the paper is structured as follows. Section 2 presents some related work. Section 3 introduces the concept of bag-of-tasks application and describes the semantic application that has to be migrated to the cloud. Section 4 describes a method for minimizing the cost of computing resources needed for solving a bag-of-tasks problem. Then, in Sect. 5 this method is used to find the cheapest combination of computing instances for executing the considered application.

The obtained results are compared with those that were experimentally calculated in a previous work and presented in this same conference. Finally, Sect. 6 presents some conclusions and future work.

2   Related Work

Some research work has concentrated on evaluating the cost of executing applications in the cloud [12–14]. These applications are data-intensive and the execution time of their processing tasks is very short. Therefore, instead of analysing the most suitable type of computing instances to execute their tasks, these approaches are interested in exploring the cost of storing their data using the different facilities offered by cloud providers. Unlike these works, in [15] the speed-up of an application in the field of information retrieval is evaluated using different types of computing cloud instances. Nevertheless, the experiment is constrained to the use of only 10 computing instances in the most complex experiment and does not consider cost aspects. In any case, the main disadvantage of these experimentation-based techniques is the price to pay for the execution of the experiments.

The definition of models for estimating costs is an alternative and interesting approach [4,5,16]. In general, these solutions require that customers know/estimate the requirements of their applications (such as execution times, input and output data, or storage requirements, for instance). Then, these operational parameters are mapped onto the basic prices provided by cloud providers in order to estimate execution costs. As a particular case, [3] discusses the need of defining a different cost formula for families of applications, and propose a set of workflows and formulas for sequential, multi-thread, parallel or MPI programs.

In this paper we are interested on research approaches looking at minimizing the cost of executing applications in the cloud. Let us now discuss the methods proposed by these approaches and their main contributions. Some approaches calculate the maximum number of computing instances that could be provisioned based on the available budget and time and, then, adjust the number of resources according to how well they would be used by the application [6]. These solutions ignore the heterogeneity of computing resources offered by the IaaS cloud providers because all the computing instances provisioned before starting the application execution have to be of the same instance type. Unlike these proposals, [7–9] consider the heterogeneity of the computing resources from different perspectives. [7] proposes an auto-scaling mechanism able to compute the cheapest plan for starting up new computing instances when a workload increase is detected. This plan considers the deadline of submitted jobs and the instances that were previously hired. On the other hand, [8,9] focusses on cost-driven provisioning and scheduling activities. In [8] the goal is to minimize the cost of executing workflows in IaaS cloud providers. At the beginning, a cost-driven schedule is computed for each workflow. This schedule determines the computing resources needed to execute the workflow and the mapping of tasks to resources, taking into account the data-flow and control-flow dependencies among tasks, as well as the computing requirements of each task. Then, during the workflow execution resources will be reserved and released with the aim of minimizing the total execution cost according to the computed schedule. Instead of provisioning and scheduling resources in advance, [9] divides the execution timeline in one or more stages. In each stage, the previous provisioning decisions is evaluated, adapting them to the future computing requirements. These cost-driven evaluations try to minimize the cost of provisioned resources being able to manage the uncertainty of consumer's future demand and provider's resource prices.

3   Bag-of-Tasks Applications and Its Application to a Linked-Data Related Problem

In this section the features of bag-of-tasks applications will be introduced, and a problem related to the semantic annotation of a large repository of educational units [17] will be depicted.

A *bag-of-tasks application* is a type of parallel application whose tasks are independent. Typically, all tasks execute the same code with different input data. Therefore, these applications can be successfully executed on computing environments composed of a large number of resources (IaaS platforms of cloud computing, for instance, but also cluster or grid environments). The goal is to keep all computing resources busy throughout the application execution, ensuring that the application as a whole finishes as fast as possible. On the other hand, we are specially interested in bag-of-tasks applications whose tasks have high computation requirements (compute-intensive applications). This interest is motivated by the type of problems that we are currently solving in the field of linked-data and bioinformatics. From an economic perspective, the cost of transferring the input/output data of a compute-intensive task to the computing resource where it will be executed is rather small compared to the cost of processing the data. Therefore, our cost-driven method concentrates on minimizing the cost of provisioning the computing resources needed to execute these tasks.

In a previous work [17] we semantically annotated a large-scale repository composed of more than 15 million of educational resources. The ADEGA algorithm [18] was used to create the metadada of these resources using the categories of DBpedia. For each educational resource a set of significant terms (between 5 and 10 in mean) were extracted and, subsequently, these terms were semantically annotated by means of an RDF-based graph. The resulting graphs were used to classify the corresponding educational resources, and provided a semantic description of the resource richer than a traditional description based on just one instance of the ontology. A bag-of-tasks application was programmed to annotate all the resources stored in the given repository. This application consisted of a (big) set of compute-intensive tasks, being each one in charge of analyzing a set of educational resources. We first executed the application in three different and heterogeneous computing infrastructures, two grids and a cluster; the annotation process completed in about 178 days.

Nevertheless, the use of the grid and cluster infrastructures at our disposal reported both technical and human problems: (1) the reluctance of system administrators to install and configure new software, mainly when this software has special requirements or needs to be customized for a specific problem; (2) the computing infrastructures were shared among different research groups and were frequently unavailable due to technical reasons; (3) their execution policies were very restrictive (users had a limited usage rate, being the infrastructures configured to efficiently execute specific types of tasks, for instance); and, finally, (4) the failure rate of the cluster was very high (we measured about a 20 % of failing processes when conducting the experiments) and, despite this fact, neither efficient fault handling mechanisms nor checkpointing mechanisms were available.

As new educational resources were being continuously added to the repository, that led us to assess the possibility of migrating the application to the Amazon EC2 cloud in order to move to a more reliable computing environment. The execution cost was one of the most important aspects to consider as a part of this decision and, therefore, a rough cost estimation was empirically calculated: firstly, a set of cloud resources were experimentally selected; then, the operational parameters of the application were mapped onto the basic prices of these resources in order to calculate this estimation, being the estimated cost about 158, 457.46€ (with a fixed deadline of 178 days) [10].

4 A Method for Minimizing the Cost of Resource Provisioning

Our goal is to determine the cheapest combination of computing instances needed to execute a bag-of-tasks application in the Amazon cloud. We propose a minimization method that considers the heterogeneity of IaaS cloud providers, that is, the wide catalogue of computing resources, the geographical distribution of resources or the different purchasing and payment options. Although in this paper the method has been applied to the Amazon infrastructure, it could be also applied to other cloud providers.

In this section, the price model of Amazon computing instances and the procedure for estimating the performance of these instances are detailed. Both price and performance are relevant variables in the proposed method for minimizing the execution costs. The method to determine the cheapest combination of computing instances considering the application workload and a deadline provided by the customer will be then presented.

4.1 Price and Performance of Computing Instances

Nowadays, IaaS cloud providers offer a wide range of computing instances optimized for different purposes. The price of those instances mainly depends on their hardware configuration (CPU, memory, storage, and networking capacity) and follows a full-hour billing model. Nevertheless, other factors also have influence in the final price of an instance, such as the geographical location or the purchasing and payment options offered by the cloud provider. Let us now concentrate on the pricing of the Amazon cloud. Firstly, Amazon instances are hosted in multiple Regions and Availability Zones whose prices vary depending on the region in which it is running. Secondly, a same instance can be hired according to three different purchasing models (*on-demand*, *1-year/3-year reserved* or as *spot instances*). In the case of a reserve instance, it can be paid according to three different payment options (*all*, *partial* or *no upfront* options). These payment options provide the customer with the largest discount compared to *on-demand* instances, combining a fixed cost with a payment-per-usage cost. In any case, the final price of a computing instance will depend on the combination of all these options. In our method we have defined the concept of *logical instance*: an instance of a specific type, located in a specific region and hired according to a purchasing model and a payment option. On the other hand, local and persistent storage volumes must also be hired and, whose cost must also be added to the final costs. In Amazon these storage volumes are provided by the Amazon Elastic Block Store (Amazon EBS).

On the other hand, the minimization method also requires to know the performance of each type of (logical) instance. We define this performance as the number of tasks that the instance will be able to execute per time unit. Given that IaaS cloud providers follow a full-hour billing model, the hour has been selected as time unit. Obviously, the performance of an instance depends on the problem to be solved and will be usually computed by simulation or experimentation-based techniques. Once the price per hour and the performance of an instance have been computed, the cost per task can also be estimated for each instance type.

Let us now focus on the annotation problem. Table 1 summarizes the performance of the selected set of Amazon instances from the perspective of the problem. We have only considered the *M1* and *M3* generation of instances (*m1.small, m1.medium, m1.large, m1.xlarge, m3.xlarge* and *m3.2xlarge*) and the family of storage optimized instances (*i2.xlarge* and *i2.2xlarge*). This decision was motivated by the cost that implies the use of experimentation techniques for computing the performance of instances. Considering the available instances, we are interested in obtaining the number of terms per time unit each type of instance can process (which is related to how powerful the instance is). In order to measure the computational power of the instances, we have experimentally estimated the mean time required to annotate a term using the chosen Amazon instance types (for that, 10, 000 terms were randomly selected from the input repository and then annotated, using in all cases the same Amazon Machine Image -AMI-). With respect to the Amazon region, we used the US West (Oregon) region in order to compare the results of the minimization method with the results presented in [19]. For each instance as many parallel tasks as the number of processors provided by the instance are allocated. Table 1 summarizes, for each instance type, its number of processors, the mean time required to annotate a term as observed in the experiments (including data movement and other management delays) and the resulting computational power expressed as the number of terms that each instance can process in an hour.

Table 1. Evaluation of the time required to annotate a term using different Amazon EC2 instances (prices to 1 January, 2015).

Instance type	m1.small	m1.medium	m1.large	m1.xlarge	m3.xlarge	m3.2xlarge	i2.xlarge	i2.2xlarge
Number of cores	1	1	2	4	4	8	4	8
Execution time (sec/term)	152.38	59.03	41.39	38.97	38.04	37.69	33.80	33.04
Computational power (terms/hour)	23.63	60.99	173.96	369.52	378.55	764.13	4526.04	871.67

The process of computing the performance of the chosen instances has been simplified. Firstly, in Amazon EC2, acquiring a new instance, completing the virtual machine startup and starting the application execution can take several minutes. We have ignored this startup delay when the performance of instances has been computed. Secondly, the performance of two virtualized instances of the same type may be different under certain conditions. Predicting and detecting these conditions is very complex and, therefore, we have assumed that the performance of computing instances of the same type is homogeneous.

4.2   Minimizing the Cost of Resource Provisioning

The goal of the method is to determine the cheapest combination of computing instances to execute a bag-of-tasks application. The workload of the application (W_{app}) and a deadline (T_{max}) will be previously defined by the customer. Obviously, this deadline will influence the selected purchasing model for hiring the computing instances needed to execute the application. Intuitively, for short deadlines reserved instances would be a bad solution, while long deadlines would prefer that kind of instances (the effective hourly price is less in that cases). In any case, the cost per hour associated to the different types of computing instances will be calculated in order to solve the provisioning problem.

The minimization method has been defined as a quadratic function where there are two sets of variables. One set corresponds to the number of logical instances that will be used to process the input workload. The second set of variables establishes, for each one of the machines, how long it will have to be computing. The objective will be to minimize the cost ensuring the input workload will be processed and the deadline will be met.

The problem is shown in Eq. 1. It belongs to the class of Mixed Integer Non-Linear Programming problems (MINLP) and includes the following elements:

- As stated, we are considering that there are LI different types of *logical instances*. Let $N = (n_1, n_2, \ldots, n_i, \ldots)$ be the integer variables indicating how many instances of each logical machine will be engaged in solving the problem and $T = (t_1, t_2, \ldots, t_i, \ldots)$ the time, in hours, the instances will be used.
- Let T_{max}, in hours, the deadline provided by the customer and W_{app} the input workload to be processed.

- Let $CH = (ch_1, ch_2, \ldots, ch_i, \ldots)$ be the real vector of $euro/hour$ costs and $CF = (cf_1, cf_2, \ldots, cf_i, \ldots)$ be the real vector of fixed costs ($euro$). Fixed costs include the upfront cost and the monthly cost, if any.
- Let $TPH = (tph_1, tph_2, \ldots, tph_i, \ldots)$ be the real vector of the performance of each instance type. For example, in the annotation problem the performance will be expressed in $terms/hour$: tph_i indicates how many terms instance type i processes per hour.
- Let $size$, in GB, the size of the disk attached to each instance (in this problem this value is 70 GB [10]) and c_{EBS}, in $GB/hour$, the cost per hour of the local storage.

$$\text{minimize} \sum_{i=1}^{LI} ((size \cdot c_{EBS} + ch_i) \cdot t_i + cf_i) \cdot n_i$$

$$\text{subject to} \sum_{i=1}^{LI} t_i \cdot n_i \cdot tph_i \geq W_{app} \tag{1}$$

$$0 \leq n_i, i \in \{1..LI\}$$

$$0 \leq t_i \leq T_{max}, i \in \{1..LI\}$$

$$t_i \leq 24 \cdot 365, \text{i corresponds to Res-1-year inst.}$$

$$t_i \leq 24 \cdot 3 \cdot 365, \text{i corresponds to Res-3-year inst.}$$

Restriction $\sum_{i=1}^{LI} t_i \cdot n_i \cdot tph_i \geq W_{app}$ imposes that the hired computing instances will be enough to complete the execution of the application. Constraint $t_i \leq 24 \cdot 365$ imposes that Reserved-1-year logical instances can only be used for 1 year. Analogously, constraint $t_i \leq 24 \cdot 3 \cdot 365$ states that the instances hired with a Reserved-3-years purchasing model can only be used for 3 years.

As a result, the MINLP problem (Eq. 1) returns the combination of instances and the time each instance must be running to meet the problem constraints and requirements with a minimal cost. The problem has been programmed using the AMPL language (A Mathematical Programming Language, http://ampl.com/) and executed by the filterSQP solver and the NEOS server (Network-Enabled Optimization System) [20].

The fact of defining the concept of logical instance makes the proposed method to be flexible enough to support changes in types of instances, purchasing models or payment options offered by cloud providers. Therefore, we strongly believe that it can be applied to future changes in the Amazon cloud infrastructure and to products and services provided by other cloud vendors, such as Google Cloud Platform or Microsoft Azure, for instance.

5 Deploying the Annotation Application in the Amazon Cloud

In this section we analyze the cost of executing the semantic application in the Amazon cloud. Firstly, we will compare the execution cost that was estimated in our previous work with the cost computed by the minimization method defined. Both execution costs have been calculated for a specific deadline provided by the customer (178 days). Then, the customer constraint will turn into a flexible variable and the goal will be to reduce the computing cost independently from the execution time.

Table 2 depicts the cost of executing the semantic application in Amazon AWS. A similar table was presented in [10], where we concluded that the problem could be carried out in 178 days using 95 *m1.xlarge* instances located in the US West (Oregon) region. The price of Amazon services (Amazon EC2, EBS and S3) has been updated to January 1st 2015 in order to compare the estimated cost and the minimized cost. For a detailed description of instance types used and the deployment schema, please refer to [10].

Table 2. Cost estimation of executing the application on Amazon.

Executing the application				129,010.36	euros
Amazon EC2 - Cost of Computation					
Exec. environment	Terms processed	Exec. time (sec/term)	CPU price (€/h)	Cost euros	% Faults
EC2 (95 m1.xlarge)	149,427,907	38.97	0.31	125,359.20	0,00
Amazon EBS - Cost of Data Storage					
Exec. environment	Data stored (GB)	Months	€ per GB-month	Cost euros	
EC2 (95 m1.xlarge)	6,650	5.93	0.09	3,549.11	
Amazon S3 - Cost of Data Storage				37.32	euros
Exec. environment	Data stored (GB)	Months	€ per GB-month	Cost euros	
S3 (Input data)	618.88	1	0.0264	16.34	
S3 (Output data)	794.63	1	0.0264	20.98	
Amazon S3 - Cost of Data Requests				64.74	euros
Exec. environment	# requests	€ per 10,000 reqs	€ per 1,000 reqs	Cost euros	
S3 (GET requests)	165,178,886	0.0035	-	57.81	
S3 (PUt requests)	1,575,098	-	0.0044	6.93	

Briefly, the total cost of executing the application on Amazon is €129,010.36. Amazon EC2 service represents a 97.16 % of the total cost, whereas Amazon EBS represents the 2.75 % and Amazon S3 represents the remaining 0.08 %.

5.1   Minimizing the Cost of the Deployment

Let us now to use the minimization method to determine the cheapest combination of computing instances to execute the semantic application. The input workload and deadline are the same than those defined in the estimated solution (149, 427, 907 terms to be annotated and 178 days, respectively).

The minimization problem gives as a result that the terms can be annotated with a minimum computing instances cost of €86, 432.79. The combination of logical instances that achieve that cost is 45 *m3.2xlarge* on-demand instances running for 178 days (42, 472 hours), 1 *m3.2xlarge* on-demand instance running for 138.04 days (3313 hours) and 1 *m3.xlarge* on-demand instance running for 1 hour.

The computing cost has been reduced by 31.05 %, from €125, 359.20 to €86, 432.79. The combination of instances proposed by the minimization method is mainly composed by *m3.2xlarge* instances, whereas we proposed experimentally the use of *m1.xlarge* instances. From a hardware point of view, an *m3.2xlarge* instance is composed by 8 CPU cores (Intel Xeon Processor), with a clock speed of 2.5 Ghz. Therefore, 367 cores will be used to annotate the input terms (we are only considering the instances that will be purchased during all the time needed to complete the annotation process). On the other hand, an *m1.xlarge* instance was composed by 4 CPU cores (Intel Xeon Processor) and, therefore, in that case, 380 cores were to be used (95 instances). Both approaches propose a similar number of cores. The difference is motivated because *M3* instances integrate the latest Intel Xeon Processor and this provides a better and more consistent performance than *M1* instances for most use-cases. On the other hand, from an economic point of view, the cost per hour of *m3.2xlarge* and *m1.xlarge* instances is €0.492 and €0.308, respectively. The price of *M3* instances is bigger than *M1* instances. Nevertheless, if the cost of a core per hour is calculated (€0.061 in the case of *m3.2xlarge* instances and €0.077 in the case of *m1.xlarge* instances), then the difference between the total computing cost calculated by both methods is understood.

Then, why did we propose the use of *m1.xlarge* instances in [10]? In 2013, *M1* instances were cheaper than *M3* instances. Given that the performance of both type of instances was very similar, from an economic point of view purchasing *m1.xlarge* instances was better. Therefore, the new proposal of provisioning is motivated by the changes in the Amazon price policies.

Finally, the cost of data storage in the Amazon EBS is also reduced by 51.81 %, from €3, 549.11 to €1, 710.14. This reduction is because the number of computing instances that will be provisioned has reduced to half. Anyway, the cost of S3 storage is the same for both solutions.

5.2   Flexible Customer Constraints

The options of cloud-based deployment have been analyzed with the aim of solving the semantic problem in the same time as the cluster and grid-based solution (178 days). Let us now to suppose that the deadline is not a problem for the customer. Now, the goal is to find the cheapest deployment for executing the semantic application independently from the total execution time.

The cheapest solution computed by the minimization method has a cost of €33, 524.67 and a deadline of 3 years. The combination of logical instances that achieve that cost is 1 *m3.2xlarge* 3-year-reserved (All-Upfront) instance running for 3 years (26, 280 hours) and 1 *m3.xlarge* 3-year-reserved (All-Upfront) instance running for 2.67 years (23, 403 hours). This solution reduces the computing cost by 61.21 % with respect the solution whose instances are running for 178 days. Nevertheless, the deadline of the annotation process has considerably increased, from 178 to 1095 days (3 years). On the other hand, the cost of data storage in Amazon EBS will be €428.65.

Finally, a compromise between the cost of computing instances and the deadline could be also computed by this method. Let us to consider the scenario of processing the input terms in 540 days (1.5 years). The minimization problem gives as a result that these terms can be annotated with a minimum computing instances cost of €53, 742.7. The solution corresponds to a combination composed by 1 *m1.large* 3-year reserved (heavy use) instance running for 518.6 days (12, 447 hours) and 22 *m3.2xlarge* 1-year-reserved (All-upfront) instances running for 365 days (8, 760 hours). In this case, the cost of data storage in the Amazon EBS will be €1, 772.19.

6   Conclusions

In this paper we have presented a method for determining the cheapest combination of computing instances needed to execute a bag-of-tasks application in the Amazon cloud. The method has been applied to a specific bag-of-tasks application in the field of linked-data. In a previous work we estimated the cost of executing this application in the Amazon Cloud. In this one, we have compared that cost with the results provided by the new minimization method. We have improved the previous estimation and the price to pay for executing the application has been reduced by 31.05 %.

On the other hand, the method that we have proposed concentrates on minimizing the cost of computing instances. In bag-of-tasks applications whose tasks are compute-intensive the cost of instances has a significant influence on the final price of the execution. Nevertheless, the method also should consider the cost of data involved into the execution of applications. Defining equations to estimate this cost for a general problem is not easy because it depends on technical and deployment issues that are specific of each application: the storage service (or services) selected for storing the application data, the number of input/out operations, the architecture of each application (the components are running in the same computing instance or in many distributed instances; in the last case data communications should be considered, for example), each application has its own data constraints, strategies and policies (centralized/distributed data, strategies for the data replication, or synchronization of data between instances or storage services, for instance), etc. In any case, an estimation of the cost of data involved into the execution of a concrete application could be easily made using the calculators offered by cloud providers.

Unlike other existing approaches, this method considers the heterogeneity of cloud providers (instance types, geographical location of resources, or purchasing and payment options, for instance), and it is flexible enough as to support changes on both resources catalogue and purchasing options of current vendor as well as other service models from different cloud vendors. For example, let us assume that we have decided to execute the application in the Google Cloud platform. We will have to update the pricing of the Google cloud resources and to experimentally measure the time these resources require to process a work unit. With these data input we can directly apply the proposed minimization problem in order to get, once a deadline is provided, the number and types of required instances, as well as the estimated cost.

As future work we are interested in integrating this cost-driven method into the provisioning and scheduling mechanisms of the framework that we proposed in [21]. This framework integrates cluster, grid and cloud infrastructures in order to execute compute-intensive and data-intensive applications (scientific workflows, for instance). Additionally, we would like to extend and improve monitoring aspects of the framework, which could be useful for improving both cost estimations and the provisioning process [16], as well as auto-scaling mechanisms for monitoring and managing the changing workload of the applications. On the other hand, we would like also to define new models to minimize the cost of executing other type of applications (Workflow applications, for instance) or to address some open issues closely related to the Amazon instances (new types of computing instances are being continuously added to the Amazon instance catalogue whose performance/cost ratios and purchasing options should be dynamically analyzed and integrated).

Acknowledgements. This work has been supported by the research projects TIN2014-56633-C3-2-R granted by the Spanish Ministerio de Economía y Competitividad, project 287230/2 granted by the Gobierno de Aragón, and project UZ-2015-TEC-04 granted by the University of Zaragoza.

References

1. Tak, B.C., Urgaonkar, B., Sivasubramaniam, A.: To move or not to move: the economics of cloud computing. In: Proceedings of the 3rd USENIX Conference on Hot Topics in Cloud Computing, HotCloud 2011, p. 5. USENIX Association, Berkeley (2011)
2. Hajjat, M., Sun, X., Sung, Y.W.E., Maltz, D., Rao, S., Sripanidkulchai, K., Tawarmalani, M.: Cloudward bound: planning for beneficial migration of enterprise applications to the cloud. SIGCOMM Comput. Commun. Rev. **40**(4), 243–254 (2010)
3. Truong, H.L., Dustdar, S.: Composable cost estimation and monitoring for computational applications in cloud computing environments. In: Proceedings of the International Conference on Computational Science, ICCS 2010, pp. 2175–2184 (2010)
4. De Alfonso, C., Caballer, M., Alvarruiz, F., Moltó, G.: An economic and energy-aware analysis of the viability of outsourcing cluster computing to a cloud. Future Gener. Comput. Syst. **29**(3), 704–712 (2013)
5. Kashef, M.M., Altmann, J.: A cost model for hybrid clouds. In: Altmann, J., Rana, O.F., Vanmechelen, K. (eds.) GECON 2011. LNCS, vol. 7150, pp. 46–60. Springer, Heidelberg (2012)
6. Malawski, M., Juve, G., Deelman, E., Nabrzyski, J.: Cost- and deadline-constrained provisioning for scientific workflow ensembles in IaaS clouds. In: Proceedings of the International Conference on High Performance Computing, Networking, Storage and Analysis, SC 2012, pp. 22:1–22:11. IEEE Computer Society Press, Los Alamitos (2012)

7. Mao, M., Li, J., Humphrey, M.: Cloud auto-scaling with deadline and budget constraints. In: Proceedings of the 11th IEEE/ACM International Conference on Grid Computing, pp. 41–48 (2010)
8. Rodríguez, M.A., Buyya, R.: Deadline based resource provisioning and scheduling algorithm for scientific workflows on clouds. IEEE Trans. Cloud Comput. **2**(2), 222–235 (2014)
9. Chaisiri, S., Lee, B.S., Niyato, D.: Optimization of resource provisioning cost in cloud computing. IEEE Trans. Serv. Comput. **5**(2), 164–177 (2012)
10. Hernández, S., Fabra, J., Álvarez, P., Ezpeleta, J.: Cost evaluation of migrating a computation intensive problem from clusters to cloud. In: Altmann, J., Vanmechelen, K., Rana, O.F. (eds.) GECON 2013. LNCS, vol. 8193, pp. 90–105. Springer, Heidelberg (2013)
11. Tian, F., Chen, K.: Towards optimal resource provisioning for running mapreduce programs in public clouds. In: Proceedings of the 2011 IEEE 4th International Conference on Cloud Computing, CLOUD 2011. IEEE Computer Society Press, Los Alamitos, pp. 155–162 (2011)
12. Deelman, E., Singh, G., Livny, M., Berriman, B., Good, J.: The cost of doing science on the cloud: the montage example. In: Proceedings of the 2008 ACM/IEEE Conference on Supercomputing, SC 2008, pp. 50:1–50:12. IEEE Press, Piscataway (2008)
13. Garfinkel, S.L.: An evaluation of Amazon's grid computing services: EC2, S3 and SQS. Technical report, Center for Research on Computation and Society (2007)
14. Juve, G., Deelman, E., Berriman, G., Berman, B., Maechling, P.: An evaluation of the cost and performance of scientific workflows on Amazon EC2. J. Grid Comput. **10**(1), 5–21 (2012)
15. Morar, G.A., Muntean, C.I., Silaghi, G.C.: Implementing and running a workflow application on cloud resources. Informatica Economica J. **15**(3), 15–27 (2011)
16. Truong, H.L., Dustdar, S.: Cloud computing for small research groups in computational science and engineering: current status and outlook. Computing **91**(1), 75–91 (2011)
17. Fabra, J., Hernández, S., Otero, E., Vidal, J., Lama, M., Álvarez, P.: Integration of grid, cluster and cloud resources to semantically annotate a large-sized repository of learning objects. Concurr. Comput.: Pract. Exp. (2014)
18. Lama, M., Vidal, J.C., Otero-García, E., Bugarín, A., Barro, S.: Semantic linking of learning object repositories to DBpedia. Educ. Technol. Soc. **15**(4), 47–61 (2012)
19. Hernández, S., Fabra, J., Álvarez, P., Ezpeleta, J.: A reliable and scalable service bus based on Amazon SQS. In: Lau, K.-K., Lamersdorf, W., Pimentel, E. (eds.) ESOCC 2013. LNCS, vol. 8135, pp. 196–211. Springer, Heidelberg (2013)
20. Czyzyk, J., Mesnier, M.P., Moré, J.J.: The NEOS server. IEEE J. Comput. Sci. Eng. **5**(3), 68–75 (1998)
21. Fabra, J., Hernández, S., Ezpeleta, J., Álvarez, P.: Solving the interoperability problem by means of a bus. An experience on the integration of grid, cluster and cloud infrastructures. J. Grid Comput. **12**(1), 41–65 (2013)

Service Selection in Clouds

Service Quality Assurance in Multi-clouds

Dana Petcu[(✉)]

West University of Timişoara and Institute e-Austria Timişoara, Timişoara, Romania
petcu@info.uvt.ro
http://web.info.uvt.ro/~petcu

Abstract. A particular problem of cloud environments is the assurance of a certain level of service quality. The problem is escalated in the case of building support platforms for using multiple clouds. Various partial solutions to ensure a certain quality level of the cloud services have been investigated in the last half decade. This paper analyzes the existing approaches to define, model, evaluate, estimate, measure of optimize the quality of services offered to cloud-based applications. A particular approach is detailed, the one that uses model-driven engineering techniques. Moreover, the special case of designing data-intensive applications, the appropriate quality of service attributes are identified.

Keywords: Quality of Service · Cloud services · Model-driven engineering · Data-intensive applications

1 Introduction

Service quality assurances are expected to reduce risks as well as allow the increase of transaction volume and thus expanding the services' market as a whole. Service quality assurances are essential in the nowadays' on-line world. Their mechanisms are causing the services with the highest quality to prosper and those having low service quality to disappear [24]. Therefore, service quality assurance can be seen as a catalyst of the evolution toward efficient service markets and customer high satisfaction.

This paper presents an overview of the current status of the quality of services (QoS) characteristics, assessment and evaluation in cloud environments. A particular attention is provided to the case of multi-clouds and the latest mechanisms for QoS assurance inspired from model-driven engineering techniques.

The paper is organized as follows. The next section is looking to the QoS definition, relationship with SLAs, evaluation and models. The third section is presenting the multi-clouds needs in terms of QoS, proposes a taxonomy, discusses the QoS procedures for service selection and composition, and underlines the need of continuous QoS assurance and optimization. The fourth section is focusing on the model-driven engineering approach for QoS assurance in multi-clouds. The fifth section is discussing the particular case of QoS in data-intensive application engineering.

© Springer International Publishing Switzerland 2016
J. Altmann et al. (Eds.): GECON 2015, LNCS 9512, pp. 81–97, 2016.
DOI: 10.1007/978-3-319-43177-2_6

2   QoS in Clouds

Definition. The Quality of Service (QoS) was defined in [16] in 2008 as the totality of characteristics of a service that bear on its ability to satisfy stated and implied needs of the user of the service. QoS is an inherent element of service-oriented architecture. Nowadays, QoS play a major role in cloud environments in order to implement the concept of measured service [18].

The QoS is determined by the fulfillment of both functional and non-functional requirements [30]. Meeting the user's requirements with regard to the functionality depends on the service's description. The amount of non-functional quality attributes that have to be considered is very high in the case of cloud services. Therefore, often QoS parameters are considered to be related to non-functional properties of a cloud service.

Relationship with Performance. The performance is the key QoS attribute that is important to both users and providers of cloud services [9]. Cloud end users are maily interested in the time behaviour of the application running on top of cloud services (like the response time, processing time, or throughput). Another concern is the resource consumption and techniques like monitoring resource utilization to identify over-provisioned, under-performance. Reliability or consumption pattern identification are essential to maintain a certain level of QoS. Guaranteed performance in the cloud is allowing to protect the rights of clients and of their suppliers [22].

Relationship with SLA. The QoS attributes are usually specified in Service Level Agreements (SLA). The SLA is an adequate solution to specify the QoS guarantees, as it specifies the service level objectives to ensure that the delivered QoS meets the user expectations.

Relationship with Monitoring. The QoS attributes like response time or throughput have a strong variability and in order to implement the contract, these parameters need to be carefully controlled. Consequently, continuous supervision of QoS attributes is necessary to honor the SLAs by the service provider [7]. SLA compliance is also often tested by the clients. Monitoring of the various parameters of SLAs is a common practice to ensure the compliance with negotiated terms. The monitoring the QoS agreements allows to observe the behaviour of the service and it is based on extracting metrics needed to make measurements of QoS. In [10,20], for example, the servers, the application, the databases and networks are monitored using agent technologies. The processes associated with monitoring that ensure prevention, correction, and control remain key issues to properly solve the trade-off between the benefit of the supplier and the customer satisfaction [22].

Optimality: A Trade-Off Between User Requirements and Provider Offers. An important challenge for cloud providers is to automate the management of cloud resources while keeping into account the QoS requirements of hosted applications as well as the resource supervision expenses [7]. For example, the paper [21] proposes a QoS-aware placement of virtual machines by using a polynomial time heuristic method that solves the problem defined as an integer linear programming model. Another paper, [8], proposes a negotiation mechanism for assuring the QoS requirements that can identify the most optimal agreement in a search space with a large number of parameters. It is based on a co-evolutionary multi-agent approach based on preference ordering.

The authors of [7] identified the quality attributes based on customers desires associated with SLA, as well as the metrics to measure the deviation of QoS from predictables, with possible resolution in the outline of architecture for spontaneous supervision of QoS without violation of SLA.

QoS Evaluation. The main challenge for the QoS evaluation is related to the fact that the performance in cloud environments (especially the response time) is varying in time due to the resource contention of concurrent competing requests. The run-time performance related parameters such as availability are changing in time. Therefore it is difficult to assure the accurate evaluation of QoS [34]. QoS should be maintained not only in the presence of background dynamic resource provisioning but also in the presence of variable capacity of the servers.

The use of quantitative indexes is an accepted practice. Usually a set of indicators is compiled in just one value [18]. In this context, the Service Measurement Index (SMI) is a clear candidate to assess the QoS. SMI [11] is designed to enable the analysis and assessment of cloud services before using a service as well as while using the service. The domains of QoS covered by the SMI are accountability, agility, assurance, financial, performance, security, privacy, usability [36].

Models. There are several reported efforts trying to model QoS in clouds or to manage non-functional properties in an intelligent fashion. The main objective of these QoS models is to support users evaluating the quality of their cloud services [30]. However, the lack of standards for QoS attributes in cloud environments is hindering the deployment of advanced techniques for QoS management [18].

The paper [1] provides an overview of research works in the cloud QoS modeling space. The survey considers QoS modeling techniques for interactive cloud services (e.g. multi-tier applications) and focus on QoS aspects related to performance, reliability and availability.

A specific direction of research consists in the definition of QoS attributes in cloud environments. The paper [15] describes the mathematical model for the QoS metrics, focusing on the QoS categories of performance and security. For performance, these metrics are delay, delay variation, throughput, information overhead. For the security, the metrics are authentication, authorization, accreditation, integrity, information availability, certification, physical security, non-repudiation. The authors of [30] extracted over two hundred relevant attributes from seven existing cloud QoS models and fifty quality aspects. The most frequently mentioned quality criteria have lead to so-called quality dimensions: reliability, flexibility, performance, data security, costs and conditions, usability, customer service, and provider's sense of responsibility.

Another concern is related to the QoS model life-cycle. The paper [13] focus on a Quality Model life-cycle that has several stages: strategy, design, transition, operation, continual improvement. Two quality models are defined: one for clients and other for providers. The authors of [36] synthesizes the existing research on approaches to the quality analysis of cloud services and they reveals multiple quality analysis approaches that focus either on specific quality aspects or on a specific step in the activity cycle. One accepted fact is that the QoS consists of three dimensions: the technical quality of the outcome, the functional quality of the process and the image of the service provider.

Final Remarks. Despite the multiple efforts which partially mentioned above, QoS assurance remains an open problem in cloud environment both from theoretical and practical point of view. With the advent of using services from multiple clouds, the complexity of the problem increases.

3   QoS in Multi-clouds

Multi-cloud Context. The multiple clouds usage scenarios are referring to the serial actions, when applications are moved from one cloud to another, or simultaneous actions, when an application is using services from various clouds. The simplest scenarios are the migration from a private cloud to a public cloud, respectively when some services are lying on the private cloud, while other services are lying on a public cloud (hybrid cloud). The reasons for using multiple clouds are various, from cost changes, availability problems, avoidance of lock-in, national law constraints, peaks, offer enhancement, service particularities, and not at least the perceived QoS [25].

The multi-cloud is a delivery model for multiple clouds which assumes that there is no priori agreement between the cloud providers and a third party is responsible for the services contacts the service providers, negotiates the terms of service consumption, monitors the fulfillment of the service level agreements, triggers the migration of codes, data and networking from one provider to another [25].

In multi-clouds the main problem is the portability [26]. Other issues are related to automated deployment, service aggregation, governance, service selection mechanism and methodology, search engines and so on. The main requirements were exposed for example in [25].

Taxonomy. We propose in Fig. 1 a taxonomy of the QoS attributes in multi-clouds. The QoS attributes included under flexibility category are of particular importance in the case of multi-cloud, by defining their reason to be.

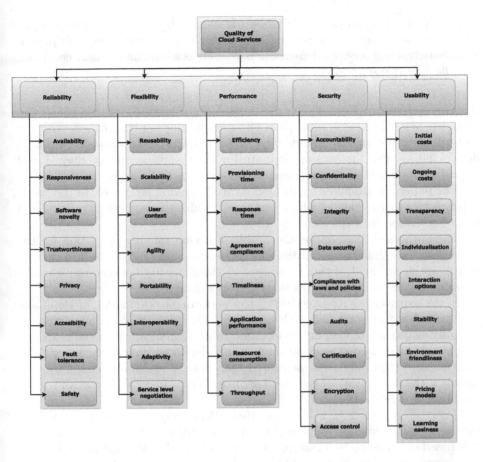

Fig. 1. QoS attributes (non-functional) in multi-clouds.

QoS Management Platforms. QoS management is usually interpreted as the process of allocating resources to the application to guarantee a SLA parameters as performance, availability or reliability. It needs an intelligent environment of self-management application components based on domain knowledge in which application components can be optimized thus facilitating the transition to an advanced governance environment. Reactive control systems taking into QoS attributes are needed to provide an intelligent cloud resource management. A QoS API is expected to be defined, maybe using the SMI indicators, in order to be able to implement a real cloud QoS management platform [18].

Cloud management platforms are currently commonly used in managing the different layers of cloud-based applications. In the ecosystem of RightScale, Enstratus, Cloudability, Cloudyn or CloudExpress, the clients can take advantage of added-value services using a common API that represent a major effort to unify information exposed by providers [18]. However, the multi-clouds supporting platforms do not had until now a clear objective to support QoS management.

The paper [32] proposed a framework named DynaQoS to provide QoS-guaranteed automatic resource management including support for multiple-objective control and service differentiation, as well as a self-tuning fuzzy controller with flexible rule selection.

Service Selection. Equal QoS is not possible to be attained by all cloud service providers [34]. The QoS of some providers are superior in performance, others in security or in offering the minimum costs. Consequently, the cloud users should decide the services that are appropriate for their applications, or they should appeal to human or semi-automated expert systems to do that.

The paper [27] discuss a set of QoS-aware brokering strategies, in the particular case of hybrid clouds, which aim to maximize the user satisfaction, cloud broker revenues and reduce energy costs.

The authors of [23] address the problem of QoS ranking prediction for the order of services under considerations for a particular user by proposing a particle swarm optimization algorithm that measure the similarity between two users by considering the occurrence probability of service pairs.

In the experiments reported in [34] the performance evaluation of cloud service providers was combined with monitored QoS data in order to obtain an accurate evaluation of QoS for cloud users. In particular, a fuzzy synthetic decision is used to evaluate the cloud service providers according to the users' preferences, and, then, based on monitored QoS data, a specific model is used to calculate the uncertainty of the cloud services. Then, fuzzy logic control is used to obtain QoS evaluation.

Smart CloudBench [9] is a system that offers automated, on-demand, real-time and customized benchmarking of software systems deployed on cloud IaaS. It is based on an analysis of run-time behavior of cloud services. It helps its users to compare available offerings in the cloud selection phase and to monitor performance for QoS assurance in the cloud consumption phase. The performance tests are referring to load, scalability, endurance, stress and spike.

The QoS attributes like trust, reliability or security can be modeled and discovered in automatic ways [18]. However, in these cases it is also required to take into account the user feedback. Therefore, the complete automation of a broker service is not possible as human validation is required to make strategic decisions.

Service Composition. QoS is increasingly significant when composing services because a degrading QoS in one of the services can dangerously disturb the QoS of the complete composition [7]. To tackle with this issue, the authors of [17] proposes building a data warehouse of QoS to achieve better service matching and enhance dynamic service composition. A centralized storage combines QoS information from various cloud sources and helps solve the cloud service selection problem through processing of large numbers of historical QoS of cloud services. The proposed QoS data warehouse model supports a deep analysis of the services interior structure and properties through online database analysis, reasoning about complex service weakness points, as well as visual representation of analysis results. The QoS attributes that are analyzed are availability, response time, documentation, best practice, throughput, latency, succcssability, reliability, and compliance.

Continuous QoS Assurance and Optimization. The cloud services evolve over time, in terms of provision, APIs, performance or availability. In these conditions, it is difficult to assess if a service keeps the compliance with current policies and regulations, with the technical specifications or SLAs, or fulfills functional and non-functional requirements of a user application. The exponential increase of the number of cloud services with similar functionality contribute also to the problem complexity, forcing the clients to invest considerable efforts in identifying the optimum cloud service for their application [19]. As continuous quality assurance and optimization of cloud is impossible for individual consumers, this reality creates the opportunities for a market of cloud service intermediaries, like the third party supporting a multi-cloud. Moreover, continuous QoS assurance and optimization is a highly required feature of cloud broker component of the multi-clouds.

Intermediation for continuous QoS assurance represents an open research topic. The paper [4] focuses on two specific forms of continuous QoS assurance intermediation, policy-driven cloud service governance and service level failure mitigation for cloud services. The scenario provided as example demonstrates the utility of continuous quality assurance intermediation capability.

The technology enabling to support continuous QoS assurance and optimization brokerage is already available [19]. The relevant tools that can provide the building blocks for an implementation of such continuous QoS assurance and optimization in brokers are the tools for monitoring and controlling services, applications, virtualised infrastructures, or even tools for integrating applications, processes and data.

In this context, the paper [19] presents the essential requirements for a software framework enabling continuous QoS assurance and optimization. Broker@Cloud is a software framework fulfilling these requirements [32]: the framework allows governance and quality control, failure prevention and recovery, as well as optimization. The broker capabilities are related to service discovery, integration, aggregation, customization, quality assurance, and optimization. Moreover, the work presented in [31] establishes a platform-agnostic ontology for the facilitation of QoS assurance brokerage.

4   QoS Assurance via Model-Driven Engineering

Model-Driven Techniques for Multi-clouds. Model-driven development techniques allow the shift of the programming paradigms from code-centric to model-centric. Models are the objects of the development process enabling the developers to work at a level of abstraction that allows them to focus on cloud

adoption rather on implementation specifics. Moreover, the model transformations help the automation of the process of going from abstract concepts to
implementation. This approach is highly relevant for the design and management
of applications across multiple clouds. Furthermore, models can also be used to
reason about the application QoS and to support design-time exploration methods that identify the best cloud deployment configuration that satisfy certain
QoS constraints.

In this context, the main goal of MODAClouds project[1] was to provide methods, a decision support system, an open source integrated development environment (IDE), a run-time environment for the high-level design, early proto-
typing, semi-automatic code generation, and automatic deployment of applications on multi-clouds with guaranteed QoS. MODAClouds envisioned to design
abstractions that help a QoS engineer to specify non-functional requirements
and tools to evaluate and compare multiple cloud architectures according their
availability, cost and performance.

MODAClouds' QoS Models. At the highest level of abstraction, independent from the cloud, the QoS model includes information concerning expected
QoS characteristics at the application level. QoS constraints can be attached
to specific application components or services. At the lowest level, closer to the
cloud environment, the QoS model includes data concerning QoS characteristics
of the specific cloud resources.

The overall process for applying the MODAClouds' model-based approach is
the following. The starting point for QoS analysis is at a first level of description
of the target application, a level that is independent from the cloud. The QoS
engineer specifies QoS constraints at the this level (e.g., constraints on the application response times). QoS constraints are then semi-automatically translated
into monitoring rules and additional monitoring rules can be also specified. At
the next level, dependent on the cloud, but independent from a specific provider,
constraints or monitoring rules predicating on specific cloud computing concepts
can be included (e.g., constraints specifying that the CPU utilization of an application container must be lower than a given threshold). The same happens for
the what concerns the cloud provider dependent level: QoS constraints (like monitoring rules) can be inherited from the previous level and new constraints (rules)
predicating on cloud specific model concepts can be introduced (e.g. cost information that offers the possibility to estimate the application costs). Monitoring
rules at all levels are feed into a monitoring engine. Then the QoS Engineer can
define the design alternatives and optimization constraints to perform the performance assessment of a given candidate solution. Finally, when the application
is fully deployed, design time parameters can be refined through the analysis of
run-time monitoring data.

In the early stage of the project, the authors of [2] described the state of the
art regarding cloud QoS modeling concepts and performance annotations and
evaluation of design-time models. The document specifies the requirements for

---

[1] www.modaclouds.eu.

QoS evaluation, design-time exploration and optimization tools developed in the frame of MODAClouds project. The investigated attributes of QoS are performance, cost and availability. The key metrics for performance were throughput, response time and system utilization. A special attention was given to model-based performance prediction.

The stochastic models considered suitable for performance analysis are Markovian chains, queueing systems, layered queueing networks, mean field model, fluid queues, or Petri nets. Such models are coupled with design exploration methods based on local search in order to examine design alternatives through what-if analyses. A QoS engineer is expected to express performance queries formulated upon QoS models (such queries allowing to verify the correctness of the performance requirements in the design phase). Quality-driven model transformation approaches can be used to navigate the design space or to specify feedback rules.

The QoS models developed in MODAClouds are based on layered queueing network models, which capture the contention between users for the available hardware and software resources, and the interaction between them. To parameterize these models, it is essential to estimate the inter-request times and the resource consumption associated with each request. Inter-request times can be extracted from the information and the data that is typically tracked by application-logs or container-level logs. Resource consumptions are harder to obtain as not being tracked by logs, and the deep monitoring instrumentations typically required pose unacceptably large overheads.

MODAClouds Toolbox. The MODAClouds model-driven approach is supported by the MODAClouds Toolbox (Fig. 2). This has three main components[2]: an IDE for high-level application design (Creator 4Clouds), a decision support system that helps decision makers identify and select the best execution venue for cloud applications, by considering technical and business requirements (Venues 4Clouds), and a multi-cloud run-time environment energized to provide automatic deployment and execution of applications with guaranteed Quality of Service (QoS) on compatible multi-clouds (Energizer 4Clouds).

Creator 4Clouds provides features to assess the QoS guarantees required by the application. It allows to analyze the QoS trade-offs of various possible application configurations (Space^{Dev}4Clouds), map high level data models into scalable NoSQL, and deploy the resulting application on multi-clouds by exploiting the CloudML[3] language. In particular, MODACloudML, a specific extension of CloudML, allows the definition of QoS constraints. A constraint is classified in hard or soft: hard constraints can never be violated, while soft constraints have certain priorities (the constraints with the highest associated priority are the ones more likely to be satisfied). The priority value associated to soft constraints are used for design time exploration [3].

---

[2] Available at http://www.modaclouds.eu/software/open-source-repositories/ as open-source codes.

[3] www.cloudml.org.

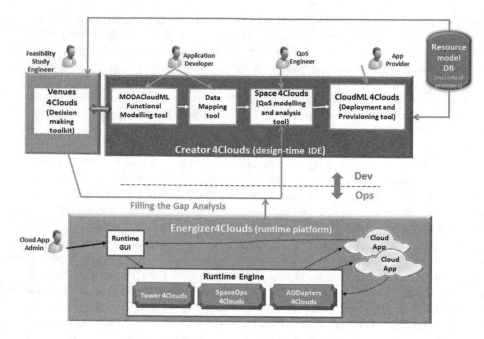

Fig. 2. Workflow of the MODAClouds Toolbox.

In Space^{Dev}4Cloud a two-step approach for search space exploration has been developed. In the first step, an initial configuration of the services is derived automatically using a partially specified application description provided by a QoS engineer. The solution is based on approximated performance models: the QoS associated to a deployment solution is calculated by means of a queuing model with processor sharing policy. In the second step, a local-search-based optimization algorithm iteratively improves the starting cloud deployment exploring several configurations. A performance model layered queueing network is employed to derive more accurate estimates of the QoS.

Energizer 4Clouds includes the frameworks to support monitoring (through Tower 4Clouds) and self-adaptation (Space^{Ops}4Clouds), together with utilities that perform auxiliary tasks in the platform (ADDapters 4Clouds). Through Tower 4Clouds, operators are able to perform complex monitoring and data analyses from multiple sources.

Space^{Ops}4Clouds identifies and actuates proper self-adaptation actions that take into account the current and foreseen state of the system under control. QoS constraints at run-time are translated into monitoring rules (inputs for the monitoring platform that is part of the Tower 4Clouds).

Monitoring rules are specifying the aggregation process of the fine grained monitoring data coming data collectors, under what conditions an alarm is raised (a condition can be a constraint on the values of the monitored data), and what actions are taken in case an alarm is triggered.

MODAClouds IDE can automatically generate monitoring rules from QoS constraints, while the QoS engineer can modify or add new rules. The QoS engineer specifies the constraints, delegates the creation of monitoring rules to the IDE, and then can modify or creates new rules. The framework allows to manipulate rules, as well as constraints, through a visual representation.

Space 4Clouds (^{Dev} and ^{Ops}) is designed to be a open source tool for the specification, assessment and optimization of QoS characteristics for cloud applications [14]. It allows users to describe a software architecture by means of MODA-CloudML models that express cloud-specific attributes. Its users can specify the models defining the cloud application using Creator 4Clouds graphical interface.

Space 4Clouds can be used either to assess the cost of an application and its cloud configuration or to find a suitable cloud configuration that e.g. minimizes the costs while meeting the QoS requirements, providing only the application model. Two possible usage scenarios are therefore possible. In the first one, the QoS engineer uses the tool in assessment mode, namely to evaluate the performance and cost based on a specific application deployment. In the second scenario, the QoS engineer provides only a partial configuration and lets the tool face the task of analyzing the possible alternatives to return a cost optimized solution that meets the constraints. In this scenario, the module returns a complete deployment description, and also reports useful information about the overall performance and cost. Then the QoS engineer can choose to accept the solution as it is, modify the constraints or change the deployment and evaluate again other configurations.

The feed-back loop technologies of MODAClouds Toolbox extend capabilities offered by the three main components: through them Tower 4Clouds is connected with Creator 4Clouds and Venues 4Clouds, respectively [12]. The first connector is responsible for providing the QoS engineers with the perspective of the application behavior at runtime in order to improve the development process. The second connector allows Venues 4Clouds to adapt its knowledge base according to monitoring data. This helps in offering to users an updated vision of services QoS for future recommendations.

To support QoS analysis, the developer may rely on performance, utilisation or reliability models. To provide reliable estimates, the input parameters must be accurately estimated. Such an estimation is challenging because not all QoS attributes are explicitly tracked by log files. The QoS models are initially parameterized using expert-knowledge or data collected in small deployments.

The Filling-the-Gap (FG) tool is a component for parametrization of performance models continuously at run time. Its objective is to provide accurate estimates to the parameters of the design-time QoS models [35]. Once the application has been deployed on the cloud, possibly in a production environment, the FG analysis is deployed to obtain estimates based on monitoring data collected at run-time. The FG tool implements a set of statistical estimation algorithms to parameterize performance models from run-time monitoring data related to response times and queue-lengths.

Final Remarks. The iterative process of QoS evaluation at different layers of application description using QoS models was proved to be useful at least in the main use cases of MODAClouds project. The iteration approach can be applied also to other use cases like the ones involving cloud-based Big Data applications.

5   QoS Assurance for Data-Intensive Cloud Applications

Data-intensive applications, like the ones with real-time requirements, are nowadays deployed in large-scale distributed storage of cloud environments. Real-time applications, like video streaming, virtual reality, digital libraries, or scientific data collection, are rely upon a certain level of QoS for their data access needs. High-throughput data-intensive processors, like MapReduce, also needs the QoS guarantees for a fast gathering of throughput for concurrent data access. Moreover, the current techniques dealing with QoS support in distributed file systems focus mainly on the network management among heterogeneous clusters and on the flow control. How to provide storage QoS in a distributed file system in cloud environments is challenging [33].

The DICE project[4] aims at developing tools that will help software designers reasoning about efficiency, reliability and safety of data-intensive cloud applications. One of its primary goals is to provide facilities to extensively model and verify the assessment of quality aspects [5]. The continuously evaluation of the QoS is important not only in the specific verification and validation phases, but through the entire life-cycle of the services.

In this context, the recent DICE project output [6] overviews on state-of-the-art research in quality testing through model-driven approaches. Testing methods that primarily focus on quality aspects like efficiency are considered. In particular, the non-functional characteristics of the software that are of interest for DICE are reliability (including availability and fault tolerance), performance (time behavior and resource utilization) and safety (acceptable levels of risk). The main quantitative analysis techniques that are measured and compared from the point of view of assessment of performance, reliability and safety are combinatorial, state-based (stochastic Petri nets, queueing networks) or Monte Carlo simulation. For QoS assurance aspects, a list of key monitoring metrics used to assess quality are provided.

The technologies and concepts analyzed in [6] are referring to: (1) frameworks for executing data-intensive applications[5] and streaming processors[6]; (2) NoSQL

---

[4] www.dice-h2020.eu.

[5] Current representative solutions: Hadoop and Spark.

[6] Current representative solutions: Apache Storm, Apache Spark Streaming, Apache Samza, Apache S4, STReamparse, Stratio.

databases[7] and in-memory databases[8]; (3) cloud-based blob storage[9]. Several conclusions of the analysis are reported in what follows.

Data-Intensive Processors. In what concerns the key metrics to assess the QoS of Hadoop or Spark services, the throughput and compliance with deadlines are the most relevant ones. Hadoop framework provides reliability guarantees by monitoring the execution of the map and reduce tasks. The QoS models for Hadoop reported in the literature are empirical models mapping data size into execution times, approximate formula evaluating jobs executions time starting from individual tasks execution time, or formal models like queueing network and colored Petri nets.

Big Data processing require at several stages of the computation to transfer partial results from one node to another (e.g. the copy shuffle phase of Hadoop and Spark). Data transfers could become the bottleneck of the computation. Therefore Software-Defined Networking (SDN) solutions are usually adopted to configure the underlying networking infrastructure to respond to this issue. Traffic engineering is ensuring the mechanism to optimise the performance of a data network at both traffic and resource level. SDN allows to have a centralised visibility of global network topology and status. The SDN traffic engineering mechanisms focus mainly on traffic analysis, fault tolerance, flow management, or topology update.

Stream processing solutions are designed to handle large data volumes in real time taking advantage of a highly available, scalable and fault-tolerant architecture. The key monitoring metrics are latency, non-stop streaming, I/O throughput, maximum delivery time. Streaming processors are fault-tolerant and inherently parallel, with different parts of the processors individually scalable.

Databases. NoSQL databases are data storage solution used nowadays for scalable web applications that have to analyze or move huge data sets. The monitoring metrics are the throughput by workload (number of operations performed on the database in the time unit, considering different types of workloads), latency by workload, and support to parallel connections. QoS attributes for NoSQL databases focuses on performance (response times, throughput, availability, scalability, consistency guarantees).

In-memory analytics aims at processing huge volumes of data in main memory, while minimising usage of disk I/O. In their case, the key monitoring metrics include CPU utilisation, query response times, threading level, thread affinity, mean memory consumption, peak memory consumption. A significant problem for quality assurance of in-memory databases is the ability to capture time-

---

[7] Current representative solutions: Amazon DynamoDB and SimpleDB, Google Datastore, Azure DocumentDB, Apache HBase, Cassandra, Hypertable, MongoDB, CouchDB, Riak, Redis, Berkeley DB, Dyomite.

[8] Current representative solutions: Apache Derby, HyperSQL, SQLite.

[9] Current representative solutions: Ceph and Amazon S3.

varying threading levels that are used internally to these databases to process queries efficiently.

Distributed Block Storage. Distributed block storage (e.g. provided by Ceph and S3) is more difficult to be administrated than centralised storage, despite its enhanced scalability. In particular, tuning it for performance can be more difficult. The key monitoring metrics of Ceph are available disk space, read/write operations per second, I/O waits, network throughput. Ceph provides scalability as being able to handle thousands of client hosts accessing exabytes of data. The key S3 monitoring metrics are the size of all objects present in buckets, the number of objects present in buckets, get/push transfer speeds. The S3 service allows by design concurrent device failures as it is quickly detecting and repairing any lost redundancy.

The provision of storage QoS allowing resource reservations and allocation of the required disk bandwidth (especially requested by real-time applications or any data transfer that needs fixed bandwidth assurance) is investigated in the paper [33].

Final Remarks. The QoS attributes used in the case of the development of cloud-based data-intensive applications are quite different from the QoS attributes were usually encountered in cloud environment (mentioned also in the first sections of this paper). Therefore the QoS assurance procedures for this special case should take into account the specific attributes.

6   Conclusions

Model-driven engineering techniques are proving their effectiveness in QoS assurance in cloud environment, and especially in the case of multi-clouds or data intensive application design. However the processes to be applied are quite complex and still require the intervention of human expert, a QoS engineer that is able to offer initial hints about the requested QoS of a certain application and to select, potentially after several refinement iterations, one of the recommended configurations for the application deployment on multi-cloud environments. This fact is due to the large search space and the multi-criteria objectives expressed in QoS requirements. In multi-cloud support systems the role of the QoS engineer is expected to be taken by automated procedures and the current status is showing that this requirement is not yet possible without making concessions on the QoS of the multi-cloud support system.

Acknowledgements. The analysis presented in Sects. 2 and 3 is partially funded by the grant of Romanian National Authority for Scientific Research, UEFISCDI, PN-II-ID-PCE-2011-3-0260 (AMICAS). Section 4 refers to the final results of the grant of European Commission FP7-ICT-2011-8-318484 (MODAClouds). Section 5 refers to the preliminary results of the grant of European Commission H2020-ICT-09-2014-644869 (DICE).

References

1. Ardagna, D., Casale, G., Ciavotta, M., Pérez, J.F., Wang, W.: Quality-of-service in cloud computing: modeling techniques and their applications. J. Internet Serv. Appl. **5**, 11 (2014)
2. Ardagna, D., Ciavotta, M. (eds.): Design-Time Quality Modelling and Evaluation: Analysis of the State of the Art and Scope Definition. Deliverable D5.1 of MODA-Clouds (2013). http://www.modaclouds.eu/publications/public-deliverables/
3. Ardagna, D., Ciavotta, M. (eds.): MODACloudML QoS Abstractions and Prediction Models Specification – Initial Version. DeliverableD5.2.1 of MODAClouds (2013). http://www.modaclouds.eu/publications/public-deliverables/
4. Bratanis, K., Kourtesis, D.: Introducing policy-driven governance and service level failure mitigation in cloud service brokers: challenges ahead. In: Lomuscio, A.R., Nepal, S., Patrizi, F., Benatallah, B., Brandić, I. (eds.) ICSOC 2013. LNCS, vol. 8377, pp. 177–191. Springer, Heidelberg (2014)
5. Casale, G., Ardagna, D., Artac, M., Barbier, F., Di Nitto, E., Henry, A., Iuhasz, G., Joubert, C., Merseguer, J., Munteanu, V.I., Pérez, J.F., Petcu, D., Rossi, M., Sheridan, C., Spais, I., Vladušič, D.: DICE: quality-driven development of data-intensive cloud applications. In: Proceedings of MiSE 2015, pp. 78–84 (2015)
6. Casale, G., Ustinova, T. (eds.): DICE Integrated Framework: State of the Art Analysis. Deliverable D1.1 of DICE (2015). http://www.dice-h2020.eu/deliverables/
7. Chana, I., Singh, S.: Quality of service and service level agreements for cloud environments issues and challenges. In: Mahmood, Z. (ed.) Cloud Computing. Computer Communications and Networks, pp. 51–72. Springer, Heidelberg (2014)
8. Chen, J.H., Abedin, F., Chao, K.-M., Godwin, N., Li, Y., Tsai, C.-F.: A hybrid model for cloud providers and consumers to agree on QoS of cloud services. Future Gener. Comput. Syst. **50**, 38–48 (2015)
9. Chhetri, M.B., Chichin, S., Vo, Q.B., Kowalczyk, R.: Smart CloudBench–a framework for evaluating cloud infrastructure performance. Inf. Syst. Front. **18**, 413–428 (2015). doi:10.1007/s10796-015-9557-2
10. Chu, W.C.-C., Yang, C.T., Lu, C.-W., Chang, C.-H., Hsueh, N.-L., Hsu, T.-S., S.H.: An approach of quality of service assurance for enterprise cloud computing (QoSAECC). In: Proceedings of TSA, pp. 7–13 (2014)
11. CSMIC: Service Measurement Index. Framework version 2.1 (2014). http://csmic.org/downloads/SMI_Overview_TwoPointOne.pdf
12. Di Nitto, E., Matthews, P., Petcu, D., Solberg, A.: Model-driven development and operation of multi-cloud applications. In: The MODAClouds Approach. SpringBriefs series. Springer (to appear)
13. Domínguez-Mayo, F.J., García-García, J.A., Escalona, M.J., Mejías, M., Urbieta, M., Rossi, G.: A framework and tool to manage Cloud Computing service quality. Softw. Qual. J. (2014). doi:10.1007/s11219-014-9248-0
14. Franceschelli, D., Ardagna, D., Ciavotta, M., Di Nitto, E.: Space4cloud: a tool for system performance and cost evaluation of cloud systems. In: Proceedings of MultiCloud 2013, pp. 27–34 (2013)
15. Hershey, P.C., Rao, S., Silio, C.B., Narayan, A.: System of systems for quality-of-service observation and response in cloud computing environments. IEEE Syst. J. **9**(1), 212–222 (2015)
16. International Telecommunication Union, E.800 : Definitions of termsrelated to quality of service (2008). http://www.itu.int/rec/T-REC-E.800-200809-I

17. Karawash, A., Mcheick, H., Dbouk, M.: Quality-of-service data warehouse for the selection of cloud services: a recent trend. In: Mahmood, Z. (ed.) Cloud Computing. Computer Communications and Networks, pp. 257–276. Springer, Heidelberg (2014)

18. Kourtesis, D., Alvarez-Rodríguez, J.M., Paraskakis, I.: Semantic-based QoS management in cloud systems: current status and future challenges. Future Gener. Comput. Syst. **32**, 307–323 (2014)

19. Kourtesis, D., Bratanis, K., Friesen, A., Verginadis, Y., Simons, A.J.H., Rossini, A., Schwichtenberg, A., Gouvas, P.: Brokerage for quality assurance and optimisation of cloud services: an analysis of key requirements. In: Lomuscio, A.R., Nepal, S., Patrizi, F., Benatallah, B., Brandić, I. (eds.) ICSOC 2013. LNCS, vol. 8377, pp. 150–162. Springer, Heidelberg (2014)

20. Lee, S.-Y., Tang, D., Chen, T., Chu, W.C.-C.: A QoS assurance middleware model for enterprise cloud computing. In: Proceedings of the IEEE 36th COMPSACW, pp. 322–327 (2012)

21. Lin, J.-W., Chen, C.-H., Lin, C.-Y.: Integrating QoS awareness with virtualization in cloud computing systems for delay-sensitive applications. Future Gener. Comput. Syst. **37**, 478–487 (2014)

22. Maarouf, A., Marzouk, A., Haqiq, A.: Automatic control of the quality of service contract by a third party in the cloud computing. In: Proceedings of WCCS, pp. 599–603 (2014)

23. Mao, C., Chen, J., Towey, D., Chen, J., Xie, X.: Search-based QoS ranking prediction for web services in cloud environments. Future Gener. Comput. Syst. **50**, 111–126 (2015)

24. McIntyre, S.H., Kirby, G.: The market for service assurance: a model and data structure. In: Proceedings of SRII Global Conference, pp. 184–192 (2011)

25. Petcu, D.: Consuming resources and services from multiple clouds. From terminology to cloudware support. J. Grid Comput. **12**(2), 321–345 (2014)

26. Petcu, D., Vasilakos, A.V.: Portability in clouds: approaches and research opportunities. Scalable Comput.: Pract. Experience **15**(3), 251–270 (2014)

27. Quarati, A., Clematis, A., D'Agostino, D.: Delivering cloud services with QoS requirements: business opportunities, architectural solutions and energy-saving aspects. Future Gener. Comput. Syst. (2015). doi:10.1016/j.future.2015.02.009

28. Rak, M., Suri, N., Luna, J., Petcu, D., Casola, V., Villano, U.: Security as a service using an SLA-based approach via SPECS. In: Proceedings of the 5th CloudCom, vol. 2, pp. 1–6 (2013)

29. Rao, J., Wei, Y., Gong, J., Xu, C.-Z.: QoS guarantees and service differentiation for dynamic cloud applications. IEEE Trans. Netw. Serv. Manag. **10**(1), 43–55 (2013)

30. Thoss, Y., Pohl, C., Hoffmann, M., Spillner, J., Schill, A.: User-friendly visualization of cloud quality. In: Proceedings of the IEEE 7th CLOUD, pp. 890–897 (2014)

31. Veloudis, S., Friesen, A., Paraskakis, I., Verginadis, Y., Patiniotakis, I.: Underpinning a cloud brokerage service framework for quality assurance and optimization. In: Proceedings of the IEEE 6th CloudCom, pp. 660–663 (2014)

32. Veloudis, S., Paraskakis, I., Friesen, A., Verginadis, Y., Patiniotakis, I., Rossini, A.: Continuous quality assurance and optimisation in cloud-based virtual enterprises. In: Camarinha-Matos, L.M., Afsarmanesh, H. (eds.) Collaborative Systems for Smart Networked Environments. IFIP AICT, vol. 434, pp. 621–632. Springer, Heidelberg (2014)

33. Wang, C.-M., Yeh, T.-C., Tseng, G.-F.: Provision of storage QoS in distributed file systems for clouds. In: Proceedings of the 41st ICPP, pp. 189–198 (2012)

34. Wang, S., Liu, Z., Sun, O., Zou, H., Yang, F.: Towards an accurate evaluation of quality of cloud service in service-oriented cloud computing. J. Intell. Manuf. **25**, 283–291 (2014)
35. Wang, W., Perez, J.F., Casale, G.: Filling the gap: a tool to automate parameter estimation for software performance models. In: Proceedinds of the 1st QUDOS, pp. 31–32 (2015)
36. Wollersheim, J., Krcmar, H.: Quality analysis approaches for cloud services - towards a framework along the customer's activity cycle. In: Krcmar, H., Reussner, R., Rumpe, B. (eds.) Trusted Cloud Computing, pp. 109–124. Springer, Heidelberg (2014)

Employing Relevance Feedback to Embed Content and Service Importance into the Selection Process of Composite Cloud Services

Dimosthenis Kyriazis[1(✉)], Nikolaos Doulamis[2], George Kousiouris[2], Andreas Menychtas[2], Marinos Themistocleous[1], and Vassilios C. Vescoukis[2]

[1] Department of Digital Systems, University of Piraeus, Karaoli & Dimitriou 80, 185 34 Piraeus, Greece
{dimos,mthemist}@unipi.gr
[2] National Technical University of Athens, Iroon Polytechniou 9, Athens, Greece
{ndoulam,v.vescoukis}@cs.ntua.gr, {gkousiou,ameny}@mail.ntua.gr

Abstract. Cloud computing is essentially changing the way services are built, provided and consumed. As a paradigm building on a set of combined technologies, it enables service provision through the commoditization of IT assets and on-demand usage patterns. In the emerging era of the Future Internet, clouds aim at facilitating applications that move away from the monolithic approach into an Internet-scale one, thus exploiting information, individual offerings and infrastructures as composite services. In this paper we present an approach for selecting the services (that comprise the composite ones) in order to meet the end-to-end Quality of Service (QoS) requirements. The approach is enhanced with a relevance feedback mechanism that provides additional information with respect to the importance of the content and the service. The latter is performed in an automated way, allowing for user preferences to be considered during the service selection process. We also demonstrate the operation of the implemented approach and evaluate its effectiveness using a real-world scenario, based on a computer vision application.

Keywords: Cloud computing · Quality of service · Composite services · Relevance feedback

1 Introduction

As the cloud service model matures and becomes ubiquitous, service-based applications are amongst the first being deployed in such platforms. In the majority of the cases, these applications move away from the monolithic approach towards a paradigm that emphasizes modular design, giving rise to the wider adoption of the cloud service model. Since these applications consist of application service components, they are considered to be composite services (often referred to as workflows even though the term workflow includes also the orchestration of the services [1]).

These application service components provide specific functionality, contributing to the overall application's one, and may be offered by different providers. There has to be

© Springer International Publishing Switzerland 2016
J. Altmann et al. (Eds.): GECON 2015, LNCS 9512, pp. 98–114, 2016.
DOI: 10.1007/978-3-319-43177-2_7

noted that this distributed paradigm is also applied across the cloud service stack since besides service components, infrastructure (e.g. networking or storage resources) may be offered as a service within the overall applications. A representative example refers to a video rendering application which consists of service components (i.e. shaders compilation, textures compilation, rendering) but could also require the provision of a storage service to for the output video file. Thus, Future Internet applications offered through cloud environments often impose the need to engage more than one providers that offer the corresponding service.

Moreover, one has to consider that the need for dependability (as one of the main Future Internet Architecture Design Principles [2]) is fundamental for the user needs, while it has been noted that focus of cloud computing is also the user experience [3]. In this context, service selection should account for both the specific requirements with respect to the Quality of Service (QoS) and the users' vision (referred as Quality of Experience - QoE). In the case of composite services, additional challenges arise given that: (i) the users set their requirements for the (overall) end-to-end QoS and not for specific service types, (ii) the users may have specific preferences according to their experience for individual services and providers, (iii) delivery of the composite service may be provided across a federation of providers. To address these challenges, we need to set new mechanisms to estimate, search and then retrieve for the most suitable selection of the most available service components of which an application/composite service consists to deliver an overall quality of a service across a federation of providers considering at the same time the users' experience and preferences.

A QoS-aware service selection approach that incorporates a relevance feedback mechanism providing additional information during the selection process with respect to the users' QoE and preferences has been studied and evaluated through experiments in this paper. The presented algorithm allows for the selection of services instances/ components (offered by different providers) that compose the overall application/ composite service based on the end-to-end QoS parameters posed by the end user. Furthermore, the QoE consists as an additional criterion within the selection algorithm. To enable the latter we have developed a relevance feedback mechanism that concludes in an automated way (i.e. without users' intervention) to the "importance" of the content and the service. This is in fact an on-line learning process that update and dynamically evolve the profile of a user with respect to the relevant items chosen in a dynamic manner. The term "importance" refers here to the user's preferences (based on QoE metrics) for specific services within the composite service, for which the users do not pose explicitly QoS requirements - these requirements remain as end-to-end ones at the overall composite service level.

The remainder of the paper is structured as follows. Section 2 presents related work in the field of the QoS-aware selection processes and relevance feedback mechanism, while Sect. 3 introduces the presented approach. The incorporated relevance feedback mechanism is addressed in Sect. 4, while the main research topic and focus of our work (QoS-aware service selection algorithm) is introduced in Sect. 5. In the last section (Sect. 6), we present an experiment which we conducted in order to demonstrate and evaluate the operation of the implemented algorithm for a real-world computer vision application in an industrial environment. The performance of the proposed mechanism is depicted in the results and the evaluation section. Section 7 concludes with a discussion on future research and potentials for the current study.

2 Related Work

Management of composite services in cloud environments is one of the main topics within the research community. Various approaches have been proposed addressing different aspects of management both of atomic and of composite services. In most cases, service management is linked with the provision of QoS guarantees and the management of SLAs, which include such QoS terms (e.g. SLA violation protection [4]). Within this section we mainly focus on research approaches in the area of service selection (in the case of composite services), service configuration and invocation as well as relevance feedback. A fair scheduling algorithm for managing composite services of 3D image rendering was proposed in [5].

QoS-aware service selection for composite services has been addressed by different researchers. Constraint Programming has been proposed in [6], while Integer Programming and Mixed Linear Integer Programming has been used in [7–9] in order to optimize composite service execution plans. Authors of [10] propose a workflow engine (namely "WSQoSX") that builds on top of [7, 9] to construct a feasible solution based on a backtracking algorithm. A heuristic method to identify services that meet local QoS parameters (resulted by the decomposition of end-to-end QoS constraints) using integer linear programming is introduced in [11, 12], while following such a decomposition method and applying fuzzy logic control to support dynamic service selection with the lowest cost is proposed in [13]. Authors in [14] propose heuristic algorithms to find near-optimal solutions in polynomial time by modeling the service selection as a 0–1 knapsack problem and a multi-constraint optimal path problem. An interesting work is presented in [15] through a reputation-aware model for service selection that takes into account the users' experience to develop a QoS similarity metric that reflects the differences between the providers' advertised QoS and the users' experience.

As regards relevance feedback, several works have been proposed mainly in the field of content-based image retrieval. In particular in [16], a heuristic methodology is adopted based on the standard deviation of the relevant selected features. The main idea of this scheme is that upon a user's selection, all features of importance should share low deviation values while the insignificant features should characterize by large deviation values. However, as mentioned in the conclusions of this paper, there is a need for an optimal weight updating strategy. An approach towards this direction has been initially reported in [17], where the parameters of the weighted Euclidean similarity metric are optimally estimated so that the distance over all selected relevant images are minimized. The generalized Euclidean allows interconnection between different feature elements though that singularities issues are observed in this work. Other works apply Support Vector Machines (SVM) [18] or semi-supervised learning frameworks [19]. Finally, discriminant analysis was introduced in [20] and content-based sampling algorithms on the use of non-linear structures in [21].

The difference between the research outcomes presented in this section and our proposed approach lies on the fact that the ones presented here address the case of selecting services and nodes based on QoS parameters by dealing only with the specific cases of minimizing one of the parameters whilst furthermore all the parameters have the same weight attribute. In our study, the QoS parameters are dealt in a combined way as well, while we also introduce a relevance feedback mechanism to identify the user preferences and affect the selection process since one of the parameters may play a more important role during the selection process. The presented QoS-aware selection mechanisms develop execution plans that enable QoS optimization. Nevertheless, what is of major importance in clouds (especially in federated ones) is the potential network overhead that affects the end-to-end QoS level of composite services (e.g. increase of overall time due to data move across sites). To this direction we introduce the importance of the content and the service in the selection process, which may alter the selection (and as a result the execution plan) accordingly. To some extent, users' experience (and as a result importance) has been discussed in the literature, but the limitations of the corresponding works refer both to the non-automated way to obtain the QoE and to the appliance of such approaches only to services and not to content as well which may be utilized by the services.

3   Composite Service Management Overview

As already mentioned, the aim of the work presented in this paper is to identify and describe the processes that need to be completed in order to select services/components (of which a composite service consists) with regard to the provided QoS metrics. To achieve the latter we introduce a selection algorithm along with its implementation. Each composite service contains processes - service types - that can be executed from a set of service candidates, which are annotated with QoS information. The proposed approach allows the selection of these candidates for each service type based on the user constraints and the QoS parameters exposed from the service providers for each candidate. The approach is depicted in the following figure (Fig. 1) through a data flow diagram to clarify the required and generated information for each mechanism:

- The end user and the service provider are external entities. The end user sets constraints on specific QoS parameters (e.g. completion time, availability, cost, etc.). The service providers offer services annotated with QoS information. This information along with the user constraints consist as input for the selection algorithm.
- Two (2) datastores are used. The first one holds the monitoring information (both on application level and on infrastructure level) which is exploited by the relevance feedback mechanism. The second store holds the outcome of the selection process.
- The service management approach includes four (4) main processes: (i) a monitoring mechanism (namely "Application & Infrastructure Monitoring") providing monitoring information for the infrastructure (i.e. use of resources) and the application (i.e. number of requests to a service), (ii) an enactment service (namely "Composite Service Enactment") that configures and invokes the corresponding services, (iii) a relevance feedback mechanism (namely "Content & Service Importance") that

provides in an automated way the user preferences with respect to different service types based on monitoring information (e.g. for a response time QoS parameter the weight factor of it during the selection process should be decreased if the user consumes the service regardless of its response time), (iv) a selection algorithm (namely "QoS-aware Service Selection") that obtains the information from the user and the providers as well as the preferences from the relevance feedback mechanism in order to make the optimum service selection of the available candidates. In this paper we present the relevance feedback mechanism and the selection algorithm (green highlighted in Fig. 1 and further described in Sects. 4 and 5 accordingly). The monitoring and the enactment services (developed in [22, 23]) are used during our experimentation and for completion reasons are cited in Fig. 1.

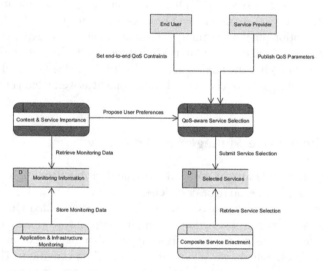

Fig. 1. Composite service management overview. (Color figure online)

4   Content and Service Importance

Let us assume that we have a set of N available services, denoted as $\mathbf{S}_i$, with $i = 1, 2, \ldots, N$. Each service is characterized by a list of M attributes $\mathbf{S}_i = [s_1^{(i)} \ s_2^{(i)} \ \cdots \ s_M^{(i)}]^T$. For this reason, we denote a service through a vector in contrast to a scalar. Examples of service attributes $s_{j,i}$ can be precision, execution time, availability, purchase cost, size and even service metadata (e.g., in a TV content service provision, service metadata refer to content type, resolution, overlays, or visual properties of TV stream). For each attribute, we set a weight, $w(s_j)$, which expresses the degree of importance concerning the attribute a_j. In this notation, we have omitted superscript (i) since we assign the same weight attribute for all service types. In conventional service selection mechanisms, equal weights are assigned for all attributes, meaning that the selection is independent from the significance of a service, or in other words that all service attributes equally contribute to the selection process. Another case is to manually set the weights $w(s_j)$ by the users. This, however, implies that the user is forced to obtain cloud computing knowledge and technical details, while in fact those details should be implicit. An alternative is to employ a relevance feedback strategy, which implicitly evaluates a set of service selections and then using an on-line learning strategy, estimates the contribution of each attribute (degree of importance) to the final service selection process. Thus, the optimization strategy is adjusted according to information as regards service relevance with respect to user's preferences (Fig. 2).

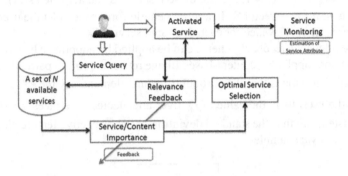

Fig. 2. Relevance feedback mechanism overview.

Upon a query, a set of K services are selected from the pool of all N available services by the application of an optimal selection algorithm. The user evaluates the retrieved services and selects a small number L out of the K retrieved as relevant. Then, the relevance feedback mechanism is activated to dynamically update importance weights of each service attribute. This way, at the following service selection process the K retrieved services are more relevant to user's preferences. The relevance feedback algorithm uses information derived from the monitoring module which dynamically calculates the current values of the attributes of a selected service. Relevance feedback leads to a dynamic selection of the services attribution, under a transparent and hidden to the user way without imposing him/her to get cloud computing or software engineering knowledge. Instead, the schemes just receive an evaluation of the system performance via the service monitoring process, and then the schemes applies intelligent learning algorithms to modify the decision rules and conclude to a concrete, user-centric judgment as regards service selection process. Two types of relevance feedback schemes are exploited in this paper. The first one updates the degree of service weights importance exploiting only service observations, i.e. using only the statics of service monitoring (i.e. the query vector is not taken into account within the relevance feedback scheme). Instead, the dynamic updating is accomplished on the activated services statics being extracted through the service monitoring process. The second type is an optimal methodology that estimates new weight factors so that, after the adaptation of the content/service importance coefficient the new retrieval results to trust current service requests as being submitted by the user while simultaneously retaining the "relevant" services selection at a maximum possible degree.

4.1 Service Observation-Based Relevance Feedback

In this approach, service attributes are selected via the activated services, i.e., the ones which accept the user since they satisfy his/her information needs and preferences. Let us recall that upon a service request, K services have been retrieved from the system to the user. Let us also recall that a small number L of them is chosen by the user, implicitly implying that these L services are within his/her preferences. Let us denote as $\mathbf{E}_i = [e_1^{(i)}\ e_2^{(i)} \cdots e_{L'}^{(i)}]^T$, with $i = 1, 2, \ldots, L$ these L selected and activated services. Vector $\mathbf{E}_i$ is of the same form as vector $\mathbf{S}_i$. In a more generic form we can let the user to assign different degrees λ of relevance for each activated service $\mathbf{E}_i$.

Then, the relevance feedback scheme can be applied by adopting a heuristic scheme similar to the ones applied to content-based image retrieval [16]. In particular, the main concept of this heuristic is that if a particular feature element, say the $e_j^{(i)}$ is a preferred attribute by the user, then, the value of $e_j^{(i)}$ over all selected L services, $i = 1, 2, \ldots, L$ will be consistent and thus the standard deviation of the respective feature element over all selected L relevant samples

$$\sigma_j = \frac{1}{L}\sqrt{\sum_{i=1}^{L}(e_j^{(i)} - \mu_j)^2} \tag{1}$$

should be small [24]. In Eq. (1), μ_j is the average value of the j-th feature element over the L selected samples, i.e. $\mu_j = 1/L \sum_{i=1}^{L} e_j^{(i)}$. On the other hand, if the standard deviation σ_j takes large values over the selected L services, this implies that the respective feature is not of user's interest. This idea simply means that the weights $w(s_j)$ can be estimated as

$$w(s_j) = \frac{1}{\sigma_j} \tag{2}$$

Though the idea behind the proposed system is quite reasonable, it still remains an ad hoc method. For this reason, as mentioned in the conclusions of [25], there is a need for an optimal updating scheme to estimate the weights $w(s_j)$.

4.2 Optimal Relevance Feedback Constrained by User's Demands and Service Observations

The second approach improves the performance of the first ad hoc methodology. The idea here is to optimally calculate the new weight attributes for a service taken into account both the activated services, i.e. the vectors $\mathbf{E}_i = [e_1^{(i)}\ e_2^{(i)} \cdots e_{L'}^{(i)}]^T$ and the user's demands being expressed through a service request vector say $\mathbf{Q} = [q_1\ q_2 \cdots q_L]^T$. Again, vector $\mathbf{Q}_i$ is of the same form as vectors $\mathbf{E}_i$ and $\mathbf{S}_i$. The proposed notation also support some attributes of the query vector $\mathbf{Q}$ not to be defined. In other words, this simply let these attributions undefined. As it has been proven in [26], the cross correlation similarity measure is a more suitable distance metric compared to conventional Euclidean distance and variations of it, like the weighted and the generalized one. Cross correlation criterion is a normalized measure, which expresses how similar two feature vectors are and thus it indicates a metric of their similarity. Furthermore, correlation remains unchanged with respect to feature vector scaling and/or translation. For example, adding or multiplying a constant value to all elements of a feature vector affects the Euclidean distance but not the correlation. The cross correlation metric can be expressed as:

$$\rho(\mathbf{E}_i, \mathbf{Q}) = \frac{\sum\limits_{i=1}^{N} e_j^{(i)} \cdot q_j}{\sqrt{\sum\limits_{i=1}^{N} (q_j)^2} \cdot \sqrt{\sum\limits_{i=1}^{N} (e_j^{(i)})^2}} \tag{3}$$

While its weighted version can be given as:

$$\rho_w(\mathbf{E}_i, \mathbf{Q}) = \frac{\sum\limits_{i=1}^{M} w(s_j) \cdot e_j^{(i)} \cdot q_j}{\sqrt{\sum\limits_{i=1}^{M} (w_j q_j)^2} \cdot \sqrt{\sum\limits_{i=1}^{M} (e_j^{(i)})^2}} \tag{4}$$

Let us now assume that L out of the K best retrieved services have been selected by the user. Then, assuming that all the L services are relevant to the actual users' information needs, the optimal weight $w(s_j)$ is estimated so that the following criterion is maximized,

$$A_w = \sum\limits_{i=1}^{L} \rho_w(\mathbf{E}_i, \mathbf{Q}) = \sum\limits_{i=1}^{L} \frac{\sum\limits_{i=1}^{M} w(s_j) \cdot e_j^{(i)} \cdot q_j}{\sqrt{\sum\limits_{i=1}^{M} (w(s_j) \cdot q_j)^2} \cdot \sqrt{\sum\limits_{i=1}^{M} (e_j^{(i)})^2}} \tag{5}$$

Differentiating the quantity A_w with respect to all weights attributes $w(s_j)$ and then setting their values equal to zero, we derive, i.e., $\partial A_w / \partial w(s_j) = 0$, for all weights attributes $w(s_j), j = 1, 2, \ldots, M$, we have that

$$\frac{\partial A_w}{\partial w(s_n)} = 0 \Rightarrow \sum\limits_{i=1}^{L} \frac{e_j^{(n)}}{G_{\mathbf{E}_i}} \cdot (\sum\limits_{m=1}^{M} w(s_m)^2 (q_m)^2) = (\sum\limits_{i=1}^{L} \sum\limits_{m=1}^{M} w(s_m) \cdot q_m \cdot \frac{e_m^{(i)}}{G_{\mathbf{E}_i}}) \cdot w(s_n) \cdot q_n \quad \forall n = 1, 2, \ldots, M \tag{6}$$

In Eq. (6), $G_{\mathbf{E}_i} = \sqrt{\sum\limits_{i=1}^{M} e_j^{(i)}}$ is the energy of vector $\mathbf{E}_i$. The previous equation refers to a linear system of M equations (as the number of unknown weights). By dividing two equations of the form shown in (3) one over the other, for example the ones corresponding to $\partial A_w / \partial w(s_n)$ and $\partial A_w / \partial w(s_k)$, $n \neq k$, the following relation of weights $w(s_n)$ and $w(s_k)$ is obtained

$$w(s_n) = w(s_k) \cdot \frac{q_k}{q_n} \cdot \frac{\sum_{i=1}^{L} \dfrac{e_n^{(i)}}{G_{E_i}}}{\sum_{i=1}^{L} \dfrac{e_k^{(i)}}{G_{E_i}}} \quad \forall n \neq k \tag{7}$$

Equation (7) is a linear system of M equations with M-1 unknowns. However, substituting the weight ratio expressed in (6) to the system of (5), all the M non-linear equations are satisfied. This means that (7) is the solution of the maximization problem of (5) and thus one weight out of M is a free variable. An explanation of this is due to the properties of A_w. Indeed, scaling the feature vector has no impact on the correlation. For this reason, among all possible solutions, we select the one in which the L_2-norm of the weights is equal to one, i.e., $\|\mathbf{w}\|_2 = 1$, where $\mathbf{w} = [w(s_1)\ w(s_2)\ \cdots\ w(s_M)]^T$. Assuming without loss of generality that the first weight, $w(s_1)$ is the free variable then, we have that

$$w(s_1) = \pm \sqrt{\frac{1}{1 + \sum_{i=2}^{M} B_i}}, \quad \text{where } B_k = \frac{q_1}{q_k} \cdot \frac{\sum_{i=1}^{L} \dfrac{e_k^{(i)}}{G_{E_i}}}{\sum_{i=1}^{L} \dfrac{e_1^{(i)}}{G_{E_i}}} \tag{8}$$

In Eq. (8), we have selected the positive solution since this leads to the maximization of A_w. The other negative solution results in the minimization of the normalized cross correlation.

Introducing **recursive implementation**, the main advantage of (9) is that it can be recursively estimated as more and more services being activated through the monitoring module. This means that, if we have estimated the weights upon a given user's demands, at the following iterations, we do not need to re-calculate the weights from scratch, but we can exploit the previous estimated weights to update the current ones.

To estimate the weights recursively, we denote as $F_l^{(r)}$ the following quantities

$$F_l^{(r)} = \sum_{m=0}^{r} \beta^{r-k} \sum_{i=1}^{L(k)} \frac{e_l^{(i)}(k)}{G_{E_i}(k)} \quad \forall l = 1, 2, .., M \tag{9}$$

where we recall that ε is a forgetting factor. In this equation, we denote as $L(k)$ the number of selected services at the k-th iteration of the algorithm. Then, the weights at the final r-th iteration are expressed by

$$w^{(r)}(s_n) = w^{(r)}(s_l) \cdot \frac{q_l}{q_n} \cdot \frac{F_n(r)}{F_l(r)} \tag{10}$$

However, $F_l(r)$ can be estimated recursively using only information of the current iteration step and the previously obtained $F_l(r - 1)$. In particular, we have that $F_l(-1) = 0$

$$F_l(r) = \delta \cdot F_l(r - 1) + \sum_{i=1}^{L} \frac{e_l^{(i)}(r)}{G_{E_l}} \quad \forall l = 1, 2, \dots, M \tag{11}$$

5 Service Selection

In this section we describe the algorithm used within the service selection mechanism in order to conclude to the components/candidates per service type of the composite service based on the QoS parameters. The main goal of the algorithm is to result to an optimum selection with regard to the QoS metrics set by the user and the corresponding ones published by the service providers. The algorithm's strategy is initially to select candidates in a way that the constraints set by the user are met (e.g. select services that meet the requested availability level without violating the budget constraint). Afterwards, the instances that offer higher level of QoS (e.g. in terms of availability or execution time) are defined and replacements on the initial selection take place.

Within the algorithm, the user's preferences are expressed with the weights $w(s_n)$ for the corresponding parameters (obtained by the relevance feedback mechanism). These values express how important each parameter is considered to be by the user and are expressed through the weight factor of Eq. (10).

Following, we describe in detail the major steps of the algorithm along with their sub-steps:

1. "Characterisation" of the provided QoS per service type taking into account all providers' offers for the specific service type
   1.1. Calculation of the minimum and maximum values for each one of the QoS parameters (set by the user) for each service type of the composite service based on their service instances (candidates).
   1.2. Computation of the pilot values for the parameters based on the minimum and maximum values of them with the use of the following function:

$$F_{Paramn}(x) = \exp\left(wn * \frac{x - MinParamnValue}{MaxParamnValue - MinParamnValue}\right) \tag{12}$$

   In the above functions, x is the value of QoS parameter for each service instance and $MinParamValue, MaxParamValue$ are the minimum and maximum values of the parameter (as described in the previous sub-step).
   1.3. Calculation of the new parameters' values that will be used further on based on the aforementioned functions (with the use of Eq. (12)):

$$NewParamnValue = InitialParamnValue * F_{Paramn}(InitialParamnValue) \tag{13}$$

In the above equation, *InitialParamnValue* refers to the value of the parameter that was initially obtained by the service providers as their offer.

1.4. Calculation of the following *ConvertedIndex* that will be used in sequel in order to proceed with the selections:

$$ConvertedIndex = \frac{\prod_{i=x}^{y} NewParamiValue}{\prod_{j=k}^{l} NewParamjValue} \qquad (14)$$

This index is the major criterion during the selection process since it shows for each service instance the offered level of quality for specific parameters with regard to the corresponding values of other parameters. We set in the numerator the parameters for which a decrease in their values optimizes the overall quality (e.g. completion time) and in the denominator the parameters for which an increase in their values optimizes the overall quality.

2. Initial service selection for one parameter
   2.1. For each service type, a candidate is selected that meets the user's parameter constraint according to the importance sorting provided by the relevance feedback mechanism (e.g. selection based on availability).
   2.2. Calculation of the overall parameters values (e.g. for cost, completion time) for the composite service according to the services selected in the previous sub-step. If these exceed the user's constraints, a selection cannot be made and the algorithm ends, otherwise it continues with the next step.
3. Identification of a candidate for each service type. The reason for this step is to discover the candidates that provide higher level of QoS for each service type.
   3.1. For each service type, the candidate with the lowest value of the *ConvertedIndex* is defined in comparison with the one selected in Step 2 of the algorithm. If no instances are defined, the service type is excluded from the rest of the algorithm execution since no optimization can be performed. If this applies for all service types, the algorithm ends and the initial selection is considered to be the final one. Otherwise, it continues with the next sub-step.
   3.2. Selection of the candidates for each service type with the lowest value of the ConvertedIndex.
   3.3. Calculation of the differences in the values of the parameters between the initial service selection (from Step 2) and the replacement one (from step 3.2).
4. Creation of a list with the "best candidates" for each service type in order to find possible replacement(s)
   4.1. For each difference that has been calculated in Step 3, the *ConvertedIndex* is re-calculated. Basically, Step 1 of the algorithm is re-executed considering as initial values for the service instances the aforementioned differences and the replacements are made based on their differences.
   4.2. The services with the lowest new ConvertedIndex are selected.

4.3. Based on the new selection, the overall parameters values are re-calculated. If the user's QoS constraints are met, the new services are the ones identified in the previous sub-step, otherwise they are excluded as candidates.

4.4. The algorithm is looped and continues from Step 3 for all service types.

6 Evaluation

The experiment used to validate our approach was performed for a real-world composite service that has been developed in the framework of the SCOVIS EU-funded project [27]. The computer vision application consists of two services *Object Identification* and *Process Recognition* [28]. For this application, we use as input three (3) real-world datasets (videos) recorded in NISSAN Iberica automobile construction industry. They capture complex industrial processes which have as a goal the assembly of a car in the factory. The recorded frames depict metal sparks, cars' equipment racks, and workers performing the assembly as well as robotic movements and fires.

Besides these application-oriented services, the composite service of our experiment includes an infrastructure-level service to depict the applicability of the algorithm along the cloud model stack. This service refers to a storage service that is used to store the output of the process recognition service as well as the output of the object identification service (providing also input for the process recognition service).

We have used as a cloud infrastructure for our experiment the one developed in the framework of IRMOS EU-funded project [29]. The infrastructure consisted of four sites acting as providers, which offer all the three services described in the previous paragraphs. In sequel, we published different SLA offers to demonstrate the different QoS offers from the providers' side for the offered services. We have selected as representative parameters Cost (denoted as C), Performance (denoted as P and referring to the accuracy for the object identification and process recognition services and the availability of the storage service), and Time (denoted as T and referring to the execution time of the application services and the storage time for the storage service). The corresponding offers for each provider are presented in the following Table 1.

Table 1. Published QoS parameters.

	Object identification service			Process recognition service			Storage service		
	C	P	T	C	P	T	C	P	T
Prov. #1	77.07	90.19	318.07	45.89	92.12	52.12	32.47	93.91	0.93
Prov. #2	93.12	98.19	371.12	36.04	99.03	67.93	28.22	94.09	0.23
Prov. #3	73.33	81.42	484.21	33.81	97.85	72.33	12.13	71.14	0.34
Prov. #4	89.03	92.17	336.48	45.46	85.19	50.54	19.28	88.77	0.32
Prov. #5	92.17	89.92	343.21	37.08	83.12	64.88	23.27	65.53	0.12
Prov. #6	85.12	90.13	331.98	35.77	93.99	68.85	32.32	97.23	0.46
Prov. #7	62.03	86.07	459.32	41.01	93.29	68.63	19.83	91.19	0.43
Prov. #8	79.01	89.18	350.13	29.99	89.14	82.49	28.22	91.03	0.99

For the sake of the experiment, we set the following end-to-end QoS requirements from the user side for the complete composite service: (i) Cost: threshold at 150 account units, (ii) Performance: at least 90 %, (iii) Time: threshold to 400 time units. We have also utilized the information from the relevance feedback mechanism to conclude on the QoS parameters that are of importance for the user and thus proceed with the service selection accordingly. The following table (Table 2) provides information on the user's selections from different providers (obtained by SLA monitoring data). According to these values and Eq. (10), the weight values of the parameters are the following: (i) Cost = 0.15, (ii) Performance = 0.78, (iii) Availability = 0.07.

Table 2. User's selections normalized monitoring data

	Object identification service	Process recognition service	Storage service
Prov. #1	7	12	25
Prov. #2	27	33	15
Prov. #3	3	28	2
Prov. #4	15	4	6
Prov. #5	5	3	22
Prov. #6	5	10	12
Prov. #7	9	20	15
Prov. #8	10	11	13

Based on the algorithm's execution, while the initial selection was Prov. #1 for the Object Identification Service, Prov. #3 for the Process Recognition Service and Prov. #7 for the Storage Service, based on the new values of the *ConvertedIndex* for the new weights (given the relevance feedback outcomes), replacements are suggested concluding to the following selected services:

− Object Identification Service: Prov. #4
− Process Recognition Service: Prov. #2
− Storage Service: Prov. #3.

We observe that due to the input obtained by the relevance feedback mechanism with respect to the user preferences, the algorithm concluded to a different selection of services. For the Object Identification Service, Serv. Provider #4 was selected instead of Serv. Provider #1. This was done due to the importance of the Performance QoS parameter in comparison to the Cost and Availability parameters. Besides, for the Storage Service, Serv. Provider #3 was selected instead of Serv. Provider #7 (done in order to meet the end-to-end Cost constraint for the composite service).

In sequel we present the evaluation of the proposed approach with respect to the user's QoE. To compare the performance of the proposed relevance feedback service selection algorithm, we use objective metrics, which are used for performance evaluation of database management architectures. In particular, our evaluation is based on the calculation of the precision-recall curve, which has been used in text-based information retrieval systems [30]. The following figure (Fig. 3) presents the precision-recall curve using three versions as regards the service selection algorithms. The first two employ relevance feedback mechanisms, while the last applies service selection without relevance fee. As observed among the two proposed feedback mechanisms, the constrained one outperforms precision for all recall values among the other two schemes. In particular, the proposed constrained relevance feedback algorithm gives the maximum precision (e.g. satisfaction of user's preferences) at a given recall (e.g. retrieval of relevant services out of a specific threshold). The worst case occurs in case that no relevance feedback is deployment. This is expected since in that case all the service attributes are considered of the same importance. In all schemes, we also observe that the precision accuracy drops as recall increases. It is quite reasonable since as more relevant services are retrieved by the system, the probability of recalling irrelevant services among the relevant ones also increases dropping the precision accuracy. The proposed constrained relevance feedback algorithm is iteratively implemented at each observation cycle. The following figure presents the effect of the number of observations on the precision-recall performance. As is observed, as the number of observations increases precision also increases at the same recall value. However, the improvement rate decreases, meaning that beyond a certain threshold of the number of iterations no further improvement is observed (we conclude to a saturation).

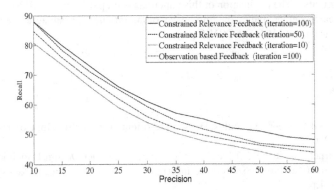

Fig. 3. Precision-recall curve for constrained and for selection without any relevance feedback for different number of observations.

7   Conclusions

Cloud environments have not yet adopted an effective scheme that will facilitate end-to-end QoS provisioning for Internet-scale composite applications [31]. Accounting for the particularities of clouds and such applications, in this paper we have introduced a mechanism for service selection with regard to quality of service information which is expected to increase the effort to provide cloud environments with a dynamic QoS capability. The aim of our work is to conclude to the selected services of which a composite service consists, based on the QoS requirements from the users and the published QoS parameters from the service providers. Moreover, we have enhanced the proposed algorithm with metrics expressing the user preferences. These metrics are defined by a relevance feedback mechanism reflecting the content and service importance within the selection process since for each parameter the mechanism proposes a weight factor that is taken into consideration during the selection process. As a result the offered services/candidates are prioritized according not only to their QoS parameters but also to the weight factor of them, which affects the selection process. The feedback mechanism doesn't require user intervention since the required information is obtained from monitoring data.

The proposed approach enables the adoption of different business models since it allows for the evaluation of alternative strategies (e.g. different QoS parameters being published by the provider) and monitoring any changes/violations that may occur, which will have an important impact on the strategies, methodologies, and structure of business processes. When adaptation is necessary, a set of potential alternatives is generated (since the algorithm providers a prioritized list of candidates per service type), with the objective of updating the service composition as its QoS continues to meet initial requirements and user expectations. Notwithstanding, it is within our future plans to attempt to comprise parameters dependencies in the selection process, which should also be reflected in the content and service importance metrics.

Acknowledgements. The publication of this paper has been partly supported by the University of Piraeus Research Center, and by the European Community under grant agreements n° 214777 (IRMOS project) and n° 216465 (SCOVIS project).

References

1. Papazoglou, M.P., Georgakopoulos, D.: Service-oriented computing. In: Communications of the ACM (2003)
2. Future Internet Architecture (FIArch) Group: Future Internet Design Principles. European Commission (2012). http://ec.europa.eu/information_society/activities/foi/docs/fiarchdesign principles-v1.pdf
3. IBM White Paper: The Benefits of Cloud Computing: A New Era of Responsiveness, Effectiveness and Efficiency in IT Service Delivery (2009)
4. Kyriazis, D.: Cloud computing service level agreements–exploitation of research results. Technical report, European Commission, Brussels (2013). http://ec.europa.eu/digital-agenda/ en/news/cloud-computing-service-level-agreements-exploitation-research-results
5. Doulamis, A.: Fair QoS resource management and non-linear prediction of 3D rendering applications. In: IEEE International Symposium on Circuits & Systems, Vancouver, Canada (2004)
6. Zilci, B.I., Slawik, M., Küpper, A.: Cloud service matchmaking using constraint programming. In: IEEE International Conference on Enabling Technologies: Infrastructure for Collaborative Enterprises (2015)
7. Zeng, L., Benatallah, B., Ngu, A.H., Dumas, M., Kalagnanam, J., Chang, H.: QoS-aware middleware for web services composition. IEEE Trans. Softw. Eng. **30**, 311–327 (2004)
8. Ardagna, D., Pernici, B.: Adaptive service composition in flexible processes. IEEE Trans. Softw. Eng. **33**(6), 369–384 (2007)
9. Zeng, L., Benatallah, B., Dumas, M., Kalagnanam, J., Sheng, Q.Z.: Quality driven web services composition. In: International Conference on World Wide Web, Hungary (2003)

10. Berbner, R., Spahn, M., Repp, N., Heckmann, O., Steinmetz, R.: Heuristics for QoS-aware web service composition. In: IEEE International Conference on Web Services, USA (2006)
11. Alrifai, M., Skoutas, D., Risse, T.: Selecting skyline services for QoS-based web service composition. In: International Conference on World Wide Web, USA (2010)
12. Alrifai, M., Risse, T.: Combining global optimization with local selection for efficient QoS-aware service composition. In: International Conference on World Wide Web, Madrid, Spain (2009)
13. Sun, Q., Wang, S., Zou, H., Yang, F.: QSSA: a QoS-aware service selection approach. Int. J. Web Grid Serv. **7**(2), 147–169 (2011)
14. Yu, T., Zhang, Y., Lin, K.J.: Efficient algorithms for web services selection with end-to-end QoS constraints. ACM Trans. Web (2007)
15. Zhao, S., Chen, G., Chen, H.: Reputation-aware Service Selection based on QoS Similarity. J. Netw. (2011). Academy Publishers
16. Rui, Y., Huang, T.S., Ortega, M., Mehrotra, S.: Relevance feedback: a power tool for interactive content-based image retrieval. IEEE Trans. Circ. Syst. Video Technol. **8**(5), 644–655 (1998)
17. Doulamis, A., Avrithis, Y., Doulamis, N., Kollias, S.: Interactive content-based retrieval in video databases using fuzzy classification and relevance feedback. In: IEEE International Conference on Multimedia Computing and Systems, Florence, Italy (1999)
18. Wang, X.Y., Zhang, B.B., Yang, H.Y.: Active SVM-based relevance feedback using multiple classifiers ensemble and features reweighting. Eng. Appl. Artif. Intell. (2012)
19. Zhang, L., Wang, L., Lin, W.: Semisupervised biased maximum margin analysis for interactive image retrieval. IEEE Trans. Image Process. **21**(4), 2294–2308 (2012)
20. Zhang, L., Wang, L., Lin, W.: Generalized biased discriminant analysis for content-based image retrieval. IEEE Trans. Syst. Man Cybern. (2012)
21. Doulamis, A., Tziritas, G.: Content-based low adaptation in low/variable bandwidth communication networks using adaptable neural networks structures. In: IEEE International Joint Conference on Neural Networks (2006)
22. Katsaros, G., Kousiouris, G., Gogouvitis, S., Kyriazis, D., Menychtas, A., Varvarigou, T.: A self-adaptive hierarchical monitoring mechanism for clouds. J. Syst. Softw. (2012). Elsevier
23. Gogouvitis, S., Konstanteli, K., Waldschmidt, S., Kousiouris, G., Katsaros, G., Menychtas, A., Kyriazis, D., Varvarigou, T.: Workflow management for soft real-time interactive applications in virtualized environments. Future Gener. Comput. Syst. (2012)
24. Papoulis, A.: Probability, Random Variables, and Stochastic Processes. McGraw Hill, New York (1984)
25. Doulamis, N., Doulamis, A.: Evaluation of relevance feedback in content-based in retrieval systems. Sig. Process. Image Commun. (2006)
26. Voulodimos, A., Kosmopoulos, D., Vasileiou, G., Sardis, E., Anagnostopoulos, V., Lalos, C., Doulamis, A., Varvarigou, T.: A threefold dataset for activity and workflow recognition in complex industrial environments. IEEE Multimedia **19**(3), 42–52 (2012)
27. Voulodimos, A., Kosmopoulos, D., Vasileiou, G., Sardis, E., Doulamis, A., Anagnostopoulos, V., Lalos, C., Varvarigou, T.: Dataset for workflow recognition in industrial scenes. In: IEEE International Conference on Image Processing, Brussels (2011)
28. Xiang, T., Gong, S., Parkinson, D.: Autonomous visual events detection and classification without explicit object centred segmentation and tracking. In: British Machine Vision Conference, pp. 233–242 (2002)

29. Kyriazis, D., Menychtas, A., Kousiouris, G., Oberle, K., Voith, T., Boniface, M., Oliveros, E., Cucinotta, T., Berger, S.: A real-time service oriented infrastructure. GSTF Int. J. Comput. (2011)
30. Rui, Y., Huang, T.S.: Optimizing learning in image retrieval. In: IEEE International Conference on Computer Vision and Pattern Recognition (2000)
31. Cloud Computing Expert Group Report. The Future of Cloud Computing. European Commission (2010). http://cordis.europa.eu/fp7/ict/ssai/docs/cloud-report-final.pdf

The Open Service Compendium

Business-Pertinent Cloud Service Discovery, Assessment, and Selection

Mathias Slawik[(✉)], Begüm İlke Zilci, Fabian Knaack, and Axel Küpper

Service-centric Networking Telekom Innovation Laboratories,
Technische Universität Berlin, Berlin, Germany
{mathias.slawik,ilke.zilci,fabian.knaack,axel.kuepper}@tu-berlin.de

Abstract. When trying to discover, assess, and select cloud services, companies face many challenges, such as fast-moving markets, vast numbers of offerings, and highly ambiguous selection criteria. This publication presents the Open Service Compendium (OSC), an information system which supports businesses in their discovery, assessment and cloud service selection by offering a simple dynamic service description language, business-pertinent vocabularies, as well as matchmaking functionality. It contributes to the state of the art by offering a more practical, mature, simple, and usable approach than related works.

Keywords: Cloud service selection · Cloud service brokering · Service matchmaking · Cloud computing · Information system

1 Introduction

There is a major trend within enterprise IT to fundamentally embrace cloud computing. The most recent 2015 "State of the Cloud Survey" reveals that 93 % of large enterprises (i.e. 1000+ employees) are already using cloud computing solutions, 82 % follow a multi-cloud strategy, while only 3 % do not have plans for adopting cloud computing[1].

Before companies contract and consume cloud services, they have to carry out *discovery*, i.e., finding cloud services in the vast Internet, *assessment*, i.e., matching services to requirements, and *selection*, i.e., choosing the best service for subsequent booking and consumption, e.g., by making a shortlist and ranking services. These tasks are challenging: cloud markets are fast-moving, have a vast numbers of offerings, selection criteria are highly ambiguous, marketplaces sometimes unorganized, and price structures and feature combinations complex and opaque. These challenges impede optimal service selection and sometimes hinders cloud adoption generally.

Our contribution was conceived within two research projects targeting specific domains: TRESOR[2] targeting the German Health sector and CYCLONE[3]

---

[1] http://goo.gl/eloh66.
[2] http://www.cloud-tresor.com.
[3] http://www.cyclone-project.eu.

© Springer International Publishing Switzerland 2016
J. Altmann et al. (Eds.): GECON 2015, LNCS 9512, pp. 115–129, 2016.
DOI: 10.1007/978-3-319-43177-2_8

targeting users of federated, multi-cloud applications. TRESOR developed a cloud ecosystem featuring a cloud broker and marketplace and was thoroughly presented in our previous works [21, 26–28]. CYCLONE is a Horizon 2020 innovation action which aims at integrating existing cloud management software to allow unified management of federated clouds. Both projects also address discovery, assessment, and selection challenges due to the lack of a suitable information systems: The TRESOR health centers cannot assess legal cloud consumption prerequisites, e.g., how and where medical data is processed. This leads to higher costs for local IT infrastructure and less functionality available to personnel. Many of the CYCLONE multi-cloud application developers face challenges in selecting optimal offerings for use in their applications, e.g., IaaS VMs and storage services. Suboptimal offerings can cause higher costs as well as lower Quality of Experience by the end-users of such applications.

Our previous work [20] establishes basic technologies for addressing these issues: a textual domain specific language for describing services, a pertinent business vocabulary of selection criteria, and a brokering component. The analysis of related work showed a particular lack of pertinent service selection criteria in description languages as well as contemporary and future marketplaces, although there has been extensive empiric research in this area. Also, the benefits of using textual domain-specific languages [6] is not utilized in any of the examined approaches, which predominantly use semantic technologies for capturing service information. The main contribution of this publication is the design, implementation, and evaluation of a first iteration of the OSC, which is an information system supporting business users in their cloud service discovery, assessment, and selection activities. For this, we employ and extend former contributions and address the following research questions in this publication:

Q1 What are the main business challenges the OSC has to address and where should it differentiate itself from the state-of-the-art and related works?
Q2 Which use cases should the OSC architecture implement and how should it be designed to be suitable, scalable, and state-of-the-art?
Q3 How does the current OSC implementation meet its requirements, as well as the needs of its first users?

By addressing these research questions we extend existing research on description languages, matchmakers, and marketplaces, by including real-world requirements to further mature this area of research. By designing the system to be "wiki-like" and having it used by regular Internet users we hope to increase the volume of empiric knowledge.

We apply the Information Systems Research Framework by Hevner et al. [7] which also structures this publication: Sect. 2 iterates prevalent business challenges and derives eight main OSC requirements. These requirements are contrasted with the related work in Sect. 3 to guide the OSC use case definition in Sect. 4. Based on these use cases we design the OSC architecture in Sect. 5 and present its current implementation status. After showing first evaluation results in Sect. 6, we conclude this publication in Sect. 7.

2   Cloud Service Business Challenges

This section structures the discovery, assessment, and selection challenges into three problem areas, describes them, and specifies requirements for the OSC, numbered **R1** to **R8**.

Cloud Market Characteristics: Fast-Moving Vastness. The cloud market is *vast* and *fast-moving*: Current forecasts demonstrate its increasing *vastness*: the total end-user spending on public cloud services is expected to grow by almost 60 % between 2015 and 2018 to a staggering \$290bn[4]. Some cloud vendors are also astonishingly large: Amazon Web Services, for example, has more than 1 million customers, achieved more than 40 % year-over-year revenue growth, and generates an estimated yearly revenue of \$4 billion[5]. The "Google Memorial"[6] highlights the velocity of a *fast-moving* cloud market participant: it lists 66 discontinued services which were sometimes highly popular, for example, the Google Reader service had more than 24 million users[7] before it was suddenly discontinued in 2013. These examples highlight that the cloud market is too vast for companies to obtain an optimal overview and it is too fast-moving to keep up with ever-changing service offerings. These cloud market characteristics require a *structured service repository* (**R1**), which integrates *dynamic information* (**R2**), e.g., IaaS spot-market prices. For maximum impact, it should be *"wiki-like"*, i.e., any Internet user should be able to create and edit service descriptions (**R3**). A *matchmaking* between requirements and contained knowledge should support service selection (**R4**).

Ambiguous Criteria and Scattered Knowledge. Assessing service offerings raises two questions: *what criteria to use* and *where to get the required information*. Deciding what criteria to use is hard: they are sometimes highly ambiguous (e.g., data privacy criteria as shown by Selzer [19]) and sometimes empirically identified, yet neither integrated into service description languages, nor existing marketplaces and repositories, as we'll show in the next section. Gathering information to apply these criteria is also a challenging task: First of all, companies conceal knowledge about unfavorable service aspects. For example, cloud backup providers label services "unlimited", while they have in fact bandwidth and storage limits[8]. The "Fair Use" clause of Backblaze, which allows the provider to cancel the contract anytime[9], and the CrashPlan "Unlimited" limits which are concealed in the EULA[10] highlight this practice. Secondly, some companies provide insufficient information: for example, Microsoft states that OneDrive can

---

[4] http://www.ft.com/cms/s/2/b3d40e7a-ceea-11e3-ac8d-00144feabdc0.html.
[5] http://goo.gl/5vHSom.
[6] http://goo.gl/YdN2np.
[7] http://googlesystem.blogspot.de/2013/03/google-reader-data-points.html.
[8] http://goo.gl/nVqeA3.
[9] https://www.backblaze.com/terms.html.
[10] http://support.code42.com/CrashPlan/CrashPlan_For_Home_EULA.

only be used with the Windows 8.1 Explorer if users use their live.com accounts for logging on to Windows[11]. On the contrary, many companies are reluctant to allow their corporate users to use such accounts, thus hindering them to use OneDrive effectively. Only private blogs offer workarounds which are not always discovered by companies wishing to assess OneDrive[12]. In summary, as provider information does not suffice and knowledge becomes more scattered, the efforts for assessing IDL services rise constantly unless there is a vocabulary of *selection criteria pertinent to businesses* (**R5**), as well as means of *integrating external information* (**R6**).

Features and Prices: Complex and Incomparable. In his seminal 1956 paper, Smith outlined that product differentiation and market segmentation are viable marketing strategies [22]. This observation still holds true almost sixty years later: to compete with cloud market leaders, service providers differentiate products and segment their market. One example is the online storage market, which is segmented into related categories, such as "remote backup", "cloud storage", and "file sharing". Different needs of consumers are addressed by different features and pricing schemes. "Cloud storage" services, such as Google Drive, allow flexible sharing of data, but incur additional costs for extending the free quota. "Backup services", such as CrashPlan, allow "unlimited" data storage for a fixed price but have only limited sharing functionality, e.g., backup family plans, such as "CrashPlan for Home". Thus, comparing different services becomes challenging if cloud consumers need to both share and backup large volumes of data. The price structure and feature combinations can also become complex: for example, Amazon EC2 offers 32 VM types in 10 locations with 6 operating systems, resulting in 1920 configuration options to choose from; in addition to opting for either on-demand, reserved, or spot market instances. Thus, comparing different competitors to find an optimal product implies an enormous effort, unless there is a suitable *price model* (**R7**) as well as a mechanism for describing different *variants* of a service (**R8**).

3   Related Work

The preceding business challenges are addressed by a number of related works from academia and practitioners in the areas of *service description languages, repositories and marketplaces, service matchmaking approaches*, as well as *cloud-selector frameworks*.

Service Description Languages. Service description languages capture relevant aspects of services for a specific use case. For example, WSDL[13] and the CORBA IDL describe the technical service interface for the main use case of

---

[11] http://windows.microsoft.com/en-us/windows-8/onedrive-app-faq.
[12] http://goo.gl/PZ7d6p.
[13] http://www.w3.org/TR/wsdl20/.

automated code generation of service skeletons. There is a wealth of service description approaches in the field of semantic web services, e.g., OWL-S [12], WSMO [18], SAWSDL[14], WSDL-S[15], SWSF[16], and others. Other languages focus on business-related information, such as WSMO4IoS [23] as well as the Linked-USDL [15] which is derived from the earlier USDL [14]. Other researchers, e.g., Breskovic et al., create standardized products for electronic markets [3], based on description languages, such as the CRDL [17]. At last, some authors focus on price and cost modeling of cloud services (**R7**), for example Kashef and Altmann in [1,9]. While these works provide interesting application areas for the OSC, they are not based on an existing service description language.

Seminal works by Fensel et al. [5] as well as Studer et al. [25] present semantic web services in detail. Studer et al. summarizes the focus areas of semantic web services: reasoning-based matching of service functionality, harmonizing data formats and protocols, and automated Web Service composition. Semantic functionality requires service knowledge expression, e.g., service inputs and outputs, preconditions, and service effects. Therefore related languages have a broad scope and aims: for example, "maximise to the extent possible the level of automation" [15] or "covering as many XaaS domains as possible" [24]. In contrast, cloud service discovery, assessment and selection activities by SMEs require merely a small set of relevant information, which has to be pertinent to business users. Yet, no approach meets the business challenges sufficiently: they do not handle *dynamic information* (**R2**) well, cannot be used *wiki-like* (**R3**), nor can easily *integrate external information* (**R6**). While there are empiric studies on service selection criteria, e.g., [16] and the CloudServiceCheck[17], the languages do not capture such service knowledge *pertinent to businesses* (**R5**). Another issue is the missing service variant management[18]. Without having a rich variant model, describing real-world cloud services becomes a major challenge, demonstrated by the example Amazon EC2 Linked-USDL description[19]. It only considers one type of instance and only one location, but consists of 1899 lines. We approximate a complete EC2 description to be 300.000 lines in length. This shows the prohibitive complexity of real-world USDL descriptions leading to inefficient processing and low human comprehensibility.

We argue that the failure to address existing SME challenges is the reason for its missing industry adoption outside of their funding scope. Many languages are abandoned, e.g., OWL-S (2006), SAWSDL (2007), WSMO (2008), and USDL (2011), and the associated tools are not updated anymore, e.g., the WSMO Studio[20]. Therefore we do not consider Semantic Web Service approaches suitable as the basis of the Open Service Compendium.

---

[14] http://www.w3.org/TR/2007/REC-sawsdl-20070828/.
[15] http://www.w3.org/Submission/WSDL-S.
[16] http://www.w3.org/Submission/SWSF/.
[17] http://www.value4cloud.de/de/cloudservicecheck.
[18] The USDL "variant management" connotes variants *of the language*.
[19] https://goo.gl/ZrMCWk.
[20] http://sourceforge.net/projects/wsmostudio.

Repositories and Marketplaces. They address the vastness of the Cloud market by managing a large number of service descriptions. They can be divided into academic marketplace research platforms and high-volume SaaS marketplaces. There are academic marketplace research platforms which are relevant to our contribution: The USDL marketplace[21], a proof-of-concept marketplace prototype based on USDL. The FI-Ware Marketplace and Repository[22] provide APIs to manage USDL service descriptions, as well as support discovering and matching application and service offerings. At last, Spillner and Schill offer an extensible XaaS Service Registry which is based on WSMO4IoS [24].

We observe that no approach overcomes the explicated limitations of its SDL. Furthermore, none is designed to be used by regular Internet users, thus hindering their broad adoption and lowering their pertinence to businesses. Prototypical high-volume commercial SaaS marketplaces are the Google Marketplace[23] and Salesforce AppExchange[24]. Instead of an elaborate cloud service formalization, they utilize very simple data models consisting of free-text, images, provider info, and a categorization. As they lack a service formalization, they are only marginally able to support users in their service discovery, selection, and assessment.

Service Matchmaking. The related work on service matchmaking is highly divergent in its contexts (e.g., Cloud Services, SOA, the Semantic Web), as well as on its opinions about what constitutes a matchmaking problem (e.g., the types of variables and the desired matchmaker functionality). We examine, if the existing service matchmakers are *business-pertinent* (**R5**). Our previous survey [29] divides approaches into *syntactic, constraint based, ontological* and *Fuzzy Set Theory based*: *Syntactic* approaches are limited to numeric QoS parameters [4,10]. *Constraint based* transforming the service request into a set of constraints and match it to a set of service descriptions [10]. Afterwards, the "closest" service can be found using the Euclidean distance between the request and the description [4]. *Ontological* approaches utilize OWL-S and reasoners, for example, to calculate the semantic similarity of method signatures [11], and to define the constraints as SWRL rules [8]. *Fuzzy Set Theory* based approaches aim to match numeric QoS parameters in a flexible manner, sometimes extending syntactic approaches, for example, by allowing "good", "medium", and "poor" value intervals [13], or using trapezoidal fuzzy numbers [2].

While being extensive, none of the related approaches addresses current business challenges: most of them only consider numeric QoS parameters, such as availability, response time, and throughput[25], which are not independently and objectively measurable. Furthermore, pertinent selection criteria which are not numeric, e.g., feature lists, are not considered, as was shown in our previous publication [30]. The referenced empiric studies show that only a small subset

---

of relevant selection criteria are numeric. At last, none of these approaches uses more sophisticated description formats than WSDL.

Cloud-Selector Frameworks. These frameworks help cloud users in assessing different aspects of cloud providers. One example is PlanForCloud[26] which allows users to create deployment descriptions and specify their planned usage of cloud resources, e.g., servers, storage, and databases. CloudHarmony[27] is a bundle of services by Gartner: a provider directory, a benchmark database for network performance, and a service status dashboard. CloudSpectator[28] offers performance measurements for different IaaS providers. Many limitations persist: PlanForCloud contains only services supported by RightScale software. CloudHarmony is quite extensive, yet lacks information about pricing and other business-pertinent selection criteria. None of the platforms offers matchmaking functionality or crowdsourcing data. The criteria are also limited, e.g., PlanForCloud offers only "price", while CloudSpectator supports only a "Multi Core Score".

4 OSC Use-Cases

This chapter derives the OSC use-cases which address the business challenges and their requirements illustrated in the preceding section. The use-cases are numbered U1 to U6 and are described in detail while Fig. 1 provides the UML use-case diagram for easy reference.

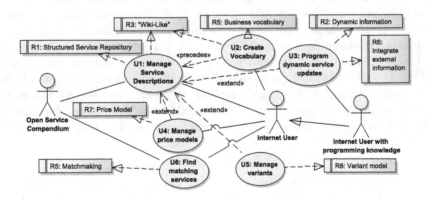

Fig. 1. OSC use cases.

---

[26] https://planforcloud.rightscale.com.

[27] https://cloudharmony.com.

[28] http://cloudspectator.com.

U1: Manage Service Descriptions. The OSC should provide functionality for Internet users to manage service descriptions, i.e., to create, show, edit, and delete structured service descriptions to provide a *structured service repository* (R1). As the OSC is "wiki-like" (R3), the use-case should allow a comprehensible, text-based language for service descriptions.

U2: Create Vocabulary. The *business-pertinent vocabulary* (R5) provides the structure for service descriptions managed by Use Case U1. Thus, the OSC should provide Internet users the functionality to create such a vocabulary. To preserve the "wiki-like" characteristic of the OSC, the vocabulary definition has to be based on a comprehensible, text-based language. In order to support companies with their assessment, the vocabulary should also contain additional information on *why* a certain property is important for service selection.

U3: Program Dynamic Service Information Updates. To *integrate external information* (R6) and to also allow service knowledge to be *dynamically updated* (R2), the OSC should give Internet users with programming knowledge the ability to implement dynamic service information updates. For reduced complexity, dynamic and static parts of a service descriptions should be integrated tightly, e.g., by having both in the same document. Dynamically updated service descriptions can lower the authoring effort considerably.

U4 and U5: Manage Price Models and Service Variants. In order to handle complex price and variant structures, the OSC should manage *price models* (R7) as well as *variants* (R8) of services including creating, showing, editing and deleting these models, as well as presenting a price calculator, a variants overview, and using the price and feature model within service comparisons. The OSC should evaluate these models when finding services, i.e., it should find the respective variant of a service matching the search request as well as calculating the prices of those variants. This model should be integrated into the description language in order to reduce complexity and to allow features to be linked to their impact on the price of service consumption.

U6: Find Matching Services. All of the previous use-cases culminate in the pivotal use-case of enabling Internet users to *find matching services to their requirements* (R5). For this, end-users should be able to define their requirements in an interactive fashion. The OSC should then evaluate services, price, and feature models to present matching services. In addition to basic selection, the OSC should also contain a matchmaking component in order to rank services and provide a more comprehensive selection result.

5   Open Service Compendium Architecture

This section presents the Open Service Compendium architecture which is designed to implement the OSC use cases by providing insight on three layers: the conceptual architecture, its implementation, as well as its future expansion.

The Conceptual Architecture. Figure 2 presents the conceptual architecture in form of a UML component diagram. There are six main components, which are described in the following paragraphs.

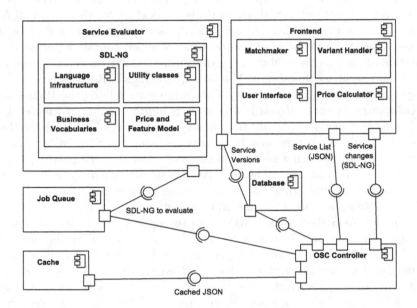

Fig. 2. Conceptual architecture.

The pivotal **OSC controller** is responsible for providing a service list as JSON to the *Frontend*, either by querying the *Database* or using the *Cache*. Changes to service descriptions are recieved from the *Frontend* in SDL-NG form and submitted to the *Job Queue* for subsequent evaluation. The **Job Queue** can additionally save the evaluation status, e.g., in cases of erroneous SDL-NG documents. The **Service Evaluator** takes SDL-NG documents from the *Job Queue*, executes them in a specially secured container to prevent malicious code execution, and writes the resulting service descriptions to the *database*. The **Frontend** provides the end-user interface for the use cases U1 through U6. It is designed as a JavaScript "Single Page Application" and is responsible for querying the OSC controller for JSON service descriptions, service matchmaking, service variant handling, price calculation, as well as submitting new and modified service descriptions to the OSC controller. A number of factors led to our adoption of the emerging "Single Page Application" style, instead of having the OSC controller render all the pages: the *back end simplicity*, the *swiftness* of the user interface, as well as the *decoupling* of back end and front end. As our architecture is well decoupled, each component can be scaled independently.

Implementation. The OSC prototype can be accessed online[29] and its current source code can be found on Github[30]. While we describe the final implementation, some of the components are currently under development and not publicly available for testing.

We used the brokering component of the TRESOR project as the base for creating the OSC controller, a Ruby on Rails application offering RESTful APIs for creating, querying, updating, and deleting services stored in a MongoDB database. The database holds service documents which contain a persisted representation of the executed ruby service description as well as meta-information, such as the execution timestamp. The Job Queue uses a Redis key-value store managed by the Resque Ruby library. For caching, we rely on the Rails-default `ActiveSupport::Cache` infrastructure, as it is highly flexible in its use of different caching stores, for example, in-memory, plain files, MemCache, or Redis. The service evaluator is a regular Ruby process using the SDL-NG to evaluate the service descriptions in a secure context and persisting the resulting service descriptions in the database. The SDL-NG contains a language infrastructure (e.g., a type system and exporters), utility classes for scraping websites, business vocabularies (e.g., for cloud storage and IaaS offerings), as well as a price and feature model. As SDL-NG descriptions can scrape websites with changing content, e.g., Amazon Spot Market prices, the service evaluator can be instructed to regularity check the description for changes and update the database records accordingly. This functionality can handle dynamic aspects of cloud systems, e.g., pricing and capability changes. Historical service records can be retrieved using the OSC controller, for example, to detect modifications of certain services and to make predictions about future changes (e.g., price drops). Our previous publication [20] provides an in-depth explanation of the SDL-NG.

The frontend is built and assembled using a Grunt JavaScript workflow. It is based on AngularJS and a number of additional Javascript and CSS libraries, e.g., Angular UI Router, Twitter Bootstrap, Less, SASS, and CoffeeScript. It integrates a Java applet containing a constraint programming matchmaker using the Choco Solver[31] to implement different constraint models for different matchmaking functionality: *discrete value matching* with hard and soft constraints, *interval matching* for negative and positive tendencies, and *matching of feature lists*. Our previous work [30] includes a detailed description of the constraint models and their implementation. Figure 3 shows some example screenshots of the user interface. In general, there are three main views for users to realize service *discovery, assessment,* and *selection.* First, a list of all services in a spe-

---

[29] http://www.open-service-compedium.org.

[30] https://github.com/TU-Berlin-SNET/open-service-compendium.

[31] http://www.emn.fr/z-info/choco-solver/.

Fig. 3. User interface: faceted search, service comparison, and storage vocabulary.

cific category (e.g., cloud storage and IaaS solutions) allows users to *discover* all available services. Users can use a faceted search to filter the list based on their selection criteria, such as company jurisdiction, payment options, and certifications. For *assessment* there is a "detail" view, where users can see the whole service description, including extensive documentation about all properties and their meaning, as well as a comparison view. To support their final *selection*, users can employ the matchmaking component for ranking services based on user defined constraints and getting the "best" service for their needs.

Future Expansion. Through eventual OSC advancements, we foresee some prospective components: first of all, there has to be some kind of basic *user management* to protect descriptions from vandalism or malicious editing. Secondly, to strengthen the usefulness of the OSC, additional external information sources should be included and managed by OSC components, e.g., external service reviews, user ratings, and benchmarking data. At last, the RDF/OWL export capabilities of the *Service Description Language* could be used to implement a *Semantic Data Store* component in order to publish an OSC dataset in the *Linked Open Data Cloud*. This has two main goals: raising the business relevance of related approaches by offering semantic descriptions of real-world services as well as enabling the OSC to benefit from advanced functionality, such as machine learning and reasoning.

6   Evaluation

This chapter presents the evaluation of the OSC architecture and its implementation: *analytical*, comparing it to the set of general requirements, *experimental*, gathering knowledge from using it in practice, as well as *empirical*, carrying out interviews and surveys.

Analytical Evaluation. Carrying out the analytical evaluation is straightforward and highlights the fitness of the OSC to cover all enumerated requirements: we have created a *structured service repository* (**R1**) using a comprehensive Service Description Language. *Dynamic information* (**R2**) can be continuously integrated by frequently running the *Service Evaluator*, as explained in Sect. 5. As we have chosen a simple to use textual DSL, the OSC becomes a *"wiki-like"* information system (**R3**), which was also highlighted in our recent publication [20]. We integrated a *service matchmaker* (**R4**) to match requirements with structured service knowledge. The business and category-specific vocabularies contain empirically determined *selection criteria*, which are pertinent to businesses (**R5**), which is highlighted by our empirical evaluation. Internet Users with programming knowledge can *integrate external information* (**R6**) using the Utility Classes of the SDL, as exemplified in the service description examples[32]. The SDL-NG contains an additional *price model* (**R7**) as well as a model to capture service *variants* (**R8**).

For **experimental evaluation**, we have applied the OSC in practice to validate its functionality by implementing an automated test suite, as well as manual usage. So far, the OSC functions as specified. For example, users can have a look at the vocabulary "cheat sheet" to get an overview of all properties and types, use a code editor to create service descriptions, view the output of the service evaluation, search for services, and compare them.

Additional **empirical evaluation** was carried out for the OSC components *service description language*, *business vocabulary*, and the *cloud storage vocabulary*. The *service description language* was presented to a group of experts from other Trusted Cloud projects having been involved in related research, e.g., the USDL [14]. A group discussion about the relevance of the OSC for the field resulted in the following statements: the textual DSL is a major simplification in describing services, especially in comparison to the USDL and semantic approaches. Deriving the vocabulary from empiric research strengthens the usefulness of the DSL in practical contexts. The utility value of a central repository with matchmaking capabilities was regarded as very high. An expert group evaluated the *business vocabulary* with respect to its relevance for service selection. Participants were one publication author, the CIO, and two IT project managers of a large German health center. They had to come up with a mutual importance rating of the individual criteria on a 5-step scale from "indispensable" (1) to "irrelevant" (5). The left pie chart in Fig. 4 groups the categories by their rated importance: 86.5 % of the 52 criteria were rated important and higher, while only 13.5 % were rated less important or irrelevant. Evaluation of an intermediate version of the *Cloud Storage Vocabulary* was performed using an online questionnaire in which participants rated the importance of the 27 criteria for their selection of a cloud storage service. The respondents were mostly students

---

[32] https://github.com/TU-Berlin-SNET/sdl-ng/tree/master/examples/services.

of computer science and related fields of study, providing valuable insight into the usefulness for generic Internet users, as most other people involved in our research are either professionals or academics. Of 35 respondents, 18 (51.4 %) completed the questionnaire. The right pie chart in Fig. 4 shows the distribution of the average importance of all criteria, which is grouped into 1–1.5 (indispensable), 1.5–2.5 (very important), and 2.5–3.5 (important). These results show that the generic OSC business vocabulary is able to capture some of the most important selection criteria of this specific client. For generalization, we will conduct an extensive questionnaire in the future and adjust the business vocabulary according to its results. The results promise a high relevance of the vocabulary for Internet users, yet the absence of less important and irrelevant criteria could also point at the inability of our respondents to differentiate the importance of their criteria. The low completion rate could imply that people either could not understand the criteria or did not know their cloud provider selection process.

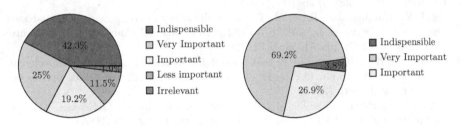

Fig. 4. Survey results for business (left) and cloud storage vocabulary (right). (Color figure online)

7 Conclusion

We have delineated the challenges in discovery, assessment, and selection of cloud services and revealed the failure of both academic and commercial approaches to address these challenges properly. By using real-world requirements as the basis for the OSC use cases as well as designing a modern solution architecture, we hope to create a practical, mature, simple and usable information system. Preliminary evaluation results are promising and we are looking forward to presenting and discussing our contribution with practitioners and researchers at GECON. We also hope to maximize the impact of the OSC by creating a "wiki-like" information system and publishing it as free and open source (FOSS) software. In the future, we will use the OSC as a basis to tackle upcoming challenges within federated, multi-cloud environments and the Intercloud in the CYCLONE project.

Acknowledgments. This work is supported by the Horizon 2020 Innovation Action CYCLONE, funded by the European Commission through grant number 644925.

References

1. Altmann, J., Kashef, M.M.: Cost model based service placement in federated hybrid clouds. Future Gener. Comput. Syst. **41**, 79–90 (2014)
2. Bacciu, D., Buscemi, M.G., Mkrtchyan, L.: Adaptive fuzzy-valued service selection. In: Proceedings of the 2010 ACM Symposium on Applied Computing, pp. 2467–2471. ACM (2010)
3. Breskovic, I., Altmann, J., Brandic, I.: Creating standardized products for electronic markets. Future Gener. Comput. Syst. **29**(4), 1000–1011 (2013)
4. Eleyan, A., Zhao, L.: Service selection using quality matchmaking. In: 2011 International Conference on Communications and Information Technology (ICCIT), pp. 107–115. IEEE (2011)
5. Fensel, D., Facca, F.M., Simperl, E., Toma, I.: Semantic Web Services. Springer, Heidelberg and New York (2011)
6. Fowler, M.: Domain-Specific Languages. Addison-Wesley, Boston (2011)
7. Hevner, A.R., March, S.T., Park, J., Ram, S.: Design science in information systems research. MIS Q. **28**(1), 75–105 (2004)
8. Jie, L.Y., Kanagasabai, R., et al.: Dynamic discovery of complex constraint-based semantic web services. In: 2011 Fifth IEEE International Conference on Semantic Computing (ICSC), pp. 51–58. IEEE (2011)
9. Kashef, M.M., Altmann, J.: A cost model for hybrid clouds. In: Vanmechelen, K., Altmann, J., Rana, O.F. (eds.) GECON 2011. LNCS, vol. 7150, pp. 46–60. Springer, Heidelberg (2012)
10. Kritikos, K., Plexousakis, D.: Mixed-integer programming for QoS-based web service matchmaking. IEEE Trans. Serv. Comput. **2**(2), 122–139 (2009)
11. Liu, M., Shen, W., Hao, Q., Yan, J.: An weighted ontology-based semantic similarity algorithm for web service. Expert Syst. Appl. **36**(10), 12480–12490 (2009)
12. Martin, D., et al.: Bringing semantics to web services: the OWL-S approach. In: Cardoso, J., Sheth, A.P. (eds.) SWSWPC 2004. LNCS, vol. 3387, pp. 26–42. Springer, Heidelberg (2005)
13. Mobedpour, D., Ding, C.: User-centered design of a QoS-based web service selection system. In: Service Oriented Computing and Applications, pp. 1–11 (2013)
14. Oberle, D., Barros, A., Kylau, U., Heinzl, S.: A unified description language for human to automated services. Inf. Syst. **38**(1), 155–181 (2013)
15. Pedrinaci, C., Cardoso, J., Leidig, T.: Linked USDL: a vocabulary for web-scale service trading. In: Presutti, V., d'Amato, C., Gandon, F., d'Aquin, M., Staab, S., Tordai, A. (eds.) ESWC 2014. LNCS, vol. 8465, pp. 68–82. Springer, Heidelberg (2014)
16. Repschläger, J., Zarnekow, R., Wind, S., Klaus, T.: Cloud requirement framework: requirements and evaluation criteria to adopt cloud solutions. In: Pries-Heje, J., Chiasson, M., Wareham, J., Busquets, X., Valor, J., Seiber, S. (eds.) Proceedings of the 20th European Conference on Information Systems (2012)
17. Risch, M., Altmann, J.: Enabling open cloud markets through WS-agreement extensions. In: Wieder, P., Yahyapour, R., Ziegler, W. (eds.) Grids and Service-Oriented Architectures for Service Level Agreements, pp. 105–117. Springer, Boston (2010)
18. Roman, D., Keller, U., Lausen, H., Bruijn, J.d., Lara, R., Stollberg, M., Polleres, A., Feier, C., Bussler, C., Fensel, D.: Web service modeling ontology. In: Applied Ontology, vol. 1, pp. 77–106. IOS Press (2005)

19. Selzer, A.: Datenschutz bei internationalen Cloud Computing Services. Datenschutz und Datensicherheit - DuD **38**(7), 470–474 (2014)
20. Slawik, M., Küpper, A.: A domain specific language and a pertinent business vocabulary for cloud service selection. In: Altmann, J., Vanmechelen, K., Rana, O.F. (eds.) GECON 2014. LNCS, vol. 8914, pp. 172–185. Springer, Heidelberg (2014)
21. Slawik, M., Zickau, S., Thatmann, D., Repschläger, J., Ermakova, T., Küpper, A., Zarnekow, R.: Innovative Architektur für sicheres Cloud Computing: Beispiel eines Cloud-Ecosystems im Gesundheitswesen. In: Goltz, U., Ehrich, H.D. (eds.) Informatik 2012, GI-Edition: Thematics, vol. 208, pp. 1075–1082. Ges. für Informatik, Bonn (2012)
22. Smith, W.R.: Product differentiation and market segmentation as alternative marketing strategies. J. Mark. **21**(1), 3–8 (1956)
23. Spillner, J.: WSMO4IoS (2013). http://serviceplatform.org/spec/wsmo4ios/
24. Spillner, J., Schill, A.: A versatile and scalable everything-as-a-service registry and discovery. In: Desprez, F., Ferguson, D., Hadar, E., Leymann, F., Jarke, M., Helfert, M. (eds.) CLOSER 2013 Proceedings, pp. 175–183. SciTePress (2013)
25. Studer, R., Grimm, S., Abecker, A.: Semantic Web Services: Concepts, Technologies, and Applications. Springer, Berlin and New York (2007)
26. Thatmann, D., Slawik, M., Zickau, S., Küpper, A.: Towards a federated cloud ecosystem: enabling managed cloud service consumption. In: Vanmechelen, K., Altmann, J., Rana, O.F. (eds.) GECON 2012. LNCS, vol. 7714, pp. 223–233. Springer, Heidelberg (2012)
27. Thatmann, D., Slawik, M., Zickau, S., Küpper, A.: Deriving a distributed cloud proxy architecture for managed cloud service consumption. In: IEEE 6th International Conference on Cloud Computing (CLOUD), pp. 614–620 (2013)
28. Zickau, S., Slawik, M., Thatmann, D., Uhlig, S., Denisow, I., Küpper, A.: TRESOR - towards the realization of a trusted cloud ecosystem. In: Krcmar, H., Reussner, R., Rumpe, B. (eds.) Trusted Cloud Computing, pp. 141–157. Springer, Heidelberg (2014)
29. Zilci, B.I., Slawik, M., Küpper, A.: Cloud service matchmaking approaches: a systematic literature survey. In: Proceedings of the 26th International Workshop on Database and Expert Systems Applications, DEXA 2015. IEEE (2015)
30. Zilci, B.I., Slawik, M., Küpper, A.: Cloud Service Matchmaking Using Constraint Programming. IEEE (2015)

Energy Conservation and Smart Grids

Optimizing Data Centres Operation to Provide Ancillary Services On-Demand

Marcel Antal, Claudia Pop, Dan Valea, Tudor Cioara, Ionut Anghel[✉],
and Ioan Salomie

Technical University of Cluj-Napoca, Cluj-Napoca, Romania
{marcel.antal,claudia.pop,dan.valea,tudor.cioara,ionut.anghel,
ioan.salomie}@cs.utcluj.ro

Abstract. In this paper a methodology for optimizing Data Centres (DCs) operation allowing them to provide various types of Ancillary Services on-demand is proposed. Energy flexibility models have been defined for hardware devices inside DCs aiming at optimizing energy demand profile by means of load time shifting, alternative usage of non-electrical cooling devices (e.g. thermal storage) or charging/discharging the electrical storage devices. As result DCs are able to shape their energy demand to provide additional load following reserve for large un-forecasted wind ramps, shed or shift energy demand over time to avoid an coincidental peak load and feed back in the grid the energy produced by turning on their backup fossil fuelled generators to maintain (local) reactive power balance under normal conditions. Experiments via numerical simulations based on real world traces of DC operation highlight the methodology potential for optimizing DC energy consumption to provide Ancillary Services.

Keywords: Data centre · Energy consumption optimization · Ancillary Services · Energy flexibility · Demand shifting

1 Introduction

The Data Centre (DC) services business is blooming but, as it is usually the case, this is only one side of the story: the growing demand of their services increases their demand on energy resources, which directly translates to increasingly higher operational costs, not to mention the detrimental impact to the environment and, as such, society as a whole. Besides, the significant economic and environmental impact, the annual increasing energy demand of the DC poses another severe risk: the risk of supply shortage and instability of the electricity network. This may cause exponentially increasing side effects. On one hand to the local economy, which may suffer accidental black-outs, and on the other hand to the normal operation of the DC itself, as it is expected to provide continuous operation and guaranteed availability ranging from 99.671 % (Tier 1 DC) to 99.995 % (Tier 4 DC). All these factors are putting DC business in a risky position and creating higher pressure on the DC administrators on cutting down the energy demand and bills.

© Springer International Publishing Switzerland 2016
J. Altmann et al. (Eds.): GECON 2015, LNCS 9512, pp. 133–146, 2016.
DOI: 10.1007/978-3-319-43177-2_9

At the same time with the latest developments in the areas of digital technologies and renewable energy production the Smart Grid concept has emerged. It allows for two-way communication between the utility and its customers, the sensing along the distribution lines and combines traditional brown energy sources with green energy sources such as photovoltaic panels, wind turbines, geo-thermal power plants, etc. However, the main problem of this grid is that it cannot store energy, thus forcing the energy producers to shed their generation to match their customers' energy demand. Variations of the production, either surplus or deficit can cause serious problems in the grid, leading to the overload of energy components and culminating with power outage or service disruptions. To make the problem more difficult to solve, the integration of renewables into the grid has added a level of uncertainty because of the intermittent and unpredictable nature of green energy generation. The lack of storage forces the grid operators to continuously deploy fast-reacting power reserves to maintain grid balance. To help solving this problem, utility companies developed Ancillary Services programs that allow them to ensure the energy balance in their grids, including mechanisms such spinning and non-spinning reserves or regulation. At the beginning of a billing period, a regulation signal is sent to every customer in the regulation market specifying the type of the Ancillary Service required as well as the desired power demand profile for that specific customer. If the customer accepts the signal, it is required to adjust its power demand after the profile received.

In our vision the DCs are great candidates for providing Ancillary Services when requested because of their huge flexibility given by their positioning at the crossroads of energy, thermal and digital information networks, thus having the opportunity to transform themselves into key players within their local, sustainable energy systems. Thus we propose a DC optimization methodology that aims at integrating the DCs into the Smart Grid scenarios and enacting them to respond to various Ancillary Services Requests coming from Distribution System Operator (DSO). The methodology is leveraging on flexibility mechanisms such as load time shifting, alternative usage of non-electrical cooling devices (e.g. thermal storage) or charging/discharging the electrical storage devices, etc. As result of using our optimization methodology the DCs could: (i) shape their energy demand to provide additional load following reserve for large un-forecasted wind ramps, (ii) shed or shift energy demand over time to avoid an coincidental peak load in the grid, (iii) feed in the smart energy grid the energy (either power or heat) produced by turning on their backup fossil fuelled generators, despite quite inefficient and above all highly pollutant, gaining a net financial reward by the energy provider, which, in that way will avoid to turn on fossil-fuelled standby power generation plants. In this way energy providers can leverage on financial incentive as a concrete way to involve DCs in more systemic energy efficiency programs. We have conducted experiments via numerical simulations based on real world traces of DC operation from production systems which highlight the potential of our methodology to optimize DC energy consumption and to shape its profile to provide Ancillary Services.

The rest of the paper is structured as follows: Sect. 2 shows related work, Sect. 3 presents the proposed optimization methodology leveraging on flexibility mechanisms defined, Sect. 4 presents numerical simulation based experiments and results, while Sect. 5 concludes the paper and presents the future work.

2   Related Work

Recent studies have shown that DCs are great candidates for participating in demand-response programs due to the following reasons [1]: (i) are large energy consumers or producers if they have on-site renewable energy production facilities, (ii) are highly automated and may respond fast to demand response (DR) signals and (iii) are characterized by a large energy flexibility due to the nature of their hardware components and workload executed. One of the most comprehensive studies describing the potential of different DC's hardware components and strategies providing demand response was released by Lawrence Berkeley National Laboratories [2]. The strategies are referring to: shutting down IT equipment, load shifting or queuing IT Jobs, temperature set point adjustment, load migration and IT equipment load reduction. Even though the results were promising the DCs being able to adjust the demand profile with 10–12 % the approach fail to take into consideration the correlations and combination among strategies to obtain a stronger response as well as new technologies such as non-electrical cooling or batteries. Also even if the report shows that it is feasible for a DC to respond to DR signals no DC operation optimization algorithm is presented.

We have classified literature techniques for optimizing DCs operation to participate in demand response programs and provide Ancillary Services according to the leveraging mechanism used in: (i) techniques based on load migration and consolidation, (ii) techniques exploiting electrical batteries and (iii) techniques based on cooling system intensity adjustments and heat removal strategies.

Time and spatial load migration and consolidation techniques are usually used for voluntary reduction of DC's energy demand. Authors of [14] evaluate the DCs that offer Ancillary Services in form of voluntarily load reduction using an analytical profit maximization framework and propose an optimization technique based profit maximization strategy. The authors propose a mathematical model that includes: DC's internet service revenue, the cost of electricity and the compensation it may receive by offering Ancillary Services. Furthermore, it takes into consideration the servers' power consumption, DCs Power Usage Effectiveness (PUE), workload statistics and SLAs. This approach interferes with the workload behaviour, resulting in performance degradation. Also, it does not consider any other form of energy flexibility mechanisms, such as, electrical storage devices, non-electrical cooling devices, etc. In [3] the authors present a solution for minimizing the electrical bill in a smart grid that employs both day ahead dynamic pricing and regulation signals. At the beginning of a billing period (several minutes to one day), the market participants (DCs) receive a regulation signal which specifies the trend of energy consumption during that period. During the billing period, DSO updates the initial trend, by sending regulation signals. A two tier DC controller is implemented, which performs resource allocation and schedules task dispatch, achieving optimality in minimizing the overall cost. A more complex approach is presented in [1]. It takes advantage of two DC flexibility mechanisms: workload shifting and local generation (local diesel generators and local renewable energy). Using these mechanisms, algorithms are developed in order to avoid the coincidental peak and reduce the energy costs. They rely on the prediction of coincident peak occurrence based on historical data to optimize the workload allocation and local generation and to minimize the expected cost. The authors of [15] present a dynamic pricing system for a federation of DCs and use a distributed constraint optimization solver to negotiate a mutually optimal price. Workload relocation between DCs is used to meet the energy need at various DCs from different geographic locations. This technique is limited by several factors, such as DC capacity, workload security and SLAs, as well as extra energy needed for data transportation.

Lately with the advent *of batteries technologies* and due to the fact that they don't pose any workload degradation overhead they are starting to be considered as important resources for helping DCs to participate in demand response. One of the first approaches of using batteries as a flexibility element within the DC is presented in [12]. The authors propose exploiting the batteries as an energy buffer with three functionalities: first it can shave power peaks; secondly it can store energy when it is cheap and third it can increase the DC power consumption when requested. In [13] a technique is proposed for balancing and keeping the DCs' peak power under a given threshold (because of the electricity pricing) but in the same time allowing DCs to respond to the regulation control signals that may request an increase in power consumption. A detailed energy storage scheme is presented in [10] in which uninterrupted power supply (UPS) units are used as energy storage devices. Based on the existence of delay-tolerable workload, it tries to reduce the time average electricity costs using Lyapunov optimization. The control algorithm will decide at each time moment how much energy to draw from the grid, how much of it to save into the energy storage and how much energy to draw from the storage such that the time average cost of these operations is minimized.

Even though efforts have been made to reduce the cooling system energy consumption it is still is responsible for as much as 50 % of the energy consumption in a DC thus it is important resource for energy flexibility. In [6] a strategy of optimizing the energy consumption of the cooling system, by evaluating the time-varying power prices is presented. The system checks the prices in the hour-ahead market, and precools the air masses. In this way, later, when the power prices increase, the thermal masses can absorb heat for a given period of time. The electrical cooling system of a DC is detailed in [9], where a hybrid cooling system composed of traditional CRAC cooling, free air cooling and liquid cooling is presented. The authors propose a power optimization scheme that combines the different cooling techniques and dynamically adjust the cooling source to minimize the overall power consumption. Furthermore, the heuristic is extended to handle a network of DC by dynamically dispatching the incoming requests among a network of DC with various cooling systems. New approaches are consider the DCs energy producers and target the reuse of the heat generated by the DC for heating nearby residential or commercial buildings is presented in [16]. Under certain conditions, the extra energy from the DCs renewable sources may be fed back to the grid. In this context, the authors propose a solution that aims to integrate the DCs with smart grids. To prove their results the authors use a grid simulation integrated with a DC operation simulation in which the DC observes the grid and adapts its internal state to meet grid's conditions.

In this context our approach paves the way for next generation energy sustainable DC which is able to optimize its overall energy consumption considering the installed hardware components and available flexibility mechanisms in a holistic and integrated manner. To increase and exploit the potential of DC to provide Ancillary Services along with load time shifting load or using diesel generators to feed energy to the grid we will also investigate and define flexibility mechanisms non electrical cooling devices such as the thermal storage as well as electrical storage devices.

3 DC Optimization Methodology

Ancillary Services address short-term imbalances in the grid and the DC as a demand response player has the role of providing help in balancing the grid on short time basis. We have defined an optimization methodology which exploits the available levels of electrical energy demand flexibility offered by the following DC's components: IT Computing Resources (i.e. servers), Electrical Cooling System, Electrical Storage System (i.e. batteries) and Thermal Storage System [21] (allow for excess thermal energy to be collected for later use). The overall goal is to provide an optimal capacity and operational planning for the DC to provide Ancillary Services if requested. It uses a discrete modelling of DC as a system and defines the current energy state of each component at timeslot t as a function of previous states at timeslots $t - 1, t - 2 \ldots t - k$.

The *flexibility mechanism for the IT Computing Resources* energy demand is leveraging on the time-shifting of delay tolerant workload. The real-time workload must be executed as soon as it arrives, while the delay-tolerant workload can be executed in the future but no later than a given deadline. The DC's energy demand is reduced at timeslot t with the amount of energy needed to execute the delay-tolerant load that is shifted at timeslot $t + u, u \in [1, T - t]$ while the DC's energy demand at timeslot $t + u$ is increased with the amount of energy needed to execute the delay-tolerant load shifted from timeslot t. To decide on the optimal timeslot and amount of delay tolerant workload to be shifted we define a model for estimating the energy consumption of the DC IT servers for a given workload configuration. We define a workload scheduling matrix $S = \left(s_{i,j} \right)_{T \times T}$ where its element $s_{i,j}$ represents the percentage of the delay-tolerant workload, with i representing the arrival timeslot, j the execution timeslot and T the maximum dimension of the time window based on the Ancillary Service response length:

$$S = \begin{pmatrix} S_{11} & \cdots & S_{1T} \\ \vdots & \ddots & \vdots \\ 0 & \cdots & S_{TT} \end{pmatrix} \tag{1}$$

Due to the fact that the execution of a delay-tolerant workload cannot be scheduled before its arrival timeslot, the scheduling matrix is an upper triangular one having zero values under its main diagonal. A matrix row i represents all the workload received at timeslot i and divided in percentages associated to the delayed execution timeslot until its deadline. As a consequence, the sum on each matrix row is 1. A matrix column j represents all the workload scheduled for execution at timeslot j. By summing all the workload elements of a column and translating them in energy values we obtain the estimated amount of energy needed to execute the delay-tolerant workload at timeslot j (relation 2), while the energy demand for executing all DC workload is calculated using relation 3:

$$E_{w\_delayed}(j) = \sum_{i=1}^{j} E(s_{i,j})$$ (2)

$$E_{workload}(t) = E_{w\_real-time}(t) + E_{w\_delayed}(t)$$ (3)

The *flexibility mechanism of electrical cooling system* is leveraging on the usage of non-electrical cooling systems such as the Thermal Aware Storage (TES). The DC's energy demand at timeslot t is decreased with the amount of energy discharged from the TES (as consequence of lowering the intensity and demand of the electrical cooling system), while at timeslot $t + u, u \in [1, T - t]$ the DC's energy demand is increased with the amount of energy charged in TES (as consequence of increasing the intensity of the electrical cooling system to overcool the TES tanks). To estimate the amount of flexibility that can be offered by the TES we compute the TES level at timeslot t, denoted by $E_{TES}(t)$, based on the previous state and the actions of charging and discharging at timeslot t, denoted by $E_{C-TES}(t - 1)$ and $E_{D-TES}(t - 1)$, respectively (see relation 4). We have considered the following characteristics of the TES device: charge loss factor during operation (ρ_{TES}), discharge loss factor during operation (δ_{TES}), and time discharge factor when it is not operated (φ_{TES}).

$$E_{TES}(t) = \varphi_{TES} * (E_{TES}(t - 1) + (1 - \rho_{TES}) * E_{C-TES}(t - 1) \\ - (1 + \delta_{TES}) * E_{D-TES}(t - 1))$$ (4)

To estimate the level to which the electrical cooling system can be lowered due to the fact that its operation is compensated by TES discharging we have estimated how much power is used by the electrical cooling system. We use [7] assumption that all the electrical power consumed by the DC IT resources to execute the workload is transformed into heat and must be dissipated by the cooling system. To estimate the actual cooling power needed to deal with the dissipated heat, the formula provided by [6] is used and enhanced with the TES flexibility mechanism described above where COP is the cooling system Coefficient of Performance:

$$E_{cooling}(t) = \frac{Heat_{removed}}{COP} + (-E_{D-TES}(t) + E_{C-TES}(t))$$ (5)

. The *flexibility mechanism defined for an energy electrical storage device (ESD)* is based on reducing at timeslot t the DC energy demand with energy discharged from the batteries and increasing at timeslot $t + u, u \in [1, T - t]$ the DC energy demand with the energy charged in batteries. A DC is equipped with batteries that store energy to cover its energy consumption needs for a short period of time. The state of the art ones have a higher charge-discharge life-cycle that allows them to be used more frequently thus offering a certain level of flexibility for the DC energy demand. Being similar with the TES, we need also to estimate the amount of energy that is discharged from the devices when they are used to power the DC ($E_{D-ESD}(t - 1)$) and the amount of energy that is charged in the devices from the DC surplus energy ($E_{C-ESD}(t - 1)$) this time taking into consideration the operating parameters of the ESD, such as: energy losses incurred during both charge and discharge cycles and also during the time the device is not used (we denote the charge loss, discharge loss and time discharge factors by ρ_{ESD}, δ_{ESD} and φ_{ESD}, respectively), and the percentage of maximum energy removal during a discharge, Depth of Discharge (DoD).

$$DoD * E_{MAX-ESD} < E_{ESD}(t) = \varphi_{TES} * (E_{ESD}(t-1) + (1 - \rho_{ESD}) * E_{C-ESD}(t-1)$$
$$- (1 + \delta_{ESD}) * E_{D-ESD}(t-1)) \tag{6}$$

Using the above presented model at each timeslot t we can determine the DC energy demand as:

$$E_{DC}(t) = E_{workload}(t) + E_{cooling}(t) + E_{C-ESD}(t) - E_{D-ESD}(t) - E_{Diesel-Gen}(t) \tag{7}$$

To shift the energy demand profile for *providing Ancillary Services* the following optimization function need to be minimized:

$$f\_Objective = (\frac{\sum_{t=TE}^{TS} (E_{DC}(t) - E_{signal}(t))^2}{TE - TS} + \frac{\sum_{t=0}^{TS} (E_{DC}(t) - E_{baseline}(t))^2 * (TS - t)}{TS}$$
$$+ \frac{\sum_{t=TE}^{T} (E_{DC}(t) - E_{baseline}(t))^2 * (t - TE)}{T - TE}) \tag{8}$$

The optimization function aims at shedding the DC energy demand profile to match a requested energy profile by the DSO for the response interval $[TE, TS]$ while reducing the energy consumption alteration impact on the rest of the optimization time window: $[1, TE]$ before and $[TS, T]$ after DC's response interval. Thus the function computes the normalized distance between the DC energy demand curve $E_{DC}(t)$, and the reference values requested by the DSO $E_{signal}(t)$ during the demand response period $[TE, TS]$ on one side and the DC energy demand baseline (i.e. expected energy consumption estimated based on the workload the DC has to execute) $E_{baseline}(t)$ for the rest of the prediction window $[1, TE] \cup [TS, T]$ on the other side. Furthermore, in order to minimize the DC energy consumption changes from the initial baseline, the distances outside the demand response interval $[TE, TS]$ are weighted with a function that increases with the distance from the interval, thus assuring that the changes in the DC energy consumption from the initial baseline are kept as close as possible to the demand response period.

4   Use Case Evaluation

To demonstrate the viability of our proposed optimization methodology, numerical simulation based experiments have been carried out, with a view to subsequently apply and validate the approach in the coming months in real pilot DCs of GEYSER EU FP7 project [19]. To that end, we have developed a simulation environment in which the hardware systems' characteristics and operation (see Table 1) of a real DC are modelled. The workload energy demand was taken from the IT power consumption logs of the DC [18] considering 5 min samples normalized using the maximum power consumption of modelled DC.

Table 1. DC's hardware components characteristics.

Component	Hardware characteristics simulated
Electrical cooling system	Cooling Capacity = 4000 kWh, Minimum Cooling Load = 200 kWh, Maximum Cooling Load = 2000 kWh, COP Coefficient = 3.5
IT computing resources	11000 SERVERS with: P_MAX = 325 W, Memory, Processor, Hard Drive = RAM 8 GB, CPU 2.4 GHz, HDD 1 Tb
Electrical storage system	Charge Loss Rate = 1.2, Discharge Loss Rate = 0.8, Energy Loss Rate = 0.995, Max Charge and Discharge Rate = 1000 kWh, Max Capacity = 1000 kWh
Thermal storage system	Charge Loss Rate = 1.1, Discharge Loss Rate = 0.99, Energy Loss Rate = 0.999, Max Charge and Discharge Rate = 1000 kWh, Maximum Capacity = 3000 kWh

The proposed methodology was used to shape the energy demand profile of the simulated DC aiming at providing the Ancillary Services described in Table 2. The services are distinguished by their following requirements: (i) how fast the DC must respond if it can fulfil the requested service (response time), (ii) the minimum length of the DC response, and (iii) the hardware resources on which the DC is leveraging on generating the requested output considering factors such as the modelled hardware devices inertia in providing flexibility.

Table 2. Ancillary services the DC may provide.

Service name	Description	Time to full response	Response length	DC mechanism
Regulation	Increase demand for large un-forecasted renewable energy production	20 min	1 h	Load time shifting, ESDs, electrical cooling system adjustments using TES
Scheduling	Shed or shift energy consumption over time to match a requested profile	10 min	>1 h	Load time shifting, ESDs, electrical cooling system adjustments using TES
Reserve	Provide fast ramping power	<10 min	30 min	ESDs and diesel generators

The optimization objective function (see relation 8) needs to be minimized considering the following input data for the response length time window: requested energy profile for the prediction window associated with the Ancillary Service signal, DC energy demand baseline without optimization and DC predicted energy demand. To solve the minimization problem Mixed Integer Nonlinear Programing [20] was used.

4.1 DC Providing Regulation Ancillary Service

In this scenario we assume that in the energy grid there is large un-forecasted renewable energy production that may threaten the grid stability. In consequence the DSO sends a regulation signal to the DC connected to the grid at 12 pm requesting to increase its energy demand between 12:25 pm and 1:15 pm and consume as must as possible the energy surplus. Figure 1 top presents the DC energy demand baseline with orange line and requested profile with blue line. In response DC takes advantage of our methodology to optimize its demand using the available flexibility mechanisms such that it consumes more energy in the requested period (see Fig. 1 bottom).

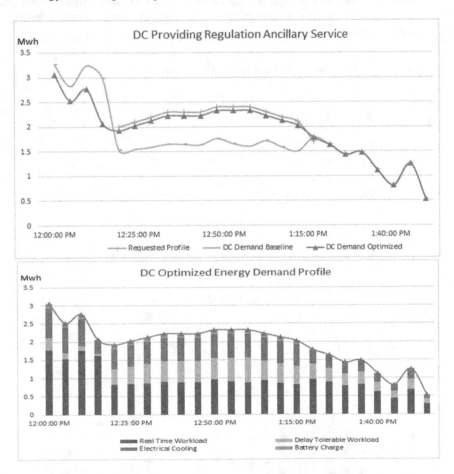

Fig. 1. DC providing regulation ancillary service. (Color figure online)

By applying the optimization techniques proposed, the DC energy demand profile is adapted to the Regulation Ancillary Service signal request. Consequently, it can be seen that most of the delay tolerable workload arrived in the interval 12–12:25 pm has been delayed to fill the energy demand gap in the interval 12:25–1:15 pm. Also, the electrical cooling system is used more in this interval to overcool the TES, such that they can be used later to reduce the energy consumption if needed by substituting the electrical cooling system. As a result, the DC energy demand was increased by 34 % from original baseline on the service response length.

4.2 DC Providing Scheduling Ancillary Service

In this scenario we assume that in the Smart Grid there is predicted energy consumption coincident peak and in order to avoid it the DC is requested to shed or shift energy consumption over time. In consequence the DSO sends a scheduling signal to the DC connected to the grid at 12 pm requesting to decrease its energy demand between 12:30 pm and 2 pm.

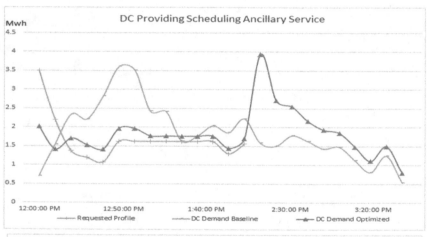

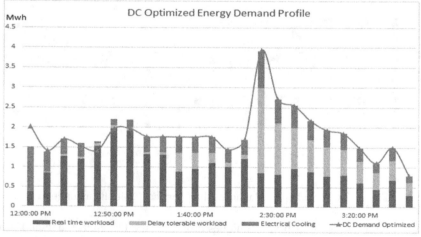

Fig. 2. DC providing scheduling ancillary service. (Color figure online)

Figure 2 presents the DC energy demand baseline; the requested profile with blue line and the DC optimized energy demand profile obtained using our methodology and the flexibility actions used. As it can be noticed using our methodology the DC is able to reduce the energy consumption over the service response period with 32 % to meet the request. Most of the delay tolerant workload from the service response period is delayed after 2:30 pm. The electrical cooling device is used less with 20 % during the response period by leveraging on the TES device which was prior overcooled. Also no charging batteries actions are taken during this period. Total amount of flexible energy shifted to provide the requested services is 8.43 MWh.

4.3 DC Providing Reserve Ancillary Service

In this scenario we assume that the DSO in order to maintain the (local) reactive power balance under normal conditions and to ensure a stable grid operation with adequate

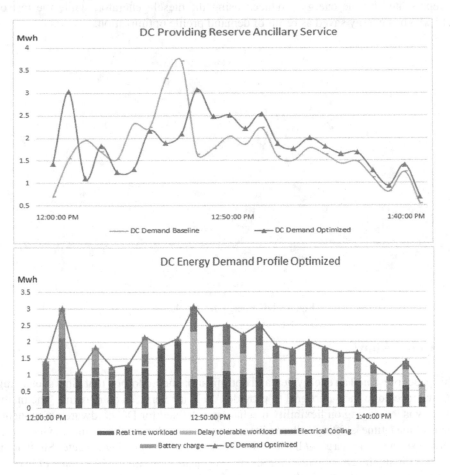

Fig. 3. DC providing reserve ancillary service. (Color figure online)

voltage control requests the DC to provide reserve Ancillary Service. In consequence it sends a reserve signal to DC to produce energy using its diesel generator (the greener biomass-fuelled generators are not yet considered for DC backup power generation) and feed it back to grid. To increase the amount of energy fed to the grid the DC uses our optimization methodology to shift as much as possible the energy demand away from the time interval when the service is expected by using at minimum the electrical cooling system and shifting the execution of delay tolerant workload. Also it leverages on the batteries to feed extra power to the grid.

Figure 3 presents the optimized DC energy demand profile while Fig. 4 presents the diesel energy generated and feed to the grid. We have considered that the Reserve Ancillary Service signal is received at 12:00 pm, the DC will provide fast ramping power starting from 12:10 pm and the service response length is 30 min until 12:40 pm. During the reserve service duration the using our methodology the DC manages to shift about 4.15 MWh of flexible energy resulting in a temporary decrees of energy consumption with 15 %. Also the amount of energy feed to the grid is 8.79 MWh out of which 52 % is represented by the energy produced using the diesel generator, while the rest of 4.15 MWh is energy saved as result of demand profile optimization.

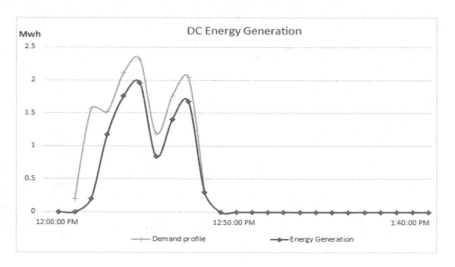

Fig. 4. DC Energy feed to the grid.

5   Conclusion

This paper presented an energy demand optimization methodology that aims at enacting DCs connected to the smart grid to provide Ancillary Services on demand. The methodology is leveraging on flexibility mechanisms defined for DC hardware components such as load time shifting, alternative usage of non-electrical cooling devices (e.g. thermal storage) or charging/discharging the electrical storage devices, etc. Simulation results validate the DC potential for shaping its energy profile to meet goals of diverse energy networks and provide three types of Ancillary Services: Regulation, Scheduling and Reserve. The approach is about to be validated within the context of four operational DCs of the GEYSER project (Pont Saint Martin and Terni in Italy, Alticom in the Netherlands and RWTH Aachen in Germany).

Acknowledgements. This work has been conducted within the GEYSER project Grant number 609211 [19], co-funded by the European Commission as part of the 7th Research Framework Programme (FP7-SMARTCITIES-2013).

References

1. Liu, Z., Wierman, A., Chen, Y., Razon, B., Chen, N.: Data center demand response: avoiding the coincident peak via workload shifting and local generation. In: ACM SIGMETRICS/ International Conference on Measurement and Modeling of Computer Systems, pp. 341–342. ACM, New York (2013)
2. Ghatikar, G., Ganti, V., Matson, N., Piette, M.A.: Demand Response Opportunities and Enabling Technologies for Data Centers: Findings from Field Studies (2012). http:// eetd.lbl.gov/sites/all/files/LBNL-5763E.pdf
3. Ghasemi-Gol, M., Wang, Y., Pedram, M., Hsieh, M.: An optimization framework for data centers to minimize electric bill under day-ahead dynamic energy prices while providing regulation services. In: Green Computing Conference (IGCC), Dallas, pp. 1–9. IEEE (2014)
4. Koomey, J.: Growth in data center electricity use 2005 to 2010. Analytics Press, Oakland, CA, 1 August 2010
5. Ma, O., Alkadi, N.: Demand response for ancillary services. IEEE Trans. Smart Grid (99) (2013). IEEE
6. Zhang, Y., Wang, Y., Wang, X.: TEStore: exploiting thermal and energy storage to cut the electricity bill for datacenter cooling. In: 8th International Conference and Workshop on Systems Virtualization Management, Las Vegas, pp. 19–27 (2012)
7. Tang, Q.: Sensor-based fast thermal evaluation model for energy efficient high-performance datacenters. Intel Corporation. In: Intelligent Sensing and Information Processing (ICISIP) 2006, Bangalore, pp. 203–208, IEEE (2006)
8. Sawyer, R.L.: Calculating Total Power Requirements for Data Centers, Whitepaper. http:// www.apcmedia.com/salestools/vavr-5tdtef/vavr-5tdtef_r1_en.pdf?sdirect=true
9. Li, L., Zheng, W., Wang, X.: Coordinating liquid and free air cooling with workload allocation for data center power minimization. In: 11th International Conference on Autonomic Computing (ICAC 2014), Philadelphia. USENIX (2014)
10. Urgaonkar, R., Urgaonkar, B., Neely, M., Sivasubramaniam, A.: Optimal power cost management using stored energy in data centers. In: ACM SIGMETRICS Joint International Conference on Measurement and Modeling of Computer Systems, pp. 221–232, ACM, New York (2011)
11. Zheng, W., Ma, K., Wang, X.: Exploiting thermal energy storage to reduce data center capital and operating expenses. In: 20th International Symposium on High Performance Computer Architecture (HPCA), Orlando. IEEE (2014)
12. Govindan, S., Sivasubramaniam, A., Urgaonkar, B.: Benefits and limitations of tapping into stored energy for datacenters. In: Proceedings of the 38th Annual International Symposium on Computer Architecture (ISCA), San Jose, pp. 341–352. IEEE (2011)
13. Aksanli, B., Rosing, T.: Providing regulation services and managing data center peak power budgets. In: Design, Automation and Test in Europe Conference and Exhibition (DATE), Dresden, pp. 1–4. IEEE (2014)

14. Ghamkhari, M. Mohsenian-Rad, H.: Data centers to offer ancillary services. In: Proceedings of IEEE International Conference on Smart Grid Communications (SmartGridComm), Tainan City. IEEE (2012)
15. Li, Y., Chiu, D., Liu, C., Phan, L.T.X., Gill, T., Aggarwal, S., Zhang, Z., Thau Loo, B., Maier, D., McManus, B.: Towards dynamic pricing-based collaborative optimizations for green data centers. In: Data Engineering Workshops (ICDEW), Brisbane, pp. 272–278. IEEE (2013)
16. Janacek, S., Schomaker, G., Nebel, W.: Data center smart grid integration considering renewable energies and waste heat usage. In: Klingert, S., Hesselbach-Serra, X., Ortega, M.P., Giuliani, G. (eds.) E^2DC 2013. LNCS, vol. 8343, pp. 99–109. Springer, Heidelberg (2014)
17. Chen, Y., et al.: The case for evaluating mapreduce performance using workload suites. In: Modeling, Analysis and Simulation of Computer and Telecommunication Systems (MASCOTS), Singapore, pp. 390–399. IEEE (2011)
18. Nord Pool Spot Market Data. http://www.nordpoolspot.com/Market-data1/Elspot/Area-Prices/ALL1/Hourly/?view=table
19. GEYSER – Green Energy Data Centers as Energy Prosumers in Smart City. http://www.geyser-project.eu/
20. LINDO™ Software for Integer Programming, Linear Programming, Nonlinear Programming, Stochastic Programming, Global Optimization. http://www.lindo.com/
21. Zheng, W., Ma, K., Wang, X.: Exploiting thermal energy storage to reduce data center capital and operating expenses. http://www2.ece.ohio-state.edu/~xwang/papers/hpca14.pdf

A Specification Language for Performance and Economical Analysis of Short Term Data Intensive Energy Management Services

Alberto Merino, Rafael Tolosana-Calasanz, José Ángel Bañares$^{(\boxtimes)}$,
and José-Manuel Colom

Dpto. de Informática e Ingeniería de Sistemas,
Universidad de Zaragoza, Zaragoza, Spain
albertomerort@gmail.com, {rafaelt,banares,jm}@unizar.es

Abstract. Requirements of Energy Management Services include short and long term processing of data in a massively interconnected scenario. The complexity and variety of short term applications needs methodologies that allow designers to reason about the models taking into account functional and non-functional requirements. In this paper we present a component based specification language for building trustworthy continuous dataflow applications. Component behaviour is defined by Petri Nets in order to translate to the methodology all the advantages derived from a mathematically based executable model to support analysis, verification, simulation and performance evaluation. The paper illustrates how to model and reason with specifications of advanced data flow abstractions such as smart grids.

Keywords: Energy · Cloud computing · Specification language

1 Introduction

The Smart Power Grid (SG) domain is a prototypical scenario to illustrate the need of different services that will require short and long term processing. The existing paradigm of passive distribution and one-way communications from large suppliers to final consumers will be replaced by an active and responsive system. The development of not only generation but also micro generation at a large scale may pose a big challenge for different actors interacting within a physically constrained network through various ICT systems to efficiently operate the power grid. Actors in SG comprise Bulk Generation, Transmission System Operators, Distribution System Operators, End-users becoming proactive actors, markets, and third service providers to support processes of others actors [5].

From the ICT point of view, data flow applications processing real-time data from thousands of devices make possible new ways to monitor the grid networks and provide new means to accurately predict and effectively respond to events. In the SG scenario events related to different actors occur anywhere in

© Springer International Publishing Switzerland 2016
J. Altmann et al. (Eds.): GECON 2015, LNCS 9512, pp. 147–163, 2016.
DOI: 10.1007/978-3-319-43177-2_10

the power generation, distribution and demand chain requiring the joint analysis of heterogeneous massive data sources. It implies different coordinated data flows (forecasting, monitoring, control, etc.) that should be fed with several heterogeneous data sources and that will require the composition of different data flow abstractions to define its functionality.

Recently, several works have presented the benefits of using large data centers with massive computation and storage capacities operated by Cloud providers [4]. Traditional electric utilities and new actors in the SG lack the resources and expertise on all ICT background. Cloud service providers will be in charge on the design, deployment, maintenance and upgrades of the plethora of data intensive services that will make possible the next power system generation. Sharing services executed on scalable platforms that adapt the resources to the evolving demand of the different actors in the SG domain allow electric utilities reduce operational cost. From the cloud service provider point of view, it requires the orchestration of different expertise by means of a common framework that facilitates the integration of data intensive analysis tools, and provides data-intensive engineers the mechanisms to deploy services on cloud infrastructures. This trend may also inspire new services in the SG domain, such as personal services derived from smart meters that analyze user behaviors and optimize the appliance consumption; planning electrical vehicle charges to protect components of the distribution network from being overloaded; or advanced trading services to support more flexible power grid asset buying and selling operations.

The requirements for several Energy Management services that will facilitate effortless energy monitoring and control have been presented in [1]. These requirements of combining long and short-term processing in different scenarios have motivated the Lambda Architecture proposed by Nathan Marz [9]: a generic, scalable and fault-tolerant data processing architecture. In a Lambda architecture data entering the system are dispatched to both the *batch layer* and the *speed layer* for processing. The batch layer manages dataset and precomputes batch views; and the speed layer compensates high latency of batch layer dealing with recent data only and providing real-time views. The speed layer is fundamental to develop services related to network operation or real state estimation of the grid network. Uncertainties in the real-time views of the system state will still remain, but a certain amount of unpredictability should be assumed, as the expected systems behaviour is intrinsically random, heterogeneous and adaptive. One of the Lambda Architecture strengths is the complexity isolation, meaning that complexity is pushed into the speed layer whose results are only temporary. However, isolating complexity does not means it disappears resulting in a speed layer that is far more complex than the batch layer.

In our previous paper [15], we presented the principles of a methodological approach to specify and analyze real-time data intensive applications executed over a general cloud software architecture. The execution may incur an economical cost, and it can be therefore important to conduct an analysis prior to any execution. Such an analysis can explore how economic cost is interrelated to performance and functionality. The proposed methodology is based on the intensive use of formal executable models used to obtain qualitative information and analysis on performance and economic behaviours under different scenarios. The use of formal executable specifications has a twofold objective: (1) To allow the engineer to conduct and analyse the models in an intensive way before the deployment of the application in order to understand its behavior, and to identify the boundaries of QoS parameters of the different adopted solutions; and (2) Reason on functional and non-functional requirements with functional and performance models, which constitute an essential element of the system knowledge.

In this paper we go on in the development of the methodology presenting a specification language to support the proposed methodology. Then, we show the reasoning capabilities that provides the use of a formal model. The rest of this paper is structured as follows. In Sect. 2 a brief overview of the data flow language specification is presented. It is illustrated by means of the Matrix-Vector Multiplication problem in streaming fashion, an example of the kind of advanced data flow abstractions required for real-time SG state estimations in the cloud. This problem can be adequately modeled by the wavefront pattern [18]. Section 3 analyses the use of different analysis possibilities of the Petri net (PN) underlying the model, and finally conclusions are given in Sect. 4.

2 Specification Language for Basic and Advanced Data Flow Applications

Once delegated the ICT complexity to third cloud service providers, the first step is the definition of a methodology providing the strategy to afford the complexity and defining the framework to support it. Different aspects of information processing, information integration, data mining, complex event processing, and machine learning and SG state monitoring must be considered and coordinated. Several of the focus areas identified above resemble those seen in eScience and the Big Data.

In [15] we presented the principles of the methodology to cope with the inherent complexity of Continuous Data Flow Applications (CDFAs). The methodology considers all involved elements at different abstraction levels. In this paper, we present the specification language to support the methodology with the following requirements that go beyond pure functionality: (1) The development of CDFAs must be supported by a specification language that provides different views of the constructive elements at different abstraction levels. The language should support complementary capacities for the description of the application or components of the application: behavioral specification of concurrent processes, transformations operated over the data flow, and structural description of components that configure the application. (2) A formal component-based development to build models from existing components and capability to reason about the resulting composition. Reuse of components allows developers to use knowledge of their properties to predict the new system properties [12]. (3) Workflow and data flow patterns have been widely studied [11,18]. More advanced data flow abstractions such as MapReduce, or Bulk Synchronous parallel (BSP) constitute the essence of parallel programming frameworks such as Hadoop and Hama. However, these frameworks are only instances of many possible parallel execution templates. The reasonable approach is a general specification language that combines eScience workflow and large-grain dataflow abstractions [13].

These principles have guided the design of our component based specification LANGuage of Layers and tIERS (*Langliers*) to support a methodology for building trustworthy CDFAs. That is, the design of layers concerned with the logical division of components and functionality, and the design of tiers concerned with the physical distribution of components. The Hierarchical construction of the specification of CDFAs requires the definition of composition and refinement primitives. The semantics of the component-based language will be defined formally through standard PNs in order to translate to the methodology all the advantages derived from a mathematically based model: Analysis, Verification, Equivalence Relations, etc. Due to space limitations, the paper sketches a CDFA language specification focusing on the structural and behavioural specifications.

There are many ways in which a system can be built to provide the same functionality with different concurrent behaviours and different deployments over distributed infrastructures [11]. Our methodological approach to identify the elements to compound our hybrid specification can be summarised with the equation'Specification of CDFA = Functional Entities + Communication / Synchronisation mechanisms + Data Dependencies + Resources'. The identification and characterisation of each building block of the proposed equation defines the basic specification elements.

The constructive elements of a CDFA application are presented in this section, starting from the most basic building blocks and their interpretation as constructive primitives of distributed applications and continuing with their composition by means of simple operators (Subsect. 2.1). Composition operators provide the way to configure components with complex behaviours. Then, we show how *Langliers* represents the basic components identified in [15], Computational and Data Transmission Processes, to describe a CDFA network as a graph showing various connected processing components that operates over a data stream. This processing network model is an abstraction that describes the **functional** behaviour of a CDFA made up of a number of platform-independent components. The explicit network specification allows developers to visualize the functional model and apply analysis techniques. The last remaining step to specify a complete model is to set the implementation of the functional model with the specification of the resources that will be used to execute the model. This **operational** specification can be used to conduct performance optimizations selecting a good mapping of Computational Processes and Data Transmission Processes to computational and network resources.

2.1   Basic Building Blocks and Composition Operators

The precise and formal specification of components requires a description beyond architectural units. It is not enough to specify the interface. Specification of nonfunctional or quality attributes is also required to enable different types of reasoning. In *Langliers* a component is expressed in the form of an *interface* and a *behaviour* description [12]. The **interface** provides a specification for the services the component provides and publishes its input and output points. It gives information at the syntax level that enables *data type checking*, and publishes the *events* that trigger computations and state changes. This way, our data stream model follows a data driven execution model where events lead to computations that may generate events on other components. The **behaviour** represents components internal states and state changes. A component behavior description is specified either by one explicit PN or by the PN resulting from the behavior composition of subcomponents.

Once defined the elements of a component description, we present the basic building primitive components to describe a distributed system. The behaviour specification of these building primitives is represented by one of the PNs shown in Fig. 1. Transitions and places used for the composition of behaviours are part of the interface declaration and can have respectively associated a set of parameters or data type. Behaviour specification can have inscription expressions labelling arcs in the same way as high-level PNs (HLPNs) [6] (e.g., colored PNs or predicate/transition nets), which provides more compact and manageable descriptions. Internal transitions can also be labelled with actions to represent atomic actions that may be executed after the firing of the transition. It allows conventional programming language methods to describe operations and provides an executable functional specification in a similar way to Renew[1], which utilises tuples and Java expressions as the primary inscription language. For the sake of simplicity, in this paper a detailed description of parameters and PN inscriptions are left out of the specification.

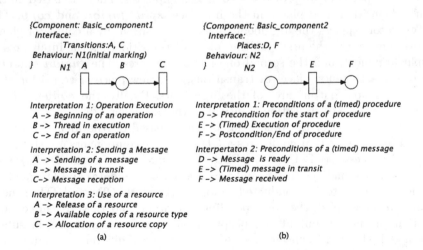

{Component: Basic_component1
  Interface:
      Transitions:A, C
  Behaviour: N1(initial marking)
}   N1   A   B   C

Interpretation 1: Operation Execution
A -> Beginning of an operation
B -> Thread in execution
C -> End of an operation

Interpretation 2: Sending a Message
A -> Sending of a message
B -> Message in transit
C-> Message reception

Interpretation 3: Use of a resource
A -> Release of a resource
B -> Available copies of a resource type
C -> Allocation of a resource copy

(a)

{Component: Basic_component2
  Interface:
      Places:D, F
  Behaviour: N2
}   N2   D   E   F

Interpretation 1: Preconditions of a (timed) procedure
D -> Precondition for the start of procedure
E -> (Timed) Execution of procedure
F -> Postcondition/End of procedure

Interpretaton 2: Preconditions of a (timed) message
D -> Message is ready
E -> (Timed) message in transit
F -> Message received

(b)

Fig. 1. Component specification of basic component primitives and interpretations.

---

[1] http://www.renew.de.

We propose two basic building-blocks with different precise interpretations. Figure 1(a) shows the *Basic Component1* that declares as behaviour the Petri net $\mathcal{N}_1$. Interface Transition A requires a component with a Transition (output port) that triggers transition A. Transition A represents the beginning of the execution of an operation in the first interpretation, the beginning of the sending of a message in the second interpretation and the release of a resource in the third interpretation. Interface Transition C requires a component to trigger the execution of an event synchronised with the end of the operation in the first interpretation, the reception of a message in the second interpretation and the allocation of a resource copy in the third interpretation. Place B in Fig. 1(a) is an internal state with the interpretations presented. An initial marking can be defined when this component is declared as subcomponent of another component.

Figure 1(b) shows the *Basic Component2* that declares as behaviour the PN $\mathcal{N}_2$. Interface Place D represents events received and requires a component that sends events to this place, and Interface Place F represents generated events waiting to be consumed requiring a component that consumes these events. Place D represents preconditions to start the execution of an operation in the first interpretation and that a message is ready in the second interpretation. Place F represents the ending of an operation or a received message waiting to be consumed. Transition E represents an internal action, for example a procedure executed in a machine or a network transmission. It can be timed to represent non-instantaneous actions.

The declaration of a "Composite" component is similar to a basic component with an additional declaration of subcomponents, connection of subcomponents and definition of its interface (ports and data-flow) as a mapping of input and output ports to the input and output ports of subcomponents. Three simple composition operators are provided to define Composites. They are based on the fusion of transitions and places in the interface: *split*, *fusion* and *copy*. The *split* operator replaces the argument, place or transition, by a couple of places or transitions, where the first resulting place or transition has the input arcs of the split argument, and the second one the output arcs. The *fusion* operator replaces the arguments, places or transitions, by a new place or transition that has the input and output arcs of the arguments. Finally, the *copy* operator creates a new place or transition identical to the argument.

The construction of the functional model is based on the identification of the basic components that configures a CDFA. These components are the Computational Processes (CPs) and the Data Transmission Processes (DTPs). CPs accomplish functional operations and transformations on data, and DTPs allow data dependencies to be conducted among CPs. Both CPs and DTPs need resources to accomplish the corresponding operation, and these resources also appear in the model, but at a conceptual, and generic way. Later in subsequent model refinements, specific resource constraints of different computational infrastructures will be added, such as limitations in parallelism, capacity, etc. The behavioural description of CPs and DTPS was presented in [15]. Figure 2 shows the *Langliers* specification of an untimed and timed CPs.

Figure 2(a) shows a CP defined by *Op_Component*. This basic component is defined by the composition of two instances of *Component_1*, the first one with the first interpretation and the second with the third interpretation semantic. The second component declaration includes an initial marking of one token in Place *B*. On the left is represented the composition of PNs describing the sub-components behaviour, and on the right the textual component specification. Composites consist in a declaration of subcomponents, and a declaration of port mappings or links by means of the PN based composition operators. The rename declaration is used to rename places and transitions of subcomponents or the result of composition operators.

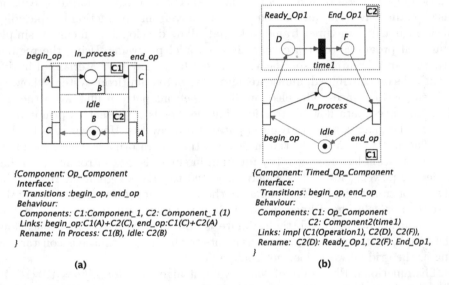

{Component: Op_Component
Interface:
  Transitions :begin_op, end_op
Behaviour:
  Components: C1:Component_1, C2: Component_1 (1)
  Links: begin_op:C1(A)+C2(C), end_op:C1(C)+C2(A)
  Rename: In Process: C1(B), Idle: C2(B)
}

(a)

{Component: Timed_Op_Component
Interface:
  Transitions: begin_op, end_op
Behaviour:
  Components: C1: Op_Component
             C2: Component2(time1)
  Links: impl (C1(Operation1), C2(D), C2(F)),
  Rename: C2(D): Ready_Op1, C2(F): End_Op1,
}

(b)

Fig. 2. A Computational Process with Resources. (a) A CP composed by 1 state. (b) Timed model assigning $time_i$ units of time to the execution of the $operation_i$. **Legend:** Textual representation of components on the right follows the frame-based tradition of concepts as attribute-value pairs: **Component:** Name of component; **Interface:** List of Place and Transitions that can be used to compose components; **Behaviour:** Either a reference to a PN $\mathcal{N}$, or a list of **Components**, **Links** that connect components, and **Rename** declarations; **Places** and **Transitions** are referenced by the component name followed by the Place/Transition name placed in parenthesis.

The model presented in Fig. 2(a) is untimed. The addition of timed information to a CP is introduced by the addition of a sequence place-transition-place in parallel with a process place representing an operation of the computational task that consumes time. The transition added is labelled with time information representing the duration of the computational operation. In Fig. 2(b), the CP from Fig. 2(a) is refined by assigning *time1* units of time to the execution of the operation 1. Note that the **Link** declaration can be complex enough to require the use of a procedural language for the composition of operators. Two new operators are defined using basic operators. *Split-Copy* splits a copy of a place, and *impl* operator specifies the way an operation is implemented. The *impl* makes a *split-Copy* of the first argument and fusions the first returned place with the second argument, and the second place with the third argument. The Links declaration in Fig. 2(b) uses the *impl* operator to refine *In_process*.

2.2 *Langliers* Specification of a Cloud Based Operational Model of a Matrix-Vector Multiplication in Streaming

To illustrate a more complex specification with *Langliers* we present the specification of an operational model for Matrix-Vector Multiplication in streaming based on the wavefront abstraction [18]. The wavefront abstraction is a paradigmatic regularly structured framework that allow developer to focus on simple sequential programs to create very large parallel programs. Using the regular structure and declarative specification, a wavefront may be materialized in different ways on distributed, multicore, and distributed multicore systems showing different performances. The election of a wavefront pattern illustrates the use of an advanced data flow abstraction that neither is it present as primitive in workflow languages, nor in advanced parallel frameworks. However, this kind of data flow abstraction is essential in SG real time monitoring services. Accurate state estimation has become a key function in supervisory control and planning of electric power grids and is widely expected to play a significant role in the advance of smart grid [8]. Traditional methods compute state estimations by the least squares solution of linear equations. In the more simple case, as soon the measurements are obtained, the estimate is obtained by matrix multiplication. The matrix that converts the measurements to the state estimate is constant as long as the grid network does not change [3].

The functional PN model of the wavefront algorithm for $Z^{(k)} = Y^{(k)} + A \cdot X^{(k)}$, $k = 1, 2, \ldots$ was presented in [15]. In this section is presented a functional and operational specification in *Langliers*.

The untimed functional PN specification of the wavefront algorithm is shown in the upper part of the Fig. 3. The functional model is constructed in a modular fashion. Each element of the wavefront array is defined as a composite *Cell* component made up of basic subcomponents (see upper Fig. 3 *Cell* component specification): (1) A subcomponent to describe the Computational Process carried out in a node of the wavefront array; and (2) two subcomponents to describe Data Transmission Processes of the data streams from *Cells* at the north/east to *Cells* in the south/west. Observe that OP_ij places are refined adding a sequence place-transition-place in parallel with the place representing the operation that is executed over each data of the data flow. The new added transition is labeled with the procedural action that must be carried by each *Cell* component: $op = aij * xj + yi$. Each *Cell* component is initialised with its aij element of matrix A. Arcs and transitions are annotated with variables defining a complete functional specification.

To construct the global functional model, nine instances of the *Cell* component are needed (Fig. 3). Each *Cell_ij* component is connected by a *Sync_ij* transition resulting from the fusion of the transition *begin_opij* with the transition *end_HTransi(j − 1)* of the east *Cell* and the the transition *end_VTransij* with the *begin_op(i + 1)j* of the south *Cell*.

Each one of *Sync_1j* transition at the first row does not have a *Cell* component connected at the North, and constitute the *IYi* interface transitions representing the input stream of the corresponding i-th component of the vector $X^{(k)}$ via the fusion of the transitions *begin_op_1j* with a the *end_Transmission* of a DTP component. In the same way, each one of *Sync_i1* transition at of the first column does not have a left *Cell* component, and constitute the *IXj* interface transitions representing the input stream of the corresponding j-th component of the vector $Y^{(k)}$ via the fusion of the transitions *begin_op_i1* with a the *end_Transmission* of a DTP component. Each one of *End_HTransi3* transitions in *Cell* components of the last column is the output stream of the corresponding i-th component of the vector $Z^{(k)}$ and constitute the *OZi* interface transitions.

Timed Operational Specification for the Wavefront Algorithm. We consider a cloud computing infrastructure where each *Cell* component can be executed over a different Virtual Machine (VM). We assume a cloud platform (OpenNebula, OpenStack, etc.) provides networking and computing virtualisation. For each token in the Idle places *Idle_ij* we assume that there is a VM implementing a computational resource that can accomplish the same functionality with similar performance, and for each token in the *CijH* and *CijV* places we assume a transmission over the network assuming than the use of virtualisation technologies does not alter the original incoming data injection rate at each data flow [16]. In this case, the addition of time to the model of Fig. 3 will be done in the way described in the previous section: adding a sequence place-transition-place in parallel with the places representing the activities that consume time by the *Cell* located at row i-th, column j-th: *OP_ij* representing the duration of the computation, and in parallel with places *CijH* and *CijV* representing the consumption of time in the transmission of a data element in the corresponding DTPs. Following this approach we obtain an operational net model that is isomorphous to the functional model in Fig. 3.

An alternative more complex operational model is shown at the bottom part of the Fig. 3. It shows a pipeline of three nodes and graphically the *Node* component specification. Each node component is composed of: (1) A subcomponent to describe the available Computational Resources at each node, and (2) two subcomponents to describe DTPs between computational resources in the same node, and to the computational resources of the next step. Each *Node* component has a *Ci_OP* component with a *PU_i* place representing the VM resources in use, and an *IdlePU_i* place representing available VM allocated for this step. Transition labelled with time *timePU_i* represents the time for a VM to execute the operation in a wavefront *Cell*. The timed *C1_Cx* subcomponent represents

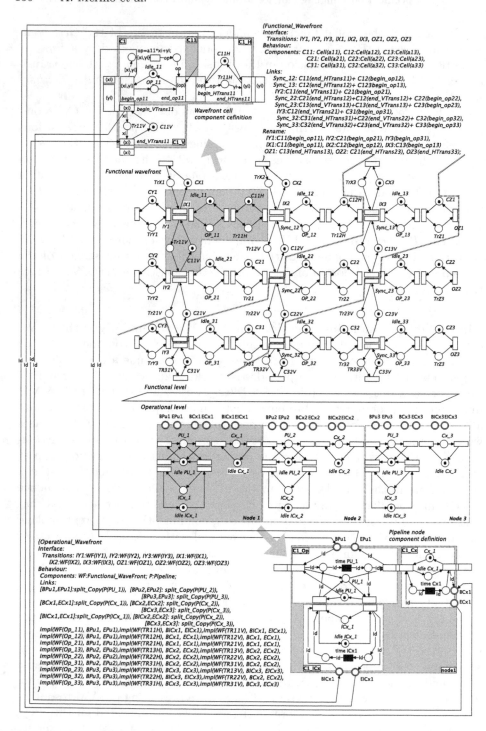

Fig. 3. Operational 3×3 wavefront array executed over a cloud VM pipeline in 3 steps.

the DTPs with the next step in the pipeline or with the component that receives the OZi output of the wavefront; and the timed $C1\_ICx$ subcomponent represents DTPs between VM in the same node.

CPs in a left to right diagonal can operate concurrently and propagate in wavefronts. For this reason, a balanced deployment of the wavefront $Cell$ components over the pipeline steps is executed in the first node $Cell11$, $Cell12$ and $Cell21$ that corresponds from left to right to the first and second diagonal. $Cells$ in the middle diagonal are executed in the second step, and the rest of $Cells$ are executed in the last node. Observe that the horizontal connection of the $Cell11$ is an internal transmission between VM executing in the same node, while its vertical connection is a transmission with a VM in the second node. In the case of the $Cell22$, all its connections are external transmissions, and the same happens with the $Cells$ in the diagonal deployed in the middle step. In this case, the addition of time to the pipeline model will be done by adding a sequence place-transition-place at each node i in parallel with the places PU_i representing the execution of procedures in VMs and places Cx_i and ICx_i representing respectively external and internal transmissions. The textual component specification of the operational wavefront model is presented at the bottom of Fig. 3.

The $Operational\_Wafefront$ component refines the $Functional\_wavefront$ with a $Pipeline$ by means of the **split-Copy** operator of timed activities represented by places PU_i, Cx_i and ICx_i, and the **impl** operator applied to map activities in the functional model with this timed activities in the pipeline. All mappings are specified in the $Links$ of the $Operational\_Wavefront$ component, and a sample of the result of the mapping is illustrated with the arcs connecting the $Cell11$ with places PU_1, Cx_1 and ICx_1. Observe than arcs are labelled with the id label. It represents the identifier of the $Cell$ instance to differentiate the beginning and ending of activities of cells deployed in the same node. Finally, observe that in the case that only one VM is used at each node, internal communications will be with the same machine.

3   PN Models for Performance and Economical Analysis

The proposed methodology supported by a PN based component language aims at providing different analysis and prediction techniques that allow developer assessing functional and non-functional properties. *Qualitative analysis*, that is desirable/good properties can be formulated and validated with PN models of complex concurrent and distributed systems. *Qualitative analysis* can be conducted by different techniques: (1) The construction of the state space of the model (Reachability analysis) providing a complete knowledge of all is properties if sate explosion does not hamper the use of this technique; (2) Structural techniques that allow to reason about some properties of the model just from the structure of the net using graph theory, linear algebra, convex geometry, or linear programming. The use of this technique is not constrained by the state explosion, however it has a limited decision power (semidecision algorithms) except for syntactical subclasses of PNs. On the other hand, reduction techniques allow the simplification of the nets preserving some properties. It is intimately bound up with the top-down and bottom-up design supported by the proposed methodology.

Quantitative analysis allows performance-oriented interpretations of the model such as throughput, utilization rates, queue lengths, etc. from which is possible compute *reward functions*. PNs are executable models, therefore extensive simulations may detect errors, which are rare and elusive, and provide us with some performance and reward functions. However simulation cannot guarantee the absence of errors neither identify under with conditions the simulated performance values will be reproduced. The most common analytical model used for the derivation of exact performance measures are stochastic PNs. The techniques consist on the derivation of performance measures from the reachability graph of the model from which a Markov Chain is obtained, under certain assumptions on the stochastic specification. Once again state explosion can hamper the use of the technique. Additionally, the model assume exponential distributions for transition delays, which may not be acceptable to model CPU performance, memory speed, sequential and random I/O, or network bandwidth.

Let us to explore the analysis possibilities of the presented model in Fig. 3 considering the operational net model that is isomorphous to the functional flow model. We add a sequence place-transition-place in parallel with the places representing the activities that consume time by the *Cell* located at row i-th, column j-th: OP_ij representing the duration of the computation, and in parallel with places $CijH$ and $CijV$ representing the consumption of time in the transmission of a data element in the corresponding DTPs.

Qualitative Analysis Based on Structural Analysis. In [15] we shown how the structural analysis could be used to determine the correction of the obtained design. The functional model obtained was a strongly connected marked graph. From this characteristic we recovered some interesting analysis results that we summarize: (1) The net is live, therefore the modeled solution is deadlock-free. (2) The wavefronts propagate in a orderly manner without colliding one into another validating the functional results. (3) The original solution presented in [15] showed the model cannot fully operate concurrently, and a solution based on the structural analysis was suggested to get all CPs working concurrently. The solution is shown in *Cell* Component of Fig. 3 that incorporates two $DTPs$. In this way, we can observe that the 4 transitions $Sync\_ij$, $Sync\_i(j + 1)$, $Sync\_(i + 1)j$ and $Sync\_(i+1)(j+1)$ are covered by an elementary circuit containing four tokens. All these results can be obtained using the structure net resulting from the component based language. A survey of PN tools can be found in [14].

Quantitative Analysis Based on Stochastic PNs. A stochastic PN is a Timed PN that adopts a probability density function (pdf) for the specification of random delays. Only the use of negative exponential pdf for the specification of temporal characteristics makes the analysis mathematically tractable. Let us assume that processors service delivery time $(1/\lambda)$ and injection timed transitions $(1/\gamma)$ follow an exponentially distributed random amount of time with average 100ms (rate $=10$ data/sec); and a transmission time 100 times faster with average $(1/\beta=1$ms$)$ also following an exponential distribution. From the structural analysis it is derived that all transitions will have the same throughput: The minimal repetitive sequence of transition firings contains all transitions of the net exactly once (it is guaranteed from the existence of only one T-invariant: right annuller of the incidence matrix of the net). Therefore, the relative firing frequency vector is $\mathbf{1}$, and we have the same mean cycle time for all transitions.

We translated our *Langliers* resulting operational PN to the GreatSPN2.0.2. The tool generates the reachability state with 1392640 states from which a Markov chain is derived. The steady-state numerical analysis compute performance indices (place markings probability distribution and transitions throughputs). The calculated throughput for all transition is 3,99258 data/sec. The result obtained by the GSPN analysis shows a poor throughput with a performance lost of 60 % for each processor. If we repeat the analysis with a wavefront of dimension 2×2 the throughput for all transitions is 4.69182 data/sec with a performance lost of 53 % for each processor.

Quantitative Analysis Based on Structural Analysis: Computing Performance Bounds. The use of stochastic PNs for the derivation of exact performance measures and rewards functions is hampered by two factors: (1) The explosion of the computational complexity of the analysis algorithm and (2) Only the use of n exponential pdf for the specification of temporal characteristics makes the analysis mathematically tractable.

In [2] is shown that it is possible to compute, in polynomial time, upper and lower bounds for the performance of timed and stochastic marked graph. This bounds are computed with independence of the probability distribution function of random variables that describe the timing of the system. The lower bound for the mean cycle time is obtained by solving the following linear programming problem:

$$\Gamma^{min} = \text{maximum } Y^T.Pre.\theta$$
$$\text{subject to} \qquad Y^T.C = 0, Y^T.M_0 = 1, \qquad (1)$$
$$Y \geq 0$$

Where Γ^{min}, minimum mean cycle time, Y^T is the left annuller of the incidence matrix of the net (P-semiflow), Pre is the pre incidence matrix (denoting tokens removed by transition firing), and M_0 is the initial marking. This means that the mean cycle times can be computed by the summation of all time delays involved in a circuit (P-semiflow) divided by the tokens in the circuit. And we obtain the Γ^{min} finding the maximum value of mean cycle times computed by each circuit. In our model Γ^{min} is 100 ms $(1/\lambda)$, i.e., a maximum throughout of 10 data/sec. On the other hand, the upper bound for the mean cycle can be computed by:

$$\Gamma^{max} = \sum_{j=1}^{m} \frac{\theta_j}{LB(t_j)} \qquad (2)$$

Where θ_j denotes the average service time of transition t_i, and $LB(t_j)$ the liveness bound of t_j, i.e., its maximum degree of concurrency. In our sample, the maximum liveness noun is 1 for all transitions. Therefore, Γ^{max} is given by the addition of $theta_j$ corresponding to the longer circuit given $\Gamma^{max} = 404$ ms and a minimum throughput of 2.47 data/sec.

Quantitative Analysis Based on Simulation. The distribution of response time for a cloud modeled as a queue system when service time is not exponential is complex and rely in some approximation. These approximations are very sensitive to the probability distribution of task service times, and they become increasingly inaccurate when the Coefficient of Variation (CoV) increase towards the value of 1 [7,10,17]. The difficulty increases when we try to analyze performance of applications implementing advanced data flow abstraction with a high level of concurrency constraints. In our previous quantitative analysis based on stochastic PNs throughput is near the minimum bound. The election of a exponential distributions for task service times is not adequate and results in poor and not realistic performance results.

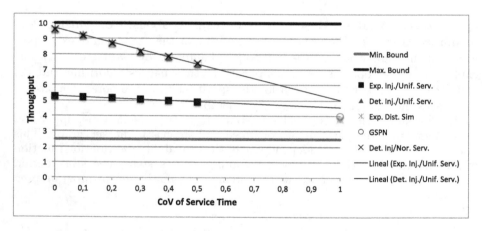

Fig. 4. Simulated throughputs with different coefficient of variation of the service time. (Color figure online)

Once known the throughput bounds, and the fact that CoV can have a high impact on performance, we conducted simulations to evaluate its impact. Figure 4 shows the results of different Renew simulations with mean services and injection times of 10 data/sec. The Figure also shows the point *GSPN* that represents the computed performance by the GSPN tool[2], and the *Exp. Dist. Sim.* shows the point with the same scenario obtained by simulation, i.e., assuming both service delivery times and interarrival times are exponential. The proximity of these points shows the accuracy of simulations. Assuming the computing

---

[2] http://www.di.unito.it/~greatspn.

nodes in the cloud are heterogenous and that the performance capabilities of these computing nodes are uniformly distributed [17] between the time of the faster node and the time of the slower node we conduct different simulations in Renew. *Exp.Inj./Unif. Serv.* shows the impact of CoV on performances assuming an exponential distribution in injections, and uniform distributions of service delivery times. *Det.Inj./Unif. Serv.* shows the same simulations with a deterministic injection time. Finally, *Det.Inj./Nor. Serv.* shows that simulations with normal distribution of service delivery times provide the same results than uniform distribution. These results shows that some mechanism is required to regulate injections rates because assuming exponential distribution of interarrival times result in performance near 50 %. On the other hand with deterministic injection, it is clear the impact of CoV on performance.

In our previous paper [15] we computed the costs for the processing of streams of length $k = n$, assuming the cost of the time unit per CPU, p: $Cost_{functional} = max\{\alpha, \beta, \gamma\} * n * p * 9$ from the functional level analysis. In this paper we have shown this costs will be proportional to the service time Coefficient of Variation CoV of the cloud platform $Cost_{operational} = k * CoV * Cost_{functional}$ assuming a mechanism to regulate the data injection to the wavefront is provided and approximately $2 * Cost_{functional}$ in case this mechanism is not provided. Depending of the CoV value of the platform, the developer can evaluate the costs of alternative operational models such as the pipeline version presented in Fig. 3.

4   Conclusions and Future Work

The SG scenario is a prototypical scenario for the Big data where a trusthworthy design of real time streamming applications is essential. Although the design of real time streaming applications is recognised as a complex task in the Big Data context [9], neither of proposed development languages and frameworks allow developers a component based reasoning that guides design decisions at all phases of the life cycle, and to address functional and non-functional requirements together with the specification of the execution infrastructure and the involved resources. This work has presented a component PN based specification language that allows developers to specify functional and operational levels at different levels of abstraction and reason with the models. A complex wavefront operational model for the Matrix-Vector Multiplication problem in streaming fashion has been presented and the way the developer can reason with the model has been illustrated. A detailed analysis of advanced data flow abstraction, or a composition of them, allow the developer reason about the functional correctness of the proposed solutions, and guide the simulations to evaluate different proposals to obtain the best performances as the base to analyze alternative solution costs.

Future work will consider the characterization of models and the definition of a limited set of building blocks that will allow us to know the limits of the formal analyses and develop tools to validate the models.

Acknowledgments. This work was co-financed by the Industry and Innovation deparment of the Aragonese Government and European Social Funds (COSMOS research group, ref. T93); and by the Spanish Ministry of Economy under the program "Programa de I+D+i Estatal de Investigación, Desarrollo e innovación Orientada a los Retos de la Sociedad", project id TIN2013-40809-R.

References

1. Aman, S., Simmhan, Y., Prasanna, V.: Energy management systems: state of the art and emerging trends. IEEE Commun. Mag. **51**(1), 114–119 (2013)
2. Campos, J., Chiola, G., Colom, J.M., Silva, M.: Properties and performance bounds for timed marked graphs. IEEE Trans. Circuits Syst. I: Fundam. Theory Appl. **39**(5), 386–401 (1992)
3. Elizondo, D., Gardner, R., Leon, R.: Power and energy society general meeting. In: 2012 IEEE Synchrophasor Technology: The Boom of Investments and Information Flow From North America to Latin America, pp. 1–6, July 2012
4. Fang, X., Misra, S., Xue, G., Yang, D.: Managing smart grid information in the cloud: opportunities, model, and applications. IEEE Netw. **26**(4), 32–38 (2012)
5. Government, U: NIST Framework and Roadmap for Smart Grid Interoperability Standards, Release 3.0. General Books, September 2014
6. Jensen, K., Rozenberg, G. (eds.): High-level Petri Nets: Theory and Application. Springer, London (1991)
7. Khazaei, H., Misic, J., Misic, V.: Performance analysis of cloud computing centers using m/g/m/m+r queuing systems. IEEE Trans. Parallel Distrib. Syst. **23**(5), 936–943 (2012)
8. Maheshwari, K., Lim, M., Wang, L., Birman, K., van Renesse, R.: Toward a reliable, secure and fault tolerant smart grid state estimation in the cloud. In: IEEE PES Innovative Smart Grid Technologies Conference, ISGT 2013, pp. 1–6 (2013)
9. Marz, N., Warren, J.: Big Data: Principles and Best Practices of Scalable Realtime Data Systems. Manning Publications Co, Greenwhich (2015)
10. O'Loughlin, J., Gillam, L.: Performance evaluation for cost-efficient public infrastructure cloud use. In: Altmann, J., Vanmechelen, K., Rana, O.F. (eds.) GECON 2014. LNCS, vol. 8914, pp. 133–145. Springer, Heidelberg (2014)
11. Pautasso, C., Alonso, G.: Parallel computing patterns for grid workflows. In: Proceedings of the HPDC 2006 Workshop on Workflows in Support of Large-Scale Science, WORKS 19–23 June 2006, Paris, France, pp. 1–10 (2006)
12. Seceleanu, C.C., Crnkovic, I.: Component models for reasoning. IEEE Comput. **46**(11), 40–47 (2013)
13. Simmhan, Y., Kumbhare, A.G.: Floe: a continuous dataflow framework for dynamic cloud applications. CoRR abs/1406.5977 (2014)
14. Thong, W., Ameedeen, M.: A survey of petri net tools. In: Sulaiman, H.A., Othman, M.A., Othman, M.F.I., Pee, N.C., Rahim, Y.A. (eds.) Advanced Computer and Communication Engineering Technology. Lecture Notes in Electrical Engineering, vol. 315, pp. 537–551. Springer International Publishing, Switzerland (2015)
15. Tolosana-Calasanz, R., Bañares, J.Á., Colom, J.-M.: Towards petri net-based economical analysis for streaming applications executed over cloud infrastructures. In: Altmann, J., Vanmechelen, K., Rana, O.F. (eds.) GECON 2014. LNCS, vol. 8914, pp. 189–205. Springer, Heidelberg (2014)

16. Tolosana-Calasanz, R., Bañares, J., Rana, O.F., Pham, C., Xydas, E., Marmaras, C.E., Papadopoulos, P., Cipcigan, L.: Enforcing quality of service on OpenNebula-based shared clouds. In: CCGRID 2014 Workshop on Data-Intensive Process Management in Large-Scale Sensor Systems, DPMSS 2014, Chicago, IL, USA, May 26–29, 2014. pp. 651–659. IEEE (2014)
17. Yeo, S., Lee, H.H.: Using mathematical modeling in provisioning a heterogeneous cloud computing environment. Computer 44(8), 55–62 (2011)
18. Yu, L., Moretti, C., Thrasher, A., Emrich, S.J., Judd, K., Thain, D.: Harnessing parallelism in multicore clusters with the all-pairs, wavefront, and makeflow abstractions. Clust. Comput. 13(3), 243–256 (2010)

Utility-Based Smartphone Energy Consumption Optimization for Cloud-Based and On-Device Application Uses

Baseem Al-athwari[✉] and Jörn Altmann

Technology Management, Economics and Policy Program College of Engineering, Seoul National University, Gwanak-Ro 1, Gwanak-Gu, Seoul 151-742, South Korea
Baseem_cs@yahoo.com, jorn.altmann@acm.org

Abstract. As the use of smartphones and its applications continue their rapid growth, prolonging the smartphone battery lifetime has become one of the main concerns for smartphone users if re-charging is not possible. In this paper, we show that, by taking into account the user preferences, the energy consumption of smartphones can be adjusted to maximize the user utility. The user preferences are reflected through the type of application uses, the perceived costs of energy allocation for the different types of applications, and the perceived value of energy remaining in the battery of the smartphone. In particular, we optimize the energy consumption of smartphones through the use of a utility-based energy consumption optimization model, which we developed. We demonstrate the workings of our model by applying it to a simple scenario, in which we vary the perceived value of energy remaining in the smartphone battery and the user's perceived costs for energy consumed by the two types of application uses: cloud-based application uses and on-device application uses. Our results show that, by letting users express their preferences, users can allocate the remaining smartphone energy such that it maximizes their utilities.

Keywords: Smartphones · Apps · Energy consumption optimization · Utility function · Usage behavior · Cloud computing · Off-loading · Application classification · Energy allocation

1 Introduction

The use of smartphones (including PDAs and tablets) together with the applications running on them evolved rapidly [1]. The most popular mobile activities performed with smartphones are web browsing, video watching, gaming, e-mailing, and social networking [2]. Even though battery technology has steadily been improved, it has not been able to match the demand for power for mobile activities. The development of past battery technology could enhance battery capacity by only 5 % annually [3]. This limitation of the smartphone batteries results in a limited use of smartphones. Therefore, energy consumption of smartphones has become one of the critical research issues.

Sometimes, users like to get their smartphone battery to last for an entire day [4]. Moreover, it might became important to the user to make the smartphone battery last as

© Springer International Publishing Switzerland 2016
J. Altmann et al. (Eds.): GECON 2015, LNCS 9512, pp. 164–175, 2016.
DOI: 10.1007/978-3-319-43177-2_11

long as possible. This, for example, can be achieved by reducing the execution of some applications. Then, the user can execute the most important applications on his smartphone more.

There are many other situations, in which users can make energy preserving decisions. These decisions of a smartphone user can range from choosing which applications to use, how to use an application, to how long the application should be used. For example, it could consider when to make a phone call, what to browse on the Internet, and which video to watch [4]. Consequently, the amount of energy consumed per application is different and the overall energy consumption depends on the user behavior.

Many studies have been conducted on smartphone usage. Some of these studies have investigated how users interact with their phones in the real world [5–12]. Other studies have focused on the charging behavior of users [13–20]. The relationship between the user behavior and the power consumption has also been examined in literature [5, 7–9, 12, 14, 20, 21, 31–39]. Their common findings are that all users have a unique usage pattern. Therefore, it is clear that a one-size power management solution cannot fit all and, hence, an appropriate solution must adapt to the behavior of the user [4]. Only then, it is possible to improve the smartphone user experience.

Despite the significant efforts by these studies about human behavior and energy efficiency for mobile devices, they did not consider the user preferences in using the applications. Especially, they did not ask what kind of preference the user has for different types of applications.

The main objective of this work is to understand how the user utility can be maximized, subject to the remaining energy in the battery and the user preferences for different types of applications.

For the purpose of our study, we classify application uses into two categories: on-device application uses, which refer to application uses that do not need Internet connectivity; and cloud-based application uses, which refer to application uses that require Internet connectivity and the cloud.

To address the research objective, we conduct the following steps: First, we propose a utility-based consumption optimization model to describe the user preferences with respect to energy allocation to the two types of smartphone application uses (i.e., on-device application use and cloud-based application use). The shape of the user utility function is defined by the Cobb-Douglas function. Second, considering a scenario that includes on-device and cloud-based application uses, we demonstrate our model and how the optimal energy allocation yields maximum utility subject to the remaining energy and the user preferences for the two types of smartphone application uses.

This work can be used by smartphone users, helping them to get the maximum utility from the remaining energy in their smartphone battery. In detail, we make the following two contributions: (1) a utility-based energy consumption optimization model; (2) the demonstration of the application of the optimization model to two types of application uses (on-device application uses, cloud-based application uses).

The remainder of this paper is structured as follows. In the next section, we present a literature overview about smartphone user behavior and energy consumption of smartphones. Section 3 introduces our utility-based energy consumption optimization model.

Section 4 presents the scenario and the workings of our model. Section 5 concludes the paper with a brief overview, the research limitations, and our future work.

2 Background

2.1 Smartphone Usage

Smartphones are used to perform many jobs such as phone calling, Internet browsing, watching videos, downloading files, and sending emails. User behavior has a significant effect on the energy consumption. Many studies on smartphone usage have been conducted to understand how users interact with their phones in the real world [5–12]. A typical methodology that has been used is to install a logger application on smartphone of the users and collect actual usage data. Their common findings are that all users have a unique device usage pattern. For example, Kang et al. [9], who analyze high-level smartphone usage patterns, developed a battery logger for the Android mobile platform and collected usage log data from 20 smartphone users over a two-months period. Their results showed that all 20 users have their own usage pattern. They also presented a case study, in order to show how to apply usage pattern information to smartphone power management. Another example is the work of Froehlich et al. [11], who developed MyExperience for gathering traces from user's smartphones and for analyzing the smartphone usage differences in user activities.

Many user studies have also focused on the relationship between the user behavior and the energy consumption of devices [5, 7–9, 12, 14, 20, 21, 31–39]. For example, Kang et al. [8] proposed a method of predicting the battery lifetime of mobile devices based on usage patterns. Using detailed traces from 255 users, Falaki et al. [5] have conducted a comprehensive study of smartphone use. They measured the energy consumption and application usage behavior of 33 Android and 222 Windows Mobile devices. They also found immense diversity among users' behaviors. They make important observations that are relevant to our work. That is, they found that users do not use a large number of different applications (much less than the number of installed applications) but give a large portion of their attention to a small subset of the applications installed. With a large-scale smartphone user study, Oliver [12] examines how users interact and how users consume energy on their personal mobile devices. Shye et al. [7] presented a comprehensive analysis of high-level characteristics of smartphone power consumption. They developed a logger application for Android G1 mobile phones and used it to collect smartphone usage data over a 6-months period from 20 users. Using this data, they applied a linear regression method to build a power model describing the relationship between the power consumption and the user activities. With this model, they also explored optimization potentials.

2.2 Human-Battery Interactions

Many studies have been devoted to the human-battery interaction [13–20]. The term human-battery interaction (HBI) was first coined by Banerjee et al. [13], to describe mobile phone users' interactions with their cell phones and to manage the battery energy available. In their user studies on HBI [14, 15], Rahmati et al. investigated users' attitudes and perceptions of mobile battery life. In particular, they evaluated various aspects of human battery interactions, including charging behavior, battery indicators, user interfaces for power saving settings, user knowledge, and user reaction. In their experiments, users had to use unfamiliar devices for a period of a month. According to their results, most mobile users had no knowledge of the power characteristics of their devices and applications. Moreover, most mobile users underused the power saving settings of their devices. Although the studies of Rahmati et al. were the first to qualitatively and quantitatively assess how users consumed energy [14, 15], their studies were conducted in 2006–2007, still before the market launch of the iPhone. Due to the rapid growth of smartphones and their applications, the user behavior (e.g., multimedia playing, gaming) has significantly changed.

In addition to enhancing the energy efficiency by taking into account the user behavior, is also believed that tools for predicting battery life by considering the relationship between power consumption and user activities can help users to extend their mobile battery life [4]. Athukorala et al. [22] conducted a study with 1140 users on how the mobile battery-awareness application changes user behavior. The Carat application provides a user with information on the energy consumption of applications. In their study, they classified users into two groups. Users, who had used Carat for more than three months, were considered Advanced Users. Users, who had used it for a shorter time period, were classified as Beginners. Their result showed that advanced users stop using applications that were identified by Carat as highly energy-consuming applications more often than beginners. All users learned to better manage their battery over time.

3 Utility-Based Energy Consumption Optimization Model

3.1 Classification of Application Uses on Smartphones

Given that smartphones are rich in the number of applications installed, some applications (e.g., video streaming and gaming [24]) are very much resource intensive in terms of processing power and data transfer [23]. They are highly energy-consuming applications and, consequently, drain smartphone batteries very quickly.

Many of the popular activities (e.g., messaging, multimedia streaming, gaming, and e-mailing) on smartphones can be performed either local or through cloud-based services. For example, if a smartphone user wants to answer an email, the user can perform the activity online or the user can perform it off-line and send the email later. Another example is that a user wants to modify her time scheduler, where the user has the choice of synchronizing the scheduler with the cloud-based scheduler immediately or later. Therefore, we classify these smartphone application uses into two categories: on-device application uses, referring to applications that can be executed on the smartphone locally; and cloud-based application uses, referring to applications, which require data transfer and processing power on the cloud. We consider these two application use categories to differ in their utility to the user, depending on the energy stored in the battery.

3.2   Utility Function

In spite of the large number of applications installed on smartphones, users do not use them equally. In fact, as users have different preferences for their application uses, their valuation of the amount of energy consumed per type of application use is different. Some users may value playing online games very highly, while others are content playing local games. Within this paper, we consider the preferences for two types of application uses (Sect. 3.1), namely on-device application use and cloud-based application use.

For smartphone users, the trade-off between using an application on-device or cloud-based is significant. That is, both alternatives can be thought of as representing a bundle of different characteristics: execution time, energy consumption, and monetary cost. For example, considering the battery constraint of the smartphone, the user might wish to maximize her utility from the amount of energy remaining on her smartphone, as an opportunity for charging the smartphone does not exist in the near future. To express the user preference for each type of application use, it is necessary to apply the theory of consumer behavior [29] and define the user's utility function.

With respect to the utility function, the Cobb-Douglas is useful, as it is well-behaved (i.e., more of a good is preferred to less of a good [29]). Furthermore, Cobb-Douglas functions are widely used in economics to represent the preferences between goods and the utility that can be obtained by those goods [25, 26]. Hasan et al. [27] used a Cobb-Douglas stochastic frontier model to measure the domestic bank efficiency in Malaysia. Hayes [28] applies the Cobb-Douglas model to the association of research libraries.

The Cobb-Douglas indifference curves show combinations of on-device application use and cloud-based application use, which result in the same utility for the user. Therefore, our user utility function is represented by the following Cobb-Douglas function:

$$U\left(E_{local}, E_{cloud}\right) = (E_{local})^{\alpha}(E_{cloud})^{\beta} \tag{1}$$

where E_{local} is the energy planned to be consumed through on-device application use, E_{cloud} is the energy planned to be consumed through cloud-based application use. The unit of E_{local} and E_{cloud} is [Wmin].

The exponents, α and β, of the Cobb-Douglas utility function should be defined, such that they express the long-term preferences of the user for the two types of energy use. For our model, we consider the past consumption of energy for on-device application use E_{local}^{H} and the past consumption of energy for cloud-based application use E_{cloud}^{H}. The past consumption of energy can be obtained through monitoring applications, running on the smartphone of the user. The relative ratio of E_{local}^{H} and E_{cloud}^{H} is used to set α and β as shown in the following two equations:

$$\alpha = \frac{E_{local}^{H}}{E_{local}^{H} + E_{cloud}^{H}} \tag{2}$$

$$\beta = \frac{E_{cloud}^H}{E_{local}^H + E_{cloud}^H} \tag{3}$$

According to the definition of Eqs. 2 and 3, the factors α and β are positive and fulfil $\alpha + \beta = 1$.

To calculate the optimal allocation of energy E_{local}^* and E_{cloud}^* to the two types of application use, we also need to consider the budget constraint, which is expressed with the following equation:

$$E_{local} * P_{local}^E + E_{cloud} * P_{cloud}^E = m \tag{4}$$

To be able to use Eq. 4, a user is asked to express her perception of the budget m (i.e., express her valuation of the amount of energy that is left in the battery) and her preferences for consuming energy for on-device application uses and for cloud-based application uses.

The user's preference for using an application type can be expressed by stating the perceived cost (P_{local}^E and P_{cloud}^E [\$/Wmin]) for the energy for both types of application uses. In this regard, we would like to note that user's perceived cost refers to the user's valuation for energy planned to be consumed by on-device applications or cloud-based applications but not to the real prices of energy. Different users may have different perceived costs.

With respect to the user's perception of the budget, the budget m can be interpreted as the user's monetary valuation of the available energy in the battery. This way, the budget can be used to capture the time before it is possible to recharge the battery again. As only the user knows how long it will take before the battery can be recharged, the user needs to express this information. For example, the longer it takes before the battery can be recharged, the lower the budget is. If the battery can be recharged immediately, the budget is 100 \$. For our model, we assume to have values of m between 0 \$ and 100 \$.

As the budget is an abstract construct, it is also sufficient to state the rate of substitution RS for the cost of the two types of application uses. Therefore, a user must only state how much of the energy for one type of application use she is willing to substitute for consuming one more unit [Wmin] for the other type of application use:

$$RS = \frac{P_{local}^E}{P_{cloud}^E} \tag{5}$$

For example, if the perceived cost of energy consumption by on-device application uses is 2\$/Wmin and the perceived cost of energy consumption by cloud-based application uses is 1\$/Wmin, then the rate of substitution for this user is 2. That means, the user is willing to give up 1 unit [Wmin] of energy for cloud-based application uses only if the user obtains 2 units [Wmin] of energy for on-device application use.

With input values for E_{local}^H, E_{cloud}^H, P_{local}^E, P_{cloud}^E, and m, the utility-maximizing allocation to on-device application uses E_{local}^* and cloud-based application uses E_{cloud}^* can be calculated by using the Lagrange multipliers theorem [30]. The results provide the optimal amounts of energy that should be consumed through on-device application uses and through cloud-based application uses. They also provide the level at which the energy should be consumed at most (i.e., the amount of units [Wmin]). In detail, the results are as follows:

$$E^*_{local} = \frac{\alpha}{\alpha + \beta} \frac{m}{P^E_{local}} \tag{6}$$

$$E^*_{cloud} = \frac{\beta}{\alpha + \beta} \frac{m}{P^E_{cloud}} \tag{7}$$

4   Application Example of the Optimization Model

4.1   Parameter Settings

To demonstrate the workings of our utility-based energy consumption optimization model, we assume a simple scenario with 5 users:

Each user is assumed to have an average amount of battery energy consumed through on-device application uses E^H_{local} and cloud-based application uses E^H_{cloud} during the past month. The values have been obtained by monitoring the users' application uses.

Based on these data of past behaviors, we can model the long-term preferences for each user using the utility function (Eq. 1) with α (Eq. 2) and β (Eq. 3) based on the two types of application uses for each user. Columns 2 and 3 of Table 1 show the preferences for the on-device application uses and cloud-based application uses for the five users according to their average energy consumption through the two types of applications uses during the past month.

Table 1. The long-term preferences based on the past energy consumption through on-device application uses and cloud-based application uses for five users are shown.

User	E^H_{local} [Wmin]	E^H_{cloud} [Wmin]	α	β
1	40	60	0.40	0.60
2	66.7	33.3	0.67	0.33
3	50	50	0.50	0.50
4	33.3	66.7	0.33	0.67
5	70	30	0.70	0.30

Table 1 shows that users' past consumptions for the two types of applications uses set the two exponents of the utility function, α and β, in the same ratio. For example, for User 2, the ratio of the past energy consumption for on-device application uses and cloud-based application uses has been 2:1. In the same ratio, the exponents α and β are set. That means that User 2's preference for on-device application uses is twice as high as User 2's preference for cloud-based application uses. In case of User 3, the ratio of the past energy consumption through the two types of application uses is 1:1. As the ratio of the exponents α and β is also 1:1, User 3 is modeled to be indifferent to the two types of application uses.

4.2 Modeling Results

Assuming that User 4 wants to maximize the utility from the energy remaining in the smartphone battery, the smartphone user needs to express the perceived energy budget m in [$]. In our scenario, User 4 states that the remaining energy in her smartphone is worth m = 60 $.

The perceived costs for allocating energy to on-device application uses and to cloud-based application uses (P_{local}^E and P_{cloud}^E [$/Wmin]) also needs to be set by User 4. To see the effect of setting those two values, six different pairs of values are analyzed in Table 2. All of these pairs of values have the same rate of substitution (Eq. 5), namely RS = 1/2. That means that User 4 would be willing to sacrifice two units of energy of on-device application uses to consume one more unit of energy for cloud-based application uses.

Based on these values, the utility-maximizing combination of on-device application uses E_{local}^* and cloud-based application uses E_{cloud}^* can be calculated using Eqs. 6 and 7. The results are also shown in Table 2.

Table 2. Utility-maximizing combination of energy allocation to on-device application uses E_{local}^* and to cloud-based application uses E_{cloud}^* for User 4 ($\alpha = 0.33$ and $\beta = 0.67$). While the budget has been fixed (m = 60 $), different values for P_{local}^E and P_{cloud}^E have been used.

m[$]	P_{local}^E [$/Wmin]	P_{cloud}^E [$/Wmin]	RS	E_{local}^* [Wmin]	E_{cloud}^* [Wmin]
60	0.5	1	0.5	39.60	40.20
60	1	2	0.5	19.80	20.10
60	2	4	0.5	9.90	10.05
60	3	6	0.5	6.60	6.70
60	4	8	0.5	4.95	5.03
60	5	10	0.5	3.96	4.02

The results of Table 2 show that, if User 4's perceived value for the energy allocation to on-device application uses is 0.5 $/Wmin and for the energy allocation to cloud-based application uses is 1 $/Wmin, then the energy allocation ratio for cloud-based application uses is 1.015 of the on-device application uses. This combination of the energy allocation to the two types of application uses maximizes the utility of User 4. Table 2 also shows that the energy allocation ratio for the other pairs of values of P_{local}^E and P_{cloud}^E is also 1.015. The knowledge, which can be gained about User 4 preferences, is that the battery energy can be consumed much faster for the values 0.5 $/Wmin and 1 $/Wmin than for the other pairs of values. If the pair of values is 5 $/Wmin and 10 $/Wmin, then the battery energy should be consumed very slowly.

Table 3 shows that, if the perceived budget of the remaining energy in the battery is high, the utility-maximizing energy allocations to on-device application uses E_{local}^* and cloud-based application uses E_{cloud}^* are high. For instance, for the battery energy budget m = 90 $, the energy allocation to on-device application uses is 33 Wmin. The values of the energy allocation decrease, as the perceived budget of the remaining energy in the battery gets low. For instance, if m = 10 $, the energy allocation to on-device application uses is 3.3 Wmin only. This difference of the energy allocation shows the User 4 preferences for the battery energy consumption. User 4 states with a perceived low energy budget that the energy consumption should be much slower than for a perceived high energy budget. The energy of the battery should last for very long.

Table 3. Utility-maximizing combination of energy allocation to on-device application uses and cloud-based application uses for User 4 (with $\alpha = 0.33$ and $\beta = 0.67$). While the energy budget m is varied, the values of P^E_{local} and P^E_{cloud} are set to 1 $/Wmin and 2 $/Wmin, respectively.

m [$]	P^E_{local} [$/Wmin]	P^E_{cloud} [$/Wmin]	E^*_{local} [Wmin]	E^*_{cloud} [Wmin]
100	1	2	33	33.5
90	1	2	29.7	30.15
80	1	2	26.4	26.8
70	1	2	23.1	23.45
60	1	2	19.8	20.1
50	1	2	16.5	16.75
40	1	2	13.2	13.4
30	1	2	9.9	10.05
20	1	2	6.6	6.7
10	1	2	3.3	3.35

Since our study focuses on applying the consumer behavior theory in studying the energy consumption, all results presented in Tables 1, 2, and 3 show the workings of our proposed model. That is, a smartphone user with a Cobb-Douglas utility function can maximize her utility by allocating a fraction of her remaining energy to each type of application uses. The size of the fraction is determined by the user's preference for both types of application uses, the perceived cost of energy for both types, and the perceived value of the energy remaining in the smartphone battery.

5 Conclusion

In this paper, we propose a utility-based energy consumption optimization model, which considers the user's preferences with respect to energy consumption aspects when using smartphone applications. Compared to other studies about smartphone usage and energy consumption, our study represents a novel approach to allocate energy to applications. It considers two types of application uses: on-device application uses and cloud-based application uses. These two types of application uses are the goods considered in the user's utility function, which is based on a Cobb-Douglas function. The users' preferences are described through past patterns of energy consumption, the perceived value of energy remaining in the smartphone battery, and the perceived costs for allocating energy to each type of application uses.

To demonstrate the working of our approach, we apply our approach to a simple scenario. The results based on the scenario show that an optimal (i.e., utility maximizing) allocation of energy to different types of application uses is possible for a user. The allocation by the user determines not only the ratio between the two types of application uses but also the quantity with which the energy in the battery should be consumed. The user only needs to specify the perceived cost of energy for each type of application and the perceived value of energy remaining in the smartphone battery.

We argue that this work will contribute to the line of studies assessing the effect of usage behavior on energy consumption optimization of smartphones. It can be used by smartphone users to obtain the maximum utility from the remaining energy in their smartphones battery.

In the future, we plan to conduct studies with real smartphone users and to analyze their value setting for perceived costs and perceived energy budget.

References

1. Dinh, H.T., Lee, C., Niyato, D., Wang, P.: A survey of mobile cloud computing: architecture, applications, and approaches. Wireless Commun. Mobile Comput. **13**(18), 1587–1611 (2013)
2. Mobiforge: Global mobile statistics 2014 part A: mobile subscribers; handset market share; mobile operators (2015). http://mobiforge.com/research-analysis/global-mobile-statistics-2014-part-a-mobile-subscribers-handset-market-share-mobile-operators
3. Robinson, S.: Cellphone energy gap: desperately seeking solutions. Strategy analytics. Technology report, Chicago, IL, USA (2009)
4. Tarkoma, S., Siekkinen, M., Lagerspetz, E., Xiao, Y.: Smartphone Energy Consumption: Modeling and Optimization. Cambridge University Press, Cambridge (2014)
5. Falaki, H., Mahajan, R., Kandula, S., Lymberopoulos, D., Govindan, R., Estrin, D.: Diversity in smartphone usage. In: 8th International Conference on Mobile Systems, Applications, and Services, pp. 179–194. ACM (2010)
6. Pasricha, S., Donohoo, B.K., Ohlsen, C.: A middleware framework for application-aware and user-specific energy optimization in smart mobile devices. Pervasive Mobile Comput. **20**, 47–63 (2015)
7. Shye, A., Scholbrock, B., Memik, G.: Into the wild: studying real user activity patterns to guide power optimizations for mobile architectures. In: 42nd Annual IEEE/ACM International Symposium on Microarchitecture, pp. 168–178 (2009)
8. Kang, J.-M., Park, C.-K., Seo, S.-S., Choi, M.-J., Hong, J.W.-K.: User-centric prediction for battery lifetime of mobile devices. In: Ma, Y., Choi, D., Ata, S. (eds.) APNOMS 2008. LNCS, vol. 5297, pp. 531–534. Springer, Heidelberg (2008)
9. Kang, J.-M., Seo, S.-S., Hong, J.W.K.: Usage pattern analysis of smartphones. In: 13th Asia-Pacific Network Operations and Management Symposium (APNOMS), pp. 1–8. IEEE (2011)
10. Demumieux, R., Losquin, P.: Gather customer's real usage on mobile phones. In: 7th International Conference on Human Computer Interaction with Mobile Devices and Services, pp. 267–270. ACM (2005)
11. Froehlich, J., Chen, M.Y., Consolvo, S., Harrison, B., Landay, J.A.: MyExperience: a system for in situ tracing and capturing of user feedback on mobile phones. In: 5th International Conference on Mobile Systems, Applications and Services, pp. 57–70. ACM (2007)
12. Oliver, E.: The challenges in large-scale smartphone user studies. In: 2nd ACM International Workshop on Hot Topics in Planet-Scale Measurement, p. 5. ACM (2010)

13. Banerjee, N., Rahmati, A., Corner, M.D., Rollins, S., Zhong, L.: Users and batteries: interactions and adaptive energy management in mobile systems. In: Krumm, J., Abowd, G.D., Seneviratne, A., Strang, T. (eds.) UbiComp 2007. LNCS, vol. 4717, pp. 217–234. Springer, Heidelberg (2007)

14. Rahmati, A., Qian, A., Zhong, L.: Understanding human-battery interaction on mobile phones. In: 9th International Conference on Human Computer Interaction with Mobile Devices and Services, pp. 265–272. ACM (2007)

15. Rahmati, A., Zhong, L.: Human–battery interaction on mobile phones. Pervasive Mobile Comput. **5**(5), 465–477 (2009)

16. Ferreira, D., Dey, A.K., Kostakos, V.: Understanding human-smartphone concerns: a study of battery life. In: Lyons, K., Hightower, J., Huang, E.M. (eds.) Pervasive 2011. LNCS, vol. 6696, pp. 19–33. Springer, Heidelberg (2011)

17. Oliver, E.A., Keshav, S.: An empirical approach to smartphone energy level prediction. In: 13th International Conference on Ubiquitous Computing, pp. 345–354. ACM (2011)

18. Heikkinen, M.V., Nurminen, J.K., Smura, T., Hämmäinen, H.: Energy efficiency of mobile handsets: measuring user attitudes and behavior. Telematics Inf. **29**(4), 387–399 (2012)

19. Ferreira, D., Ferreira, E., Goncalves, J., Kostakos, V., Dey, A.K.: Revisiting human-battery interaction with an interactive battery interface. In: ACM International Joint Conference on Pervasive and Ubiquitous Computing, pp. 563–572. ACM (2013)

20. Vallina-Rodriguez, N., Hui, P., Crowcroft, J., Rice, A.: Exhausting battery statistics: understanding the energy demands on mobile handsets. In: 2nd ACM SIGCOMM Workshop on Networking, Systems, and Applications on Mobile Handhelds, pp. 9–14. ACM (2010)

21. Ravi, N., Scott, J., Han, L., Iftode, L.: Context-aware battery management for mobile phones. In: 6th International Conference on Pervasive Computing and Communications (PerCom 2008), pp. 224–233. IEEE (2008)

22. Athukorala, K., Lagerspetz, E., von Kügelgen, M., Jylhä, A., Oliner, A.J., Tarkoma, S., Jacucci, G.: How carat affects user behavior: implications for mobile battery awareness applications. In: 32nd Conference on Human Factors in Computing Systems, pp. 1029–1038. ACM (2014)

23. Carroll, A., Heiser, G.: An analysis of power consumption in a smartphone. In: USENIX Annual Technical Conference, p. 14 (2010)

24. Falaki, H., Lymberopoulos, D., Mahajan, R., Kandula, S., Estrin, D.: A first look at traffic on smartphones. In: 10th SIGCOMM Conference on Internet Measurement, pp. 281–287. ACM (2010)

25. Brenes, A.: Cobb-Douglas Utility Function (2011)

26. Yan, B., Shi, F., Yu, R.-Q.: Exploring utility function in utility management: an evaluating method of library preservation. SpringerPlus **2**(1), 1–11 (2013)

27. Hasan, M.Z., Kamil, A.A., Mustafa, A., Baten, M.A.: A Cobb Douglas stochastic frontier model on measuring domestic bank efficiency in Malaysia. PLoS ONE **7**(8), 1–5 (2012)

28. Hayes, R.M.: An application of the Cobb-Douglas model to the association of research libraries. Library Inf. Sci. Res. **5**(3), 291–325 (1983)

29. Allen, W.B., Doherty, N., Mansfield, K.W.E.: Managerial Economics: Theory, Applications, and Cases. Norton, New York (2005)

30. Varian, H.R.: Intermediate Microeconomics, 9th edn. Norton, New York (2014)

31. Altmann, J., Varaiya, P.: INDEX project: user support for buying QoS with regard to user's preferences. In: 6th IEEE/IFIP International Workshop on Quality of Service (IWQOS), pp. 101–104 (1998)

32. Altmann, J., Rupp, B., Varaiya, P.: Internet demand under different pricing schemes. In: ACM Conference on Electronic Commerce (EC) (1999)

33. Altmann, J., Chu, K.: A proposal for a flexible service plan that is attractive to users and internet service providers. In: IEEE Conference on Computer Communications (InfoCom) (2001)

34. Altmann, J., Rohitratana, J.: Software resource management considering the interrelations between explicit cost, energy consumption, and implicit cost: a decision support model for IT managers. In: Multikonferenz Wirtschaftsinformatik (MKWI) (2010)

35. Altmann, J., Rupp, B., Varaiya, P.: Effects of pricing on internet user behavior. NetNomics **3**(1), 67–84 (2000)

36. Kim, J., Ilon, L., Altmann, J.: Adapting smartphones as learning technology in a Korean university. J. Integr. Des. Process Sci. **17**(1), 5–16 (2013)

37. Haile, N., Altmann, J.: Estimating the value obtained from using a software service platform. In: Altmann, J., Vanmechelen, K., Rana, O.F. (eds.) GECON 2013. LNCS, vol. 8193, pp. 244–255. Springer, Heidelberg (2013)

38. Haile, N., Altmann, J.: Value creation in software service platforms. In: Future Generation Computer Systems. Elsevier (2015). doi:10.1016/j.future.2015.09.029

39. Haile, N., Altmann, J.: Structural analysis of value creation in software service platforms. Electron. Markets (2015). doi:10.1007/s12525-015-0208-8

Optimizing the Data Center Energy Consumption Using a Particle Swarm Optimization-Based Approach

Cristina Bianca Pop[(✉)], Viorica Rozina Chifu,
Ioan Salomie Adrian Cozac, Marcel Antal, and Claudia Pop

Computer Science Department, Technical University of Cluj-Napoca,
Cluj-Napoca, Romania
{Cristina.Pop, Viorica.Chifu, Ioan.Salomie,
Marcel.Antal, Claudia.Pop}@cs.utcluj.ro

Abstract. This paper presents a Particle Swarm Optimization-based method for optimizing the energy consumption in data centers. A particle position is mapped on a data center configuration (i.e. allocation of virtual machines on the data center's servers) which is evaluated using a fitness function that considers the energy consumed by the servers' hardware resources and by the data center's cooling system as evaluation criteria. The Particle Swarm Optimization-based method is triggered each time a workload arrives to be accommodated on the data center's servers. The proposed method has been integrated in the CloudSim framework and has been evaluated on randomly generated logs.

Keywords: Data center · Energy consumption optimization · Particle Swarm Optimization

1 Introduction

The extreme increase in CO_2 emissions of the currently existing data centers worldwide has determined authorities to declare the efficient management of IT systems and data centers as one of the most critical environmental challenge we have to deal with. Additionally, it has been registered an increase of the costs for producing and delivering the electrical energy for IT systems as well as for their cooling. In this context, the statistics are worrying. For example, in the United States, the data centers and their cooling systems consume around 1.2 % of the national energy and this percent is likely to double each five years [2, 8]. Also, starting with 2002, the costs for electrical energy have increased with approximately 5.5 %/year and there are organizations in which up to 50 % of the expenses on hardware systems are on the electrical energy required by the systems to function and for cooling [1]. As a result, the optimization of energy consumption of IT systems and data centers has become a high priority for both the authorities and the industry.

Through this paper we aim to address the problem of optimizing the energy consumption of data centers by proposing a Particle Swarm Optimization-based method which accommodates the incoming workload in a data center in such a way that the

© Springer International Publishing Switzerland 2016
J. Altmann et al. (Eds.): GECON 2015, LNCS 9512, pp. 176–189, 2016.
DOI: 10.1007/978-3-319-43177-2_12

energy consumption is reduced. We consider that a solution of the optimization problem is represented as a data center configuration which implies re-allocating the set of virtual machines already running on the data center's servers as well as accommodating the virtual machines part of the incoming workload. Such a data center configuration is evaluated using a fitness function that takes into account both the energy consumed by each server's hardware resources as well as by the data center's cooling system. To evaluate the Particle Swarm Optimization-based method we have developed an experimental prototype which integrates the method in the CloudSim infrastructure [10]. As test scenarios we have used randomly generated workloads.

The paper is structured as follows. Section 2 presents related work. Section 3 defines the problem of optimizing the energy consumption in data centers as an optimization problem. Section 4 presents the proposed Particle Swarm Optimization-based model for optimizing the data center's energy consumption, while Sect. 5 presents the associated Particle Swarm Optimization-based algorithm. Section 6 discusses experimental results. The paper ends with conclusions.

2 Related Work

The research literature reports several heuristic-based approaches for accommodating the incoming workload and re-organizing the current running workload in data centers such that several criteria ranging from computation time, cost and energy consumption are optimized. For example, in [3] authors propose a method for workload distribution in a cloud infrastructure that is based on a heuristic approach. The main contribution of this approach consists of: (1) modeling the workloads distribution problem as an optimization problem and (2) solving the considered optimization problem by using a heuristic approach. The proposed heuristic approach consists of two main steps. In the first step a packing list consisting of a set of jobs that have not been assigned yet is created for each virtual machine type, while in the second step the most efficient virtual machine type is determined based on the packing lists created in the previous step. In this approach, the quality of a solution is evaluated by taking into consideration the computation time and the total leasing cost.

In [9], authors propose an Ant Colony System-based method for dynamically consolidating virtual machines such that the energy consumption of the available physical machines is reduced. The method relies on a structure of triples which is processed by a set of ants in search of a migration plan, where each triple is composed of a virtual machine and its possible source and destination physical machines. A physical machine can be set as a source only if it is under loaded or if it is/might be overloaded. Each triple has a pheromone value which influences the ants' decisions of selecting the triple. The choice of a new triple is done probabilistically by considering the CPU and memory utilization levels of the source and destination physical machines.

In [4], authors propose a Particle Swarm Optimization-based method to optimize the energy consumption in heterogeneous virtualized data centers while ensuring the CPU and memory requested levels. The particle position is defined using a two-dimension encoding scheme indicating a valid allocation of virtual machines on the data center's servers. The particle velocity is defined as a vector of 0s and 1s used to adjust the particle position by indicating the servers whose virtual machines need to be reorganized or not. Authors redefine the subtraction, addition and multiplication operators to fit the proposed representation of a particle. Additionally, authors introduce an energy-aware local fitness first strategy to improve a particle position. A first fit strategy is used to generate the initial population of particles.

In [5], authors dynamically migrate virtual machines in an energy efficient manner using a modified Particle Swarm Optimization method such that the Quality of Service is ensured. The proposed method is triggered when an overloaded or under loaded physical node is detected. In this approach, the particle position represents an allocation of virtual machines on the existing physical nodes and is evaluated based on CPU and disk utilization. To generate the initial population of particles the First Fit algorithm is used for determining the first physical node that can accommodate a virtual machine. During an algorithm iteration, the position of each particle is updated and validated; if invalid allocations are found the original allocation is kept.

3   Problem Definition

The problem of optimizing the energy consumption in data centers can be formally defined as:

Given the incoming workload (composed of a set of virtual machines) and the current data center configuration, find a new configuration of the data center, which accommodates the incoming workload, such that a fitness function evaluating the energy consumed by the servers and cooling system of the data center is minimized.

Given the above formal definition, we model the concepts of virtual machine, workload, server, data center, and fitness function as follows.

Virtual Machine. A virtual machine, *VM*, is modeled as the set of server hardware requirements needed by the virtual machine to properly execute the associated task:

$$VM = \{HDD_{req}, MIPS_{req}, CPU_{req}, RAM_{req}\} \tag{1}$$

where HDD_{req} represents the virtual machine's hard-disk requirements, $MIPS_{req}$ represents the number of instructions that will be occupied by the virtual machine, CPU_{req} represents the virtual machine's required number of CPU cores, and RAM_{req} represents the virtual machine's required RAM memory.

Incoming Workload. The incoming workload, *WKLD*, is modeled as a set of virtual machines that need to be deployed on the servers of the data center:

$$WKLD = \{VM_1, \ldots, VM_p\} \tag{2}$$

where VM_i is a virtual machine defined using Formula 1, and p is the number of virtual machines part of the workload *WKLD*.

Server. A server, S, part of the data center is modeled using the degrees of utilization/energy consumption of its hardware components and the server's state as follows:

$$S = \{(CPU_S, RAM_S, HDD_S), OTHERS_S, CoolSys_S, state_S\} \tag{3}$$

where CPU_S represents the server's CPU degree of utilization, RAM_S represents the server's RAM degree of utilization, HDD_S represents the server's HDD degree of utilization, $OTHERS_S$ represents the energy consumed by other hardware components part of the server (e.g. UPS, video and network boards, etc.), $CoolSys_S$ represents the energy consumed by the server's cooling system, and $state_S$ represents the server's state (i.e. running, stopped).

Data Center. A data center, DC, is modeled as a matrix, in which each column is associated to a server part of the data center, and each row is associated to a virtual machine that must be/is deployed in the data center:

$$DC = [dc_{ij}]_{i=1,n;j=1,m} \tag{4}$$

where n is the number of virtual machines, m is the number of servers part of the data center, and dc_{ij} represents the energy consumed by the virtual machine VM_i if it is deployed on the server j, otherwise the value of dc_{ij} is set to 0.

Fitness Function. A data center configuration, DC, (i.e. deployment of virtual machines on the data center's servers) is evaluated using the following fitness function which needs to be minimized:

$$E(DC) = (\Lambda_0 |E_S(DC) - X|^2 + \Lambda_1 |E_{CS}(DC) - Y|^2)^{\frac{1}{2}} \tag{5}$$

where (i) E_S evaluates the total energy consumed by the servers of the data center, (ii) E_{CS} evaluates the energy consumed by the data center's cooling system, (iii) Λ_0 and Λ_1 are weights with values in the interval $[0, 1]$, $\Lambda_0 + \Lambda_1 = 1$, which are assigned to each fitness component to indicate their importance in evaluating the overall fitness, and (iv) X and Y are the targeted values for the energy consumed by the servers of the data center and by the data center's cooling system respectively.

4 Particle Swarm Optimization-Based Model for Optimizing the Data Center Energy Consumption

In this paper we aim to solve the problem of optimizing the energy consumption at the data center level using the Particle Swarm Optimization meta-heuristic [6]. This section describes how the concepts defined in Sect. 3 have been mapped to the concepts from Particle Swarm Optimization.

4.1 Overview of the Particle Swarm Optimization Meta-Heuristic

The Particle Swarm Optimization [6], inspired by the behavior of birds during their search for food, relies on a number of particles with positions and velocities associated to search for the optimal or near-optimal solution of an optimization problem. This search is an iterative process in which each particle adjusts its position and velocity according to its best position encountered so far and the global best position encountered at the swarm level. The position update is performed as follows [6]:

$$x_i^{t+1} = x_i^t + v_i^{t+1} \tag{6}$$

where x_i^{t+1} is the new position, x_i^t is the current position and v_i^{t+1} is the new velocity obtained using the formula below [6]:

$$v_i^{t+1} = c_x * v_i^t + c_p * \left(x_i^{pb} - x_i^t\right) + c_q * \left(x_i^{gb} - x_i^t\right) \tag{7}$$

where c_x, c_p, and c_q are weights associated to each component of the velocity update formula, x_i^{pb} is the particle's personal best, and x_i^{gb} is the swarm's global best.

4.2 Particle Swarm Optimization-Based Model

Following the Particle Swarm Optimization concepts, a particle is mapped on a software agent whose position represents a data center configuration defined using Formula 4. The velocity of a particle is defined similar to a position (i.e. data center configuration) except that the containing values can be either 0 or 1. The velocity will be used to update a data center configuration. We have adapted the formulas for updating the position and velocity of a particle by considering the following interpretations (adapted from [7]) of the mathematical operators (for simplicity we consider the case of two data center configurations DC_p and DC_q with three servers each):

Subtraction of Two Positions. We define the subtraction of two positions x_p and x_q as:

$$x_p - x_q = DC_p - DC_q = \begin{pmatrix} d?_{p_1}^1 & \cdots & dc_{p_m}^1 \\ \vdots & \ddots & \vdots \\ dc_{p_1}^n & \cdots & dc_{p_m}^n \end{pmatrix} - \begin{pmatrix} dc_{q_1}^1 & \cdots & dc_{q_m}^1 \\ \vdots & \ddots & \vdots \\ dc_{q_1}^n & \cdots & dc_{q_m}^n \end{pmatrix} =$$
$$\begin{pmatrix} \left|dc_{p_1}^1 - dc_{q_1}^1\right| & \cdots & \left|dc_{p_m}^1 - dc_{q_m}^1\right| \\ \vdots & \ddots & \vdots \\ \left|dc_{p_1}^n - dc_{q_1}^n\right| & \cdots & \left|dc_{p_m}^n - dc_{q_m}^n\right| \end{pmatrix} \tag{8}$$

where:

$$\left| dc_{p_i}^{\ j} - dc_{q_i}^{\ j} \right| = \begin{cases} 0, if\, dc_{p_i}^{\ j} = dc_{q_i}^{\ j}, i \le m, j \le n \\ 1, otherwise \end{cases} \tag{9}$$

Weighted addition of Two Velocities. We define the weighted addition between two velocities v_p and v_q as follows:

$$c_p * v_p + c_q * v_q = \begin{cases} v_p,\ if\ v_p = v_q \\ ApplyMutation(c_p * v_p) + c_q * v_q, otherwise \end{cases} \tag{10}$$

where c_p and c_q are numerical weights associated to the velocities, and *Apply_Mutation* is a method by which two elements of the matrix resulted by multiplying c_p with v_p are randomly chosen and swapped. In the matrix resulted after adding two velocities the elements with values higher than 1 will be normalized to 1. In addition the elements that have been involved in the mutation process will be marked.

Addition of a Position and a Velocity. We define the addition between a position x_p and a velocity v_p as follows:

$$x_p + v_p = DC_p + v_p = \begin{pmatrix} dc_{p_1}^{\ 1} & \cdots & dc_{p_m}^{\ 1} \\ \vdots & \ddots & \vdots \\ dc_{p_1}^{\ n} & \cdots & dc_{p_m}^{\ n} \end{pmatrix} \oplus \begin{pmatrix} v_{p_1}^{\ 1} & \cdots & v_{p_m}^{\ 1} \\ \vdots & \ddots & \vdots \\ v_{p_1}^{\ n} & \cdots & v_{p_m}^{\ n} \end{pmatrix} =$$

$$\begin{pmatrix} dc_{p_1}^{\ 1} * v_{p_1}^{\ 1} & \cdots & dc_{p_m}^{\ 1} * v_{p_m}^{\ 1} \\ \vdots & \ddots & \vdots \\ dc_{p_1}^{\ n} * v_{p_1}^{\ n} & \cdots & dc_{p_m}^{\ n} * v_{p_m}^{\ n} \end{pmatrix} = \begin{pmatrix} dc_{p_{1,1}}^{add} & \cdots & dc_{p_{1,m}}^{add} \\ \vdots & \ddots & \vdots \\ dc_{p_{n,1}}^{add} & \cdots & dc_{p_{n,m}}^{add} \end{pmatrix} \tag{11}$$

where:

$$dc_{p_{i,j}}^{add} = \begin{cases} dc_{p_i}^{\ j},\ if\ v_{p_i}^{\ j} == 1 \\ Random\_Replace(dc_{p_i}^{\ j}),\ if\ v_{p_i}^{\ j} == 0 \\ Rotate(DC_p, 1), if\left(v_{p_i}^{\ j}\, has\, been\, mutated \right) \wedge \left(c_p > c_q \right) \wedge r[0, c_p] \\ Rotate(DC_p, 2), if\left(v_{p_i}^{\ j}\, has\, been\, mutated \right) \wedge \left(c_p < c_q \right) \wedge r[c_p, 1] \\ Rotate(DC_p, 3), if\left(v_{p_i}^{\ j}\, has\, been\, mutated \right) \wedge \left(c_p > c_q \right) \wedge r[0, c_q] \\ Rotate(DC_p, 4), if\left(v_{p_i}^{\ j}\, has\, been\, mutated \right) \wedge \left(c_p < c_q \right) \wedge r[c_q, 1] \end{cases} \tag{12}$$

where (*i*) *Random_Replace* is a function that randomly selects a virtual machine from a server part of DC_p and migrates it on another server, (*ii*) r is a randomly generated number, (*iii*) c_p and c_q are the constants that appear in the position update formula (see Formula 7), and (*iv*) *Rotate* is a function that rotates the matrix elements with 1, 2, 3, or

4 positions, i.e. each column i < number of columns becomes column $i + 1$ and the last column becomes the first column.

5 Particle Swarm Optimization-Based Algorithm for Optimizing the Data Center Energy Consumption

The Particle Swarm Optimization-based algorithm (see Algorithm 1) proposed in this paper adapts the Particle Swarm Optimization meta-heuristic [6] to the problem of optimizing the data center energy consumption by using the model defined in Sect. 4. The proposed algorithm takes as input the parameters: (*i*) $DC_{current}$ – the current data center configuration, (*ii*) WKLD – the incoming workload, (*iii*) X – the targeted energy consumption of the servers from the data center, (*iv*) Y – the targeted energy consumption of the data center's cooling system, (*v*) noParticles – the number of particles, (*vi*) noIt – the number of algorithm iterations, (*vii*) c_x, c_p and c_q – the weights used in the formulas for updating the velocity and the position. The algorithm returns the optimal or near-optimal data center configuration that accommodates the incoming workload. The algorithm consists of an initialization and an iterative stage. In the initialization stage, the set of particles is initialized by assigning to each particle position a data center configuration randomly generated based on the current data center configuration $DC_{current}$ and incoming workload WKLD. Also, the global best data center configuration, DC_{opt}, is identified from the particles' configurations.

Algorithm 1. Particle Swarm Optimization-based Algorithm

---

1 **Inputs:** $DC_{current}$, WKLD, X, Y, noParticles, noIt, c_x, c_p, c_q
2 **Output :** DC_{opt}
3 **Begin**
4   *Particles* = **Initialize_Particles**(*noParticles, $DC_{current}$, WKLD*)
5   DC_{opt} = **Get_Global_Best**(*Particles*)
6   *iteration = 0*
7   **while** (*iteration < noIt*) **do**
8   **for** $i = 1$ **to** *noParticles* **do**
9   *Particles$_i$.velocity* = **Update_Velocity**(*Particles$_i$, X, Y, c_x, c_p, c_q*)
10   *Particles$_i$.position* = **Update_Position**(*Particles$_i$, X, Y, c_x, c_p, c_q*)
11   *Particles$_i$.localBest* = **Update_Local_Best**(*Particles$_i$*)
12   DC_{opt} = **Update_Global_Best**(*Particles*)
13   **end for**
14   *iteration++*
15   **end while**
16   **return** DC_{opt}
17 **End**

The iterative stage, which is run for a number of *noIt* iterations, aims to identify the optimal or near-optimal data center configurations by continuously modifying each particle as follows:

- The velocity and position of each particle are updated according to the Particle Swarm Optimization-based Model (see sub-Sect. 4.2).
- The local best position (i.e. data center configuration) of each particle is modified if it is the case.
- The global best data center configuration is updated if it is the case.

To determine the local best position (i.e. data center configuration) and the global best data center configuration the fitness function defined in Formula 5 is used.

6 Evaluation

This section presents how we have evaluated the Particle Swarm Optimization-based method for optimizing the energy consumption in data centers by describing the used experimental prototype and discussing experimental results.

6.1 Experimental Prototype

To evaluate the proposed Particle Swarm Optimization-based method we have developed an experimental prototype whose architecture is illustrated in Fig. 1. The architecture is divided in two logical parts: (1) one part composed of the *Particle Swarm Optimization-based Module* which generates the optimal or near optimal data center configuration by accommodating the current incoming workload in the current data center configuration, and (2) one part composed of the *CloudSim*a framework for modeling and simulation of cloud computing infrastructures and services [10]. *CloudSim* simulates the application of the optimal or near-optimal data center configuration (i.e. virtual machines migration on the data center's servers) provided by the *Particle Swarm Optimization-based Module* on the current data center.

6.2 Experimental Results

This section discusses the experimental results we obtained by running the Particle Swarm Optimization-based method on randomly generated workloads which have to be accommodated on randomly generated datacenter configurations (with maximum 50 hosts and 50 virtual machines in our case). The workloads and the initial data center configurations were generated using the CloudSim infrastructure. First, we have performed a set of experiments which focused on identifying the optimal values of the Particle Swarm Optimization-based method's adjustable parameters, namely the number of particles ($noParticles \in [10, 100]$), the maximum number of iterations ($noIt \in [10, 100]$), and the weights used in the velocity update formula ($c_x, c_p, c_q \in [0, 1]$). In these experiments we considered 10 simulations, each lasting 802500 ms, in which several randomly generated workloads had to be deployed on the servers' of the data

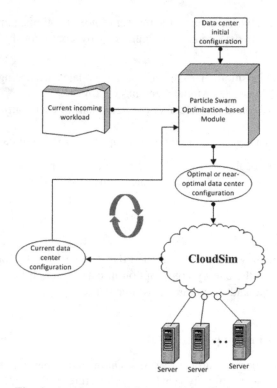

Fig. 1. Architecture of the experimental prototype.

center leading to several executions of the Particle Swarm Optimization-based algorithm. Experiments have demonstrated that the following values for the adjustable parameters provide the best results for all the considered simulations: *noParticles* = 30, *noIt* = 10, $c_x = 0.1$, $c_p = 1$, $c_q = 0.5$. Tables 1, 2, 3 and 4 present a fragment of the experimental results obtained for this configuration in one of the 10 simulations.

To better analyze the experimental results we have divided the simulation in 2675 intervals, each lasting 300 ms. Tables 1 and 2 present the experimental results obtained within the first two intervals, while Tables 3 and 4 present the experimental results obtained within the last two intervals, namely the virtual machines (*VM ID*) allocated on the first 10 hosts (*Host*) together with the following hardware features and consumption data: *pes* - the host's number of physical CPUs, *freq* - the CPU frequency, *alloc mips* - the number of instructions allocated to a virtual machine, *req mips* - the number of instructions required by a virtual machine, *total mips* - the total number of instructions per host, *usage* - the impact a virtual machine has from the host's usage degree perspective, *old usage* - the impact a virtual machine has from the host's usage degree perspective for a simulation in the last interval, and *energy* - the total energy consumed by the host.

By analyzing the experimental results we have noticed that for the interval [300, 600] the total consumed energy is equal to 660543.8 W*sec (i.e. 660.54 kW/sec), for the interval [801900, 802200] is equal to 242233 W*sec (i.e. 242.23 kW/sec), while for the

Table 1. Experimental results obtained for the interval [0, 300].

Host	VM ID	Pes	Freq	Alloc MIPS	Req MIPS	Total MIPS	Usage	Old Usage	Energy
0	26	2	1860	545.09	545.09	1000	54.51 %	0.00 %	0
	27			714.64	714.64	1000	71.46 %		
	39			87.30	87.30	500	17.46 %		
1	0	2	2660	601.34	601.34	2500	24.05 %	0.00 %	0
	1			1025.2	1025.20	2500	41.01 %		
2	28	2	1860	562.36	562.36	1000	56.24 %	0.00 %	0
	29			731.9	731.90	1000	73.19 %		
	40			11.16	11.16	500	2.23 %		
3	2	2	2660	2253.62	2253.62	2500	90.14 %	0.00 %	0
	3			177.48	177.48	2500	7.10 %		
4	30	2	1860	223.27	223.27	1000	22.33 %	0.00 %	0
	31			392.81	392.81	1000	39.28 %		
	41			95.93	95.93	500	19.19 %		
5	4	2	2660	2296.79	2296.79	2500	91.87 %	0.00 %	0
	5			220.65	220.65	2500	8.83 %		
6	32	2	1860	665.96	665.96	1000	66.60 %	0.00 %	0
	33			835.5	835.50	1000	83.55 %		
	42			341.61	341.61	500	68.32 %		
7	6	2	2660	1449.06	1449.06	2500	57.96 %	0.00 %	0
	7			1872.92	1210.94	2500	74.92 %		
8	34	2	1860	326.87	326.87	1000	32.69 %	0.00 %	0
	35			496.41	496.41	1000	49.64 %		
	43			426.38	426.38	500	85.28 %		
9	8	2	2660	1492.23	1492.23	2500	59.69 %	0.00 %	0
	9			1916.09	1167.77	2500	76.64 %		
10	36	2	1860	344.13	344.13	1000	34.41 %	0.00 %	0
	37			513.68	513.68	1000	51.37 %		
	44			350.24	350.24	500	70.05 %		

interval [802200, 802500] is equal to 240250 W*sec (i.e. 240.25 kW/sec). For the interval [0, 300] the total energy is 0 because at that point the energy could not have been measured. As a result of the migrations which have been performed in previous intervals, Tables 3 and 4 contain some hosts which have been shut down as no virtual machines have been allocated to them; as a result no energy is consumed by these hosts (e.g. hosts 1, 3, 5).

Figure 2 illustrates how the energy consumption decreases significantly throughout the simulation's intervals when running the Particle Swarm Optimization-based method. The high energy consumption from the beginning of the simulation is due to the "warm-up" process which takes place within computing systems.

We have also evaluated the Particle Swarm Optimization-based method by comparing it with the CloudSim implementation using the same workloads and initial data center configuration. For CloudSim we have used the minimum utilization policy.

Table 2. Experimental results obtained for the interval [300, 600].

Host	VM ID	Pes	Freq	Alloc MIPS	Req MIPS	Total MIPS	Usage	Old Usage	Energy
0	26	2	1860	934.44	934.44	1000	93.44 %	46.72 %	29903.16
	27			504.74	504.74	1000	50.47 %		
	39			298.91	298.91	500	59.78 %		
1	0	2	2660	1593.54	1593.54	2500	63.74 %	39.71 %	32271.67
	1			519.29	519.29	2500	20.77 %		
2	28	2	1860	356.23	356.23	1000	35.62 %	40.52 %	29611.89
	29			926.53	926.53	1000	92.65 %		
	40			224.66	224.66	500	44.93 %		
3	2	2	2660	1242.06	1242.06	2500	49.68 %	26.50 %	32552.83
	3			167.8	167.8	2500	6.71 %		
4	30	2	1860	215.63	215.63	1000	21.56 %	27.19 %	28105.28
	31			785.93	785.93	1000	78.59 %		
	41			9.81	9.81	500	1.96 %		
5	4	2	2660	2296.52	2296.52	2500	91.86 %	66.14 %	30218.55
	5			1222.26	1222.26	2500	48.89 %		
6	32	2	1860	886.93	886.93	1000	88.69 %	40.28 %	30218.55
	33			457.23	457.23	1000	45.72 %		
	42			154.36	154.36	500	30.87 %		
7	6	2	2660	1945.03	1945.03	2500	77.80 %	52.93 %	35916.25
	7			870.77	870.77	2500	34.83 %		
8	34	2	1860	746.34	746.34	1000	74.63 %	40.39 %	29528.24
	35			316.64	316.64	1000	31.66 %		
	43			439.51	439.51	500	87.90 %		
9	8	2	2660	499.49	499.49	2500	19.98 %	45.58 %	35395.95
	9			1925.24	1925.24	2500	77.01 %		
10	36	2	1860	168.12	168.12	1000	16.81 %	34.19 %	29149.8
	37			738.42	738.42	1000	73.84 %		
	44			365.25	365.25	500	73.05 %		

Figure 3 illustrates how the energy consumption varies throughout the intervals of the simulation when only the CloudSim implementation is used. By comparing Fig. 2 with Fig. 3 we can notice a small improvement in energy consumption when using the Particle Swarm Optimization-based method as opposed to the case when only the CloudSim implementation is used. Overall the Particle Swarm Optimization-based method introduces an energy saving improvement of 2.85 % compared to the CloudSim implementation.

Table 3. Experimental results obtained for the interval [801900, 802200].

Host	VM ID	Pes	Freq	Alloc MIPS	Req MIPS	Total MIPS	Usage	Old usage	Energy
0	39	2	1860	361.06	361.06	500	9.25 %	9.71 %	26766.66
1							0.00 %	0.00 %	0
2	40	2	1860	245.44	245.44	500	12.33 %	6.60 %	26758.20
3							0.00 %	0.00 %	0
4	41	2	1860	122.31	122.31	500	2.19 %	3.29 %	26079.41
5							0.00 %	0.00 %	0
6	42	2	1860	491.69	491.69	500	5.72 %	13.22 %	26756.12
7							0.00 %	0.00 %	0
8	43	2	1860	368.56	368.56	500	9.02 %	9.91 %	26765.48
9							0.00 %	0.00 %	0
10	44	2	1860	252.94	252.94	500	12.10 %	6.80 %	26757.70

Table 4. Experimental results obtained for the interval [802200, 802500].

Host	VM ID	Pes	Freq	Alloc MIPS	Req MIPS	Total MIPS	Usage	Old usage	Energy
0	39	2	1860	242.12	242.12	500	48.42 %	0.27 %	26145.96
1								0.00 %	0
2	40	2	1860	465.1	465.1	500	93.02 %	9.73 %	26926.58
3								0.00 %	0
4	41	2	1860	409.7	409.7	500	81.94 %	6.25 %	26677.38
5								0.00 %	0
6	42	2	1860	75.91	75.91	500	15.18 %	3.26 %	26070.45
7								0.00 %	0
8	43	2	1860	20.51	20.51	500	4.10 %	13.22 %	26492.61
9								0.00 %	0
10								0.00 %	0

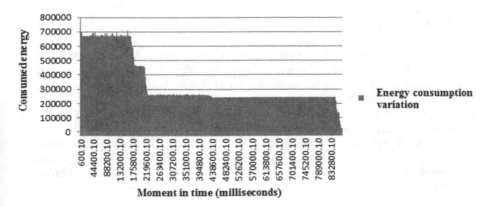

Fig. 2. Energy consumption variation when running the Particle Swarm Optimization-based method with CloudSim.

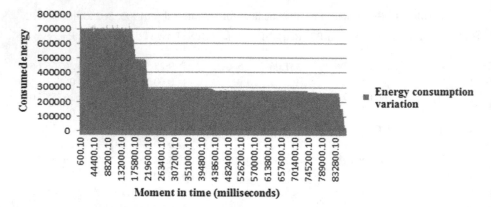

Fig. 3. Energy consumption variation when running the CloudSim without the Particle Swarm Optimization-based method.

7   Conclusion

In this paper we have presented a method for optimizing the energy consumption in data centers. The method adapts the Particle Swarm Optimization meta-heuristic to find the optimal or near-optimal data center configuration that accommodates the virtual machines from the incoming workload and re-organizes the virtual machines currently running on the data center's servers such that the energy consumed by the servers' hardware resources and data center's cooling system is minimized. The Particle Swarm Optimization-based method has been integrated in the CloudSim framework, and has been evaluated on randomly generated workloads. By comparing the obtained experimental results, we have noticed that the Particle Swarm Optimization-based method brings an improvement of 2.85 % in the energy consumption as opposed to the CloudSim implementation.

References

1. CERN openlab, Reducing Data Center Energy Consumption – A summary of strategies used by CERN, the world largest physics laboratory White Paper (2008). https://openlab-mu-internal.web.cern.ch/openlab-mu-internal/03_Documents/3_Technical_Documents/Technical_Reports/2008/CERN_Intel_Whitepaper_r04.pdf
2. U.S. Environmental Protection Agency: Report to Congress on Server and Data Center Energy Efficiency: Public Law 109-431 (2007)
3. Lampe, U., Siebenhaar, M., Hans, R., Schuller, D., Steinmetz, R.: Let the clouds compute: cost-efficient workload distribution in infrastructure clouds. In: Vanmechelen, K., Altmann, J., Rana, O.F. (eds.) GECON 2012. LNCS, vol. 7714, pp. 91–101. Springer, Heidelberg (2012)

4. Wang, S., Liu, Z., Zheng, Z., Sun, Q., Yang, F.: Particle swarm optimization for energy-aware virtual machine placement optimization in virtualized data centers. In: Proceedings of the International Conference on Parallel and Distributed Systems, pp. 102–109 (2013)
5. Li, H., Zhu, G., Cui, C., Tang, H., Dou, Y., He, C.: Energy-efficient migration and consolidation algorithm of virtual machines in data centers for cloud computing. Comput. J. (2015)
6. Kennedy, J., Eberhart, R.C.: Particle swarm optimization. In: Proceedings of IEEE International Conference on Neural Networks, pp. 1942–1948 (1995)
7. Chen, M., Wang, Z.: An approach for web services composition based on QoS and discrete particle swarm optimization. In: Proceedings of the Eighth ACIS International Conference on Software Engineering, Artificial Intelligence, Networking, and Parallel/Distributed Computing, pp. 37–41 (2007)
8. Yuan, J., Miao, X., Li, L., Jiang, X.: An online energy saving resource optimization methodology for data center. J. Softw. 8(8), 1875–1880 (2013)
9. Farahnakian, F., Ashraf, A., Liljeberg, P., Pahikkala, T., et al.: Energy-aware dynamic VM consolidation in cloud data centers using ant colony system. In: Proceedings of the 7th International Conference on Cloud Computing, pp. 104–111 (2014)
10. CloudSim: A Framework for Modeling and Simulation Of Cloud Computing Infrastructures and Services. http://www.cloudbus.org/cloudsim/

Towards an Energy-Aware Cloud Architecture for Smart Grids

Richard Kavanagh[1][(✉)], Django Armstrong[1], Karim Djemame[1],
Davide Sommacampagna[2], and Lorenzo Blasi[2]

[1] School of Computing, University of Leeds, Leeds LS2 9JT, UK
{R.E.Kavanagh,D.J.Armstrong,K.Djemame}@leeds.ac.uk
http://www.comp.leeds.ac.uk
[2] Hewlett Packard Italiana Srl, Millan, Italy
{Davide.Sommacampagna,Lorenzo.Blasi}@hp.com

Abstract. Energy consumption in Cloud computing is a significant issue in regards to aspects such as the cost of energy, cooling in the data center and the environmental impact of cloud data centers. Smart grids offers the prospect of dynamic costs for a data center's energy usage. These dynamic costs can be passed on to Cloud users providing incentives for users to moderate their load while also ensuring the Cloud providers are insulated from fluctuations in the cost of energy. The first step towards this is an architecture that focuses on energy monitoring and usage prediction. We provide such an architecture at both the PaaS and IaaS layers, resulting in energy metrics for applications, VMs and physical hosts, which is key to enabling active demand in cloud data centers. This architecture is demonstrated through our initial results utilising a generic use case, providing energy consumption information at the PaaS and IaaS layers. Such monitoring and prediction provides the groundwork for providers passing on energy consumption costs to end users. It is envisaged that the resulting varying price associated with energy consumption can help motivate the formation of methods and tools to support software developers aiming to optimise energy efficiency and minimise the carbon footprint of Cloud applications.

Keywords: Cloud computing · Energy efficiency · Energy · Power · Monitoring · IaaS · PaaS

1 Introduction

Energy efficiency in Cloud computing is fast becoming a primary concern of Cloud providers. Cloud computing is undergoing rapid adoption which is consequently giving rise to a dramatic increase in energy consumption. Data centers consequentially have an ever increasing importance in regards to attempts to save on energy consumption. In addition to this they are important in regards to demand response [2] both due to their high energy usage and the prospect of

© Springer International Publishing Switzerland 2016
J. Altmann et al. (Eds.): GECON 2015, LNCS 9512, pp. 190–204, 2016.
DOI: 10.1007/978-3-319-43177-2_13

smoothing their demand through the use of dynamic pricing. Dynamic pricing can therefore be utilised to align a Cloud's power demand to the smart grid.

The first step in creating a pricing mechanism is choosing the correct granularity of product [1] and ensuring the relevant data is available to support the billing process. The fundamental unit of trade remains a virtual machine (VM). However either the price charged for the VM must be able to change during the day or the resource allocation of the VM, in order to cope with the fluctuations in the smart grid's energy market. These changes would be based on both demand for VMs and the current cost of the power consumption of the data center. Thus ensuring end users are motivated to reduce their energy consumption at times when it is most costly.

To this end we present a framework that enables the measurement of the energy efficiency of service deployments in Cloud environments. We discuss this framework and in particular focus on its energy modelling and profiling capabilities at both the Platform as a Service (PaaS) and Infrastructure as a Services (IaaS) layers. The framework is capable of modelling, measuring and reporting on energy efficiency for both billing purposes. These monitoring capabilities offer further advantages in that they support active demand [6], enabling those deploying applications in the Cloud to be made aware of the energy consumption of their applications. This is expected to lead to tooling that can assist developers in understanding and minimising their overall energy consumption.

We demonstrate its capabilities by utilising a 3-Tier web application [20] as a generic cloud use case. We utilise this use case as a means of testing the framework and representing a general workload that might be experienced within a Cloud environment, showing the power utilisation of the distributed application and that of its sub-components. This paper's main contributions are:

- A Cloud architecture that is energy aware.
- Support for energy modelling at both the PaaS and IaaS layers, within the architecture.
- A demonstration of recording power consumption via a 3-Tier Web application use case, thus enabling the prospect of billing for energy usage and informing users of the origins of the cost of VMs.

The remaining structure of the paper is as follows: The next section discusses related work. Section 3 discusses the framework's architecture and in particular the energy modelling components at the IaaS and PaaS layers. This is followed by Sect. 4 that discusses in depth the IaaS and PaaS models that support energy modelling and future predictions of overall energy consumption. The presented architecture and models are then evaluated in Sect. 5 via a use case in order to demonstrate the effectiveness of the overall architecture, both in the deployment and operation phases. Finally we conclude and present our future work in Sect. 6.

2   Related Work

The All4Green [2] project focused on Service Level agreements, including supply demand agreements, between energy providers and data centers. These form the basis of providing more flexible tariffs for a data center's energy usage and enabling a demand response mechanism between energy providers and data centers. The architecture proposed in this paper [5] focuses upon energy awareness inside the data center, which is achieved for physical resources, Virtual Machines (VMs) and applications running within the cloud infrastructure. This awareness thus leads towards enabling billing based in part upon energy consumption.

The characterisation of the resources is an important step in regards to accurate energy predictions for software usage. This gives rise to profiling and testing frameworks such as JouleUnit [21] that enable the profiling of hardware systems in order to understand their power consumption profiles. In order to utilise profiling in a more general case monitoring frameworks such as Zabbix [23] or other frameworks [8] may be used. Kwapi [17] is the most closely related monitoring tool to our own work, in that it focuses on power and energy monitoring, however the focus of our framework is upon extending this to both VMs and applications.

Data for resources' power consumption is principally obtained either by direct measurement [9] or inferred via software and physical performance counters [13, 21]. Direct measurement obtains the wall power [13] value via the use of Watt meters [9], providing an aggregation of the current power usage of a physical resource [4]. Performance counters [3, 10, 22] are a non-invasive means of determining energy usage, by utilising performance counters located within the CPU and Operating System. Wall power measurements have the advantage of accuracy but require the specialist physical hardware to be attached into the infrastructure, while the performance counters are indirect measures of power consumption and requires a model to derive an estimate of the energy consumed.

In order to determine VM or host energy usage various frameworks have been developed. The majority of cases use linear models [3, 7, 13, 19] while others lookup table structures [12] have been used or other techniques [22]. In most cases linear models have provided power estimates with a high degree of accuracy for VMs and their underlying resources, usually within 3 W of the actual value or within 5 % error. Additive models such as [13, 19] utilise load characteristics for each of the major physical components such as CPU, disk and network, each of which is considered separately and summed together. In these cases idle power consumption is treated as an additional model parameter that is simply added to the other load characteristics. There are others that use a bias mechanism [3] or where each parameters importance is learned [22]. The use of performance counters can also differ among models, such as in some cases physical meters are needed during training followed by the use of counters post training [12].

The second concern after profiling a physical host's power consumption is to determine its future energy consumption, which can then be used to guide both the deployment and operation of VMs. Estimating future energy consumption requires an understanding of the VMs workload over time. This can include work such as CPU load prediction in models such as LiRCUP [7] which was aimed at assisting in the maintenance of service level agreements and others [14] that search for workload patterns. Workload prediction has enjoyed a lot of attention with a particular focus on the cloud property of the scaling of resources and the maintenance of QoS parameters [11,16,18]. Workload prediction in Clouds has also been seen as a means to plan future workloads so that physical hosts may be switched off when not required [15].

3   Architecture

The architecture follows the standard Cloud deployment model and is hence separated out into the Software as A Service (SaaS), PaaS and IaaS layers. The focus here will be on the PaaS and IaaS layer in which the energy modelling and profiling is performed. Figures 1 and 2 therefore show the high-level interactions of the IaaS and PaaS layer components, in the architecture.

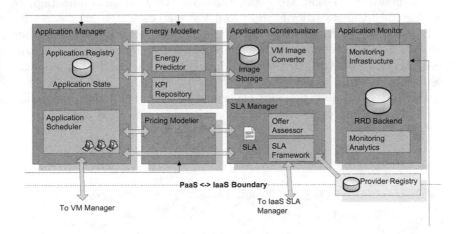

Fig. 1. The PaaS layer.

In the SaaS layer (described further in [5]) a collection of components that facilitate the modelling, design and construction of a Cloud applications, has been developed. These components aid in evaluating energy consumption of a Cloud application during its construction and are provided as plug-ins to the Eclipse Integrated Development Environment (IDE). A number of packaging components that facilitate provider agnostic deployment of cloud applications, while also maintaining energy awareness are also provided.

The PaaS layer as shown in Fig. 1 provides middleware functionality for a Cloud application and facilitates the deployment and operation of the application as a whole. Components within this layer are responsible for selecting the most energy appropriate provider and tailoring the application to the selected provider's hardware environment. Application level monitoring is also accommodated for here. The core components of this layer are discussed next:

– The **Application Manager (AM)** is the principle component in charge of this layer. It manages the user applications that are described as virtual appliances, formed by a set of VMs that are interconnected between them. It utilises information from the PaaS Energy Modeller and the Pricing Modeller in order to assist in the deployment and operation time running of applications.

- The **Virtual Machine Contextualizer (VMC)** is used to embed software dependencies of a service into a VM image and configure these dependencies at runtime via an infrastructure agnostic contextualization mechanism. This includes the insertion of probes that enable the energy modelling process.
- The **PaaS Energy Modeller** gathers and manages energy related information throughout the Cloud Service lifecycle. It provides an interface to estimate the energy cost of a PaaS KPIs in order to assist in the selection of the appropriate IaaS provider for running an application.
- The **Application Monitor (APPM)** is able to monitor the resources (CPU, memory, network ...) that are being consumed by a given application, by providing historical statistics for host and VM metrics.
- The **Service Level Agreement Manager** is responsible for managing Service Level Agreements (SLAs) at the PaaS level. This requires interacting with the Application Manager, the Pricing Modeller and the IaaS SLA Manager, to establish the terms of any SLA.
- The **Pricing Modeller** provides energy-aware cost estimation and billing information relating to the operation of applications and their VMs.

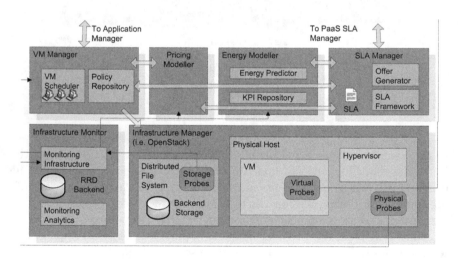

Fig. 2. The IaaS layer.

The IaaS layer as shown in Fig. 2 is responsible for the admission, allocation and management of virtual resource. This is achieved through the orchestration of a number of components, that are detailed below:

- The **Virtual Machine Manager (VMM)** component is responsible for managing the complete life cycle of the virtual machines that are deployed in a specific infrastructure provider. This is achieved with power consumption as a key concern, which is monitored, estimated and optimized using the IaaS Energy Modeller.

- The **IaaS Energy Modeller** has several key features; it is primarily aimed at reporting both host and VM level energy usage data. These values are reported as: a historical log, current values or future predictions. The historical log provides values for energy consumed over a specified time period and the average power, while the current values report power alone. Future predictions are based upon linear regression of CPU utilisation vs power consumption as found via a training phase on a per host basis. The modeller also provides automatic calibration of hosts for training. Predictions utilise either a predefined CPU utilisation level or use a sliding window where the average CPU utilisation over the last N seconds is used as an estimate of future CPU utilisation levels.

- The **SLA Manager** is responsible to manage SLA negotiation requests at IaaS level. This is required in order to allow the PaaS SLA Manager to provide offering for User/SaaS that want to negotiate SLA with the platform.

- The **Pricing Modeller** has the role to provide energy-aware cost estimation and billing information related to the operation of the physical resources that belong to the IaaS provider and are used by specific VMs.

- The **Infrastructure Manager (IM)** manages the physical infrastructure and redirects requests to hardware components. It maintains lists of hardware energy meters, compute nodes, network components and storage devices.

4   Energy Modelling

In this section we discuss energy modelling in the two modellers, for applications in the PaaS layer and for VMs and physical resources in the IaaS layer.

4.1   PaaS Energy Modelling

The PaaS Energy Modeller aggregates virtual machines' power measurements generated by the IaaS Layer, into energy and power measurements for applications. It gathers application events, sent by probes to the application monitor, to further support energy profiling at the level of method calls and subcomponents.

Data required by the PaaS Energy Modeller, as illustrated in Fig. 3, is made available by two interfaces. The first provided by Zabbix retrieves VM power measurements generated by the IaaS Energy Modeller. The second provided by the Application Monitor (Fig. 4), retrieves events reported by probes installed inside the application's virtual machines.

The PaaS Energy Modeller provides the following measurements:

- The **Average Power (W)** of an application (1) is the sum of the average power of each one of the n virtual machines (VM_i) where the application is running, which is calculated (2) by averaging all the instant k power measurements collected on VM_i during that application's lifetime.

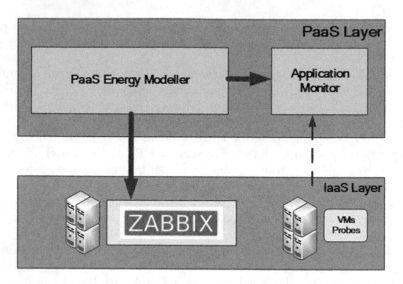

Fig. 3. PaaS energy modeller data sources.

$$\bar{P}_{Application} = \sum_{i=1}^{n} \bar{P}_{VM_i} \qquad (1)$$

$$\bar{P}_{VM_i} = \frac{1}{k} \sum_{j=1}^{k} \bar{P}_j^i \qquad (2)$$

- The total **Energy Consumed (Wh)** by the application (3) is the sum of its virtual machines' consumption, which is calculated (4) from the sum of the energy between each pair of power measurements in two consecutive instants, say t_a and t_b, by applying the trapezoidal rule (5).

$$E_{Application} = \sum_{i=1}^{n} E_{VM_i} \qquad (3)$$

$$E_{VM_i} = \sum E_{t_b t_a}^i \qquad (4)$$

$$E_{t_b t_a}^i = (t_b - t_a)\frac{P^i(t_a) + P^i(t_b)}{2} \qquad (5)$$

The two measurements of power and energy described above are about the whole application; for finer analysis, the PaaS EM, can use events' timestamps to restrict the power calculation to the time interval when the event occurred.
- Every time an event occurs, the **Event Data** is collected by probes; in this way the Energy Modeller knows when such event started, terminated and on which VM it occurred. As shown in Fig. 5, probe data provides the start and end time stamps of the event ("starttime" and "endtime"); each event also reports the identifier of its type ("eventType"), which allows identifying different types of events for the same application to be analyzed separately.

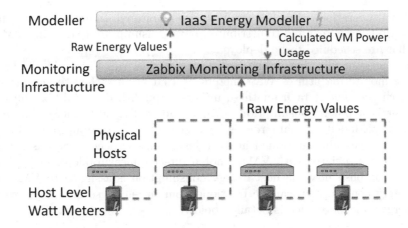

Fig. 4. Monitoring in the IaaS layer.

- **Average Power per Event Type (W)**: The PaaS Energy Modeller uses events data to collect measurements of power from the virtual machine where each event occurred, within a specified time period; then it calculates the average of all measurements for each event and finally returns the average power calculated on all events of the same type.
- **Energy Consumed per Event Type (Wh)**: The PaaS Energy Modeller collects events data and computes the discrete integral, using (5) for each pair of measurements of the power, to obtain the total energy consumption. Finally it sums the single events' consumption for each event of the same type to get the total energy consumption for that event type. In order to provide a better approximation of the energy consumed by each event, the PaaS Energy Modeller interpolates power values from the available samples. This approximation is required for events lasting a short period of time.

4.2 IaaS Energy Modelling

The IaaS Energy Modeller has two main roles, the first is at deployment time when the VM Manager utilises power consumption predictions of VMs. The

```
<event>
      <applicationID>HMMERpfam</applicationID>
      <eventType>eventA</eventType><instanceId>45</instanceId>
      <nodeId>4351a79d-75ee-42fd-b9e6-b963a10b1787</nodeId>
      <starttime>1411468096408</starttime>
      <endtime>1411468096930</endtime>
</event>
```

Fig. 5. Event data example.

second is at operation time when the VMs are monitored. In both cases the IaaS Energy Modeller is required to attribute power consumption to existing VMs or VMs that are scheduled to be deployed.

The energy monitoring in the IaaS Layer is shown in Fig. 4. At the lowest level the monitoring utilises Watt meters [9] that are attached to the physical host machines. The data from these meters is published in Zabbix [23]. The values for host power consumption is then read by the IaaS Energy Modeller. The Energy Modeller's main role is to assign energy consumption values to a VM from the values obtained at host level. This is needed because energy consumption associated with VMs is not a directly measurable concept. Rules therefore establish how the host energy consumption is assigned to VMs. The host energy consumption can be fractioned out in one of several ways, within the Energy Modeller which is detailed below:

- **CPU Utilisation Only**: This uses CPU utilisation data for each VM and assigns the energy usage by the ratio produced by the utilisation data. (Available for: Historic, Current, Predictions). This is described in the Eq. 6 where VM_P_x is the named VM's power consumption, $Host\_P$ is the measured host power consumption. VM_Util_x is the named VMs CPU utilisation, VM_Count is the count of VMs on the host machine. VM_Util_y is the CPU utilisation of a member of the set of VMs on the named host.

$$VM\_P_x = Host\_P \times \frac{VM\_Util_x}{\sum_{y=1}^{VM\_Count} VM\_Util_y} \qquad (6)$$

- **CPU Utilisation and Idle Energy Usage**: Idle energy consumption of a host can also be considered. Using training data the idle energy of a host is calculated. This is evenly distributed among the VMs that are running upon the host machine. The remaining energy is then allocated in a similar fashion to the CPU Utilisation only mechanism. (Available for: Historic, Current, Predictions). This is described in Eq. 7 where $Host\_Idle$ is the host's measured idle power consumption. This provides an advantage over the first method in that a VM is more appropriately allocated power consumption values and prevents it from using no power while it is instantiated.

$$VM\_P_x = Host\_Idle + (Host_P - Host\_Idle) \times \frac{VM\_Util_x}{\sum_{y=1}^{VM\_Count} VM\_Util_y} \qquad (7)$$

- **Evenly Shared**: In the case of predictions CPU utilisation is not always clearly estimable, thus energy consumption can be evenly fractioned amongst VMs that are on the host machine. The default for predictions is to share out power consumption evenly as per Eq. 8. A slight variation also exists which counts the CPU cores allocated to each of the VMs and allocating based upon this count (Eq. 9). Equations 8 and 9 describe this even sharing rules where $Host\_Predicted$ is the amount of power that the host on which the named VM resides is estimated to utilise and VM_VCPU_x is the amount of virtual

CPUs allocated to the named VM while VM_VCPU_y is the amount of virtual CPUs allocated to a VMs on the named host.

$$VM\_P_x = Host\_Predicted \times \frac{1}{VM\_Count} \tag{8}$$

$$VM\_P_x = Host\_Predicted \times \frac{VM\_VCPU_x}{\sum_{y=1}^{VM\_Count} VM\_VCPU_y} \tag{9}$$

The default method chosen on the IaaS Energy Modeller is option 2 for current and historic values and 3 for predictions. Once the Energy Modeller has assigned energy values to a given VM it then writes these values to disk, which are again via Zabbix_sender reported back to the monitoring infrastructure, thus providing VM level power consumption values to the PaaS layer.

5   Evaluation

In this section we present an evaluation of our framework. The overall aim of the experimentation is demonstrate the energy monitoring capabilities of the proposed architecture and show how it can ensure customers are aware of their energy usage for Cloud data centers, thus achieving the awareness aspect of active demand [6]. This is achieved by running a 3-Tier Web application [20], which has been chosen as an example of a typical Cloud/Web based application. In running this experiment we demonstrate the usage of the energy modellers at the PaaS and IaaS layers, which is the first step towards billing end users for a VM's energy consumption. The objectives of the experiment will be to find at the PaaS level the overall application's energy usage and at the IaaS level the energy usage per VM. This will be done under varying workload conditions. This will therefore highlight how the framework can both advise end users of their application's energy consumption which enables transparency during billing and provide a means for recording the energy consumption of an individual user. In the next section we discuss the experimental setup, followed by a discussion of our findings in Sect. 5.2.

5.1   Experimental Setup

The 3-Tier Web application is the RichFaces Photo Album that is provided by jboss.org. It has been configured to run on five VMs one containing haproxy and one containing a MySQL database. JMeter was utilised on a third to induce workload and simulate the users during the experimentation. The final two VMs ran instances of JBoss, to execute the workload that was induced. The VMs were deployed using OpenStack.

The experiment was run with 4 physical hosts available. Each host is equipped with two quad-core processors with 2.66 GHz, 32 GB of RAM and a 750 GB local hard disk. Each host is connected to two different networks transferring one Gbit/s each synchronously. The first is dedicated for infrastructure management as well as regular data exchange between the physical hosts. The second is for the storage area network usage only where storage nodes are accessible through a distributed file system. Monitoring data including the wall power is made available through the 1st network. Each energy-meter can measure voltage, current and power consumption. The energy meter's used are *Gembird EnerGenie Energy Meters* [9]. These energy measurements are reported once per second, through Zabbix 2.2. One host is dedicated to collecting the measurements and can share the aggregated information with the monitoring components and another hosts is dedicated towards acting as the main storage management system.

5.2 Results and Discussion

In the first experiment the 5 VMs as previously described will be run, with varying amounts of users trying to access the system. The users will vary from 0 to 1000 in increments of 200. The VMs will be started providing a deployment phase for each run, followed by a period of undergoing load from users. Each run will be repeated 5 times in order to ensure validity of the results. The PaaS level metric of the application's overall energy consumed will then be presented along with IaaS layer metric of the energy consumption per each VM.

Figure 6 shows the energy consumed by the Photo Album, for a range of different users. We can see that the amount of energy consumed for each run increases with the amount of users, up until a plateaus at 600 users due to the workload saturating the VMs.

Figure 7 shows the average power consumed by each VM in the Photo Album, for a range of different users. In a similar fashion to Fig. 6 the plateau can be

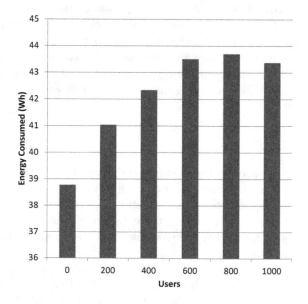

Fig. 6. The total energy consumed by the application.

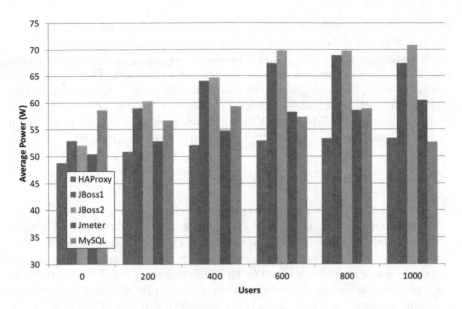

Fig. 7. The per VM average power consumption. (Color figure online)

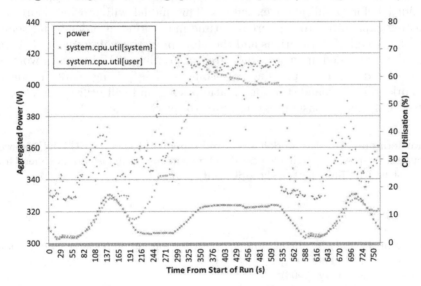

Fig. 8. Trace of the power consumed during the life of the VMs. (Color figure online)

seen. It can also be observed the relative energy usage in each of the VMs, with substantial increases in the JBoss instances power consumption and more limited increases from the JMeter instance. The HAProxy and MySQL instances have relatively modest increases in power consumption. This can be seen as a clear demonstration of how different instance types can be identified as more energy consuming than others and of their relative power consumption.

Figure 8 shows a trace of the CPU utilisation and aggregated power consumption of VMs during a single experimental run, for 1000 users. The deployment, running and undeployment phases are shown as the spikes on the graph. This illustrates the energy awareness, which can be used to choose providers and optimise placement of VMs as well as by developers to compare deployment strategies and iteratively reduce energy consumption of applications.

6   Conclusion and Future Work

We have demonstrated how the proposed framework can measure an applications overall energy consumption and how this can be broken down on a per VMs basis. This research can be leverage by future smart grids from two perspectives that help manage demand. Firstly, it enables user awareness of energy consumption and secondly, facilitates billing based on this information. This ability to measure power consumption also gives developers the opportunity to examine how their applications perform in terms of energy consumption on the Cloud. In future work the PaaS Energy Modeller will be equipped with a statistical model to be trained before application execution. This model will provide short term forecasting capabilities to support real time monitoring in order to implement early detection of SLA violations and therefore proactive enforcement. The IaaS layer will be expanded upon to include greater profiling of VM types in workload prediction and improved profiling of resources. The pricing model inside the framework will be expanded beyond static pricing and will utilise the estimates of power and energy consumption in order to set the price for VMs.

Acknowledgements. This work has received support through the EU 7th Framework Programme for research, technological development and demonstration under Grant Agreement no 610874 as part of the ASCETiC project.

References

1. Altmann, J., et al.: GridEcon: a market place for computing resources. In: Altmann, J., Neumann, D., Fahringer, T. (eds.) GECON 2008. LNCS, vol. 5206, pp. 185–196. Springer, Heidelberg (2008)
2. Basmadjian, R., Lovasz, G., Beck, M., de Meer, H., Hesselbach-Serra, X., Botero, J.F., Klingert, S., Perez Ortega, M., Lopez, J.C., Stam, A., van Krevelen, R., di Girolamo, M.: A generic architecture for demand response: the ALL4Green approach (2013)
3. Bohra, A.E.H., Chaudhary, V.: VMeter: power modelling for virtualized clouds. In: 2010 IEEE International Symposium on Parallel Distributed Processing, Workshops and Phd Forum (IPDPSW), pp. 1–8, April 2010
4. Castañé, G.G., Núñez, A., Llopis, P., Carretero, J.: E-mc2: a formal framework for energy modelling in cloud computing. Simul. Model. Pract. Theory **39**, 56–75 (2013)

5. Djemame, K., Armstrong, D., Kavanagh, R., Ferrer, A.J., Perez, D.G., Antona, D., Deprez, J.C., Ponsard, C., Ortiz, D., Macias, M., Guitart, J., Lordan, F., Ejarque, J., Sirvent, R., Badia, R., Kammer, M., Kao, O., Agiatzidou, E., Dimakis, A., Courcoubetis, C., Blasi, L.: Energy efficiency embedded service lifecycle: towards an energy efficient cloud computing architecture. In: CEUR Workshop Proceedings, vol. 1203, pp. 1–6. CEUR-WS (2014)
6. European Technology Platform on Smart Grids: Consolidate View of ETP SG on Smart Grids (European Technology Platform on Smart Grids). Technical report (2015)
7. Farahnakian, F., Liljeberg, P., Plosila, J.: LiRCUP: linear regression based CPU usage prediction algorithm for live migration of virtual machines in data centers. In: 2013 39th EUROMICRO Conference on Software Engineering and Advanced Applications (SEAA), pp. 357–364, September 2013
8. Fatema, K., Emeakaroha, V.C., Healy, P.D., Morrison, J.P., Lynn, T.: A survey of cloud monitoring tools: taxonomy, capabilities and objectives. J. Parallel Distrib. Comput. **74**(10), 2918–2933 (2014)
9. GEMBIRD Deutschland GmbH: EGM-PWM-LAN data sheet (2013). http://gmb.nl/Repository/6736/EGM-PWM-LAN_manual-7f3db9f9-65f1-4508-a986-909157 09e544.pdf
10. Hähnel, M., Döbel, B., Völp, M., Härtig, H.: Measuring energy consumption for short code paths using RAPL. SIGMETRICS Perform. Eval. Rev. **40**(3), 13–17 (2012)
11. Islam, S., Keung, J., Lee, K., Liu, A.: Empirical prediction models for adaptive resource provisioning in the cloud. Future Gener. Comput. Syst. **28**(1), 155–162 (2012)
12. Jiang, Z., Lu, C., Cai, Y.: VPower: metering power consumption of VM. In: 2013 IEEE 4th International Conference on Software Engineering and Service Science, pp. 483–486, May 2013
13. Kansal, A., Zhao, F., Liu, J., Kothari, N., Bhattacharya, A.A.: Virtual machine power metering and provisioning. In: Proceedings of the 1st ACM Symposium on Cloud Computing, SoCC 2010, pp. 39–50. ACM, New York (2010)
14. Khan, A., Yan, X., Tao, S., Anerousis, N.: Workload characterization and prediction in the cloud: a multiple time series approach (2012)
15. Prevost, J.J., Nagothu, K., Jamshidi, M., Kelley, B.: Optimal calculation overhead for energy efficient cloud workload prediction (2014)
16. Quiroz, A., Kim, H., Parashar, M., Gnanasambandam, N., Sharma, N.: Towards autonomic workload provisioning for enterprise grids and clouds (2009)
17. Rossigneux, F., Lefevre, L., Gelas, J.P., Dias De Assuncao, M.: A generic and extensible framework for monitoring energy consumption of OpenStack clouds. In: The 4th IEEE International Conference on Sustainable Computing and Communications (Sustaincom 2014). Sydney, Australia, December 2014
18. Roy, N., Dubey, A., Gokhale, A.: Efficient autoscaling in the cloud using predictive models for workload forecasting (2011)
19. Smith, J.W., Khajeh-Hosseini, A., Ward, J.S., Sommerville, I.: CloudMonitor: profiling power usage. In: 2012 IEEE 5th International Conference on Cloud Computing (CLOUD), pp. 947–948, June 2012
20. Tsebro, A., Mukhina, S., Galkin, G., Sorokin, M.: RichFaces Photo Album Application Guide (2009). http://docs.jboss.org/richfaces/latest_3_3_X/en/realworld/html_single/

21. Wilke, C., Götz, S., Richly, S.: JouleUnit: a generic framework for software energy profiling and testing. In: Proceedings of the 2013 Workshop on Green in/by Software Engineering, GIBSE 2013, pp. 9–14. ACM, New York (2013)
22. Yang, H., Zhao, Q., Luan, Z., Qian, D.: iMeter: an integrated VM power model based on performance profiling. Future Gener. Comput. Syst. **36**, 267–286 (2014)
23. Zabbix, S.I.A.: Homepage of Zabbix: An Enterprise-Class Open Source Distributed Monitoring Solution (2014). http://www.zabbix.com/

Applications: Tools and Protocols

Diameter of Things (DoT): A Protocol for Real-Time Telemetry of IoT Applications

Soheil Qanbari[1]([✉]), Samira Mahdizadeh[1], Rabee Rahimzadeh[2],
Negar Behinaein[2], and Schahram Dustdar[1]

[1] Vienna University of Technology, Vienna, Austria
{qanbari,dustdar}@dsg.tuwien.ac.at, e1329639@student.tuwien.ac.at
http://dsg.tuwien.ac.at
[2] Baha'i Institute for Higher Education (BIHE), Tehran, Iran
{rabee.rahimzadeh,negar.behinaein}@bihe.org
http://www.bihe.org

Abstract. The Diameter of Things (DoT) protocol is intended to provide a near real-time metering framework for IoT applications in resource-constraint gateways. Respecting resource capacity constraints on edge devices establishes a firm requirement for a lightweight protocol in support of fine-grained telemetry of IoT deployment units. Such metering capability is needed when lack of resources among competing applications dictates our schedule and credit allocation. In response to these findings, the authors offer the DoT protocol that can be incorporated to implement real-time metering of IoT services for prepaid subscribers as well as Pay-per-use economic models. The DoT employs mechanisms to handle the IoT composite application resource usage units consumed/charged against a single user balance. Such charging methods come in two models of time-based and event-based patterns. The former is used for scenarios where the charged units are continuously consumed while the latter is typically used when units are implicit invocation events. The DoT-enabled platform performs a chained metering transaction on a graph of dependent IoT microservices, collects the emitted usage data, then generates billable artifacts from the chain of metering tokens. Finally it permits micropayments to take place in parallel.

Keywords: Diameter protocol · Service metering · Internet of things

1 Introduction

Utility computing [1] is an evolving facet of ubiquitous computing that aims to converge with emerging Internet of Things (IoT) infrastructure and applications for sensor-equipped edge devices. The agility and flexibility to quickly provision IoT services on such gateways requires an awareness of how underlying resources as well as the IoT applications are being utilized as metered services.

© Springer International Publishing Switzerland 2016
J. Altmann et al. (Eds.): GECON 2015, LNCS 9512, pp. 207–222, 2016.
DOI: 10.1007/978-3-319-43177-2_14

Such awareness mechanisms enable IoT platforms to adjust the resource leveling to not exceed the elasticity constraints such that stringent QoS is achievable.

The quest for telemetry of the client's IoT application resource usage becomes more challenging when the job is deployed and processed in a constrained environment. Such applications collect data via sensors and control actuators for more utilization in home automation, industrial control systems, smart cities and other IoT deployments. In this context, telemetry enables a Pay-per-use or utility-based pricing model through metered data to achieve more financial transparency for resource-constrained applications.

Metering measures rates of resource utilization via metrics, such as number of application invocations, data storage or memory usage consumed by the IoT service subscribers. Metrics are statistical units that indicate how consumption is measured and priced. Furthermore, metering is the process of measuring and recording the usage of an entire IoT application topology, individual parts of the topology, or specific services, tasks and resources. From the provider view, the metering mechanisms for service usage differ widely, due to their offerings which are influenced by their IoT business models. Such mechanisms range from usage over time, invocation-basis to subscription models. Thus, IoT application providers are encouraged to offer reasonable pricing models to monetize the corresponding metering model.

To fulfill such requirements, we have incorporated and extended the Diameter base protocol defined in RFC6733[1] to an IoT domain. There are several established Diameter base protocol applications like Mobile IPv4 [2], Credit-Control [3] and Session Initiation Protocol (SIP) [4] applications. However, none of them completely conforms to the IoT application metering models.

The current accounting models specified in the Diameter base are not sufficient for real-time resource usage control, where credit allocation is to be determined prior to and after the service invocation. In this sense, the existing Diameter base applications do not provide dynamic metering policy enforcement in resource and credit allocations for prepaid IoT users. Diameter extensibility allows us to define any protocol above the Diameter base protocol. Along with this idea, in order to support real-time metering, credit control and resource allocation, we have extended the Diameter to Diameter of Things (DoT) protocol by adding four new types of servers in the AAA infrastructure: DoT provisioning server, DoT resource control server, DoT metering server and DoT payment server. Further details regarding the aforementioned entities will be discussed in a later section of DoT architecture models. In summary, our main contribution is the specification of an extended Diameter base protocol to an IoT application domain. This contributes to fully implementing a real-time policy-based telemetry and resource control for a variety of IoT applications. Our protocol supports both the prepaid and cloud pay-per-use economic models. However, in this paper, we address the metering for the prepaid model.

With this motivation in mind, the paper continues in Sect. 2, with a brief review on how the Diameter base protocol functions. Next, we introduce the

---

[1] https://tools.ietf.org/html/rfc6733.

terms and preliminaries defined in this study at Sect. 3. With some definitive clues on the Diameter architecture, we propose Diameter of Things (DoT), an extension to the Diameter on how IoT applications are to be metered and monetized. The DoT framework layered architecture together with its interacting entities are detailed in Sect. 4. In support of our model, we have defined a DoT-based IoT application topology and its associated hybrid metering policies in Sect. 5. This lets the application telemetry policies vary independently from clients as well as applications that use it. To enable this, DoT performs several interrogations which are detailed in Sect. 6. DoT commands are then described in Sect. 7. Next, in Sect. 8, we express formally the DoT application transaction models to achieve better telemetry control over computing resources. Subsequently, Sect. 9 surveys related work. Finally, Sect. 10 concludes the paper and presents an outlook on future research directions.

2   The Utility of Diameter

The Remote Authentication Dial In User Service (RADIUS) [5] as per RFC2865 is a simple but most deployed protocol which provides network access control using client/server Authentication, Authorization and Accounting (AAA) model. The IETF[2] has standardized the Diameter base protocol [6] as an enhanced version of RADIUS providing a flexible peer-to-peer operation model. It is featuring intermediary agents (Relay, Proxy, Redirect and Translation) and capabilities negotiation among servers. It enables reliable transport layer using TCP or SCTP connection. The Diameter peer connections are ensured using a Keepalive mechanism. It also supports the dynamic peer discovery and configurations in a valid session. Such specifications are achieved using set of commands and Attribute-Value-Pairs (AVPs) by collaborating and negotiating peers. Diameter has the concept of "applications", which is entirely missing in RADIUS. The protocol is enriched with a globally unique application ID. These applications benefit from the general capabilities of the Diameter base protocol while defining their own extensions on top of the base.

Some of the main features offered by Diameter are dynamic routing based on Realm, session management, accounting, agent support. It is based on Peer-To-Peer architecture as illustrated in Fig. 1, in a way that each Diameter node can behave as either a client or server based on the current deployment model. Diameter nodes can be of the type of Diameter client, Diameter server and Diameter agent. Diameter client is the node that receives the user connection request. Diameter server is the one serving the request e.g. performing user authentication based on provided information. Diameter agents themselves divide into four types of Relay, Proxy, Redirect and Translate agents. A relay agent is used to forward messages to other Diameter nodes based on the information provided in the message. Proxy agent can also act like a relay agent with the extra functionality of policy enforcement implementation via message content modification. Redirect

---

[2] Internet Engineering Task Force (https://www.ietf.org).

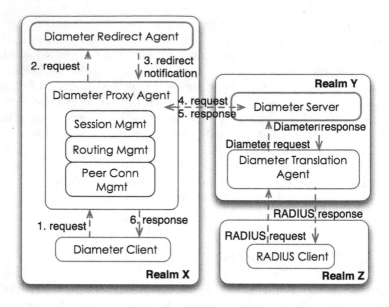

Fig. 1. Diameter base protocol architecture

agents act as a centralized configuration repository by returning information necessary for Diameter agents to communicate directly with another node. Translation agents provide translation between two distinct AAA protocols.

3   DoT Preliminaries and Terms

In this section we present basic conventions, terms together with their definitions considered in the DoT protocol:

- **Diameter of Things (DoT)**: DoT implements a mechanism to provision IoT deployment units, control resource elasticity, meter usage, and charge the user credit for the rendered IoT applications.
- **IoT Microservice**: A fine-grained atomic task performed by an IoT service on a device.
- **IoT Application Topology**: It contains the composition of hybrid collaborating IoT microservices to meet the user's request. The topology is packages with the elasticity requirements and constraints (hardware or software) which will dictate our schedule and credit allocation within the runtime environment.
- **Metering Server**: A DoT metering server performs real-time metering and rating of IoT applications deployment.
- **Metering Agent**: The agent transfers the metered values to the metering server via tiny tokens.
- **Provisioning Server**: Provisioning server refers to initial configuration, deployment and management of IoT applications for subscribers. It also deals with ensuring the underlying IoT device layer is available to serve.

- **Payment Server**: The micropayment transaction charges subscribers upon relatively small amounts for a unit of usage. It basically transfers a certain amount of trade in the payWord or microMint micropayment schemes [7]. In the payWord scheme a payment order consists of two parts, a digitally signed payment authority and a separate payment token which determines the amount. A chained hash function, is used to authenticate the token. The server then calculates a chain of payment tokens or paychain. Payments are made by revealing successive paychain tokens.
- **Rating**: The process of giving price to an IoT application usage events. This applies to service usage as well as underlying resource usage.
- **Resource-Control Server**: Resource control server implements a mechanism that interacts in real-time with a resource and credit allocation to an account as well as the IoT application. It controls the charges related to the specific IoT application usage.
- **One-Cycle Event**: It indicates a single-request-response message exchange pattern which one specific service is invoked by one consumer at a time while no session state is maintained. One message is exchanged in each direction between requesting and responding DoT nodes.

4   DoT Architecture Models

Figure 2 illustrates a schematic view on collaborating components of our proposed DoT architecture. It contains of a DoT client, Provisioning server, Resource control server, Metering server, and a Payment server.

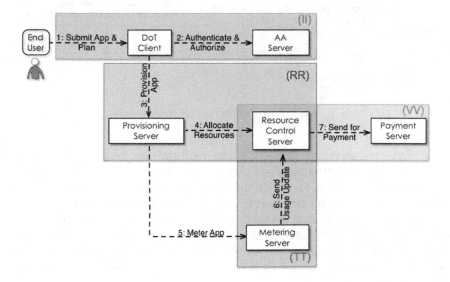

Fig. 2. Typical diameter of things (DoT) application architecture.

As the end user defines and composes an IoT application, the request is forwarded to the DoT client. The DoT client submits the composed application to the DoT infrastructure which determines possible charges, verifies user accounts, controls the resource allocation to the application, meters the usage, and finally generates a bill and deducts the corresponding credit from the end user's account balance.

DoT client contacts the AAA server with the AA protocol to authenticate and authorize the end user. When the end user submits the IoT application topology graph, the DoT client contacts the provisioning server to submit an application topology. Afterwards, the provisioning server contacts the resource control server with information of required resource units. The resource control server reserves the resources that need to be allocated to the service. When user's credit is locked for the application provisioning, the DoT client receives the grant resource message and informs the end user that the request has been granted. As soon as the IoT application is deployed and instantiated, the submitted topology is registered to the metering server for telemetry and credit control purposes.

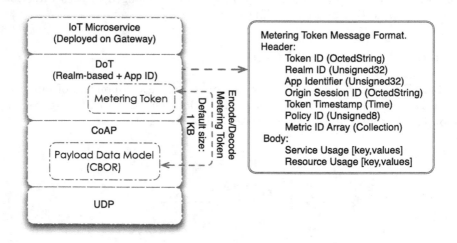

Fig. 3. Typical DoT metering token structure.

The metering server is responsible to perform the metering transaction according to the submitted topology and meter the services by calling metering the tasks of each service in the chain. Metering transactions will remain running until the termination request is sent from DoT client to the provisioning server. After receiving a termination request, the resource control server releases the resource and sends the billable artifacts related to the user usage to the payment server. The payment server, then, invokes the payment transaction and deducts credit from the end user's account and refunds unused reserved credit to the user's account.

In DoT application architecture, metered values are transfered via tokens. The metering token message attributes as shown in Fig. 3 must be supported by all DoT implementations that conform to this specification. The CBOR[3] message format is considered for the metering tokens transmission as it can decrease payload size compared to other data formats.

5 DoT-Based IoT Application Overview

The DoT application defined in this specification implements flexible metering policy as well as the definition and constraints of the application topology.

5.1 DoT-Based Application Topology

The main responsibility of the provisioning server is the actual provision of the requested IoT application package. It contains the composition of collaborating IoT microservices to meet the user's request. Each IoT microservice is predefined with a detailed specification such as its ID, constraints and various usage patterns and policies. For instance, as defined in Listing 1.1 they can be advertised with diverse pricing models due to the event-based or time-based patterns for specific subscribers. The IoT microservices elasticity requirements and constraints (hardware or software resources) are also defined in the topology which will dictate our schedule and credit allocation within the runtime environment. The end user's request can be received in the form of a JSON object. It contains user information as well as the user requirements in terms of IoT composite application topology and its specification, to realize the intended behavior. After receiving the request, a provisioning server generates a dependency graph of the application topology complying with its specification.

The Dependency graph displays dependencies between different microservices which are requested to be in topology. In the DoT protocol, this dependency graph is used in forming the transaction model for metering the IoT deployment unit. The dependency graph is a directional graph where each node of the graph represents an available microservice in the service package registry. Similarly, each edge of the graph shows dependencies between two microservices (two nodes). The edge has a direction that shows the execution order of microservices involved in this edge. Additionally, each edge has a label which shows the policy to be in effect for this connection. The Resource control server realizes such metering policies using a predefined incident matrix. This incident matrix represents the metering policies for our directed acyclic graph (DAG) of IoT services. The metering policy incident matrix P_t is a $n*m$ matrix of P_{ij} policies, where n is the number of nodes (vertices) and m is number of lines (Edges). In the cell of N_i and V_j, the P_{ij} indicates the rate of call per granted unit (time &events). It enables each service to invoke its neighbor with the attached policy. Therefore, when a client sends a request containing a tailored IoT application topology, the Resource control server is able to rate the request based on the enforced metering policies of time (duration) and event-based usage patterns.

---

[3] The Concise Binary Object Representation: http://cbor.io.

5.2 DoT-Based Metering Plans

The metering plans define the allocation mechanism for granting the required resource units to an IoT application/constituent microservices. It is an indication that the following assumptions underlying our IoT telemetry solution has been considered for the proper positioning of DoT protocol. The IoT applications are advertised with an associated charging plans. In case of cloud-based model, there may be a subscription fee for pay-per-use plans. The cost of obtaining such plans is known as the plan's "premium" which is the price that is calculated and offered in the subscription phase by the provider. The estimation of the plan's premium is out of the scope of the DoT protocol. The plan indicates the composed services pricing schema and comes in two models of predefined as well as customized. The plan will be built to be consistent with the composed application topology in the rate setting.

The subscribed metering plan indicates: (i) the price of granted units for every IoT application constituent microservice. For instance, 5 h for Humidity sensor and 10 invocations for Chiller On/Off actuator. (ii) the resource Used Unit Update (U3) frequency for all associated units which are defined in the provider's plan. (iii) the manual/automatic payment configuration. So that the provider can handle the payment transactions automatically while informing the user. (iv) container instance fee, which is the fee that user pays for underlying resource usage. Instance usage can be time based or underlying resource-usage based which is defined by the provider's policy. (v) finally, subscription time for pay-per-use model and subscription fee for prepaid model.

Listing 1.1. Excerpt of an IoT application spec and policy in a JSON object.

```
{    "microserviceID":"01",
     "microserviceName":"getTemperature",
     "uri":"getTemperature.py",
     "execute":"python_getTemperature.py",
     "constraints":{"runtime":  "python_2.7","memory":  " ... "}
     "policies":[{"policyID":"PL_01_01",
                   "cost":"$2/week",
                   "desc":"time_mode_-_$2_per_week"},
                  {"policyID":"PL_01_02",
                   "cost":"0.01cent/invoke",
                   "desc":"event_mode_-_0.01cent_per_invoke"},
                  {"policyID":"PL_01_03",
                   "cost":"$1",
                   "desc":"subscription_fee"}
                 ] }
```

6 DoT Interrogations

For a Hybrid DoT, four main interrogations are performed for a well-functioning protocol. The first interrogation is called Initial Identification (II) which basically deals with clients' identification, for instance the user authentication and authorization processes. The second interrogation is Request Realization (RR) that aims to provision the clients' IoT applications as well as scheduling their resource allocation upon agreed terms and subscribed plan. The third interrogation is called Telemetry Transmission (TT) that deals with metering the running services as well as the granted units usage data transmission for charging purposes. The final interrogation, entitled Value Verification (VV), ensures value generation and delivery to the interested stakeholders. The hybrid metering is carried out in main DoT sessions which hold globally unique and constant Session-IDs. The whole DoT-based metering life-cycle including the II, RR, TT, and VV interrogations are presented in Fig. 4.

6.1   Initial Identification (II)

The end user subscribes the application as well as the chosen plan to the DoT client. The DoT client submits the IoT deployment units to the Provisioning server to ask for the required resource units it needs to run. In this case, the Provisioning server queries for resources (including underlying resources and credit allocation) from Resource control server. The Resource control server is responsible for the device resource reservation. It also keeps track of user credit fluctuations.

In this phase, the end user requirements are modeled into an application topology using a directed acyclic graph. This graph can connect various IoT microservices available in diverse usage units. The deployment of such hybrid applications will result in one global constant Session-ID followed by related sub-session-IDs as well as transaction-IDs. Note that the IoT application might send a (re)authorization request to the AAA server to establish or maintain a valid DoT session. However, this process does not influence the credit allocation that is streaming between the DoT client and provisioning server, as it has already been authorized for the whole transaction before.

6.2   Request Realization (RR)

The Resource control server analyzes the IoT service and allocates resources to the requested service. It also considers the subscription time/fee in order to notify user when this value elapses.

When the new usage update arrives at the Resource control server, it charges the credit based on the usage summary received from the Metering server. It also validates subscription by checking the status of credit (as in prepaid model) or elapsed time (in pay-per-use model) against a certain threshold. Upon reaching the threshold, the Resource control server sends an update notification request to the user. DoT protocol makes it possible to define a default action for this purpose. This default action can be to perform update automatically or to ask user to take the desired action.

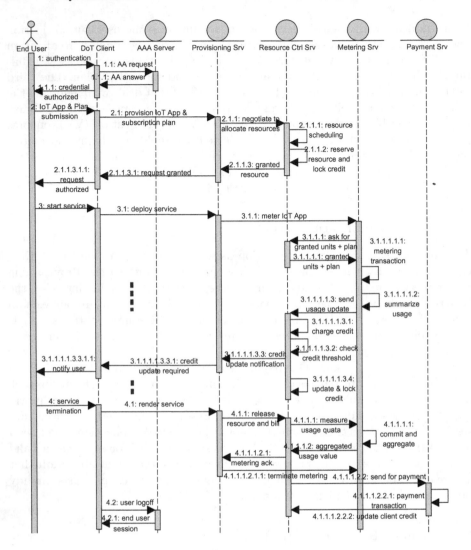

Fig. 4. The sequence of DoT interrogations to enable hybrid metering.

6.3   Telemetry Transmission (TT)

As soon as the end user sends the Start service request to the DoT client, the DoT Client asks the Provisioning server to initiate the service and start monitoring and metering processes. In this regard, the Provisioning server submits the IoT application to the Metering server and asks to establish a metering mechanism for the newly opened session.

Having an IoT application deployed, the metering server monitors the real usage of each service element including service usage and resource usage at a certain frequency rate called Unit Usage Update (U3). The U3 frequency determines the rate of sending updates regarding unit usage of each service. It is independent of the type of service. For example, the $U3$ set to 25 %, implies that for a time-based microservice with granted units of 100 min, the usage update should be provided every 25 min; and for an event-based microservice with granted units of 100 invocations, the usage update will be sent after every 25 invocations.

To make it more clear, after identification of an IoT application to the Metering server, the Metering server sends a request to the Resource control server asking for the amount of granted units as well as the plan, which includes the U3 value for each microservice as defined by the provider. The U3 values are then provided to the Metering agents, as the metering server starts the metering transaction.

During deployment of an IoT application, each Metering agent meters the actual resource and service usage of its associated/assigned microservice. If the actual service usage value reaches an integer multiples of $U3$, the Metering agent will send a notification message to the Metering server. The Metering server then uses these feedbacks to gain a realistic perception of the usage of each microservice and to charge the user credit accordingly. Next, if the application usage of a microservice reaches the threshold value, the Metering Server informs the Resource control server issuing a resource-update request for the service. For instance, when the actual usage of a certain microservice reaches a certain threshold, e.g. more than 70 %, metering server informs the resource control server. This contributes to a continuous and consistent service delivery. The detailed flow of TT phase is presented in Fig. 5.

In the DoT credit allocation model, the provisioning server asks the resource control server to reserve resources and to lock a suitable amount of the user's credit. Then it returns the corresponding amount of credit resources in the form of service specific usage units (e.g., number of invocations, duration) to be metered. The granted and allocated unit type(s) should not be changed during an ongoing DoT session.

6.4   Value Verification (VV)

When the end user terminates the service session, the DoT client must send a final service rendering request to the Provisioning server. The Provisioning server should ask the Resource Control server to release all the allocated resources to an IoT application and perform payment transaction. As such, the Resource control server deallocates the granted resources and asks the Metering server to commit the measured metering tokens and report the quota value to it. Then the Resource Control server sends the billable artifacts to the Payment Server to charge the client account respectively. Finally, the Payment server sends the updated client credit to the Resource control server. Meanwhile, the DoT Client drops the user session via AAA server.

Upon each deduction from user credit, the DoT protocol verifies the credit value. As soon as the credit value drops below a certain threshold, it informs the user to perform credit update automatically or to take the desired action manually.

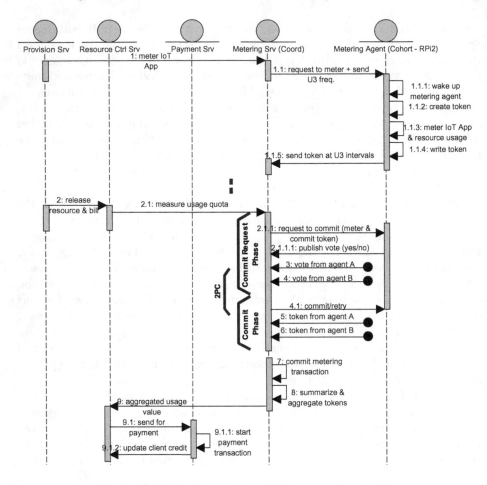

Fig. 5. DoT hybrid metering - 2PC transaction model.

7   DoT Command Messages

The DoT messages contain commands and Attribute Value Pairs (AVP) to enable metering and payment transactions for DoT-based applications. The messaging structure should be supported by all the collaborating peers in the domain architecture. Four main commands are explained here in more details.

7.1   Provision-Application-Topology-Request/Answer

The SATR command is a message between DoT client and Provisioning server. Via this command, the DoT client submits the IoT App (defined by the Client) to the Provisioning server and inquiry resources needed for the application delivery in II or RR interrogations. Following the request, the PATA response with an acknowledgment of resources reserved for the client's IoT App request.

For instance, the PATR message format is: [<Session-Id>, <Client-Id>, <Request-action>, <Dest-Realm>, <User-Name>, <IoT-App-Id>, <AVPs>]. In return, the PATA response will contain the <Granted-Service-Units> attribute in addition to the original request.

7.2 App-Resource-Allocation-Request/Answer

The CAMR command is used in RR interrogation. As soon as the Provisioning server receives Terminate-IoT-App-Request command, it sends a Commit-App-Metering-Request command message to the Metering server asking resource usage quota measurement for a specific user. Another use case is to ask for resource usage during service delivery. In return, the Commit-App-Metering-Answer command is used to report the measured quota value for the requested user and the metered IoT application.

7.3 Commit-App-Metering-Request/Answer

The SMR command is used in RR interrogation. As soon as the Provisioning server receives Terminate-Service-Request command, it sends a Start-Metering-Request command message to the Metering server asking resource usage quota measurement for a specific user. Another use case is to ask for resource usage during service delivery. In return, the Start-Metering-Answer command is used to report the measured quota value for the requested user and a metered IoT application.

7.4 Start-Bill-Payment-Request/Answer

The Start-Bill-Payment-Request command which should be invoked in VV interrogation, is used between the Resource control server and the Payment server to establish a payment mechanism and initiate a fund transfer. In response to the request, the Start-Bill-Payment-Answer command contains the state of payment transaction and the updated user credit information.

8 DoT Transaction Model

The runtime of a DoT application is carried out in four "nested chained" transactions. In this respect, the DoT transaction model preserves consistency by defining conflict serializability. In order to prevent the conflict between operations in the DoT transaction model, a schedule pattern is defined to force the logical temporal order in transactions execution. In this case, recoverability is an argument in favor of transaction processing with a rollback mechanism. In the DoT model there exists four transactions prone to inconsistency: (T1) Identification, (T2) Provisioning, (T3) Metering and (T4) Payment transaction. The Identification transaction embeds two sub-transactions of Authorization and Authentication. As such, the Payment transaction has also two sub-transactions

Table 1. The scheduled chronological execution sequence of DoT transactions.

T1: Identification	T2: Provisioning	T3: Metering	T4: Payment
:	:	:	:
Lock-S (credit)	Lock-X (credit)	Lock-X (credit)	Lock-X (credit)
Read (credit)	Read (credit)	Read (credit)	Read (credit)
Authenticate and authorize	Reserve (premium)	Calculate (credit)	Paychain (credit/debit)
Unlock (credit)	Deploy (IoT appID)	Write (credit)	Write (credit)
:	Write (credit)	Commit	Commit
	Commit	Unlock (credit)	Unlock (credit)
	Unlock (credit)	:	:
	:		

of Credit and Debit. Here is the schedule of conflict serializability for read(), write(), and commit() operations on the credit resource object of the client.

We use the following notation: Let T_i be a transaction and *credit* be a relation or a data resource of a relation. Assuming $O_{ij} \in R(credit), W(credit)$ be an atomic read/write operation of T_i on data item *credit*. Then the two operations O_{ij} and O_{ik} on the same *credit* data resource are in conflict if at least one of them is a write operation. To avoid such conflicts, we have come up with the DoT transaction schedule in Table 1.

9   Related Work

In relation to our work, there is some commendable research regarding the cloud service usage metering. Elmsroth et al. [8] proposed a loosely coupled architecture solution for an accounting and billing system for use in the RESERVOIR [9] project. There are some alternatives that propose billing and metering solutions, Narayan et al. [10]. Petersson [11] describes cloud metering and billing solution. Naik et al. [12] proposed a solution for metering of services delivered from multiple cloud providers. They incorporate the cloud service broker together with a metering control system to report metered data at configurable intervals. Meanwhile, there are some prominent studies on capturing pricing models for IoT domains. Aazam and Huh [13] provided a resource prediction, resource price estimation and reservation for the Fog which resides between underlying IoTs and the cloud. Their proposed model does not support the real-time session and event-based metering models.

Mazhelis et al. [14] studies the applicability of the Constrained Application Protocol (CoAP), a lightweight transfer protocol under development by IETF, for efficiently retrieving monitoring and accounting data from constrained devices. Their results indicate that CoAP is suited for efficiently transferring monitoring and accounting data, both due to a small energy footprint and a memory-wise compact implementation. This work relies on using the accounting and monitoring infrastructure produced by the Accounting and Monitoring of Authentication and Authorization Infrastructure Services (AMAAIS) project [15]. Our work elevates the metering to an IoT domain by proposing an extended Diameter protocol that enables IoT infrastructures to incorporate the DoT protocol in their deployment models. This contributes to a real-time resource utilization awareness by constructing and allocating flexible metering models to IoT deployment units.

10 Conclusion

In this study, we have presented a metering protocol, called the Diameter of Things (DoT), that enables real-time telemetry and automatic resource allocation control of IoT applications. The DoT is designed to enhance the resource utilization by extending the Diameter base protocol. The authors offered the DoT architecture, its interrogations as well as its transaction model for accounting for the resource usage of constrained devices. The DoT offers considerable benefits, such as granular metering of lightweight applications, real-time transparency over resource usage in edge devices and transporting and exchanging application-specific metering policies in an IoT domain. As an outlook, our future work includes the DoT implementation together with an evaluation of the proposed DoT architecture in terms of scalability, performance and session management. A concise evaluation of the requirements[4] for the Diameter-based protocols is proposed that will be considered for the DoT implementation as well as evaluation purposes. We envision the DoT protocol to gaining acceptance as a de facto metering standard in IoT.

Acknowledgments. The research leading to these results is sponsored by the Doctoral College of Adaptive Distributed Systems (ADSys) (http://www.big.tuwien.ac.at/adaptive) at the Vienna University of Technology.

References

1. Buyya, R., Yeo, C.S., Venugopal, S., Broberg, J., Brandic, I.: Cloud computing and emerging it platforms: vision, hype, and reality for delivering computing as the 5th utility. Future Gener. Comput. Syst. **25**(6), 599–616 (2009)
2. Calhoun, P., Johansson, T., Perkins, C., Hiller, T., Mccann, P.: Diameter mobile IPv4 application. In: IETF, RFC 4004, August 2005
3. Hakala, H., Mattila, L., Koskinen, J.-P., Stura, M., Loughney, J.: Diameter credit-control application. In: IETF, RFC 4006, August 2005
4. Garcia-Martin, M.: Diameter session initiation protocol (SIP) application. In: IETF, RFC 4740, April 2006
5. Rigney, C., Rubens, A., Simpson, W., Willens, S.: Remote authentication dial in user service (RADIUS). In: IETF, RFC 2138, June 2000
6. Calhoun, P., Loughney, J., Guttman, E., Zorn, G., Arkko, J.: Diameter base protocol. In: IETF, RFC 3588, September 2003

---

[4] https://tools.ietf.org/html/draft-zander-ipfix-diameter-eval-00.

7. Rivest, R.L., Shamir, A.: PayWord and MicroMint: two simple micropayment schemes. In: Lomas, M. (ed.) Proceedings of the International Workshop on Security Protocols, pp. 69–87. Springer, London (1997)
8. Elmroth, E., Marquez, F.G., Henriksson, D., Ferrera, D.P.: Accounting and billing for federated cloud infrastructures. In: Proceedings of the 2009 Eighth International Conference on Grid and Cooperative Computing, GCC 2009, Washington, DC, USA, pp. 268–275. IEEE Computer Society (2009)
9. Rochwerger, B., Breitgand, D., Levy, E., Galis, A., Nagin, K., Llorente, I.M., Montero, R., Wolfsthal, Y., Elmroth, E., Cáceres, J., Ben-Yehuda, M., Emmerich, W., Galán, F.: The reservoir model and architecture for open federated cloud computing. IBM J. Res. Dev. **53**(4), 535–545 (2009)
10. Narayan, A., Rao, S., Ranjan, G., Dheenadayalan, K.: Smart metering of cloud services. In: 2012 IEEE International Systems Conference (SysCon), pp. 1–7, March 2012
11. Petersson, J.: Cloud metering and billing. http://www.ibm.com/developerworks/cloud/library/cl-cloudmetering. Accessed 08 Aug 2011
12. Naik, V.K., Beaty, K., Kundu, A.: Service usage metering in hybrid cloud environments. In: 2014 IEEE International Conference on Cloud Engineering (IC2E), pp. 253–260, March 2014
13. Aazam, M., Huh, E.-N.: Fog computing micro datacenter based dynamic resource estimation and pricing model for IoT. In: 2015 IEEE 29th International Conference on Advanced Information Networking and Applications (AINA), pp. 687–694, March 2015
14. Mazhelis, O., Waldburger, M., Machado, G.S., Stiller, B., Tyrväinen, P.: Retrieving monitoring and accounting information from constrained devices in internet-of-things applications. In: Doyen, G., Waldburger, M., Čeleda, P., Sperotto, A., Stiller, B. (eds.) AIMS 2013. LNCS, vol. 7943, pp. 136–147. Springer, Heidelberg (2013)
15. Stiller, B.: Accounting and monitoring of AAI services. Switch J. **2010**(2), 12–13 (2010). IETF

Automatic Performance Space Exploration
of Web Applications

Tanwir Ahmad$^{(\boxtimes)}$, Fredrik Abbors, and Dragos Truscan

Faculty of Science and Engineering, Åbo Akademi University,
Joukahaisenkatu 3-5 A, 20520 Turku, Finland
{tanwir.ahmad,fredrik.abbors,dragos.truscan}@abo.fi

Abstract. Web applications have become crucial components of current service-oriented business applications. Therefore, it is very important for the company's reputation that the performance of a web application has been tested thoroughly before deployment. We present a tool-supported performance exploration approach to investigate how potential user behavioral patterns affect the performance of the system under test. This work builds on our previous work in which we generate load from workload models describing the expected behavior of the users. We mutate a given workload model (specified using Probabilistic Timed Automata) in order to generate different mutants. Each mutant is used for load generation using the MBPeT tool and the resource utilization of the system under test is monitored. At the end of an experiment, we analyze the mutants in two ways: cluster the mutants based on the resource utilization of the system under test and identify those mutants that satisfy the criteria of given objective functions.

Keywords: Performance evaluation · Performance prediction · Model-based mutation · Probabilistic timed automata · Load generation

1 Introduction

Current web applications range from dating sites to gambling sites, e-commerce, on-line banking, airline bookings, and corporate websites. Web applications are becoming increasingly complex and there are many factors to be considered when the performance of web systems is concerned, for example network bandwidth, distributed computing nodes, software platform used for system implementation, etc. [19]. It is very important for companies to provide high-quality service to their customers in order to keep their competitive edge in the market [13,18]. Therefore, performance testing has become an important activity to identify the performance bottlenecks before application deployment [23].

Performance testing is a process of measuring the responsiveness and scalability of a system when it is under a certain synthetic workload [23]. The *synthetic workload* is generated by simulating the workload in a real environment. Usually, different *key performance indicators* (KPIs) are monitored during a load

© Springer International Publishing Switzerland 2016
J. Altmann et al. (Eds.): GECON 2015, LNCS 9512, pp. 223–235, 2016.
DOI: 10.1007/978-3-319-43177-2_15

generation session in order to evaluate the performance of the system under test (SUT). Generally, load is generated by executing pre-recorded scripts of user actions which simulate the expected user behavior. The approach is passive in nature and does not represent the dynamic behavioral pattern of real users [9].

In our previous work, we used *Probabilistic Timed Automata* (PTA) for specifying workload models [1,2]. PTA models allow the tester to express the dynamic behavior of real users probabilistically and at the same time increase the level of abstraction of user model. A PTA can be created using two methods. Firstly, the tester can build a workload model manually based on his/her experience or knowledge of the SUT. Secondly, the workload model can be produced by mining web access log files [3]. The models created using the latter approach are approximations of the behavioral patterns of previous real users.

At present, the complex structure of many web applications allows users to reach same resources following different navigation paths. Furthermore, the access pattern of a large scale web application is unpredictable; it could change drastically over a relatively short period, due to some global events [10]. These types of abrupt user behavioral patterns and unanticipated usage of the web application could degrade the performance or even crash the system.

The two methods comprehensively discussed above for creating workload models do not explore the potential behavioral pattern space of the user, because the inferred models are either subjective or approximated based on the previous web application usage.

Mutation testing is an approach, originally proposed by DeMillo *et al.* [7] and Hamlet [11], where a tester creates test cases which cause faulty variants of a program-under-test (PUT) to fail. During mutation analysis, the tester injects faults into the PUT by using specific mutation operators and generates faulty programs or *mutants*. A *mutation operator* is a syntactical change to a statement in a program. A mutant that is created by inserting one single fault, is called a *first order mutant* and a mutant with two or more injected faults is known as a *high order mutant* [12].

Specification mutation has been proposed by Budd and Gopal as an extension of mutation testing to specification [6]. The main idea is to create variations of an original specification which can be used to generate tests which violate the original functional specification of the SUT. If the system is specified using state machines, then specification mutation means mutating the state machine, for example, changing the sequence of transitions. However, in code mutation, changes are made to the actual implementation of the system. In our approach, we apply specification mutation for load generation. More specifically, we mutate a workload model in order to generate mutants which are then used to generate load against the SUT.

This paper investigates an approach for automatically mutating a given workload model and generating models with variant configuration, known as *mutants*, to explore the space of possible behavioral patterns of real users. We simulate these mutants for load generation against the SUT using the MBPeT [1,2] tool and observe the performance of the SUT to identify which mutant or groups of mutants saturate different resources of the SUT.

The rest of the paper is structured as follows: Sect. 2, we give an overview of the related work. In Sect. 3, we present our performance exploration process and tool chain, whereas, in Sect. 4, we demonstrate the applicability of our approach to a case-study. Finally, Sect. 5 presents conclusions and discusses future work.

2   Related Work

Several authors have proposed the use of specification mutation for test generation in the context of functional and security testing, while others have tried to explore the performance of a system via simulations. Different from them, we are applying specification mutation for performance exploration against an already implemented system. To the best of our knowledge, there is no other approach that uses the mutants for performance exploration.

Martin and Xie [17] proposes a framework that facilitates automated mutation testing of access control policies. They have defined a set of new mutation operators for XACML policies. The mutation operators are used to generate faulty policies (called mutant policies). A change-impact analysis tool is employed to detect equivalent mutants among generated mutants. The proposed approach generates test data randomly in form of requests, these requests are later used to kill the mutant policies. A mutant policy is considered killed if the response of the request based on the original policy is different from the response of the request based on the mutant policy.

Lee and Offutt [15] proposed a technique for using mutation analysis to test the semantic correctness of XML-based component interactions. They specified the web software interactions using an Interaction Specification Model (ISM) that consists of document type definitions, messaging specifications, and a set of constraints. Interaction Mutation Operators (IMO) are used to mutate the given valid set of interactions, in order to generate mutant interactions. These are mutant interactions are sent to the web component under test, if the response of a mutant interaction is different from the valid interaction, the mutant is killed. The approach is used to verify the correctness of web component interactions.

In [22], the authors propose a model-based approach for testing security features of software systems. In their approach, they define fuzzing operators for scenario models specified as sequence diagrams. The fuzzing operators are template-based and are applied to UML sequence chart messages, for example, to remove, insert, swap, or change message types. The approach differs from ours in the sense that they apply their operators on UML models for the purpose of testing security, while we apply our operators to PTA models for testing the performance.

In [5], Brillout et al. proposed a methodology for automated test case generation for Simulink models. They mutate Simulink models by injecting syntactic changes into the model. The authors proposed an algorithm to generate test cases by systematically analyzing a model and a set of mutants. They have used bounded model checking to explore the behavior of models and compute test suites for given fault models.

A model-based testing approach has been proposed by Barna et al. to test the performance of a transactional system [4]. The authors use an iterative approach to determine the workload stress vectors of a system. A framework adapts itself according to the workload stress vectors and then drive the system along these stress vectors until a performance stress goal is achieved. They use a system model, represented as a two-layered queuing network, and they use analytical techniques to find a workload mix that will saturate a specific system resource. Their approach differs from ours in the sense that they simulated model of the system instead of testing against a real implementation of a system.

3   Approach and Tool Chain

In this paper, we propose a *Performance Exploration (PerfX)* approach (illustrated in Fig. 1) which mutates a given workload model in order to generate a certain number of mutated workload models or *mutants*. We simulate the generated mutants for load generation and record the resource utilization of the SUT. Our approach makes use of the MBPeT tool [1] to simulate each mutant in a separate load generation session. MBPeT is a performance testing tool that generates load by simulating several replicas (or virtual users) of a given workload model concurrently. MBPeT generates the load in a distributed fashion and applies it in real-time to the SUT, while measuring several KPIs including SUT resource utilization.

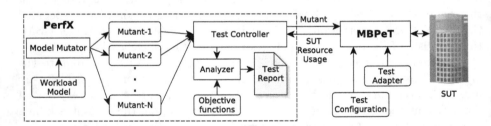

Fig. 1. Approach for performance exploration.

The expected behavior of the users is modeled using Probabilistic Timed Automata (PTA) [14]. A PTA contains a finite set of clocks, locations, and edges with probabilities. The edges are chosen non-deterministically based on probability distribution, which also makes the selection of target location probabilistic. A *clock* is a variable that expresses time in the model. The time can advance in any location as long as the *location invariant condition* holds, and an edge can be taken if its *guard* is satisfied by the current values of the clocks. In order to reduce size of a PTA, edges are labeled with three values: *probability value, think time,* and *action* (see Fig. 2(a)). A think time describes the amount of time that a user thinks or waits between two consecutive actions. An action is a request or a set of requests that the user sends to the SUT. Executing an action means making a probabilistic choice, waiting for the specified think time, and executing the actual action.

In addition to a workload model, MBPeT requires a *test adapter* and a *test configuration* file as input to run a test session. The tool utilizes a *test adapter* to translate abstract actions found in a workload model into concrete actions understandable by the SUT. For example, in case of a web application, a payment action would have to be translated into a HTTP *POST* request to a given URL. Secondly, a *test configuration* is a file which specifies the necessary information about the SUT and is used by the MBPeT tool to run a test session. The file contains a collection of different parameters which are system specific. For example, if a SUT is a web server then the IP address of the web server, test session duration, maximum number for concurrent users, ramp function, etc. The *ramp function* defines the number of concurrent virtual users at any given moment during a test session.

The *PerfX* approach can be divided into three main stages: *model mutation, running test session*, and *result analysis*.

3.1   Model Mutation

At the first stage, several *mutants* are created from an original workload model. The original workload model is created either manually from performance requirements or automatically from historic usage. For our purpose we define two operators:

- **Change Probability Distribution(CPD)**: This operator replaces the probabilistic distribution of outgoing edges of a location with random values while keeping the sum of the probabilities of all the outgoing edges from a location equal to 1
- **Modify Think Time(MTT)**: This operator randomizes the think time values of outgoing edges of a location within a given range.

A tool module, the *Model Mutator* generates the population of mutants. We adjust the number of mutants in the population by setting two parameters: *maximum mutation order* (*MMO*) and *number of mutation rounds* (*NMR*). During each round of mutation, the module generates mutants between the first order and the given *MMO*. For example, if the *MMO* is three, the module will generate the first, second and third order mutants respectively. Four parameters are provided as input to the module, which uses the following algorithm: NMR, MMO, W(workload model), and *OP* (mutation operator).

Input: NMR, MMO, W, OP
1: $P \leftarrow \{\}$ // Population set
2: **for** $round = 1$ **to** NMR **do**
3:    **for all** o such that $1 \leq o \leq MMO$ **do**
4:        $M \leftarrow GenMutants(o, W, OP)$ // Generate a set of oth order mutants of W model using OP operator
5:        $P \leftarrow P \cup M$ // Add generated mutants to P
6:    **end for**
7: **end for**

Although, the algorithm uses a same mutation operator for each mutation round, the mutants generated are different every time because the operator replaces the existing values with random ones.

We can calculate the total number of mutants in a population using the following equations:

$$M(o) = \sum_{i=1}^{o} \frac{l_e!}{i!(l_e - i)!} \tag{1}$$

$$P(o, r) = M(o) \times r \tag{2}$$

where $M(o)$ defines the number of mutants generated in a single round of mutation, based on the l_e number of locations with outgoing edges in a given model and the o order of mutation (where $o \in \{x | x \geq 1 \wedge x \leq l_e\}$) in Eq. 1. The $P(o, r)$ in Eq. 2 denotes the number of mutants in a population and $r \in \mathbb{N}$ represents the number of mutation rounds.

For example, we want to generate a population of mutants by mutating the model in Fig. 2(a). We set the order of mutation o to 2 and the number of mutation rounds r to 4. Then, in each round of mutation the module will create three first order mutants (i.e., mutant with a single mutated location) and three second order mutants (i.e., mutant with two mutated locations). In short, the module will generate six mutants in each round of mutation (i.e., $M(2) = 6$) and after four rounds, there will be a population of twenty-four mutants (i.e., $P(2, 4) = 24$). Figure 2(b) shows one of the first order mutants generated, where the CPD operator is applied to location 1, which results in a different probability distribution.

Since our approach is based on random mutation, it is impossible to estimate the optimal number of mutants required to investigate the user behavioral pattern space sufficiently. However, a population with a relatively large number of mutants is more beneficial because it covers the user behavioral pattern space more adequately and provides more conclusive results. However, the tester should also take into account the efforts of generation and simulating all those mutants when deciding the size of a population.

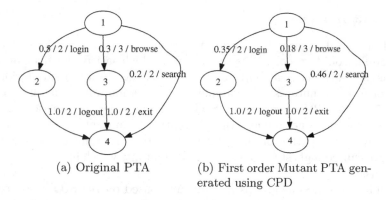

(a) Original PTA

(b) First order Mutant PTA generated using CPD

Fig. 2. CPD operator applied to a workload model.

3.2   Running Test Sessions

In the following stage, each mutant in the population is used separately for load generation session. A *Test Controller* module is responsible for orchestrating test sessions for each of the generated mutants and collecting the test results. The module selects a generated mutant and invokes the MBPeT tool with the following input parameters: mutant, test adapter and test configuration. For each session we use identical configuration of the MBPeT tool, same ramp and test adapter.

The duration of the test session is decided by the test engineer and it depends on the average duration of user sessions (sequence of actions generated from the workload model). As a rule-of-thumb, the test session duration should not be less than the maximum user sessions duration (i.e., the sum of think times and estimated response times for the longest sequence in the workload model).

At the end of a test session, the MBPeT tool calculates the average, maximum and minimum values of the resource (i.e., CPU, memory, disk and network bandwidth) usage at the SUT during the test session and forwards them to the Test Controller. Once all the test sessions have been executed, the Test Controller sends the results (an example is given in Table 1) of all the test sessions to the *Analyzer* module for analysis.

Table 1. Example of test session results.

Mutants	Resources (Avg, Min, Max)					
	CPU[a]	Memory[a]	Disk read[b]	Disk write[b]	Net send[b]	Net recv.[b]
Mutant-1	23, 2, 56	15, 5, 43	22, 4, 89	39, 4, 92	66, 3, 63	33, 1, 97
Mutant-2	32, 5, 76	11, 9, 52	37, 9, 76	19, 2, 38	34, 7, 95	45, 0, 56

[a] Measured in percentages.
[b] Measured in kilobytes (KB).

3.3 Result Analysis

The last stage takes care of analyzing the results of all test sessions. An *Analyzer* module from the tool selects the mutants which satisfy the given objective functions. An *objective function* is used to express a certain target criterion for a mutant or a set of mutants, for example, find those mutants which have caused at least 70 % of CPU usage on the SUT. Custom objective functions are also supported, allowing one to query the population of mutants in an effective and flexible way. Further, the tool has two built-in objective functions: a) mutants which have caused highest CPU usage and b) mutants which have caused highest memory usage.

Secondly, this module groups the mutants based on the SUT resources utilization using the K-means [16] algorithm. Clustering of mutants allows the tester to observe different groups of mutants where all the mutants in a group have a different probability distribution nonetheless cause approximate similar amount of stress to the SUT with respect to resource utilization.

4 Experiment

In this section, we demonstrate our approach by using it to explore performance space of an *auction web service*, called *YAAS*, which was developed as a stand-alone application. YAAS has a *RESTful* [21] interface based on the HTTP protocol and allows registered users to search, browse, and bid on auctions that other users have created. The YAAS application is implemented using Python [20] and the Django [8] framework. We have manually created the original workload model (see Fig. 3(a)) by analyzing the web application traffic.

4.1 Test Architecture

The tool and SUT run on different computing nodes. The SUT runs an instance of the YAAS application on top of an Apache web server. All nodes (tool and the server) feature an 8-core CPU, 16 GB of memory, 7200 rpm hard drive, and Fedora 16 operating system. The nodes were connected via a 1Gb Ethernet.

4.2 Generating Mutants

In this experiment, we have used one mutation operator, *CPD* which randomly alters the probability distribution of outgoing edges of a location while keeping the sum of probabilities of all the outgoing edges equals to 1. The *MMO* was set to 5 (i.e., total number of locations with outgoing edges in the workload model shown in Fig. 3(a)), which means that we generated 31 mutants in each round of mutation. We ran 3 mutation rounds and generated a population of 93 mutants in around 5 s.

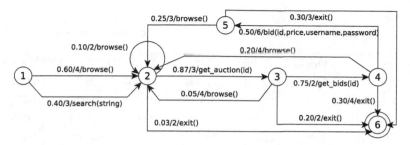

(a) Original workload model

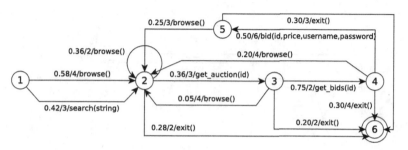

(b) MutantC workload model

Fig. 3. Comparison of original and MutantC workload model.

4.3 Running Test Sessions

The test session duration was set to 10 min because we had observed the average duration of real user sessions was 2 min. The concurrent number of users for each test session was 200. The entire experiment ran for 15 h and 30 min.

4.4 Results

We have specified 4 objective functions, one for the each resource category (i.e., CPU, memory, disk, network). Based on those objective functions, we have obtained 4 mutants: *MutantC, MutantM, MutantD* and *MutantN* that have saturated the CPU, memory, disk and network resources respectively, more than the rest of the mutants and the original model. The results are listed in Table 2 along with their resource utilization.

Figure 4 shows the CPU utilization of the SUT when comparing the Original model to the MutantC model. From the figure one can see that the average CPU utilization is much high with the MutantC model compared to the Original model. We point out that this difference in CPU utilization was achieved with only a second order mutant, MutantC. The probability distribution of the outgoing edges in the MutantC model has been changes at two locations: *1* and *2*, as shown in Fig. 3(b).

Table 2. Maximum resource utilization achieved by mutants.

Resources	Original	MutantC	MutantM	MutantD	MutantN	Maximum
CPU (%)	76.22	**92.42**	71.44	91.63	89.47	92.42
Memory (GB/s)	3.28	1.50	**3.37**	0.97	0.93	3.37
Disk write (KB/s)	117.04	76.16	104.38	**247.69**	76.56	247.69
Net send (MB/s)	1.29	2.27	1.62	2.18	**3.09**	3.09
Net recv. (KB/s)	71.62	90.02	80.12	114.11	**116.16**	116.16

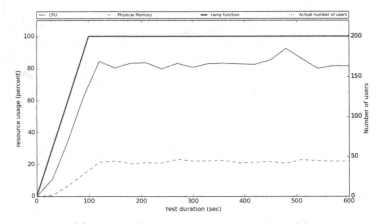

(a) CPU utilization with the original model.

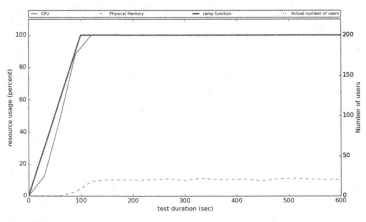

(b) CPU utilization with the MutantC model.

Fig. 4. CPU utilization using the original model vs MutantC model.

The spider-chart in Fig. 5(a) shows resource utilization of the original model, MutantC and MutantM over 5 axes. It highlights that the MutantM and the original model have approximately similar resource utilization values whereas MutantC has a distinct resource utilization trend. Despite the fact that the MutantC has saturated the CPU resource, it has also sent and receive more data over the network than the original model. Further analysis of the MutantC, exhibits a one significant change between the original model and the MutantC is that the *browse* action at the location 2 has high probability in the MutantC than the original model. This could mean that the consecutive *browse* actions can saturate the CPU of the SUT.

The black-colored polygon, named *Maximum* in Fig. 5(a), illustrates the maximum resource utilization that has been achieved by all the mutants in each resource category. The spider-chart allows the tester to visually correlate and contrast the different worst-case scenario mutants over their diverse aspects.

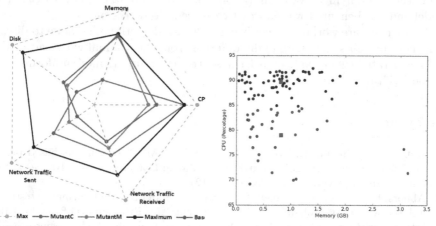

(a) Spider chart of resource utilization for 3 mutants.

(b) Two mutant clusters (blue and red) based on CPU and memory utilization.

Fig. 5. Result analysis.

Moreover, we have divided the mutants between two clusters using K-means algorithm, as shown in Fig. 5(b). The blue dots in the figure represents the cluster of mutants with more than 85 % of CPU usage and the red dots displays the mutants between 67 % to 85 % of CPU usage. The green squares express the centroids (i.e., means) of the clusters. By clustering mutants together, it is possible to focus the analysis to a particular set of workload models that have a negative impact on the performance. In Fig. 5(b), mutants are clustered based on two attributes: CPU and memory utilization. However, increasing the number of cluster and/or attributes lead to a more detailed analysis of the mutants and their impact on the performance.

5　Conclusion

In this paper we have presented an automated performance exploration approach that mutates a workload model in order to generate different mutants. These mutants reflect potential behavioral pattern space. We simulate the mutants for load generation and analyze the mutants with respect to the SUT resource utilization.

The experiment presented in the paper substantiates that the approach can be used to identify hidden or unknown weaknesses of the SUT by rigorously and automatically exploring the user behavioral pattern space. The tester can write custom objective functions to filter the behavioral patterns of interest. Those access patterns can later be employed to optimize the SUT.

For the future development, we are planning to investigate more guided methods for mutant generation which would allow us to focus the exploration on desired resource (or combination of resource utilization). Also we plan to study the effect of applying several mutation operators simultaneously to the same model and the benefits towards worst-case scenario detection.

Further, we are working on equivalent-mutant detection technique to discard equivalent mutants (i.e., marginally different from the original workload model) and regenerate new mutants in order to scatter the mutants more uniformly over the behavioral pattern space.

References

1. Abbors, F., Ahmad, T., Truscan, D., Porres, I.: MBPeT: a model-based performance testing tool. In: 2012 Fourth International Conference on Advances in System Testing and Validation Lifecycle (2012)
2. Abbors, F., Ahmad, T., Truscan, D., Porres, I.: Model-based performance testing of web services using probabilistic timed automata. In: Proceedings of the 2013 10th International Conference on Web Information Systems and Technologies (2013)
3. Abbors, F., Truscan, D., Tanwir, A.: An automated approach for creating workload models from server log data. In: Andreas, H., Therese, L., Leszek, M., Stephen, M. (eds.) Proceedings of the 9th International Conference on Software Engineering and Applications. pp. 14–25. Scitepress (2014)
4. Barna, C., Litoiu, M., Ghanbari, H.: Model-based performance testing: NIER track. In: 2011 33rd International Conference on Software Engineering (ICSE), pp. 872–875. IEEE (2011)
5. Brillout, A., He, N., Mazzucchi, M., Kroening, D., Purandare, M., Rümmer, P., Weissenbacher, G.: Mutation-based test case generation for simulink models. In: de Boer, F.S., Bonsangue, M.M., Hallerstede, S., Leuschel, M. (eds.) FMCO 2009. LNCS, vol. 6286, pp. 208–227. Springer, Heidelberg (2010)
6. Budd, T.A., Gopal, A.S.: Program testing by specification mutation. Comput. Lang. 10(1), 63–73 (1985)
7. DeMillo, R.A., Lipton, R.J., Sayward, F.G.: Hints on test data selection: help for the practicing programmer. Computer 11(4), 34–41 (1978)
8. Django, September 2012. https://www.djangoproject.com/

9. Draheim, D., Grundy, J., Hosking, J., Lutteroth, C., Weber, G.: Realistic load testing of web applications. In: Proceedings of the 10th European Conference on Software Maintenance and Reengineering, CSMR 2006, p. 11. IEEE (2006)

10. Elbaum, S., Karre, S., Rothermel, G.: Improving web application testing with user session data. In: Proceedings of the 25th International Conference on Software Engineering, pp. 49–59. IEEE Computer Society (2003)

11. Hamlet, R.G.: Testing programs with the aid of a compiler. IEEE Trans. Softw. Eng. **4**, 279–290 (1977)

12. Jia, Y., Harman, M.: Higher order mutation testing. Inf. Softw. Technol. **51**(10), 1379–1393 (2009)

13. Kao, C.H., Lin, C.C., Chen, J.N.: Performance testing framework for rest-based web applications. In: 2013 13th International Conference on Quality Software (QSIC), pp. 349–354. IEEE (2013)

14. Kwiatkowska, M., Norman, G., Parker, D., Sproston, J.: Performance analysis of probabilistic timed automata using digital clocks. Formal Methods Syst. Des. **29**, 33–78 (2006)

15. Lee, S.C., Offutt, J.: Generating test cases for xml-based web component interactions using mutation analysis. In: 12th International Symposium on Software Reliability Engineering, ISSRE 2001, Proceedings, pp. 200–209. IEEE (2001)

16. MacQueen, J.B.: Some methods for classification and analysis of multivariate observations. In: Proceedings of 5-th Berkeley Symposium on Mathematical Statistics and Probability, vol. 1, pp. 281–297. University of California Press, Berkeley (1967)

17. Martin, E., Xie, T.: A fault model and mutation testing of access control policies. In: Proceedings of the 16th International Conference on World Wide Web, pp. 667–676. ACM (2007)

18. Menascé, D.A.: Load testing of web sites. IEEE Internet Comput. **6**(4), 70–74 (2002)

19. Offutt, J.: Quality attributes of web software applications. IEEE Softw. **19**(2), 25–32 (2002). doi:10.1109/52.991329

20. Python: Python programming language, October 2012. http://www.python.org/

21. Richardson, L., Ruby, S.: Restful Web Services, 1st edn. O'Reilly, Sebastopol (2007)

22. Schieferdecker, I., Grossmann, J., Schneider, M.: Model-based security testing. In: Proceedings 7th Workshop on Model-Based Testing, MBT 2012, Tallinn, Estonia, 25 March 2012, pp. 1–12 (2012). doi:10.4204/EPTCS.80.1

23. Subraya, B., Subrahmanya, S.: Object driven performance testing of web applications. In: First Asia-Pacific Conference on Quality Software, Proceedings, pp. 17–26. IEEE (2000)

E-Fast & CloudPower: Towards High Performance Technical Analysis for Small Investors

Mircea Moca[1]([⊠]), Darie Moldovan[1], Oleg Lodygensky[2], and Gilles Fedak[3]

[1] Babeş-Bolyai University, Cluj-Napoca, Romania
{Mircea.Moca,Darie.Moldovan}@econ.ubbcluj.ro
[2] Laboratoire de l'Accélérateur Linéaire, Paris, France
oleg.lodygensky@lal.in2p3.fr
[3] INRIA, Université de Lyon, Lyon, France
gilles.fedak@inria.fr

Abstract. About 80 % of the financial market investors fail, the main reason for this being their poor investment decisions. Without advanced financial analysis tools and the knowledge to interpret the analysis, the investors can easily make irrational investment decisions. Moreover, investors are challenged by the dynamism of the market and a relatively large number of indicators that must be computed. In this paper we propose E-Fast, an innovative approach for on-line technical analysis for helping small investors to obtain a greater efficiency on the market by increasing their knowledge. The E-Fast technical analysis platform prototype relies on High Performance Computing (HPC), allowing to rapidly develop and extensively validate the most sophisticated finance analysis algorithms. In this work, we aim at demonstrating that the E-Fast implementation, based on the CloudPower HPC infrastructure, is able to provide small investors a realistic, low-cost and secure service that would otherwise be available only to the large financial institutions. We describe the architecture of our system and provide design insights. We present the results obtained with a real service implementation based on the Exponential Moving Average computational method, using CloudPower and Grid5000 for the computations' acceleration. We also elaborate a set of interesting challenges emerging from this work, as next steps towards high performance technical analysis for small investors.

Keywords: E-Fast · CloudPower · Technical analysis · Moving averages · High Performance Computing

1 Introduction

The nowadays financial markets are amongst the most competitive markets in the world. More, the specific conditions of the financial markets are rapidly changing, so that efficient data analysis, fast and well grounded reactions to market changes, multiple-source market data integration are actual challenges

© Springer International Publishing Switzerland 2016
J. Altmann et al. (Eds.): GECON 2015, LNCS 9512, pp. 236–248, 2016.
DOI: 10.1007/978-3-319-43177-2_16

concerning investors. Obviously, the big players of the market like the large capitalized banks afford to address these challenges by developing and maintaining sophisticated systems relying on modern HPC infrastructures that provide advanced financial analysis capacities. More, they support research departments with specialists that are inter-disciplinary skilled in areas like maths, finance and programming. In contrast, for smaller players that do not have access to the above described resources it is almost impossible to efficiently perform in these market conditions. The poor investment decisions lead to about 80 % of the financial market investors to fail [1].

In this paper we propose E-Fast, an innovative platform prototype for on-line technical analysis for helping small investors to obtain a greater efficiency on the market by increasing their knowledge. The prototype relies on High Performance Computing (HPC), allowing to rapidly develop and extensively validate sophisticated finance analysis algorithms. The novelty stands in the initiative of building a real technical analysis solution based on HPC for helping small investors to cope with hash market challenges. Our approach is designed with the potential of being sustainable through the specific communities' efforts. For instance, we use technologies (like XtremWeb [2] middleware) that allow an easy aggregation of computing resources from the participating individuals.

In this work, we aim at demonstrating that the E-Fast implementation, based on the CloudPower HPC infrastructure, is able to provide small investors a low-cost and meaningful service that would otherwise be available only to the largest finance institutions. We describe the architecture of our system and provide design insights. We also present the results obtained with a real implementation of the Exponential Moving Average computational method, using CloudPower and Grid5000 for the computations' acceleration. We also elaborate a set of interesting challenges emerging from this work and explain our envisioned approach.

Our efforts also come to meet a set of main objectives of the European strategy for the 2014/2020 timeframe [3], focusing on the following three priorities:

- Intelligent and sustainable growth by developing a knowledge and initiative based economy.
- Sustain a competitive and efficient economy that relies on its own resources.
- Social and territorial cohesion support. In this context, direct extensions of our approach can support the building of small investor communities.

The remainder of this paper is organised as follows. Section 2 gives the background of our work, Sect. 3 presents the architecture of the implemented E-Fast prototype, while Sect. 4 presents the experiments run with the prototype and discusses results. Further, Sect. 5 presents related work, Sect. 6 explains relevant future challenges and Sect. 7 concludes this work.

2   Background

In this section we describe the context of our work and define the concepts used in our discussion. In our approach, the user interacts with the system through a set of services. Such a **service** is characterized by:

- Service name,
- Input structure,
- Result (output) structure, and
- Other specific parameters.

The user aims at executing one or more services in order to analyze their specific results. The results can either be directly interpreted by the user or further used into third party analysis tools. The logic of a particular service is given by a stand alone or a mix of **computational method**(s). Examples of methods may be moving averages, genetic algorithms, data-mining algorithms, Monte Carlo simulations and others. For each service, the system expects to a strict definition regarding the input and output data.

A service **execution** is the process of executing the computational method(s) underlying that service on particular input and other user-defined parameters. An execution yields a result (output) with specific semantic and format. The execution is managed by the E-Fast server and may imply the delegation of the effective computational method execution to the HPC infrastructure (see system architecture in Sect. 3.1). The general execution flow for a particular service is detailed in Sect. 3.2.

2.1 Moving Averages

In this work we built a service that is simply defined by the Exponential Moving Average computational method. We chose this method because it is notorious in technical analysis, it is computing intensive, it can be run with a BoT execution approach, and it underlies other indicators like MACD, Price ROC, Momentum, and Stochastic. Forward we give a short description of this method and explain its use in technical analysis.

The employment of moving averages in technical analysis is already a common approach. Their simplicity and efficiency made them successful in industry and economics even before being applied in the financial area. By definition, the moving average (denoted by $MA(k)$) is a method to smooth the variability in time of the analyzed time series by considering the average of the most recent k observations. In technical analysis, to provide a trading signal, two moving averages for the prices of a certain stock are calculated. One of them has a larger number of observations k_l, in order to capture the **long term** trend and the other with a smaller k_s, which is more sensitive to the **recent fluctuations** in price. When the value of the short term moving average passes above the long term moving average, we have a buy signal, suggesting that the price will increase more. On the contrary, when the short term moving average crosses the long term moving average by dropping below its value, it signals sell, forecasting a drop in the price of the stock.

There are several versions of the method, like simple (SMA) and exponential (EMA) [4,5] moving averages. The simple moving average can be criticized because gives the same importance to all considered observations. In contrast, the exponential moving average gives a higher importance to the recent observations, gradually decreasing the importance for the older ones.

The calculation of EMA is given in Eq. 1, where $EMA(k)$ is the exponential moving average calculated for k periods, a is the smoothing constant, showing the importance weight to give to each component and P is the price of the stock at a certain moment in time.

$$EMA(k) = \alpha P_k + \alpha(1-\alpha)P_{k-1} + \alpha(1-\alpha)^2 P_{k-2} + \cdots + \alpha(1-\alpha)^{k-1}P_1 \quad (1)$$

The moving averages can be used in technical analysis to calculate trading signals (buy or sell). For this, the moving average must be calculated twice, with different values for k. We call long term EMA (EMA_l) the one calculated on a bigger k and short term EMA (EMA_s) the other one.

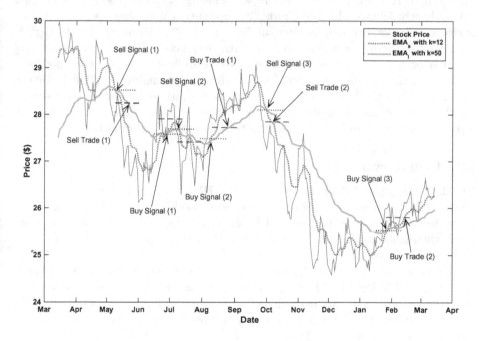

Fig. 1. Stock price, and computed moving averages and signals.

For a better understanding of using EMA in this context, in the following we provide an example, depicted in Fig. 1. For a particular stock, we show the calculated moving averages and the buy/sell signals, also marking the trading points. The chart contains data from March 2012 to March 2013 on the stock price of Microsoft, where $k = 12$ for EMA_s and $k = 50$ for EMA_l. We marked every intersection between the lines of the EMAs with a dot line. Depending on the stock's behavior on the market, this method can yield a large number of buy/sell signals. In practice, not all of the generated signals are worthy to be considered. Hence, in order to avoid noisy trading signals, generated by two or more very close in time crossovers between the two lines, we used a supplementary filter (represented by the dash line). Only when EMA_s passes the filter, a trade is generated. We also mention that our strategy permits both long and short positions and we do not discuss the profitability of this particular example.

Going into detail, we notice that the first signal (in May 2012) is a sell signal. The transaction Sell Trade (1) only occurs after the value of the EMA_s dropped below the filter value. After this transaction, we own a short position. Next we have the Sell Signal (2), which does not lead to a trade since EMA_s doesn't surpasses the filter. Forward, another sell signal is generated, but even if the value of EMA_s went bellow the filter value, the signal is ignored since we already own a short position (and we wait for a buy signal). The following signal, Buy Signal (2) flags the opportunity to buy, which occurs at the moment showed by Buy Trade (1) arrow, in this way closing the short position. Sell Signal (3) is shortly followed by Sell Trade (2), opening a new short position, which is closed only several months later, at Buy Trade (2). Although the strategy is quite simple, finding efficient values for its parameters (like k, the smoothing factor α or the size of the noise filter) can be difficult. In fact, they are very sensitive to the trends inside the analyzed time series, making it difficult for the investor to find the best solution. For this reason, an almost exhaustive search for the best parameter combinations for a strategy that works usually only for a particular stock can be very costly in terms of computational time.

2.2   CloudPower

Big Data and High Performance Computing (HPC) are key factors in knowledge and innovation in many fields of industry and service, with high economic and social issues: aerospace, finance and business intelligence, energy and environment, chemicals and materials, medicine and biology, digital art and games, Web and social networks.

Today, acquiring high-end data centers and supercomputers is very expensive, making Big Data and HPC unreachable to small business for their research and development. For reasons both technical and economic, access to such technologies is difficult to fundamental actors of growth that are small and medium-sized innovative companies. That is why it is important to support them in this process. This a fundamental tool for competitiveness and innovation capacity of service and industry enterprises.

The CloudPower project offers a low cost Cloud HPC/BigData service for small and medium-sized innovative companies. With CloudPower, companies and scientists will run their simulations to design and develop new products on a powerful, scalable, economical, reliable and secure infrastructure. CloudPower leverages on the open-source software XtremWeb-HEP previously developed by the CNRS and INRIA in France. The principle of the technology is to collect the under-exploited resources on the Internet and Data Centers to build a virtual supercomputer providing HPC and Big Data services on demand. CloudPower is supported by the French National Research Agency (ANR).

3   The E-Fast Prototype

In this section we give a detailed description of the proposed E-Fast prototype, focusing on its architecture as well as the service definition and execution.

3.1   System Architecture

In this subsection we present the architecture of the implemented E-Fast prototype. This mainly contains three components: the E-Fast client and server and the distributed computing infrastructure.

Figure 2 depicts the architecture of the prototype. First, the E-Fast client runs on the users' machines and allows them to connect to the E-Fast server and *consume* its services. This is a web interface that allows the client to set up the parameters of the execution and to inspect and analyze the results obtained from the executions. Based on the execution parameters received from client, the server extracts the appropriate input data from the database and transfers it to the distributed computing infrastructure. Then, it delegates to the infrastructure the execution of the service on the respective input data. After receiving the results from the infrastructure, the server composes the final result from a user's perspective and delivers it through the client. The database managed by the server mainly contains: financial market historical data, results of the executions and execution meta data.

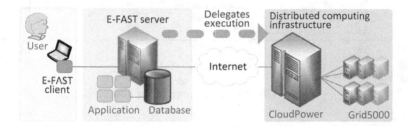

Fig. 2. Overview of the E-Fast prototype architecture.

3.2   Service Execution Flow

In this subsection, we detail the overall approach for a service execution. Figure 3 presents the general execution flow for a particular service. The process begins with the user, specifying the execution parameters through the E-Fast client. Based on these parameters the E-Fast server makes the decision whether to start a new execution or directly deliver the results corresponding to the received parameters. The direct delivery would occur when the user has already performed an execution for the same parameters. If it's not this case, the E-Fast server selects from the database the appropriate input data (according to the computational method defining the required service and the user's preferences). Forward, according to the computation distribution strategy of the service, the server creates a set of input files and uploads them to CloudPower. Then, the server starts the execution of the service by creating and launching a job on the DCI for each input file. After a while, the E-Fast server receives the results from CloudPower, aggregates them into a final result and presents them to the user within the E-Fast client.

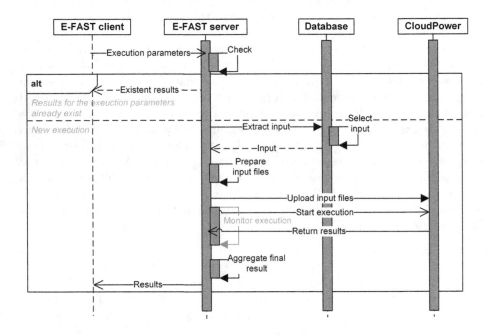

Fig. 3. General service execution flow.

3.3   Computational Method Distribution

As discussed in Sect. 1, the computational methods used in technical analysis are generally computational intensive. In this sense, our implementation relies on CloudPower for accelerating the service execution. This is capable of executing bag of tasks, these being independent one from another. In this context, for any given computational method, this aspect brings the challenge of defining a **computation distribution strategy**. This is significantly determined by the method's definition, so when a high execution performance (i.e. in terms of makespan) of the service must be attained, then the distribution strategy may be critical. In this case, it must be tailored to the method's definition. In the following we call **distribution criterion** a concept based on which a system designer defines the distribution strategy.

Since the Moving Averages are computed on a single stock at a time and the obtained results are independent from those of other stocks, we chose the stock to be the distribution criterion. Hence, our implementation executes the computational method on time series, separately for each stock. For example, if the user wants to calculate the rentability of the $S\&P500$ index, then the system runs a task for each stock from the whole set of 502 stocks (this is our experimental data and it is described in Sect. 4).

For each execution, the user specifies a time series from the available historical data. The real execution time of the service on a specific machine from the HPC infrastructure depends on the size of the specified time series. From this perspective, if one aims at optimizing the execution, then the distribution strategy can be changed - i.e. execute a task on a set of stocks, not only a single one. By this, a system designer could adjust the average real execution time of a task in order to fit the HPC infrastructure's requirements in terms of optimality.

3.4 Service Architecture

In our approach, the functionality of a service is organized in two components: the **technical** and the **business** layers. While the technical layer implements one or more computational methods, the business layer computes business key-values (like profit), with direct utility for the financial analyst, based on the technical layer's output. Figure 4 depicts the service layers and parameter types.

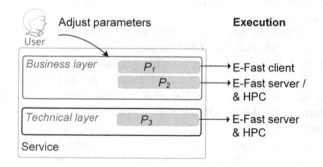

Fig. 4. Service architecture overview.

For a better understanding, we explain the parameter types that characterize the service directly referring to the Moving Averages method. Hence, the layers contain the following parameter types:

- P_1 is a parameter type that directly affects the execution of the service on E-Fast client side. For instance, the user may vary the commission value applied to the gross profit. These computations have low complexity and can be directly supported by the E-Fast client and the input data is directly available on the E-Fast server.

– P_2 has direct impact on business but the implied computations are more complex compared to those of P_1, so they need to be performed by the E-Fast server with the eventual delegation to the HPC infrastructure. Such a parameter would be the filter used to compute the effective transactions based on the signals provided by the Moving Averages method. The adjustment of the filter may lead to a significantly different number of transactions, making the service more sensitive to the stock's volatility. Consequently, more transactions lead to a greater absolute value of the calculated trading fees. Hence, the impact of this parameter is important.
– P_3 is specific to the technical layer and is related to the optimization of the computational method and generally requires the E-Fast server to coordinate the execution on the HPC infrastructure. For instance, finding optimal k_s and k_l values for the Moving Average method and particular market data implies the a costly execution of the service for a relevant set of k_s and k_l combinations on the HPC infrastructure.

4   Experiments and Results

In this section we present the execution of the implemented service in order to illustrate its use in practice.

The **experimental data** used in this work was historical market data of the companies composing the S&P500 index for the 2006–2014 period. This is one of the major indices in the United States, covering around 75 % of the equity market by capitalization. It comprises 502 stocks for which we collected daily pricing information.

In order to obtain the best parameters for the Exponential Moving Average trading strategy, one execution of the E-Fast service computes for one stock from S&P500 the return based on EMA for all combinations of k. More specifically, $k_s = \{2, 3, 4 \ldots 50\}$ and $k_l = \{4, 6, 8, \ldots 100\}$. This setup led us to a number of 496 603 profitability calculations for the whole S&P500 index. In our experiments we used the same noise filter value, but in a real system, the user must be able to tune this parameter.

Our main success criterion was the profit obtained by each combination. When calculating the profit we used the same percentage fees per trade to be extracted from the results of each sell-buy pair. Other criteria that can be used for evaluating the performance of a trading strategy can be used, depending on the investment objectives. Such criteria can be the maximum drawdown (the maximum loss of a strategy during its life), number of profitable trades/all trades, risk adjusted return, Sharpe ratio etc.

We compared the results obtained with our trading strategies against the buy and hold strategy on the S&P500 index. While the total return for the S&P500 for the entire analyzed period was a profit of 61.84 %, the results of our strategies show a profit of 77.3 %. Table 1 shows the returns obtained by the best 5 groups of strategies. We observe that there are several k_s and k_l combinations yielding significant returns, the differences among them being relevant. This demonstrates the importance of finding and using the right parameters for a certain strategy.

Table 1. Return for top 5 groups of strategies.

Strategy group	1	2	3	4	5
Return	77.3 %	73.7 %	71.3 %	69.6 %	68.5 %

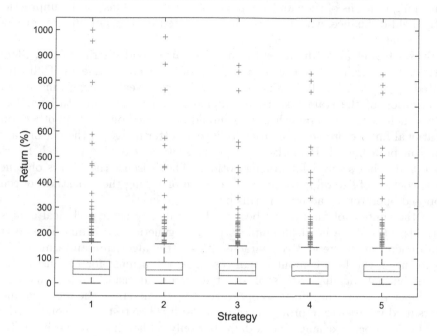

Fig. 5. Returns distribution for the S&P500 index.

In Fig. 5 we show the distribution of the obtained returns. We note that all strategies obtained positive returns, some of them with outstanding positive performance. These performances can be filtered and used as main target investments by the investors. Although they are shown as outliers, they are actually the most important strategies, the ones that provide the highest returns. For example, the best strategy for the Apple stock (AAPL) is obtained using the short term moving average with $k_s = 14$, long term moving average with $k_l = 52$ and a filter of 0.15 %. While the main focus in our work is to show how E-Fast &CloudPower can be used together for solving computational intensive financial problems, we did not focus on refining and optimizing the business results.

In practice, the methods can be optimized by periodically running the service (e.g. weekly), so that it adapts to new, recent market data. Then, the user may retain the best parameter combination till next analysis.

5   Related Work

The literature in the field of distributed and parallel computing in finance is not very rich in terms of diversity. Most of the related work is focused on solving particular computational finance problems involving Monte Carlo models for derivative pricing. Since the Black and Scholes [6] model was introduced, it was widely used, along with others, to compute derivatives prices. The iterative character of the method (usually it can reach 1 million runs) can be very consuming in terms of time and computation resources. This can be unpractical in the field of finance, where the result is expected in terms of minutes or close to real time.

Stokes-Res et al. [7] discusses the parallelization and distribution of Monte Carlo option pricing in the context of several grid environments. Difficulties related to running parallel tasks on the grid were revealed, consisting in synchronization of the start task time and partitioning the computational load. They conclude that several other tests should be carried on this and other computational finance problems in order to have a better image on the performance that can be achieved. Heinecke et al. [8] presents a scalable approach for the Black and Scholes solver for pricing options. They discuss the results obtained in the context of several hardware solutions, emphasizing the robustness of their proposed operator for addressing this particular issue.

In the context of finding the best trading rules by using technical analysis methods, Strassburg et al. [9] employs parallel genetic algorithms. Due to the data dimension, the repetitive characteristics of the algorithm and time-critical answer need, the high computational resources are a must for the institutions and individuals dealing with sophisticated trading decision support methods. The paper presents the efforts to optimize the parameters of the technical indicators used in order to improve the trading results. The tests were conducted on the Madrid Stock Exchange Index data, but only on holding long positions (not allowing short selling) aiming to demonstrate the usefulness of the parallel approach. However, the tests were made on a single machine with four cores, limiting the conclusions to this closed environment. A solution to reduce the computation time for intensive operations in financial analysis was proposed by Moreno and Balch [10]. They built a disk memoization solution to reduce repeated computations, allowing the analysts to build and debug their algorithms more quickly.

A new automated trading system architecture was introduced by Freitas et al. [11], who considers dividing the trading problem into several tasks handled by distributed autonomous agents, with minimal central coordination. Their strategy is based on obtaining a consensus trading signal based on other trading signals from multiple strategies. The results were considered very satisfactory after testing moving average crossover strategies on a large database.

6   Future Challenges

The work so far consisted in building the E-Fast prototype equipped with a first service based on the Exponential Moving Averages computational method. From both - technical and financial perspectives, the aim was to proof the concept of providing advanced technical analysis services based on distributed computing, for small investors. These achievements led us to a set of interesting challenges and motivates us to build further on this concept. Relevant developments are:

- Building **service composition mechanisms** that allow the user to combine several services in order to obtain advanced knowledge on the market. The interesting aspect of the services in this context is that based on the same market data, several computational methods can be applied in order to obtain similar or **complementary visions** and understanding of the market's behavior. For instance, the user can execute two services in order to obtain results with similar semantic but computed with different methods. In this case, the aim would be to compare the different results obtained for particular input data and assess a **degree of confidence** in them. In other situations, the user might be interested in **combining** two or more **services** by running them and using their outputs together in order to understand the market from different perspectives.
- Building advanced **collaboration mechanisms** to allow the different stakeholders work together and obtain synergy. As mentioned, players on the financial market need high expertise in fields like mathematics, finance and technical/computer science. In this sense we aim at building mechanisms that allow users to **share their resources** (i.e. computing, knowledge, expertise, skills). By this we aim at facilitating the crowding of mutually interested specialists, small investors and resource owners.
- Optimizing the prototype from two perspectives. For each service, from a technical viewpoint, the system designer should optimally decide the computations performed within the two technical and business layers of the service (presented in Sect. 3.4). This is very challenging, since the design decision is specific to each computational method. More, the solution must take into account the specifics of the HPC infrastructure and, at the same time be parametric, in order to allow the user to choose amongst several service flavours. From a financial perspective, the system must keep services up-to-date from a business viewpoint. As explained in Sect. 4, optimal key-parameter values must be found for a computational method in order to efficiently adapt to the recent market behavior. In this sense, the challenge would be to build fully or quasi-automatic mechanisms that keep the services up-to-date and adapt to market fluctuations.

7 Conclusions

In this paper, we proposed E-FAST, a service prototype for on-line technical analysis that can support small investors to obtain a greater efficiency on the market by increasing their knowledge. In this work we created a prototype that relies on High Performance Computing (HPC). This allows one to rapidly develop and extensively validate sophisticated finance analysis algorithms. We aimed at demonstrating that E-Fast based on the CloudPower HPC infrastructure is able to provide small investors a scalable, low-cost and secure service that would otherwise be available only to the largest financial institutions. We presented the architecture of our system. We also presented the results obtained with a real implementation of the Exponential Moving Average computational method, using CloudPower and Grid5000 for the computations' acceleration. Finally we presented a set of interesting challenges emerging from this work and describe our approach to address them.

Acknowledgements. This work was partially supported by project with number PN-II-PT-PCCA-2013-4-1644.

References

1. Barber, B.M., Odean, T.: The behavior of individual investors (Chap. 22). In: Handbook of the Economics of Finance, vol. 2, Part B, pp. 1533–1570. Elsevier, Amsterdam (2013)
2. Fedak, G., Germain, C., Neri, V., Cappello, F.: Xtremweb: a generic global computing system. In: Proceedings of First IEEE/ACM International Symposium on Cluster Computing and the Grid (CCGRD 2001), Australia, pp. 582–587. IEEE (2001)
3. European Commission: Europe 2020 - a strategy for smart, sustainable and inclusive growth. Technical report (2010)
4. Holt, C.C.: Forecasting seasonals and trends by exponentially weighted moving averages. Int. J. Forecast. **20**(1), 5–10 (2004)
5. Cox, D.R.: Prediction by exponentially weighted moving averages and related methods. J.R. Stat. Soc. Ser. B **23**(2), 414–422 (1961)
6. Black, F., Scholes, M.: The pricing of options and corporate liabilities. J. Polit. Econ. 637–654 (1973)
7. Stokes-Ress, I., Baude, F., Doan, V.D., Bossy, M.: Managing parallel and distributed monte carlo simulations for computational finance in a grid environment. In: Lin, S.C., Yen, E. (eds.) Grid Computing, pp. 183–204. Springer, Berlin (2009)
8. Heinecke, A., Jepsen, J., Bungartz, H.J.: Many-core architectures boost the pricing of basket options on adaptive sparse grids. In: Proceedings of 6th Workshop on High Performance Computational Finance, p. 1. ACM (2013)
9. Strassburg, J., Gonzalez-Martel, C., Alexandrov, V.: Parallel genetic algorithms for stock market trading rules. Procedia Comput. Sci. **9**, 1306–1313 (2012). Proceedings of International Conference on Computational Science, ICCS 2012
10. Moreno, A., Balch, T.: Speeding up large-scale financial recomputation with memoization. In: Proceedings of 7th Workshop on High Performance Computational Finance, WHPCF 2014, Piscataway, NJ, USA, pp. 17–22. IEEE Press (2014)
11. Freitas, F.D., Freitas, C.D., De Souza, A.F.: System architecture for on-line optimization of automated trading strategies. In: Proceedings of 6th Workshop on High Performance Computational Finance, WHPCF 2013, USA, pp. 4:1–4:8. ACM (2013)

Community Networks

Towards Incentive-Compatible Pricing for Bandwidth Reservation in Community Network Clouds

Amin M. Khan[1,2(✉)], Xavier Vilaça[2], Luís Rodrigues[2], and Felix Freitag[1]

[1] Department of Computer Architecture,
Universitat Politècnica de Catalunya, Barcelona, Spain
{mkhan,felix}@ac.upc.edu
[2] Instituto Superior Técnico, Universidade de Lisboa INESC-ID Lisboa,
Lisbon, Portugal
{xvilaca,ler}@tecnico.ulisboa.pt

Abstract. Community network clouds provide for applications of local interest deployed within community networks through collaborative efforts to provision cloud infrastructures. They complement the traditional large-scale public cloud providers similar to the model of decentralised edge clouds by bringing both content and computation closer to the users at the edges of the network. Services and applications within community network clouds require connectivity to the Internet and to the resources external to the community network, and here the current best-effort model of volunteers contributing gateway access in the community networks falls short. We model the problem of reserving the bandwidth at such gateways for guaranteeing quality-of-service for the cloud applications, and evaluate different pricing mechanisms for their suitability in ensuring maximal social welfare and eliciting truthful requests from the users. We find second-price auction based mechanisms, including Vickrey and generalised second price auctions, suitable for the bandwidth allocation problem at the gateways in the community networks.

Keywords: Community clouds · Community networks · Auctions · Resource allocation

1 Introduction

Community network clouds represent efforts to collaboratively build cloud infrastructures in the community networks [1,2], extending the ideas from the volunteer computing model to community cloud computing [12]. Community networks are a successful example of social collective for building ICT infrastructure for the communities in a bottom-up fashion, for instance Guifi.net, currently the largest community network in the world, connects more than 28,000 locations (nodes) with wireless and optical fibre links [1]. Other examples of successful community networks include Athens Wireless Metropolitan Network (AWMN) in Greece, Freifunk in Germany, FunkFeuer in Austria, and Ninux in Italy.

© Springer International Publishing Switzerland 2016
J. Altmann et al. (Eds.): GECON 2015, LNCS 9512, pp. 251–264, 2016.
DOI: 10.1007/978-3-319-43177-2_17

Community network clouds build on this success of community networks and aim to provide services and applications of local interest for the communities by applying the model cloud computing. They fit nicely with the recent shift in exploring alternative approaches to large-scale data centres based public cloud computing, which include Inter-Cloud and federated clouds (where multiple public cloud providers work together), hybrid clouds (where enterprises combine their own cloud infrastructure with the public clouds), multi-clouds (where applications procure services from different public cloud providers), community clouds (where dedicated infrastructure is provided for a specific community), and edge clouds using nano data centres [14] (where smaller clusters are deployed at the edges of the network to avoid latency and improve content-delivery). These initiatives provide an excellent backdrop to explore the role of the community network clouds in enhancing the value proposition of the community networks, since an infrastructure of nano data centres [14] to be deployed in a community network has to fit well with specific socio-economic and technical context of the community networks [10]. Figure 1 shows how such an edge cloud can be deployed within a community network. The servers are present at different locations, either caching content for media-rich applications or performing computation locally for time-critical applications, and which require connection to the data centres through the Internet, for which they rely on the gateway providers available in the community network [1].

When cloud applications are deployed within community networks, in many cases connectivity external to the community network is important. In the basic case, cloud applications may want to backup or synchronise data with servers external to the community network, or require fetching data for operating the service, for instance a video-on-demand service may download fresh content. Also, a service available in multiple community networks requires access at the gateways for exchanging data, and gateways in this case act to federate the community networks. Applications from Internet of Things and smart cities involve collecting data from the sensors, which may have to be shared with servers outside the community network for data analysis. For the case of edge clouds, the servers residing within the community networks, acting as nano data centres, require connectivity to the data centres. In all these situations, the applications deployed on servers within the community network require bandwidth at the gateways with quality-of-service (QoS) guarantees to connect to the Internet, though their requirements for prioritising, robustness, waiting time, and throughput, may vary for different scenarios.

Various mechanisms have been extensively studied in the literature for pricing bandwidth in wireless networks, including application of game theory and auctions [11]. These concepts include static pricing approaches, like fixed usage-based pricing where all users are charged the same amount per unit of bandwidth, and priority pricing where users pay differently according to the priority class of the requests, and dynamic market-based pricing mechanisms, which can be based on auctions like sealed first-price, generalised second price (GSP) [7], and Vickrey–Clarke–Groves (VCG) auctions [5]. In this paper, we study these pricing

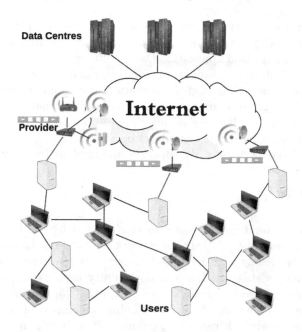

Fig. 1. Users connected to the service provider's gateway in a community network.

mechanisms with the goals of maximising social welfare (maximum utility for maximum number of users), and truthfulness (users declare their true valuation to the provider). Of the above mechanisms, only VCG ensures maximum social welfare as well as truthfulness [13], as long as the optimal allocation of resources can be computed in polynomial time. In practice, however, many resource allocation problems involve combinatorial optimisation and are NP-Hard, so often approximation [19] or heuristics [5] based approaches are employed which guarantee truthfulness but not maximal social welfare.

Recent work has explored auctions for incentivizing bandwidth sharing in community networks [18,21], and allocating bandwidth in public clouds [5,15,20] and grid systems [4]. However, the problem of bandwidth allocation for applications in community network clouds has largely been unexplored to the best of our knowledge. In community network clouds, there are multiple independent bandwidth providers with no centralised control, and, moreover, the users are connected to the providers through a multi-hop community network (in contrast to the dedicated networks within large-scale data centres). Community networks are a social collective [16], where most resources are contributed on a volunteer and reciprocal basis. The gateways provide access to the Internet on a best-effort basis, so providing guaranteed bandwidth to cloud applications is critical to the successful operation of cloud applications deployed in community network clouds.

Our contribution in this paper is showing the applicability of decentralised edge clouds model [14] to the community network clouds, and framing the problem of bandwidth reservation at the gateways as crucial for cloud applications to function and flourish in community network clouds. We provide a model that differentiates between cloud applications with different priority classes, and use this model to evaluate the suitability of different pricing mechanisms in the literature to the problem of bandwidth reservation in community network clouds.

The rest of the paper is organised as follows. We relate our work to the state-of-the-art in Sect. 2. We present our model in Sect. 3 for analysing different pricing mechanisms for reserving bandwidth, and in Sect. 4, we evaluate them through simulation experiments. We conclude and indicate future work in Sect. 5.

2   Related Work

Community clouds built using resources contributed by the community have garnered interest recently [12], with most work focusing on the exchange of virtualised resources. Along with incentives-based resource regulation for providing and consuming virtual machines in community network clouds [8,9], other approaches have focused on social cloud computing [3] to share storage and computation resources among the users of online social networks.

In respect of bandwidth resources, community networks require incentives as communication relies on cooperation among the users. The recent literature has modelled this in non-cooperative game theory [18,21]. Community networks solve this problem to a large extent through social mechanisms like enforcing reciprocal sharing agreements [1]. Bandwidth reservation has also been under focus recently in the grid systems [4], and in public clouds, both for internal bandwidth within data centre networks [6], and external bandwidth [5,15,20] to the Internet.

Our work differs since we assume the co-operation among users because of the social institution of community networks, so traffic from other nodes is guaranteed to transit on the intermediary nodes. This also follows from the fact that the bandwidth available within community networks is not priced, and is symmetric, i.e. upstream capacity is same as downstream, and under normal use sharing does not incur costs for the node owners [1]. Non-cooperative users are either excluded from the system, or correct their behaviour because they are penalised by the community. We focus on the cloud applications that are deployed in community network cloud, which can be bandwidth-intensive generating significant traffic flows within the community network, but also require guaranteed and stable connection to the Internet through the gateways in the community network.

3   System Model

We consider a bandwidth provider $\mathbb{P}$ in the community network and a set of N users $\{1, 2, \ldots N\}$. The provider operates a gateway to the Internet, allowing access external to the community network to the users. The users are connected to the provider's gateway through the wireless and fibre links in the community network [1], and the applications in community network cloud access their external servers and Internet through this gateway. Figure 1 shows the users in the community network connected to the provider through multiple such paths, where only few of these users are the clients of the provider for reserving bandwidth.

The provider processes the requests in a queue at the gateway, where time in the queue is divided into an infinite sequence of slots starting from 1, where all the available bandwidth is allocated to exactly one user in each slot. The provider allocates the slots in batch after receiving all the requests from N users and assigns the next N slots, one to each user.

For the sake of simplicity, we divide the users into two priority classes, $h \in \{0,1\}$, some have lower priority requests, h_0, and some have higher priority requests, h_1. Here in this model, the main consideration for higher priority requests is that they are more sensitive to the waiting time, and prefer to reserve earlier slots in the queue. Provider $\mathbb{P}$ aims for an optimal schedule when allocating the slots to the users, so as to maximize its revenue and the overall utility for all the users. We provide formal details below:

- **Schedule**: A schedule ϕ maps each time slot t to a user i.
- **Value**: For any schedule ϕ and user i, let t be the slot assigned to user i, then $v_i(h,t)$ is the valuation given by i being allocated for time slot t, where $h \in \{0,1\}$ is the priority class of the user. v_i is communicated by each i to $\mathbb{P}$ beforehand.
- **Utility**: For any schedule ϕ which assigns user i a slot t, the utility $u_i(\phi,t)$ for user i is difference between the value v_i and the payment $p_i(\phi,t)$ made by user i to $\mathbb{P}$.

$$u_i(\phi,t) = v_i(h,t) - p_i(h,t) \tag{1}$$

- **Restriction**: Any slot t can be assigned to at most one user.
- **Optimization**: Find ϕ that maximizes the social welfare, which is the sum of utilities u_i of all users, while fulfilling the restrictions.

$$\text{maximise } welfare(\phi) = \sum_{i \in N} u_i(\phi,t) \tag{2}$$

- **Scheduler**: Function S that maps $\boldsymbol{u} = (u_i)_{i \in N}$ to optimal ϕ.
- **Goal**: A user i when submitting the request to $\mathbb{P}$, declares the priority class h_i and value v_i, and also the bid amount b_i where applicable. When the user behaves truthfully the reported value v_i^* is the same as her inherent value v_i. We want to ensure that it is truthful for every i to declare her true value of v_i, regardless of the declared values v_j for any $j \neq i$. Such a mechanism is said to be truthful in dominant strategy, where users have no incentive to misreport their values [13].

3.1   Pricing Mechanisms

Given the above model, the prices are calculated for the bandwidth usage according to different mechanisms [11].

Fixed Pricing. In the case of fixed usage-based pricing, all the users pay the identical price c_0 for each unit of bandwidth consumed, which is constant irrespective of the priority class.

Priority Pricing. In the case of priority pricing, users pay according to the priority class h. Since in our model, there are only two priority classes h_0 and h_1, provider $\mathbb{P}$ charges two different prices c_{h_0} and c_{h_1} per unit of bandwidth, respectively.

First-Price Auction. In the case of sealed first-price auction, users make different bids b_i depending on their priority class h, with high priority requests quoting higher bid amounts in general. Each winning user pays their bid amount.

$$p_i(\phi, t) = b_i \tag{3}$$

Generalised Second Price (GSP) Auction. In a generalised second price (GSP) auction [7], users make different bids b_i but in this case the winning user pays the amount corresponding to the next highest bidder. So the user with the highest bid, pays the amount of the second highest bidder, the second highest bidder pays the amount of the third highest bidder and so on.

Vickrey-Clarke-Groves (VCG) Auction. VCG is a second-price sealed-bid auction based mechanism, which ensures truthfulness and maximum social welfare [13], if the provider $\mathbb{P}$ can calculate optimal schedule ϕ in polynomial time. Each user i provides a bid b_i to $\mathbb{P}$, and given a schedule ϕ, each user i pays the price $p_i(\phi, t)$ according to:

$$p_i(\phi, t) = \sum_{\substack{j!=i \\ j \in N}} (v_j(h, \phi') - b_j) - \sum_{\substack{j!=i \\ j \in N}} (v_j(h, \phi) - b_j) \tag{4}$$

where ϕ and ϕ' are the schedules that maximise $\sum_{i \in N} u_i$ while including and excluding the bid b_i by user i from the allocation respectively.

3.2   Scheduling Algorithm

We consider a simple scheduling algorithm which applies a greedy approach for mapping users' requests to the available slots. Algorithm 1 shows the scheduling algorithm, where $\mathbb{P}$ assigns the slots to the users in non-increasing order of their

---

Algorithm 1. Scheduling algorithm for ϕ, allocating $\overrightarrow{t}$ slots to N users

---

Input: List of users $\overrightarrow{n}$, bids $\overrightarrow{b}$, for total N users
Output: List of assigned slots $\overrightarrow{t}$, and payments $\overrightarrow{p}$
1: Sort $\overrightarrow{n}$ users in non-increasing order on their bids $\overrightarrow{b}$
2: **for** $i = 1, \ldots N$ **do**
3:     $\overrightarrow{t}[i] \leftarrow i$ ▷ Assign slots
4: **end for**
5: **for** $i = 1, \ldots N$ **do**
6:     $\overrightarrow{p}[i] \leftarrow payment(\overrightarrow{b}[i], \overrightarrow{t}[i])$ ▷ Calculate payments
7: **end for**

---

reported bids (and corresponding h_i and v_i) for the bandwidth resource. The prices calculated are dependent on the pricing mechanism, the priority class h of the requests, and the assigned slot t in the schedule ϕ. The runtime of the algorithm is $\mathcal{O}(N \log N)$ for N users, however, VCG mechanism requires computing N schedules for calculating payments for the N winning bids, so the running time in the case of VCG is $\mathcal{O}(N^2 \log N)$.

The greedy approach, in general, does not always provide an optimal allocation, which is a pre-requisite for VCG mechanism. However, in the case of the model given above and considering the step function we are going to use for $v_i(h, t)$ from Fig. 2, the greedy approach from Algorithm 1 always returns an optimal allocation. This can be proven through induction, and can be explained intuitively as choosing the requests with higher bids first (corresponding to higher h_i and v_i) always gives the maximum social welfare, since the value function in Fig. 2 is non-increasing with time and choosing a bid with lower amount causes a loss in social welfare which can't be recovered as the time progresses.

4   Performance Evaluation

We conduct the simulation experiments using the multi-agent programmable modelling environment NetLogo [17]. In all the experiments, we consider a single provider and 500 users. We run the experiments for 1000 rounds, and plot the average values in the graphs.

For different pricing mechanisms (as explained in Sect. 3.1), we use the following values. For fixed pricing, we set $c_0 = 0.5$. For priority pricing, we set $c_{h_0} = 0.25$ and $c_{h_1} = 0.75$. For auctions based pricing, the bids for lower priority requests h_0 are uniformly distributed in the range $[0.25, 0.5]$, while the bids for higher priority requests h_1 are uniformly distributed in the range $(0.5, 0.75]$. For differentiating between the two priority classes, we choose different time-utility functions (TUF), which in this case we have chosen as step functions for simplicity. According to this step function, the value $v_i(h, t)$, based on priority class h and slot t in schedule ϕ, decreases for both higher and lower priority classes after a threshold $t_0 = \frac{N}{2}$, as shown in Fig. 2. Specifically, for lower priority class h_0:

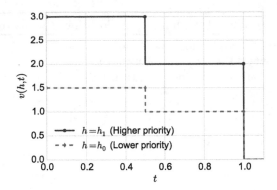

Fig. 2. Value function $v_i(h, t)$ for user i based on priority class h and slot t in schedule.

$$v_i(h_0, t) = \begin{cases} 1.5 & \text{if } t \leq \frac{N}{2} \\ 1 & \text{if } \frac{N}{2} < t \leq N \end{cases} \tag{5}$$

And for high priority class h_1:

$$v_i(h_1, t) = \begin{cases} 3 & \text{if } t \leq \frac{N}{2} \\ 2 & \text{if } \frac{N}{2} < t \leq N \end{cases} \tag{6}$$

Each user i submits exactly one request to $\mathbb{P}$, declaring her priority class h_i, value v_i, and bid amount b_i where applicable. Both the priority classes, h_0 and h_1 occur with the same probability, so almost half of the requests are of higher priority, and the rest are of lower priority. We model lying behaviour of the users, by randomly flipping their reported priority class h to $\mathbb{P}$, according to a uniform distribution. When the users lie, we observe the normalized difference from the case where all the users are truthful. Here, $u_i^*(\phi, t)$ indicates the case where the users lie to $\mathbb{P}$, and $u_i(\phi, t)$ where all the users are truthful.

$$\Delta \; welfare = \frac{\sum\limits_{i \in N} u_i^*(\phi, t) - \sum\limits_{i \in N} u_i(\phi, t)}{\sum\limits_{i \in N} u_i(\phi, t)} \tag{7}$$

Figure 3 shows how social welfare is affected when the probability of a user misreporting her value to $\mathbb{P} - p(lying)$ – increases up to the point where 90 % of the users may be lying. As expected, social welfare decreases as the probability of lying increases, since $\mathbb{P}$ fails to allocate better slots for higher priority requests. All the pricing schemes behave similarly as the proportion of lying users increases, except VCG which performs marginally better in that social welfare is slightly higher for VCG as compared to the other schemes. This shows the importance of encouraging truthful behaviour in the users for maximising social welfare.

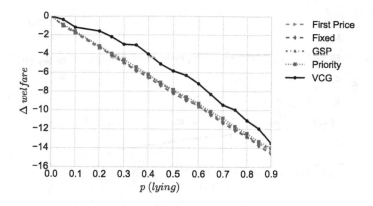

Fig. 3. Percentage difference in social welfare as more users lie.

To understand how the pricing mechanisms incentivize truthfulness for different priority classes, in the next experiment we look at the normalised difference in utility for an individual user (on average), separately for h_0 and h_1. Here again, $u_i^*(\phi, t)$ is the individual utility when some of the users lie, and $u_i(\phi, t)$ is when all the users are truthful.

$$\Delta \ utility = \frac{u_i^*(\phi, t) - u_i(\phi, t)}{u_i(\phi, t)} \tag{8}$$

Figure 4 shows the percentage difference in the average utility for all the users with low priority requests. Note that this average is over all the users in h_0, and not only those who lie. Users from h_0 may lie in order to get higher value (through reserving an earlier slot), hoping to still pay as less as possible. Figure 4 shows that for fixed usage-based price, they do gain in utility since they are paying the same amount for a better service. For priority pricing, they gain nothing as any gains in utility are offset by the higher price. For first price and GSP auctions, the results are similar and there are gains due to lying, though less than those in the case of the fixed price. The first price and GSP auctions behave similarly since expected payments are same in the first and second price auctions, when the bids are independent and identically distributed [11], as is the case in this experiment. VCG performs better since the utility decreases when the users lie.

Figure 5 shows the percentage difference in the average utility for all the users with high priority requests. Note that this average is over all the users in h_1, and not only those who lie. Users from h_1 may lie in order to save on their payments, with the hope that they can still get the same value (through keeping their earlier slot). Figure 4 shows that users from h_1, in general, lose by lying since there is little chance that $\mathbb{P}$ will assign earlier slots to the users declaring low priority to $\mathbb{P}$. So even though they save on the payments, the decrease in value because of getting assigned later slots results in net loss for users from h_1.

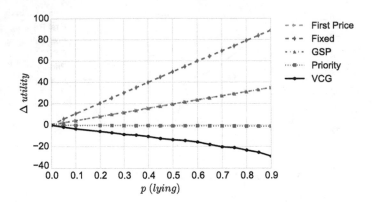

Fig. 4. Percentage difference in utility for low priority class h_0.

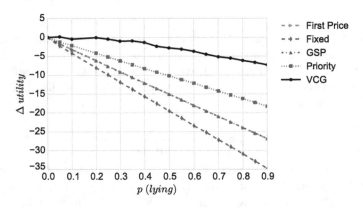

Fig. 5. Percentage difference in utility for high priority class h_1.

In the next experiment, we look specifically at the utility for the users that report untruthful values to $\mathbb{P}$, to see the maximum gain they can get in the utility under different pricing mechanisms. Figure 6 shows the maximum gain in utility a user from h_0 can get as the number of lying users increases. Note that in this case we pick only the maximum utility for a user from h_0 that is lying, averaged across all the experiment runs. The results are similar to what we observed earlier in Fig. 4.

Similarly, Fig. 7 shows the maximum gain in utility a user from h_1 can obtain through lying. We noticed in Fig. 5 that on average the users from h_1 do not gain through lying, but here we see that for all the pricing mechanisms except VCG, the utility for a lying user with high priority request increases with increase in the number of lying users, though the net gain is not significant. For VCG, the number of lying users does not have much impact, and the loss in utility for the lying user remains almost the same. Moreover, first price and GSP auctions perform better than priority pricing here. The user can have a net gain in utility by misreporting her priority class as h_0 when more than half of the users are lying in the case of priority pricing.

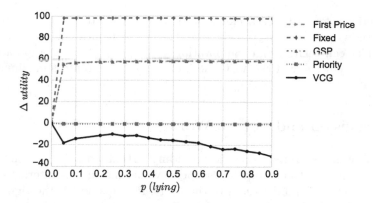

Fig. 6. Maximum gain in utility for a user from low priority class h_0.

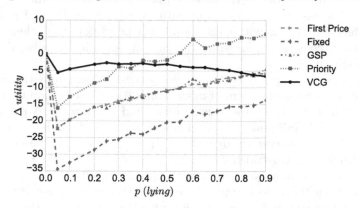

Fig. 7. Maximum gain in utility for a user from high priority class h_1.

4.1   Discussion

We find that static pricing schemes like fixed usage-based pricing and priority pricing are not very useful for arbitration between requests from different priority classes, since it is hard to avoid everyone reporting their requests as higher priority [11]. Dynamic pricing, for example, based on first-price auction can help here but with this simple auction scheme users report bid amounts lower than their true valuation of the bandwidth resource [11]. VCG mechanism, when either using with optimal allocation algorithms [13], or with approximate allocation algorithm [19], ensures truthfulness but is often computationally intensive to implement in practice. Generalised second price (GSP) auction mechanism, an extension of VCG, is not as computationally intensive as VCG and even though it doesn't guarantee truthfulness, it shares many desirable properties of VCG [11].

We think that in the context of bandwidth reservation for applications in community network clouds, GSP mechanism is a good candidate for using in allocation algorithms that need to run often, i.e. once every second. On the other hand, VCG can be used effectively where users reserve bandwidths over longer periods, for instance a cloud service may want to schedule bandwidth for performing backups every night over the whole month. In such situations, the provider can easily forgo computational efficiency of other approaches for the economic efficiency of the VCG mechanism, as it guarantees maximal social welfare.

5 Conclusion and Future Work

Cloud computing with its success in providing virtualised resources on demand has transformed the technology landscape, revolutionising how Internet applications are developed and delivered to the users. Perhaps now is the right opportunity to take full advantage of the virtualisation and distributed edge model of the cloud computing to design the killer applications for the community network clouds. The success of such cloud applications requires better and guaranteed access to the Internet from within the community network to meet their throughput and latency constraints, for which the current best-effort provisioning model doesn't match up.

In this paper, we applied various pricing mechanisms from the literature to bandwidth allocation problem of cloud applications in community networks, and studied their impact on the social welfare and truthfulness. We found that second-price based GSP and VCG mechanisms are good candidates for arbitration in bandwidth reservation algorithms. However, these mechanism assume that the provider is trustworthy, which in the case of multiple independent providers in the community network with no centralised control is difficult to ensure, and this is the focus for our future work. Another challenge is that multiple users may be connected to the provider using the same path in the community network, and reserving bandwidth for such users in the same time interval may cause congestion across some of the links, which an intelligent allocation algorithm should try to avoid. Lastly, any bandwidth reservation scheme should not negatively impact the normal operation of the community network for its users, so allocation mechanism needs to be adaptive to the network congestion and bandwidth usage in the community network.

Community network clouds build upon the vast research in peer-to-peer, volunteer and edge computing, and we see a huge opportunity in extending this work for building the core community cloud services that drive innovation in many related areas, and not just the edge cloud computing. We believe that the determinant of this success will not be just the technical sophistication with which the research challenges and open problems are solved, but also by how well the enthusiasts of the community network clouds succeed in capturing the imagination and meeting the expectations of the members of the community networks.

Acknowledgements. This work is supported by European Community Framework Programme 7 FIRE Initiative projects Community Networks Testbed for the Future Internet (CONFINE), FP7-288535, and CLOMMUNITY, FP7-317879. Support is also provided by the Universitat Politècnica de Catalunya BarcelonaTECH and the Spanish Government under contract TIN2013-47245-C2-1-R.

References

1. Baig, R., Roca, R., Freitag, F., Navarro, L.: Guifi.net, a crowdsourced network infrastructure held in common. Comput. Netw. **90**, 150–165 (2015)
2. Braem, B., et al.: A case for research with and on community networks. ACM SIGCOMM Comput. Commun. Rev. **43**(3), 68–73 (2013)
3. Caton, S., Haas, C., Chard, K., Bubendorfer, K., Rana, O.F.: A social compute cloud: allocating and sharing infrastructure resources via social networks. IEEE Trans. Serv. Comput. **7**(3), 359–372 (2014)
4. Depoorter, W., Vanmechelen, K., Broeckhove, J.: Economic co-allocation and advance reservation of network and computational resources in grids. In: Vanmechelen, K., Altmann, J., Rana, O.F. (eds.) GECON 2012. LNCS, vol. 7714, pp. 46–60. Springer, Heidelberg (2012)
5. Gui, Y., Zheng, Z., Wu, F., Gao, X., Chen, G.: SOAR: strategy-proof auction mechanisms for distributed cloud bandwidth reservation. In: IEEE International Conference on Communication Systems (ICCS 2014), pp. 162–166. IEEE, Macau, November 2014
6. Guo, J., Liu, F., Zeng, D., Lui, J.C.S., Jin, H.: A cooperative game based allocation for sharing data center networks. In: INFOCOM, pp. 2139–2147. IEEE, Turin, Italy, April 2013
7. Jana, R., Kannan, K.N., Chen, Y.-F., Jana, R., Kannan, K.N.: Using generalized second price auction for congestion pricing. In: GLOBECOM, pp. 1–6. IEEE, December 2011
8. Khan, A.M., Büyükşahin, U.C., Freitag, F.: Towards incentive-based resource assignment and regulation in clouds for community networks. In: Altmann, J., Vanmechelen, K., Rana, O.F. (eds.) GECON 2013. LNCS, vol. 8193, pp. 197–211. Springer, Heidelberg (2013)
9. Khan, A.M., Buyuksahin, U.C., Freitag, F.: Incentive-based resource assignment and regulation for collaborative cloud services in community networks. J. Comput. Syst. Sci. (2014)
10. Khan, A.M., Freitag, F.: Sparks in the fog: social and economic mechanisms as enablers for community network clouds. ADCAIJ: Adv. Distrib. Comput. Artif. Intell. J. **3**(8) (2014)
11. Maillé, P., Tuffin, B.: Telecommunication Network Economics: From Theory to Applications. Cambridge University Press, Cambridge (2014)
12. Marinos, A., Briscoe, G.: Community cloud computing. In: Jaatun, M.G., Zhao, G., Rong, C. (eds.) Cloud Computing. LNCS, vol. 5931, pp. 472–484. Springer, Heidelberg (2009)
13. Nisan, N., Ronen, A.: Algorithmic mechanism design. In: 31st Annual ACM Symposium on Theory of Computing (STOC 1999), pp. 129–140. ACM, New York, April 1999
14. Satyanarayanan, M., Bahl, P., Caceres, R., Davies, N.: The case for VM-based cloudlets in mobile computing. IEEE Pervasive Comput. **8**(4), 14–23 (2009)
15. Shen, H., Li, Z.: New bandwidth sharing and pricing policies to achieve a win-win situation for cloud provider and tenants. In: INFOCOM, pp. 835–843. IEEE, Toronto, Canada, April 2014

16. Vega, D., Meseguer, R., Freitag, F.: Analysis of the social effort in multiplex participatory networks. In: Altmann, J., Vanmechelen, K., Rana, O.F. (eds.) GECON 2014. LNCS, vol. 8914, pp. 67–79. Springer, Heidelberg (2014)
17. Wilensky, U.: NetLogo (1999)
18. Xiao, Y., Huang, J., Yuen, C., DaSilva, L.A.: Fairness and efficiency tradeoffs for user cooperation in distributed wireless networks. In: INFOCOM, pp. 285–289. IEEE, Turin, Italy, April 2013
19. Zhang, X., Wu, C., Li, Z., Lau, F.C.M.: A truthful $(1 - \epsilon)$-optimal mechanism for on-demand cloud resource provisioning. In: INFOCOM. IEEE (2015)
20. Zheng, Z., Gui, Y., Wu, F., Chen, G.: STAR: strategy-proof double auctions for multi-cloud, multi-tenant bandwidth reservation. IEEE Trans. Comput. **64**(7), 2071–2083 (2014)
21. Zhou, H., Leung, K.C., Li, V.O.K.: Auction-based bandwidth allocation and scheduling in noncooperative wireless networks. In: IEEE International Conference on Communications (ICC 2014), pp. 2556–2561. IEEE, Sydney, Australia, June 2014

On the Sustainability of Community Clouds in guifi.net

Roger Baig[1], Felix Freitag[2(✉)], and Leandro Navarro[2]

[1] Fundació Privada per la Xarxa Lliure, Oberta i Neural Guifi.net,
Gurb, Catalonia, Spain
[2] Universitat Politècnica de Catalunya, Barcelona, Spain
felix@ac.upc.edu

Abstract. The Internet and cloud services are key enablers for participation in society. The need for Internet access in areas underserved by commercial telecom operators has often been a motivation to develop community networks. Many examples around the world show successful cooperative developments of open, participatory local networking infrastructures. Such collaborative models have not yet been applied to local cloud computing resources and services. In this paper, we elaborate on the sustainability model of the http://guifi.net community network as a basis for cloud-based infrastructures and services in communities. We first look at the elements of http://guifi.net, which support the sustainability and growth of the networking infrastructure. We then discuss their application to cloud-based services within the network and come up with a framework of tools and components for community cloud resources and services. Finally, we assess the current status of the experimental community cloud in http://guifi.net, where some of the proposed tools are already operational.

Keywords: Cloud computing · Community networks · Common-pool resource · Community clouds

1 Introduction

All citizens and organizations should be able to participate and benefit in the digital society, with the Internet and cloud services as key enablers. The need for Internet access in areas which were left unattended by commercial telecom operators has often been a motivation to develop community-driven local network infrastructures. Community networks, also known as bottom-up-broadband networks, consist of a communication infrastructure in which local communities of citizens build, operate and own open IP-based networks. Hundreds of community networks operate across the globe, in rural and urban, rich and poor areas. In Europe, several community networks have been operating for more than ten years and have surpassed a thousand of nodes[1]. The participants, as

---

[1] Freifunk: http://freifunk.net in Germany, over 3,000; AWMN: http://awmn.gr in Greece, over 2,000; and guifi.net: http://guifi.net in Spain, over 29,000.

© Springer International Publishing Switzerland 2016
J. Altmann et al. (Eds.): GECON 2015, LNCS 9512, pp. 265–278, 2016.
DOI: 10.1007/978-3-319-43177-2_18

volunteers, enterprises, public and private organisations share resources, being these not only networking hardware, but also time, effort and knowledge, which are required to develop and maintain the network infrastructure used by the community. However these community networks incorporate many local services of common interest that require shared computing and storage resources. These shared computing resources, combined with Internet access, bring to users new possibilities for digital services, beyond the generic services offered mainly by global cloud service providers in the Internet. The potential lies in the application of the community cloud concept [1] to communities of citizens. In its generic form, a community cloud refers to a cloud deployment model in which a cloud infrastructure is built and provisioned for an exclusive use by a specific community of consumers with shared concerns and interests, owned and managed by the community or by a third party or a combination thereof [2]. While commercial community cloud solutions are a reality nowadays in several application areas such as in the financial, governmental and health sector, fulfilling community-specific requirements (e.g. security, performance, local content), citizen community clouds are not yet available today.

In this paper, we argue that a community network cloud, a cloud formed by community-owned local computing and communication resources able to provide services of local interest, can emerge and be sustainable if the appropriate tools and mechanisms are in place to govern the collective action of the community.

We elaborate a proposal for such a cloud for communities of citizens modelled after the model of guifi.net community network, which is the most successful and developed case among these networks in terms of size of the network, number and variety of participants, and complexity of the ecosystem.

The main contributions of this paper are the following: (a) A revision of the model that is applied in the http://guifi.net community network for the network sustainability. (b) Identification of specific issues concerning the sustainability of citizen community clouds. (c) A framework for establishing and maintaining community cloud infrastructures and services based on the http://guifi.net model. (d) An analysis of the current cloud infrastructure in http://guifi.net and assessment.

We elaborate our contributions as follows: In Sect. 2 we describe the http://guifi.net ecosystem for the access, operation and governance of the network infrastructure. We identify in Sect. 3 specific issues of cloud computing for the adoption of this sustainability model. In Sect. 4, we propose a framework containing tools and components for cloud-based service provision by a community. In Sect. 5 we describe how the framework has been implemented so far in http://guifi.net and analyze several performance indicators. In Sect. 6 we conclude outlining our findings and future work.

2   Elements of the guifi.net Ecosystem

2.1   Network Infrastructure as a Common-Pool Resource

http://guifi.net is managed as a *Common-Pool Resource* (CPR) [3], being the network infrastructure the core resource. Holding the infrastructure as a commons has some immediate effects such as the avoidance of the multiplicity of infrastructure because all participants operate on the same, and the increase of efficiency of the infrastructure in terms of costs saving and ease of participation. The CPR, i.e. the http://guifi.net infrastructure, grows by each new network segment which the participants deploy to reach the network or to improve it, and the reward for the contributors is the network connectivity that participants get [4].

For commercial services, http://guifi.net as a CPR translates into a reduced entry barrier for starting business ventures, since the network infrastructure is available for usage to everyone in the community, both to individual and professional users, and participants can benefit from pooling, with lower individual investments since resources are shared. The knowledge about the network is open and the network is neutral: no barriers that artificially limit the scope of service creations.

Nonetheless, community networks, as any other CPR, are fragile. More precisely, being non-excludable they are congestion prone, because connectivity is subtractable, and therefore subject to the free riding problem. Thus, efficient and effective governance tools are needed to protect the core resource from depletion [3], that is to say, to protect it from the *Tragedy of the commons* [5].

2.2   Stakeholders

There are four main stakeholders in guifi.net. The *volunteers*, the initiators of the project, due to their lack of economic interests, are responsible for the operation of the tools and mechanisms of governance and oversight. The *professionals* bring in quality of service, and their *customers* bring the resources which make the ecosystem economically sustainable. *Public administrations* are responsible for regulating the interactions between the network deployment and operation, and public goods, such as public domain occupation. All participants that extract connectivity must contribute infrastructure, directly or indirectly, and can participate in the knowledge creation process.

guifi.net is a success case for the coexistence of voluntarism and a well-established professional activity operating on the same CPR, i.e. the communication network. Governance tools implemented in http://guifi.net play a critical role in keeping that balance. This is critical for the sustainability of the project, because, although the economic sustainability is mostly based on the revenue generated by professional activity, the governance and the harmonisation of the ecosystem is mostly carried out by volunteers.

2.3   Communication and Coordination Tools

The technical skills among most participants, its distribution across the territory and the need to coordinate decisions to keep the network infrastructure operational has resulted in the development of many tools to facilitate communication and coordination among participants and the components of the infrastructure:

- **Software Tools for Network Management and Provisioning:** The community of http://guifi.net has developed a set of software tools to ease the design, deployment, management and operation of the network in a self-provisioning style and supporting crowd-sourced efforts by members of the community given the intrinsic inter-dependence in the computer and social network. Most of them are integrated in the http://guifi.net web site.
- **Communication Tools:** The most significant tools for communication among the participants are the *Mailing lists* with global, territorial and thematic scope, open by default. *Social Media* also open by default with a few exceptions to protect sensitive information. *Face to face meetings* play a key role in strengthening social relationships and sharing initiatives and knowledge.

2.4   Participation Framework

Participation in the community is organized by agreements: the community license shared by all participants, and a set of bilateral collaboration agreements between the entity representing the community and other organisations such as professionals or public administrations:

- **Network Commons License:** The NCL[2] is the license that every http://guifi.net participant must subscribe, developed and approved through a long standing open deliberation process. Its preamble sets the fundamental principles and the articles precisely establish the participants rights and duties to join, use, understand, offer services as long as respecting and not interfering with the operation of the network, the rights of other users, and the neutrality of the network to contents and services. It is written to be enforceable under the Spanish legislation, as legal certainty is essential to stimulate participation and investment, which in turn, is at the base of any economic activity and therefore its sustainability.
- **Reference Authority:** The guifi.net Foundation (*Fundació Privada per a la Xarxa, Lliure i Neutral guifi.net*) is a reference organisation founded by the http://guifi.net community that gives a legal identity to the community. As such, it plays a vital role for the coordination of the guifi.net ecosystem. Its foundational mission is to protect and promote the network held in commons.
- **Collaboration Agreements:** aimed at strengthening the legal certainty derived from the NCL. These agreements result from the experience of many specific agreements over the years. The main set of agreements are with:

---

[2] http://guifi.net/en/FONNC.

- **Professionals:** Any professional willing to carry out economic activities involving http://guifi.net infrastructure must sign a professional agreement with the Foundation. As part of it, the professional must state its level of commitment to the commons. There are tree options regarding contribution of his deployed infrastructure to the commons: *type A*, all of it, *type B*, a part of it only, and *type C*, nothing (that professional uses what is available but does not contribute at all). The agreement implies the acceptance of a set of Service Level Agreements (SLAs) aiming at facilitate the coexistence among the professionals. Once the agreement is signed, the professional is included in the economic compensations system.
- **Third Parties:** The Foundation also establishes agreements with third parties such as public administrations, private companies or universities.

2.5   Governance Tools

These are socio-economic tools developed by the community and managed by the Foundation to keep the infrastructure and the community operational and balanced. The pillar of this collaboration is a system with several type of agreements based on the level of commitment with the commons and an economic compensation system for investments and resource consumption.

- **Conflicts Resolution System:** A systematic and clear procedure for resolution of conflicts with a scale of graduated sanctions has been developed. It consists of three stages, conciliation, mediation and arbitration, all of them driven by a lawyer.
- **Economic Compensations System:** Developed and implemented to compensate imbalance between investment in the commons infrastructure and network usage among professionals. Expenditures declared by the professionals are periodically cleared according to the network usage. The Foundation computes and manages the billing system.

2.6   Implementation and Impact

Currently, at the physical level, the http://guifi.net infrastructure combines several technologies: wireless and optical fibre are the most common. As of July 2015, http://guifi.net has a total of 45,650 nodes, 29,200 of them declared as operational. The 10 GBps http://guifi.net optical backbone has three Internet uplink carriers. More than 400 internal application servers are announced.

The participation among stakeholders is quite diverse, with an estimate of 13,500 registered members, nine SME participating in the economic compensations system, 270 subscribers in the mailing list for professionals, and more than a hundred of councils actively collaborating with guifi.net.

Recent statistics about network penetration in households[3] [6] show the Catalan county with the best results, and the only one above the EU average, is

---

[3] Catalan Statistics Institute (IDESCAT) http://www.idescat.cat.

Osona, where http://guifi.net was born. Other counties with high guifi.net presence shown similar results contrasting with similar counties where http://guifi.net presence is irrelevant.

Currently, the main sources of economic activity in guifi.net are, on the one hand, those related to the infrastructure deployment and maintenance, and on the other hand, services delivered over the network. Although Internet access is still the most popular service, others such as VoIP, remote maintenance or backups have also been offered for a long time. New services such as video streaming and video on-demand are appearing, especially in the areas served by optical fibre. The growing trend toward local services being offered in the network infrastructure to a growing user base brings the need to a shared pool of configurable computing resources and platform services to manage that computing infrastructure.

3   The Sustainability of Community Cloud Computing

The organisational structure of the guifi.net network infrastructure, described in the previous section, follows the principles of long-enduring CPR institutions. However, when considering a shared pool of configurable computing resources and services, there are specific aspects to discuss in community clouds.

A CPR typically consists of a core resource which provides a limited quantity of extractable fringe units. In the case of a community cloud, as the core resource is nurtured by diverse contributions of networking, computing and service elements the participants deploy to expand or improve it, and the fringe unit is the service they obtain.

The following differences of cloud resources compared to the network infrastructure have been identified:

- **Building Elements:** For a community cloud, the building elements are more diverse than in the underlying network since, in addition to the physical level where host devices (*servers*) provide computing and storage services and the network provides connectivity, the cloud software stack (IaaS, PaaS and SaaS) are also building elements that provide diverse additional services.
- **Inter-Dependency Among Resources:** The resulting asset at the network level is a primary infrastructure, that is to say, it has no inherent dependencies to other infrastructures. This is not the case for the cloud, which inherently depends on network connectivity for the interaction among building elements and users. In addition there are inter-dependencies among physical resources with services and among different services. Some resources or services could be more critical or demanded than others. The consequences of the deployment of an infrastructure with such dependencies must be studied not only from the viewpoint of usage/demand/traffic on a specific class of resource, but also from a more systemic viewpoint to answer questions about the complexity of interaction and balance across classes of cloud resources, resource bundles required in services, congestion management and fairness, influence

with related infrastructures such as the underlying network, the power grid, the environment, or the socio-economic community of users and organisations around.

– **Roles and Balance Between Professionals and Volunteers:** We can expect a mix of voluntary contributions of networking and computing resources, even cloud services provided in a best-effort (or peer-to-peer) manner, together with professionally operated resources run by local or global providers, perhaps at a higher cost but also at a higher scale and with service-level commitments. As with the network, the community structure can incorporate both volunteers and professionals or SMEs, and in fact, create the opportunity for local entrepreneurs to offer tailored cloud-based services to address community needs, and develop an inclusive socio-economic ecosystem for local development. The guifi.net participation framework with the community license, the authority of its foundation, the collaboration agreements, conflict resolution and economic compensations system can be directly implemented to regulate and promote this.

– **Infrastructure vs. Services Division:** It seems that the rule applied for the network infrastructure level, "the http://guifi.net community takes care of the infrastructure as a CPR, the content is left up to the users" (considering content as pure usage and therefore external to the CPR, can also be applied to the cloud level, but the criteria to determine what must be considered external (as content) and what is considered infrastructure must be set. This boundary between internal and external services also determines how hybrid clouds should be considered.

4   A Framework for Cloud-Based Services in guifi.net

As in the case of the network infrastructure, the implementation of the CPR at the cloud level requires effective rules and tools. The design principles identified in [3] for the institutions to govern successfully collective action for a CPR inspired the tools which are presented in this section. We determine and materialize in the following the components and tools needed to implement a community cloud as a CPR.

4.1   Community Cloud Infrastructure as a Common-Pool Resource

The fundamental principles of http://guifi.net apply to a community cloud, defined to be fully inclusive, that revolve around (i) the openness of access (usage) of the infrastructure, and (ii) the openness of participation (construction, operation, governance) in the development of the infrastructure and its community. The application of these fundamental principles result in a community cloud resource and service infrastructure that is a *collective good, socially produced*, and governed as a *common-pool resource*.

The reasons that apply at network level to the conception of the contributed infrastructure as a CPR, e.g. standardisation of resource management, interoperability of individual contributed resources, need for ease of contribution by users, seem also to stand for citizen community clouds. With a set of essential IaaS and PaaS cloud services given as a CPR, enhanced and aggregated SaaS services may be built upon them and offered on a cost-sharing or a for-profit model. Previous volunteer computing proposals, e.g. [7], often addressed the trading of virtual machines (VMs) corresponding to the cloud IaaS, upon which users would deploy their services. VMs and basic cloud services are part of the CPR and therefore subject to allocation under the community license, the economic compensations and conflict resolution system. However, this scheme would enable service trading already at the level of complex services built upon this CPR. Similar to how the network CPR reduces the entry barrier (through network transparency, neutrality, cost sharing, resulting in reduced CAPEX and OPEX cost) and enables the market niche of proximity services, a cloud infrastructure held as a CPR might contribute to make it more accessible for SMEs.

4.2   Stakeholders

The coexistence of volunteer and for-profit participants, already happening at the network level, is desirable to be extended to the cloud level. Thus, the concept of the resources needed to build the cloud (the hardware and the software) as a CPR will establish a framework for contribution and collaboration between volunteers and for-profit professionals, similarly to what has been built at the network level.

4.3   Computing, Coordination and Communication Tools

As with the network infrastructure, a set of software tools and services are required to ease the tasks of deploying the components of the infrastructure and coordinating its operation and usage:

- **Cloud Access Points (CAP):** In order to facilitate the adoption of the required software components, a GNU/Linux software distribution containing all of them has been developed. The distribution, named *Cloudy*, is delivered as a standalone version and as a container to be installed in a users's computer device. Cloud participants interact with it through a Web-GUI.
- **Cloud Resource Devices:** Computing resources are also provided by a set of Resource Devices (RD), a resource aggregate. These are network-attached low-power computers deployed anywhere in the network, dedicated to provide computing and storage resources in the form of virtual machines implemented as Linux Containers with access control, resource isolation and management capabilities to grant a trusted remote user with full access to the processing, storage and network resources allocated to a given container. RDs are based on the OpenWRT GNU/Linux distribution extended with a remote control (REST API) service that can manage the life-cycle of multiple containers running concurrently in the same host. We call each of these containers a *sliver* and the set of slivers on diverse RDs belonging to a service are a *slice*.

- **Infrastructure as a Service: (IaaS)**
  - **Virtual Machines:** A service for allocating and managing virtual machines (VMs) is a key enabler of cloud uptake. In Cloudy Cloud Access Points the service is implemented using OpenVZ technology through its Web Panel, and in Cloud Resource Devices this is implemented through the Resource Controller Web Panel or its REST API.
- **Platform as a Service: (PaaS)**
  - **Distributed Announcement and Discovery of Services (DADS):** In a peer-production context it is essential to have an effective mechanism to find out the services available automatically. DADS uses the Serf gossip protocol for exchanging information about the active services available, and has been developed as a core component of Cloudy. The discovered services are presented to the user grouped by categories and can be sorted according to several metrics, including locality.
  - **Authentication Service:** This service provides user authentication by a recognised independent third party. The concept results from the evolution of the solution to authentication needs of the http://guifi.net federated proxy system. Currently, it is implemented using LDAP in a redundant master-slave architecture hosted and operated by the guifi.net Foundation.
- **Software as a Service (SaaS):**
  - **guifi.net Services:** The three main services in guifi.net have been integrated in Cloudy:
    * **DNS Service** to participate in the guifi.net DNS system for the resolution of internal addresses (RFC1918). Implemented with BIND.
    * **Network Monitoring** instance to contribute to the network monitoring system. It is implemented using SNMP feeding RRDtool buffer rings.
    * **Web Proxy** as part of hundreds of Internet gateways contributed by volunteers. That way any validated user can access any of the federated web proxies for Internet service. The service is base on the Squid proxy software.
  - **Third-Party Services:** The following third-party services are currently integrated in Cloudy:
    * **Syncthing:** A decentralised cloud storage system with cryptographic features which gives full control to the users over where their data is replicated.
    * **PeerStreamer:** A peer-to-peer media streaming framework with a streaming engine for the efficient distribution of media streams, a source application for the creation of channels and a player applications to visualize the streams.
    * **Tahoe-LAFS:** A fault-tolerant encrypted decentralized cloud storage system which distributes user data across multiple servers in replicated data chuncks. Even if some of the servers fail or are taken over by an attacker, the entire file store continues to function correctly while preserving user's privacy and security.

* **WebDAV Server:** A set of extensions to the HTTP protocol which allows users to collaboratively edit and manage files on remote web servers. Implemented with the Apache Web server DAV module.
* **Other Services:** Other services can be deployed on resource slices, a collection of virtual machines obtained and managed as IaaS using the aggregate of available cloud resource devices.
- **Communication Tools:** Two mailing lists give support to Cloudy users and developers[4]. A web site and wiki describe Cloudy[5]. To contribute to the development of Cloudy or report bugs, users can register in the dev site[6].

4.4 Participation Framework

License: A Community Cloud Commons License (CCCL) which harmonises the contribution and usage of the cloud resources will play a key role in the take-up process of the community cloud model in a similar way as the influence the network license has had on the network infrastructure. The license must take into account facts like the relationship between users and service providers, among service providers, and also the coexistence with the NCL, which, as already said in the previous section, must be accepted by any participant to join the community cloud. The CCCL has not been established yet. Similar to the NCL process, the steps to write the CCCL licence will go through deliberation with the community. We propose that the license must cover at least the following aspects:

- **Service Level Agreement:** Mainly to distinguish between best effort services given for free and paid ones. As already discussed, the promotion of economic transactions is crucial for the sustainability and expansion of the ecosystem.
- **Privacy:** In an architecture where sensible data is distributed across the network, privacy protection must start from the license.
- **Fair Use:** Rules of conduct and means of control should be specified in order to avoid abuse of the resource in commons.
- **Transparency and Accountability:** As already discussed, accountability is essential in any CPR and thus, so is the access to information.

Reference Authority: The fact of having a license is tightly related to the existence of an authority which maintains it and makes sure that it is respected. A decision on the convenience and the viability of having such organisation must be made. Existing organisations such as the http://guifi.net Foundation can be considered to fulfil this role.

---

[4] Cloudy users: https://llistes.guifi.net/sympa/info/cloudy-users and developers: https://llistes.guifi.net/sympa/info/cloudy-dev.

[5] Documentation for users: http://cloudy.community/, and developers: http://en.wiki.guifi.net/wiki/What_is_Cloudy/.

[6] Contributions to the Cloudy software: http://dev.cloudy.community.

Collaboration Agreements: As with the network infrastructure, the level of commitment of the operators with the commons is expressed through an agreement. The set of collaboration agreements for the cloud shall contribute to enhance confidence among operators offering cloud services. It must be investigated if a graduated commitment system applies to cloud services and/or if it must be service specific.

4.5 Governance Tools

The governance involves all actors to drive a community cloud infrastructure through challenges and changes to keep it operational and balanced, key to resilient and adaptive CPRs. The two main tools are the following:

- **Conflicts Resolution System:** The already existing system for the resolution of conflicts can be applied as is to community cloud related issues.
- **Economic Compensations System:** A clear economic compensations system is needed to clarify the terms of participation, promote investment, and reduce the number of disputes. The already existing compensations system adapted to fit the cloud requirements can be used to balance expenditure. In addition, the impact that the usage of the cloud services may have on the network infrastructure and its effects on the economic compensations system of the network must be investigated to determine if the current calculation system, which is based on the total amount of network traffic at the Points of Presence, must be adjusted.

5 guifi.net Community Cloud Implementation

5.1 The guifi.net Community Cloud

The most convenient way to for a participant to join and contribute to the community cloud is to install the Cloudy distribution in a small network-attached host (Cloud Access Point). Figure 1 shows its Web user interface after installation at the user's device. Cloudy ensures the provision of a basic set of common services which every participant must be able to join and interact in the community cloud. In addition, it offers an standard way to add new services.

Cloudy[7] can be installed as: (*a*) ISO installation image, to be copied to a any bootable device (e.g. USB memory)[8], (*b*) Container filesystem, to be used in LXC or OpenVZ[9], (*c*) Script, to be run on top of any Debian based distribution[10].

Cloud Resource Devices can be just installed by registering a small network-attached host on the Resource Controller and downloading a bootable firmware image to be run on the new device from a USB memory. After that the RD becomes available as part of a resource pool through its controller.

---

[7] Distributed in *stable* and *unstable* versions: http://cloudy.community/download/.
[8] http://repo.clommunity-project.eu/images/stable/cloudy.iso.
[9] http://repo.clommunity-project.eu/images/stable/cloudy.container.tar.gz.
[10] https://github.com/Clommunity/cloudynitzar.

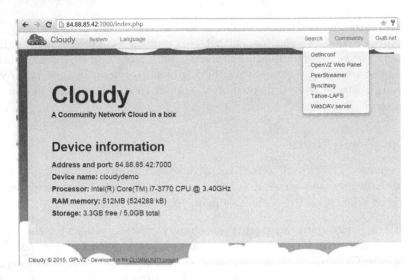

Fig. 1. Cloudy distribution web user interface.

Table 1. Community cloud indicators.

	Indicator: number of ...	Amount
Hosts	Clommunity CAP	22
	Third-party Cloudy CAP	15
	Resource Devices	83
Services	Dnsservice	5
	OWP	4
	Peerstreamer	5
	guifi-proxy3	7
	Serf	37
	Snpservice	5
	Syncthing	7
	Tahoe-lafs	3

5.2   Assessment of Usage and Engagement

The experimental http://guifi.net community cloud became operational in summer 2015. We measured the technical usage of the community network cloud in terms of instances deployed and services provided. Despite numbers may vary as it grows, a few indicators of its size are shown in Table 1. There are 37 instances in the Serf cloud, 22 contributed by the Clommunity project and 15 contributed other parties like volunteers, schools, companies. The guifi-proxy3 is the most popular http://guifi.net service and syncthing the most popular of the additional services. In addition, 83 Cloud Resource Devices are currently available for the deployment of arbitrary services. In terms of number of participants, the mailing lists show 47 subscribers to the user's list and 23 subscribers to the developer's list.

6 Conclusion

Citizen community clouds, are motivated by their disruptive potential for changing the future cloud service landscape by extending the current cloud service offerings with local cloud resource and service infrastructures open for access (usage), and open for participation (construction, operation, governance).

The paper argues to organize these citizen community clouds as common pool resources (CPR). To this end, the paper reviews first the mechanism which have led the http://guifi.net community network to become sustainable at the network infrastructure level. Then specific issues for the applicability of these mechanisms in community cloud-based services are discussed. A framework of components to govern such a community network cloud is presented, where some of these components have been already implemented. The status of the starting community cloud deployment in http://guifi.net is assessed, which reveals the user interest and acceptance of the provided tools. The deployment of the tools and usage also suggests the technical feasibility of such a cloud system to be built, used and governed by citizens.

The next steps will need to include the development of components to measure and account the contribution to and usage of the cloud CPR, to enable that the economic compensation system, already applied at the network level, can operate also at the cloud level. Initial interest from SMEs to experiment with close-to-market services upon the cloud CPR should help to develop the business models for this ecosystem.

Acknowledgements. This work was supported by the European Framework Programme 7 FIRE Initiative projects CONFINE (FP7-288535), CLOMMUNITY (FP7-317879), by the Horizon 2020 framework programme project RIFE (H2020-644663), Universitat Politècnica de Catalunya-BarcelonaTECH and by the Spanish government under contract TIN2013-47245-C2-1-R.

References

1. Marinos, A., Briscoe, G.: Community cloud computing. In: Jaatun, M.G., Zhao, G., Rong, C. (eds.) Cloud Computing. LNCS, vol. 5931, pp. 472–484. Springer, Heidelberg (2009)
2. NIST, U.S. Department of Commerce: The NIST Definition of Cloud Computing
3. Ostrom, E.: Governing the Commons: The Evolution of Institutions for Collective Action. Cambridge University Press, Cambridge (1990)
4. Baig, R., Roca, R., Freitag, F., Navarro, L.: guifi.net, a crowdsourced network infrastructure held in common. Comput. Netw. **90**, 150–165 (2015)

5. Hardin, G.: The tragedy of the commons. Science **162**, 1243–1248 (1968)
6. Statistical Institute of Catalonia: Territorial Statistics of Information and Communication Technologies in Households (2013)
7. Khan, A.M., Buyuksahin, U.C., Freitag, F.: Incentive-based resource assignment and regulation for collaborative cloud services in community networks. J. Comput. Syst. Sci. (JCSS) (2014)

Legal and Socio-Economic Aspects

Cloud Providers Viability: How to Address it from an IT and Legal Perspective?

Cesare Bartolini[1]([✉]), Donia El Kateb[1], Yves Le Traon[1], and David Hagen[2]

[1] Interdisciplinary Centre for Security, Reliability and Trust (SnT),
Université du Luxembourg, Luxembourg, Luxembourg
{cesare.bartolini,donia.elkateb,yves.letraon}@uni.lu
[2] Commission de Surveillance du Secteur Financier (CSSF),
Luxembourg, Luxembourg
david.hagen@cssf.lu

Abstract. A major part of the commercial Internet is moving towards a cloud paradigm. This phenomenon has a drastic impact on the organizational structures of enterprises and introduces new challenges that must be properly addressed to avoid major setbacks. One such challenge is that of cloud provider viability, that is, the reasonable certainty that the Cloud Service Provider (CSP) will not go out of business, either by filing for bankruptcy or by simply shutting down operations, thus leaving its customers stranded without an infrastructure and, depending on the type of cloud service used, even without their applications or data. This article attempts to address the issue of cloud provider viability, proposing some ways of mitigating the problem both from a technical and from a legal perspective.

Keywords: Cloud computing · Provider bankruptcy · Law

1 Introduction

In November 2013, an alarm rang. Nirvanix, a major provider of cloud storage services operating in California, closed down its business with very little anticipation to allow its customers to recover their cloud-stored assets. This sudden event wroke havoc in the cloud community, and revealed a significant weakness of the cloud-based business model: once an enterprise outsources services and data to a cloud provider, it is no longer in control of them, and can suffer from adverse conditions occurring to the cloud provider.

While this new business model is definitely the direction where the market is heading, it introduces new and significant challenges. While some of them are simply a new way of addressing well-known issues, such as performace issues, resource availability, service security and reliability, others are strictly related to the outsourcing of parts of the business to the Cloud Service Provider (CSP).

The risk of the CSP suddenly going out of business, either through a "soft" cessation (i.e., filing for bankruptcy), or in a more abrupt way (simply ceasing the

© Springer International Publishing Switzerland 2016
J. Altmann et al. (Eds.): GECON 2015, LNCS 9512, pp. 281–295, 2016.
DOI: 10.1007/978-3-319-43177-2_19

operations and removing the assets) concerns the uncertainty about the stability of the CSP. If the CSP faces a bad financial situation, it might decide to go out of business, and this could happen more or less abruptly. For example, the CSP might file for bankruptcy, leaving its customers to entertain their business with the trustee instead of the regular CSP management board. Even worse, the CSP might not go through the legal shutdown, and instead simply cease to do business, shutting down all operations and leaving its customers stranded and unable to use their required infrastructure anymore. And all this might occur without any forewarning to the CSP's customers.

This is the problem of the so-called *long-term viability* of CSPs, one of the main factors to take into account when moving to a cloud platform. Normally, the migration to a cloud is a one-way door. Unless there is a major change in the size of the enterprise's business (in which case there might be pressing needs to adopt an in-house architecture), the choice to rely on a CSP to run its business, both as a starting choice or after migrating pre-existing applications, is a long-term one. The relationship between the client enterprise and the CSP is likely to last until either one goes out of business. But there is a lot of difference between the client enterprise and the CSP going out of business. In the former case, the CSP would lose a customer, which might have serious repercussions from an economic point of view, but this fact does not *per se* hinder the CSP's operations. On the other side, the CSP going out of business would seriously hamper the client's operations, regardless of the client's business status. Even if the enterprise's activity were solid and growing, the CSP's end of business would block all of its IT activities, because the underlying infrastructure would not be accessible anymore.

In fact, the CSP suddenly going out of business can be a serious problem for enterprises relying on it. Of course, the client can always switch to another CSP or set up an in-house architecture to solve the problem. However, this might take some time, and a prolonged inactivity might seriously damage the client, in terms of loss of income, customers, and reputation. This might be fatal to small enterprises. Additionally, the CSP might also be used by the client as a storage resource, meaning that it might have a large amount of data used by the client, and its loss (or unavailability for a prolonged period) might be a significant damage itself.

This paper addresses the issue of CSP long-term viability, by evaluating what solutions (mostly not specifically designed for viability) the CSP and the client can adopt to avoid the consequences of the CSP suddenly going out of business, and what further problems emerge from these solutions. We discuss the issue from two perspectives, namely an IT and a legal point of view, and propose a list of technical and legal measures to mitigate the problem. In particular, Sect. 2 delves into the concept of cloud computing and illustrates the problem with respect to the various types of cloud; in that section, some real-world scenarios in which this problem was manifest are summarized. Section 3 is a survey of literature on cloud viability and some approaches that could partially address the problem. Section 4 tries to build on existing research to propose solutions or mitigators based on a technical (Subsect. 4.1) or legal (Subsect. 4.2) approaches, or mixed solutions (Subsect. 4.3). Then, Sect. 5 summarizes and evaluates the solutions in a preliminary cost analysis. Finally, Sect. 6 tries to summarize the findings and suggests future research directions.

2   Problem Statement

The impact of the problem of long-term viability increases with the pervasiveness of the cloud and depends on cloud layers. In what follows, we explore the problem of cloud providers viability with respect to the cloud delivery models and we highlight some real-life scenarios that illustrate the impact of providers going out of business.

2.1   Providers Viability and Cloud Delivery Models

Depending on how much has been outsourced, the effect of the CSP going out of business can be much different [6]. When dealing with IaaS or PaaS CSPs, the main assets (application source code and data) are under the control of the customer, who can migrate them (with different technical difficulties between IaaS and PaaS); in a SaaS environment, on the other hand, the customer normally has no access to the application source code or the datacentre where its data are stored, plus it might also lack the technical skills to perform a migration. In particular, with respect to the most common types of cloud models:

- The loss of IaaS platforms[1] would require the client to find or set up a suitable hardware architecture;
- PaaS clouds would require it to also set up the basic software platform for running its applications. This configuration is very common for those enterprises which offer web-based services to their end customers. In general, the customers of PaaS clouds[2] are application developers who offer their applications through the cloud;
- Finally, in the SaaS paradigm, the client (the end user of the IT service) normally only uses a web browser (thin client) to access the service, so a CSP going out of business completely cuts its clients off their IT applications and data.

The problem might depend not only on the CSP but also on other third-party partners going out of business in case the CSP has in turn outsourced some of its services [6], with a potential cascading effect.

Long-term viability is one of the major risks that must be taken into account when choosing to rely on a CSP to support one's software applications.

---

[1] The reference example is Amazon Elastic Compute Cloud (EC2) (http://aws.amazon.com/ec2/).

[2] Such as Google App Engine (https://appengine.google.com/start) or the Salesforce1 platform (http://www.salesforce.com/platform/solutions/connect-integrate/).

The money that can be saved by relying on an external infrastructure might be counterweighted by the risk of having the business stalled for some time, or the software and data lost due to the shutdown of the CSP.

The problem changes with the size of the CSP. Relying on major CSPs, large enterprises with an insignificant risk of abruptly shutting down, mitigates the problem. But the type of service offered by these CSPs might not be suited for the needs of the would-be customer. Additionally, while the potential customer enterprise might enjoy some negotiating power against smaller CSPs, so as to adjust the cloud functionality to its own needs, no such power will be available against major corporations, leaving the enterprise the sole options to accept or reject the standard offer. The enterprise might have political reasons to prefer a small CSP over a large one (for example nationality); the reasons might be economic (favorable offers by the small CSP); or the choice might be pushed by the need for interoperability with partners relying on a specific cloud. However, small, start-up cloud providers are more subject to market fluctuations, and might at some time decide to stop providing hosting services to their customers, or to move to another business model. This might dramatically impact cloud customers who can consequently face operational interruption of their services, business losses, reputation degradation, etc.

Long-term viability is in the interest both of the client enterprise and the CSP: the former has an interest that the cloud infrastructure will be available and able to guarantee its service, whereas the CSP wants to be seen as a reliable entity which enterprises can rely upon, so both parties might be willing to undertake some measures against the risk of a sudden disappearance of the CSP (bankruptcy, acquisition by third parties and subsequent termination, forced closure by public authorities and so on).

2.2   Cloud Providers Viability: Real-Life Scenarios

Several incidents have been reported over the last years. Probably the most outstanding example so far is the storage provider Nirvanix [5], one of the major stakeholders in cloud storage services, which went out of business in September 2013, and customers had to recur to insourcing or migrate to other cloud providers. However, Nirvanix only gave its customers two weeks before the final shutdown. The customers, hosting terabytes of data on Nirvanix services, had to deal with a considerable interruption time that resulted into a halt of their running services. The impact of this incident on some major enterprises, including IBM (who used Nirvanix's cloud storage technology) and Dell (who had some agreements with Nirvanix) has not been disclosed.

In 2012, Megaupload, one of the pioneering companies in providing storage services, has been shut down by the US Department of Justice which started an investigation against its employees [1], and its founder Kim Dotcom created a new storage service known as MegaCloud. In late 2013, this service disappeared as well [14], possibly due to an NSA blockade. Users have suddenly lost access to the areas where they had stored the files.

The case of the 2e2 company highlights other interesting consequences. After 2e2 went bankrupt, it first asked its customers (such Vodafone and Kellog) a large amount of funding to keep the service up and running [20]. Shortly after, it was discovered that the company had outsourced most of its customers' data to third-party services. After the bankrupt, the datacentres were acquired by a company that guaranteed that it would keep providing the service to customers.

Cloud providers' viability has raised several criticism over the last years. According to Gartner, one of the major risks posed by cloud adoption is the uncertainty related to providers viability, and one out of four cloud providers could go out of business in 2015 due to some reasons such as bankruptcy or acquisition [18].

In an attempt to raise the attention on the problem of cloud providers' long-term viability issues, this paper explores some research directions with the objective of setting up trustworthy cloud environments and increasing cloud services adoption.

3 Related Work

To the best of our knowledge, there does not appear to be a lot of literature addressing the issue of CSP viability. Most studies only mention it as one of the potential problems that should be accounted for when migrating to clouds, or try to address more common problems that have some connection with viability.

Reliability is seen as a major concern, and steps have been taken to address the problem. [11] surveys a number of examples in which cloud reliability became a concern. Several reliability models and approaches have been proposed (e.g., [2]). However, reliability generally refers to short-term problems, in the sense of a continuous availability of the service without interruptions or outages. While there is clearly some overlapping with the problem of long-term viability, the solutions for short-term failures are not suited for addressing the final termination of the CSP, and the other way around approaches to achieve long-term viability might be unable to solve a service downtime lasting a few hours.

The main reference to the problem of CSP long-term viability resides in a popular Gartner analysis [4] which highlights seven critical features that a business should evaluate when moving to cloud; among these is long-term viability. The report is considered a milestone concerning cloud risks. A different risk classification is provided in [19], highlighting the problem of stored data in the event of bankruptcy.

Also [15] considers the various risks associated with the migration from an insourced infrastructure to a CSP, and the set of risks includes long-term viability. The author puts it in the perspective of contractual issues that have to be addressed but again does not provide a lot of insight into the subject.

A slightly more detailed analysis is offered by [3]. This work introduces the distinction among several scenarios in which the CSP undergoes a soft shutdown (i.e., filing for bankruptcy), merges or is acquired, and abruptly ceases its business. Apart from a brief overview on software escrows (described in Subsect. 4.3), the book does not explore other solutions.

Perhaps the only work which actually attempts to address the issue of a CSP going bankrupt or ceasing its business is [12]. However, this work exclusively focuses on legal solutions, without discussing their technical implications, and moreover it puts too much emphasis on the source code of services, most likely because, despite the initial statements, it only addresses SaaS environments. Some of the solutions proposed in [12] will be discussed in this paper.

4   Addressing the Problem

This section analyses the different methods and approaches that can be used to anticipate the needs for building trustworthy cloud platforms. In what follows, these approaches are presented taking into account an information technology perspective, a purely legal perspective, and finally an approach that combines both the IT and law perspectives.

4.1   Discussion of Possible IT Solutions

The risk of a CSP failure can be mitigated by means of some preemptive technical solutions that cannot prevent the CSP from ceasing its activity, but can help avoid the consequences of such an event, especially that of preventing the cloud customer to carry on its business. Although approaches based on redundancy and standardization will involve some additional costs, they might offer a viable trade-off between expenses and benefits.

Backing Up. As obvious as it may seem, the most immediate solution to protect against the sudden disappearance of a CSP is to regularly back up one's software and data. By means of an in-house duplication of all the assets that are outsourced to the cloud, an enterprise combines the advantages of both solutions: on one side, it does not require to maintain the high-performance, 24/7-reliable infrastructures to deliver its service to its customers; on the other side, it constantly has an up-to-date version of its assets, ready for migration to another CSP (or for insourcing).

Data backup is also advisable if the service delivery is in-house. In particular, it has been suggested [14] to use a cloud backup when delivering in-house, and to use an in-house backup when the services and data are outsourced.

On the down side, backing up the software and the data has its costs, but these will reasonably be smaller than those required for in-house operation. Also, this approach does not solve every problem, because the CSP might use technologies, protocols and Application Programming Interface (APIs) that are not compatible with an in-house operation, or for migration to a different CSP. So, backed-up data might still require a lot of work to restore full business operations.

That is, unless the CSPs are based on some standard technology or structure (as described in the next paragraph).

Cloud Platforms Portability and Standardization. In the last years, several PaaS platforms have appeared as an initiative to create and manage scalable cloud-based software. When a PaaS provider goes out of business, cloud customers should be able to migrate their application to others sites.

A cloud platform should provide standard connectors, so that applications can be moved to another platform adopting the same standards. In the last few years, several PaaS tools have been proposed by different PaaS market players. Some of these tools are based on standard programming languages, however they still suffer from the lack of standard APIs in terms of interfaces and applications connectors, thus exposing customers to vendor lock-in risks. With the lack of interoperability between platforms, customers' workload migration from one cloud provider to a new one becomes a tedious task, since the customer has to adapt its migrated applications to the proprietary components of the new provider's platform in order to migrate the software and the data. To ensure high interoperability and portability between PaaS, standardization initiatives have to be developed to provide standard application dependencies mechanisms and common interfaces to ease the transfer of applications between heterogeneous PaaS platforms.

A recent initiative to enable interoperability between platforms and to ease the migration of applications is illustrated by the containers model, whose basic idea is to have an isolated packaging of an application embedded with its dependencies. Using this approach, it becomes easier to move the overall application when its hosting environment encounters some problems. "Containerization" has been promoted by Linux Dockers[3], which adds an additional layer of abstraction to virtual machines, allowing to have isolated features within the same Linux instance.

Some authors [13] have presented some proposed standard interfaces such as DMTFs Open Cloud Standards Incubator (OCSI) for resources management, the Open Cloud Computing Interface Working Group (OCCI-WG) for IaaS specification, and Cloud Data Management Interface (CDMI) for the manipulation of data elements. Others [9] have discussed some standardization challenges related to credentials and network. Another initiative to achieve cloud interoperability has been presented in the Interoperability (LISI) Maturity Model [8] published by the Department of Defense (DoD). LISI explores four levels of system interoperability related to procedures, applications, infrastructure, and data.

By defining standards for the alignment of cloud development tools and platforms, the migration from one cloud to another becomes more flexible. Standardization can have a huge impact on the costs of migration, both in money and in time, when services and data need to be transferred from one cloud provider to another one.

---

[3] https://www.docker.com/.

Service Level Agreement. A Service Level Agreement is, in its essence[4], "an agreement between the service provider and its customers quantifying the Minimum acceptable service to the customer" (capital not added) [10].

Long-term viability would clearly be one requirement that is not fit for formal specification or monitoring. Nonetheless it could be addressed in a SLA, for example by addressing issues such as disaster recovery, data portability and an exit strategy. In particular, with respect to data portability, the parties might benefit from clauses specifying:

- The use of some interface which would ease migration to other providers, to protect the customer in case of data loss or business failure of the CSP;
- Strict conditions and terms under which the customer is entitled to enact the migration, to avoid damages to the CSP due to abuse on part of the customer.

Recently, the European Cloud Select Industry Group on Service Level Agreements (C-SIG SLA)[5] has released a set of guidelines toward a standardisaztion of SLAs. Among the service level objectives that should be covered by the SLA, the guidelines suggest including a termination process [7], with steps to enable the customer to retrieve their data. The problem with this clause, however, is that it might be difficult to apply in a short time in the case of a sudden bankruptcy of the CSP.

Service Choreographies. Cloud-based services are intricate by design as they are composed of a number of software services that maintain several features which depend on different stakeholders. To maintain these dynamic interactions between stakeholders, an abstraction layer that models the different flows of communications between cloud-based software entities is needed.

Choreographies [17] have been widely used in the context of web services to specify how services interact with each other. They commonly rely on the orchestration of every entity that can be involved in this choreography. An orchestration specifies from a central view the behaviour of collaborating parties and the flow of message exchanges between the different entities. A choreography gives more visibility about the interactions between the different collaborators, since it enables each collaborator in the choreography to observe all message exchanges involved in the different.

Choreographies can be revisited in the cloud context to provide a high-level view of the interactions between the different stakeholders involved in maintaining cloud services. Maintaining the status of the different collaborations between the different entities involved in the deployment, delivery and usage of a service eases the tracking of the partners taking part in the management of cloud-based applications when the provider goes out of business.

---

[4] Other definitions of Service Level Agreement (SLAs) exist. According to [22], SLAs are "a common way to formally specify the exact conditions (both functional and non-functional) under which services are or should be delivered".

[5] Information about the group can be found at https://ec.europa.eu/digital-agenda/en/cloud-select-industry-group-service-level-agreements.

4.2   Legal Perspective and Solutions

Contractual agreements can help the stakeholders of a cloud environment avoid the worries of the CSP's bankruptcy or cessation of business. If the problem is not addressed beforehand, the customer might incur into serious trouble, because *ex post* remedies can be quite ineffective.

Once the customer's assets fall into the bankrupt estate, recovering them might prove uncertain, expensive, and long enough to seriously damage the customer's business. In addition, the liablility of a CSP for not being able to provide its service in continuity is rather blurred (whereas provisions exist concerning liability for IP violations, failure in data protection, or negligence in security [21]), and CSPs normally operate by means of non-negotiable contracts that make frequent use of liability waivers. Customers are not guaranteed in case of a prolonged inactivity of the CSP which cascades upon them.

When filing for bankruptcy, the management of the company is transferred from the CEO or board to a trustee, under the surveillance of a tribunal. Licensors or third-party providers cannot take action against the bankrupt CSP without a judicial authorization, so customers have a few days to react. However, this protection can't be relied upon if human intervention is needed, because employees cannot be guaranteed to provide customer support [6]. This problem would also impact differently depending on the size of the CSP: the customers of a major provider would have an easier opportunity to recover their data, than those of a small enterprise.

If the CSP simply ceases its activity without filing for bankruptcy, the situation can be much more complicated. The customer will simply have the normal legal remedies such as filing a suit for a breach of contract, but this does not aid in recovering the assets, especially when manual intervention would be required on the CSP's side.

An insurance of the CSP in favor of the customer can reduce the risks by covering the losses suffered by the customer, although it would not ease the recovery of the assets. Also, a simpler form of private insurance might imply the CSP requesting a few months' payment in advance from the customer; this fee would have to be bound to ensuring the temporary continuation of the service (including manual operation) even in case of bankruptcy. This solution, combined with some agreement which would grant the customer access to its assets, would allow the customer to recover the data and prepare for the migration or insourcing of the services.

CSPs might use part of their revenues to establish a special guarantee fund devoted to keep the services up and running for several months, giving their customers the opportunity to take appropriate measures (a SaaS-guarantee fund has been suggested [23], but it can be applied to other paradigms as well). The fund could also be set up in a collaboration between several CSPs, but this would have the drawback that when an individual CSP in the consortium disappears, the others might feel like they are paying for its expenses, and this would be an inhibitor against setting up such a fund. At any rate, the authors acknowledge that no such fund exists at the moment.

In 2013, the Luxembourgish Parliament tried to address the problem of a CSP going bankrupt. The Parliament introduced provisions[6] that allow owners of intangible non-fungible goods held by a bankrupt to reclaim those data at their own expenses, provided they are separable from all other assets. The provision, according to the parliamentary discussion, was introduced specifically to address the issue of a CSP going bankrupt, although its application is not limited to cloud environments.

The Luxembourgish approach is definitely a step toward addressing the problem of CSP viability. However, it only allows to recover the assets, but does not help in relocating to some other CSP or insourcing, unless the services have been designed with portability in mind. Moreover, it does not work well with SaaS platforms, because the customer will not be able to recover the software, which is a shared platform and not a proprietary asset of the customer.

The imaginative solutions suggested in [12] place too much emphasis on the source code, and appear to address the legal issues but not the technical implications. A split copyright between the CSP and the customer consists in transferring part of software copyrights to the user, whereas a joint copyright transfers a share of the ownership; in both cases, the copyright of the whole source code does not fall into the bankrupt estate. The software code could be assigned in usufruct to the customer, or IP rights transferred to a foundation or association of customers. Notwithstanding the inefficiency of these ideas, which would hinder the CSP's ability to evolve or improve the services, they place too much emphasis on the source code. They may allow its partial recovery, but not ensure the continuity of the services, as the customer might not have the technical resources to use those assets.

Data ownership, on the other hand, can be detailed in the contract, so that the customer's data do not fall into the bankrupt estate. Again, this does not help if the CSP simply shuts down the operations, as the customer will not be able to recover the data even if it has the right to do so. Therefore, the contract should either guarantee some maintenance even after the business closure, at least for a short period, or provide the customer with some means of accessing the data without the intervention of the CSP personnel.

A CSP suffering bad financial conditions might not file for bankruptcy or cease its business, but rather be acquired or merged by a financially stronger enterprise. Under these conditions, the customer is relatively safe, because the acquiring enterprise will inherit the existing contracts of the CSP, giving the customer time to renegotiate the terms or migrate to other providers.

However, there might be some issues related to the regulations on personal data, due to the change of the data controller, something that is more and more frequent. Currently, European legislation on data protection does not explicitly address the issue. However, some national rulings have filled in the gaps, by requiring that the companies involved in the merger operation notify their customers about the terms of the operation.

---

[6] Luxembourgish Code of commerce, Article 567.

4.3   Mixed Approaches

Software escrows [16] are a part of intellectual property licenses that define necessary terms to maintain a product, including software code. A software escrow is based on a relationship between a licensor and licensee, set up through an escrow agent (a trusted third party). The agent delivers the software to the licensee and manages it according to an agreement. To ensure continuity of the service, software management is delegated to the licensee in case the licensor is not able to guarantee the software service anymore, due to bankruptcy or disaster. The licensee will then provide the service continuity.

Software escrow techniques must be revisited for cloud-based services. As the hosting of data and/or software is outsourced, the availability of services is not guaranteed by securing a traditional escrow (which only covers source code), but lies in the hands of the CSP, which is a key entity to ensure continuity of the services.

Software escrow solutions raise issue concerning software synchronization and the viability of software escrow agents, which is one of the major factors that reduces the assurance of service continuity in a software escrow service. Additionally, software escrows are mainly able to address a SaaS services model, whereas solutions for IaaS and PaaS providers require mirroring the infrastructure.

Dedicated escrow solutions for cloud-based software applications offer a mirroring of the whole application execution environment [23]. To maintain cloud-based software available when the provider goes out of service, the hardware resources, application platform, dependencies and on-line status execution are continuously mirrored. Companies like Iron Mountain and EscrowTech have developed some dedicated services for SaaS systems, offering business continuity options based on backup sites mirroring the services and the data. This solution is ideal since it enables to restore the whole provider's context when it goes out of business, assuring the continuity of services. In case of a service failure, the escrow agreement enables these backup sites to ensure the continuity of services. However, it is quite expensive for both the cloud customer and the provider because each service that runs in the cloud environment must be cloned.

Recently, an escrow alliance has described the essential building blocks for a cloud escrow solution[7]:

- The contract that states relevant elements related to the source code of applications and their underlying platforms, the SLAs and the users' context;
- An online deposit as a backup environment to ensure service availability;
- Verification mechanisms to control the backup and restoration of processes.

Both cloud providers and users can benefit from software escrow techniques, but there is still a lot of effort to be done by cloud stakeholders in the domain of software escrows, particularly with respect to standard agreements.

---

[7] http://www.escrowalliance.nl/en/escrow-solutions/cloud-escrow-solutions/.

Table 1. Summary of solutions for long-term viability.

Solution	Type	Applies to	Notes
Back-ups	IT	All	Some in-house infrastructure is required, but less expensive as the one needed to deliver the service. Ready duplicate of software and data for fast redeployment
Cloud portability	IT	IaaS, partly PaaS	Requires standards for cloud support which currently do not exist. Also requires the existence of a different CSP offering the same type of service
Service Level Agreement	IT	All	A SLA can define both functional and non-functional requirements, but metrics are required for enforcement. Such metrics might help assess the CSP's financial stability
Service choreographies	IT	All	Standard interfaces between services make it easier to replace an actor in case of a cessation of business. A governing board can also remove an actor if it doesn't provide enough guarantees
Contractual remedies	Legal	All	It might be hard to obtain the fulfilment of the CSP's obligations and damage restoration once it ceases business, and damage restoration does not help the customer reenact its business in a short time
Insurance	Legal	All	Should be combined with a contractual agreement to recover the customer's own assets, without the CSP's cooperation
Recovery of own data	Legal	PaaS, SaaS	Only applicable in Luxembourg so far
Split copyright	Legal	SaaS	Problems in splitting copyright over multiple customers and about the ownership of the data. Only allows the recovery of the source code which is not the key feature of modern cloud environments
Software escrow	Mixed	All	The agreement with the original CSP must address the transmission of data to the escrow. Additionally, having a mirrored service involves additional costs

5   Summary of Proposed Solutions

Table 1 offers a quick overview of the possible approaches that can be used to tackle the problem of long-term viability described in the previous pages.

The point, then, is what solutions a CSP should adopt, and what features an enterprise should look at when selecting a CSP, to have a guarantee of long-term viability. Due to space limitations, only some preliminary considerations will follow, while a detailed cost analysis of the technical and legal solutions is out of the scope of this paper and will be reserved for a future work.

Interoperability techniques and standards for cloud portability are easy and cheap improvements if adopted early on, while they become more complex and expensive as the business size and the number of customer grows. As it is unlikely that a large CSP disappears in a short time, redesigning a non-interoperable platform to allow easy portability of the services might be an appealing solution only for small and medium CSPs.

SLAs and service choreographies are more practical solutions, because they do not involve redesigning the services but only providing a guaranteed quality of service and adequate interfaces. They are fit for both small and large CSPs, and adopting a service choreography model can improve the quality of the single actor and of the overall service composition.

From a legal standpoint, an insurance that guarantees that the services will keep running for some months after the CSP goes out of business would help medium and large providers, while for small ones it might have too high a cost against the benefits it offers. The insurance cost would be charged back on the customers, and this might be possible only in an economy of scale.

Finally, software escrows and mirroring provide huge benefits to viability, but their cost might be prohibitive. Small enterprises might not be able to afford the costs of maintaining a duplicate of their services and data at an escrow provider, whereas large CSPs might have such a technological asset that doubling the resources might be a non-feasible task. In short, escrow services seem to provide a positive benefit-cost ratio only for medium-sized CSPs.

6   Conclusion

This work analyses the current cloud landscape by focusing on the challenges related to CSPs' long-term viability. One of the main risks associated to the cloud computing model has been pointed out, analysing the current challenges behind the continuity of services when the provider goes out of business.

Several approaches can be taken in advance, to mitigate the problems into which the customer can incur in case the CSP actually (and maybe suddenly) goes out of business. These approaches can ensure that the service keeps running steadily, albeit under a different legal entity (software escrow, but this is also what happens in the case of a merger); keep the services running for some time, to allow the customer to retrieve its assets (insurances and advance payments);

allow to quickly migrate the outsourced assets (standards and federated clouds); or allow recovery of the assets in a bankrupt procedure (under Luxembourgish law). Only the first category is long-term, while all others require a fast response on the customer's side.

The viability risk is minimal for big corporations; but when outsourcing to a small enterprise, appropriate measures are needed in case the CSP vanishes from one day to the next one. The problem of cloud providers' long-term viability has no easy solution, since it is unpredictable if and when a CSP will go out of business. Most of the approaches proposed in the context of this paper were not designed to address this problem specifically but can be tailored to mitigate it. The choice of a CSP can also be based on the degree of viability offered (such as specific contractual clauses). For this reason, the above measures serve not only to protect the customer against the loss of the means of doing its business, but also to increase the trust inspired by the CSP.

The problem is largely unexplored and would need further investigation. As a possible follow-up to this work, the authors envision a detailed cost analysis of the proposed solutions, and metrics to measure their effects.

References

1. Anthony, S.: Megaupload's demise: what happens to your files when a cloud service dies? January 2012. http://www.extremetech.com/computing/114803-megauploads-demise-what-happens-to-your-files-when-a-cloud-service-dies
2. Bauer, E., Adams, R.: Reliability and Availability of Cloud Computing, 1st edn. Wiley-IEEE Press, Hoboken (2012)
3. Bowen, J.A.: Legal issues in cloud computing. In: Buyya, R., Broberg, J., Goscinski, A.M. (eds.) Cloud Computing: Principles and Paradigms, 1st edn, pp. 593–613. Wiley, Hoboken (2011). Chap. 24
4. Brodkin, J.: Gartner: seven cloud-computing security risks. Technical report, Gartner, July 2008
5. Butler, B.: The best time to prepare for getting data out of the cloud isbefore you put it in there, June 2014. http://www.networkworld.com/article/2173255/cloud-computing/cloud-s-worst-case-scenario-what-to-do-if-your-provider-goes-belly-up.html
6. Caplan, D.S.: Bankruptcy in the cloud: effects of bankruptcy by a cloudservices provider. Technical report, Law Offices of David S. Caplan, 1289 FordhamBlvd., Suite 345 Chapel Hill, NC 37514, USA, August 2010. http://ftp.documation.com/references/ABA10a/PDfs/3_3.pdf
7. Cloud Select Industry Group on Service Level Agreements (C-SIG SLA), Brussels: Cloud Service Level Agreement Standardisation Guidelines, June 2014. http://ec.europa.eu/information_society/newsroom/cf/dae/document.cfm?action=display&doc_id=6138
8. Dowell, S., Barreto, A., Michael, J.B., Shing, M.T.: Cloud to cloud interoperability. In: Proceedings of the 6th International Conference on System of Systems Engineering (SoSE), pp. 258–263. IEEE, Albuquerque, June 2011

9. Harsh, P., Dudouet, F., Cascella, R.G., Jegou, Y., Morin, C.: Using open standards for interoperability - issues, solutions, and challenges facing cloud computing. In: Proceedings of the 8th International Conference on Network and Service Management (CNSM) and 6th International DMTF Academic Alliance Workshop on Systems and Virtualization Management: Standards and the Cloud (SVM), pp. 435–440. IEEE, Las Vegas, October 2012

10. Hiles, A.: Service Level Agreements: Winning a Competitive Edge for Support & Supply Services. Rothstein Associates Inc., Brookfield (2000). Rothstein Catalog on Service Level Books

11. Hu, F., Qiu, M., Li, J., Grant, T., Tylor, D., McCaleb, S., Butler, L., Hamner, R.: A review on cloud computing: design challenges in architecture and security. J. Comput. Inf. Technol. **19**(1), 25–55 (2011)

12. Louwers, E.J.: Continuity in the cloud: new practical solutions required. In: iTech-Law 2013 European Conference, October 2013

13. Machado, G.S., Hausheer, D., Stiller, B.: Considerations on the interoperability of and between cloud computing standards. In: 27th OpenGrid Forum (OGF27), G2C-Net Workshop: From Grid to Cloud Networks, OGF, Banff, Canada, October 2009. http://dx.doi.org/10.5167/uzh-24316

14. McKendrick, J.: What to do in case your cloud provider falls off the grid, November 2013. http://www.forbes.com/sites/joemckendrick/2013/11/04/what-to-do-in-case-your-cloud-provider-falls-off-the-grid/

15. Mills, L.H.: Legal issues associated with cloud computing, May 2009. http://www.secureit.com/resources/Cloud%20Computing%20Mills%20Nixon%20Peabody\%205-09.pdf

16. Pappous, P.A.: The software escrow: the court favorite and bankruptcy law. St. Clara High Technol. Law J. **1**(2), 309–326 (1985)

17. Peltz, C.: Web services orchestration and choreography. Computer **36**(10), 46–52 (2003)

18. Thibodeau, P.: One in four cloud providers will be gone by 2015, December 2013. http://www.computerworld.com/article/2486691/cloud-computing/one-in-four-cloud-providers-will-be-gone-by-2015.html

19. Van Hoboken, J., Arnbak, A., Van Eijk, N.: Obscured by clouds or how to address governmental access to cloud data from abroad. In: Proceedings of the 6th Annual Privacy Law Scholars Conference (PLSC), June 2013

20. Venkatraman, A.: 2e2 datacentre administrators hold customers' data to 1m ransom, February 2013. http://www.computerweekly.com/news/2240177744/2e2-datacentre-administrators-hold-customers-data-to-1m-ransom

21. Weber, R.H., Staiger, D.N.: Cloud computing: a cluster of complex liability issues. Web J. Curr. Leg. Issues **20**(1) (2014). http://webjcli.org/article/view/303

22. Wieder, P., Butler, J.M., Theilmann, W., Yahyapour, R. (eds.): Service Level Agreements for Cloud Computing. Springer Science+Business Media, LLC, New York (2011)

23. van de Zande, T., Jansen, S.: Business continuity solutions for SaaS customers. In: Regnell, B., van de Weerd, I., De Troyer, O. (eds.) ICSOB 2011. LNBIP, vol. 80, pp. 17–31. Springer, Heidelberg (2011)

Evolution of the Global Knowledge Network: Network Analysis of Information and Communication Technologies' Patents

Kibae Kim[(✉)]

Technology Management, Economics, and Policy Program,
Seoul National University, Seoul, South Korea
kibaejjang@gmail.com

Abstract. In recent studies, Information and Communication Technologies have been key drivers of innovation and economic growth throughout the world. Because the Information and Communication Technology products and services require intensive knowledge, leading countries invested in their innovation systems to operate more effectively and efficiently. Studies on innovation have investigated the knowledge base of countries and their respective relationships with their national institutions, and subsequent economic growth to identify factors which have led to success. However, the approaches of previous studies omit the constituents of the knowledge base while focusing on quantitative aspects such as size. In this article, I propose a novel approach to exploring the knowledge base at a global level by undertaking a network analysis of patents. In this framework, the global knowledge network is defined as a set of countries and respective technological similarities between countries as vertices and edges. Applying this framework, the research questions are addressed qualitatively by identifying the structure of the network and how it has evolved. The analysis results indicate that the global knowledge network consists of a cluster of developed countries, and the cluster is linked with developing countries through Japan, U.S.A. and China. They also show that the Information and Communication Technology leaders changed from Great Britain and France to U.S.A. in 1920s, from U.S.A. to Japan in 1970s. The framework is expected to be applied to economic studies of innovation and knowledge bases at a global level.

Keywords: Global knowledge network · Information and Communication Technology · Technology leadership · Network analysis · Patents

1 Introduction

Business entities and governments in developed countries have been interested in Information and Communication Technologies (ICT) since the 1980 s for the reason that it can be used for consumer goods (e.g. computers and telephones), as well as helping to promote related services (e.g. banking and insurance) [15]. Furthermore, the global economy has grown in step with the ICT industry throughout the past last two decades [4]. The advancement of the ICT industry has

© Springer International Publishing Switzerland 2016
J. Altmann et al. (Eds.): GECON 2015, LNCS 9512, pp. 296–307, 2016.
DOI: 10.1007/978-3-319-43172-2_20

enabled business entities to copy, transfer and implement high-tech information services. Thanks to this advancement, people could enhance their innovative practices at an individual level, while innovation was mainly achieved by private and public organizations in the traditional way of innovation.

The key to ICT is that its outputs are based on intensive technologies. For this reason, ICT has become a topic of interest in innovation studies. Previous studies explained the relationship between ICT innovation and political implementation to identify ICT innovation success factors on the basis of quantitative analysis and case studies [16, 24]. Their theoretical background is that innovation is dependent on institutions [21] and respective knowledge base systems [5], as well as economic conditions. However, the quantitative approaches in the previous studies omit the contents of knowledge that a country possesses, while they view technologies from a quantitative perspective.

In this article, we propose a novel framework for investigating the knowledge base of countries on the basis of network theories to discuss ICT innovation at a global level. In this framework, we measure the knowledge base components from patents in the ICT field, applied to each country in the world. We identify the similarity of knowledge between a pair of countries by examining knowledge components and what they involve. With these measurements, we define a global knowledge network, consisting of countries (vertices), and similarities between pairs of countries (edges with weights). By analyzing the position of the countries within the global knowledge network as well as inspecting its structure and evolution allows us to address the issue of finding which country leads the advancement of ICT technologies in the global knowledge network.

The analysis identifies three main results. First, there is a cluster consisting of developed countries in which knowledge is vigorously exchanged. Second, the United States and Japan are the bridge connecting the cluster with developing countries. Third, the leading countries are replaced with emerging countries. That is, the United States of America caught up with Great Britain and France in 1920s, as did Japan with the United States in the 1970s. It is considerable that the position of countries in the global knowledge network reflects their economic growth, and that the role of innovation leaders (i.e., U.S.A. and Japan) was different in the global knowledge network. These findings suggest that the framework is consistent with innovative global trends, thereby desirable for economic analysis. It identifies and helps understanding the qualitative as well as quantitative perspectives.

The remainder of this paper is organized as follows. The next section gives a brief summary about the conceptual background of innovation in the field of Information and Communication Technologies and global knowledge networks. In Sect. 3, we outlines the process of defining the global knowledge network from the empirical raw data of patents. Section 4 presents the results about the global knowledge network diagram and the position of seven representative countries (i.e., U.S.A., Great Britain, France, Germany, Japan, China and Korea) in the global knowledge network.

2   Conceptual Background

2.1   Economic Growth Through Innovation in Information and Communication Technologies

By the 1980 s governments of developed countries, i.e., U.S.A. and Japan, recognized opportunities for economic growth offered by ICT. As a result, they tried to promote ICT to enhance their competitiveness [15]. New products (e.g., satellites, computers and telephones) are developed in the field of ICT, and these are then applied to various service sectors (e.g., financing, banking and customer relation management) [15]. In addition, productivity has increased in the industrial sectors that have adopted ICT through automation of manufacturing processes and efficient information sharing and storing [4]. Around the 2000s the effect of ICT innovation on economic growth was highest in U.S.A., which involved the industries that are ready to adopt ICT [13,24]. Furthermore, the strategic innovation of Korea's ICT industry (especially, Liquid Crystal Display, semiconductors and mobile phones) made it possible for Korea to complete its industrialization even though it experienced a major financial crisis in the late 1990s [6,14].

2.2   Innovation for Economic Competitiveness

Knowledge is a resource for production [9]. By definition it has various types. For example, knowledge becomes *explicit* when it is codified in documents including reports, patents and academic articles, while workers in a company accumulate *tacit* knowledge in their routine tasks [3]. Some knowledge is so *simple* that a person can obtain and transfer it easily, while other knowledge is so *complex* that it requires integrated communication and collaboration for understanding and transferring.

Because knowledge affects productivity, governments implement innovative policies to promote knowledge creation by integrating academy and industry and removing barrier for new entrants [3]. It is important that knowledge is created in a way that reflects how business entities face problems and solve them by searching for solution [10]. It is constructed by people in a society in which they share and exchange their knowledge. Due to its social aspect, innovation is dependent on the composition of people and organizations, and the institution and culture by which the business entities run. That is, innovation is performed in a system [21].

2.3   Global Knowledge Network

As ICT facilitates easier knowledge transfer between countries, the purpose of global collaboration has changed from searching for cheapest production to searching for appropriate knowledge [12]. As a result, multi-national companies form a global innovation network, defined as a set of firms and their linkages for the purpose of innovation. Transformation is affected by the nature of knowledge, the size of a knowledge base, and the ICT institutions of individual countries [12]. Knowledge transfer between multi-national companies can be tracked on the basis of patents. A previous study analyzed the network of countries linked by patents concurrently published by pairs of countries, reflecting the change of leadership from Japan, U.S.A. and Germany in 1996 to U.S.A., Germany and France in 2005 [20]. Furthermore, citations of patents reveal the knowledge flow from cited networks to citing networks; the investment of a developing country in innovation enhances the knowledge flow inside the country, which was previously from abroad [27].

3 Methodology

3.1 Data

For this analysis, patent data was gathered from the 2014 Spring Edition of the European Patent Office Statistical Database (EPO PATSTAT) [23]. This data product provides bibliographic information of patents applied for approximately 90 countries including U.S.A., Great Britain, Japan and Korea. It contains the title, the name and address of applicants, the application filing date, application authority (or country) and citation of applied patents. The patents are categorized with International Patent Classification (IPC) codes, which were designed under the Strasbourg Agreement in 1979 and managed by the World Intellectual Property Organization (WIPO) [2]. The IPC codes hierarchically classify patents on four levels: section, class, subclass, group (subgroup) in order from top to bottom [1]. The IPC codes include eight sections. In our analysis we used patents classified in Section H (Electricity), which corresponds closely with Information and Communication Technologies. This section includes six classes: H01 (Basic Electric Elements), H02 (Electric Power), H03 (Basic Electronic Circuitry), H04 (Electric Communication Technique), H05 (Other Electric Techniques), H99 (Subject Matter Not Covered in this Section). The six classes are divided into fifty one subclasses, and into more detailed groups or subgroups.

3.2 Definition of the Global Knowledge Network

To identify the constituents of the knowledge base, we define knowledge vector x_i for each country $i = 1, \cdots, n$ and year $t = 1877, \cdots, 2013$. In the vector, each element c_ν means the number that IPC code $\nu = 1, \cdots, m$ appears in the patents applied in country i in year t, where total number of IPC codes in the knowledge bases is m. Defining the knowledge vector as $x_i(t) = \langle c_1, \cdots, c_\nu, \cdots, c_m \rangle$, we measure the knowledge similarity in year t between countries i and $j \neq i$, where $1 \leq i, j \leq n$, with the inner product of a pair of knowledge vectors. It is outlined in Eq. (1).

$$v_{i,j}(t) = x_i(t) \cdot x_j(t) \tag{1}$$

Previous studies usually measured similarities using the inner product normalized by the length of vectors, or cosine similarity: $(x_i/|x_i|) \cdot (x_j/|x_j|)$ [17,19].

This normalization removes the effect of size that a country exhibits, which in turn identifies the degree that elements corresponds between the two vectors. However, we use the non-normalized metric of similarity in order to consider the size effect as well as the effect of element matching.

Using Eq. (1), we define the global knowledge network. It is a weighted, undirected graph. In the network, a vertex is a country i whose patent authority uses IPC codes. A previous study assumed that an IPC code represents a knowledge element that an innovation agent possesses [7]. With the assumption on IPC codes, we define an edge as a pair of countries that both contain common IPC codes. It is notable that knowledge is accumulated in organizations for future innovation [22], and the knowledge retained in the near past is more valid and useful than those in the far past [8,28]. Edge weight is the accumulation of similarity between countries decaying exponentially by time [26]. The weight of an edge between vertices i and j in year t, where $i \neq j$ and $1 \leq i, j \leq n$, is defined in Eq. (2).

$$w_{i,j} = \sum_{t'} v_{i,j}(t') \exp\{(t' - t)\}$$ (2)

3.3   Analysis Process

The position of each country is analyzed through the vertex "strength" [25]. Vertex strength is a weighted graph version of degree centrality. It is defined as the sum of weights between a focal vertex and its directly connected neighbour vertices. The strength i in year t is defined in Eq. (3).

$$s_i(t) = \sum_{j \neq i} w_{i,j}(t)$$ (3)

Depicting the trend of strength for each country according to time, we identify the position of the country in the global knowledge network. The network position means how much the knowledge of a country is close to the knowledge of the other countries. As a pair of countries entail common IPC codes, their knowledge constituents get similar. Therefore, the strength of a country in the global knowledge network reflects the country's leadership in terms of innovation. That is, the leading country absorbs knowledge from other countries, setting innovation trends while its neighbours follow these trends.

4   Results

The global knowledge network which we analyzed grew from five countries (i.e., U.S.A., Great Britain, France, Germany and Austria) in 1911 to 67 countries in 2011. Because the network was not stable until 1910, we analyze the network from 1911. In order to avoid the data fluctuation over the last years, we analyze the network up to and including 2011. Among the countries involved in the network, we identified four countries (i.e., China, the United States of America, Japan, Korea) in which the most patents were applied in 2011, and three countries (i.e., Germany, Great Britain and France) which were involved in the global knowledge network from 1877. From this point forward, we use the two letter country code regulated in the International Organization for Standardization (ISO) (Table 1).

Table 1. ISO 3166-1 alpha-2 two-letter country codes.

Code	Name	Code	Name	Code	Name
AR	Argentina	EP	Eur. Patent Office	MY	Malaysia
AT	Austria	ES	Spain	NL	Netherlands
AU	Australia	FI	Finland	NO	Norway
BE	Belgium	FR	France	PL	Poland
BG	Bulgaria	GB	Great Britain	RO	Romania
BR	Brazil	HU	Hungary	RU	Russia
CA	Canada	IE	Ireland	SE	Sweden
CH	Switzerland	IL	Israel	SU	Soviet Union
CN	China	IT	Italy	TR	Turkey
CS	Czechoslovakia	JP	Japan	TW	Taiwan
DD	East Germany	KR	South Korea	US	United States
DE	(West) Germany	LU	Luxembourg	YU	Yugoslavia
DK	Denmark	MX	Mexico	ZA	South Africa

We drew the diagrams of the global knowledge network for each year, and deleted the edges with a weight 0.002 times lower than the maximum weight for readability. We found three phases of network topology, which transited between approximately 1970 and 2000. Figures 1, 2 and 3 represent these three phases. Since the beginning and up to around 1970, the global knowledge network has grown from Great Britain, France, Germany and the United States, forming a cluster surrounded by newly entering countries including Austria, the Netherlands, Switzerland, and the Soviet Union (Fig. 1).

The network topology firstly changed around 1970. Since then Japan entered for the first time and was situated at the center, connecting the cluster of developed countries with developing countries. In Fig. 2, the right side consists of densely connected countries at the core of which are Great Britain, France, Germany and the United States. On the other hand, the countries in the left side are connected only with Japan, and mainly developing countries such as South Korea, Romania and Turkey.

The topology of the global knowledge network changes slightly again around 2000. Around then, there was a tendency for developing countries to be linked with the United States and soon after, China, as well as Japan. The cluster of developed countries including those three countries was maintained during the period. Finally, the location of Japan became similar to that of the

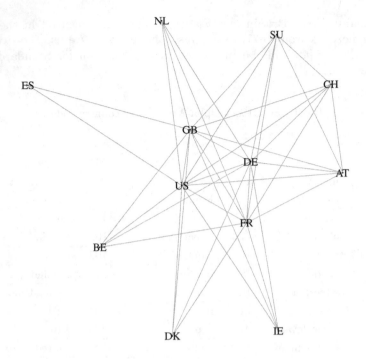

Fig. 1. Global knowledge network in 1931.

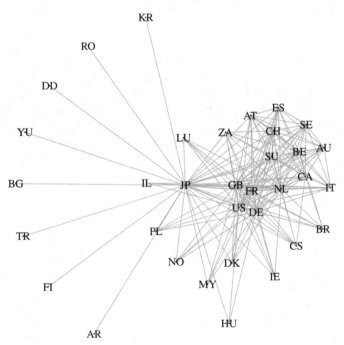

Fig. 2. Global knowledge network in 1971.

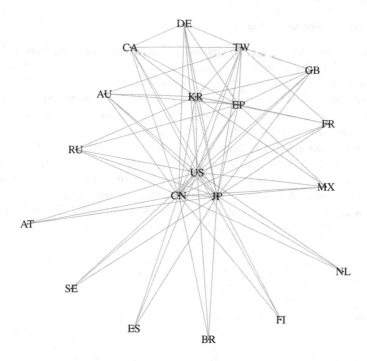

Fig. 3. Global knowledge network in 2011.

United States and China. In Fig. 3 those countries are well connected with existing developed countries including Great Britain, France and Germany, and with emerging countries such as Finland, South Korea and Taiwan. The reason that the diagram in Fig. 3 is simpler than the former ones is partly that the gap between the maximum of the weight and the remainders became broaden in this year.

In summary, the global knowledge network grew with a cluster consisting of the developed countries entering the network earlier, which are surrounded by latecomers. Reminding that the weight depicts how a pair of countries contain common knowledge elements, which are represented with IPC codes, we can imagine that the developed countries involved in the cluster advance IT with active knowledge transfer. On the other hand, other latecomers mainly surround the cluster. Japan is an interesting latecomer which entered the network late, or after World War Two, but approached the center early while linking latecoming countries with the cluster of developed countries. Consider that knowledge mainly transfers from a developed country to a developing country. Then the diagram shows that Japan has been a role model for developing countries innovating the ICT field.

4.1   Trend in Network Position

Figure 4 illustrates the selected countries's trends in the global knowledge network from 1911 to 2011, measured with the vertex strength defined in Eq. (3). This metric is also rescaled with the logarithm under 10, as outlined in the previous subsection. In 1911, Great Britain and France were situated at the central position in the global knowledge network, and Germany and the United States at the outer position in relation to the two leading countries. The United States and Germany approached the position of leading countries (i.e., Great Britain and France), and slightly surpassed them in 1920. However, the position of Germany retreated to the periphery around 1945, which may be a result of World War Two, and was restored to its former position in 1950. The network position of the US and Germany departed more from the position of Great Britain and France in the 1970s, after their position moved closer together.

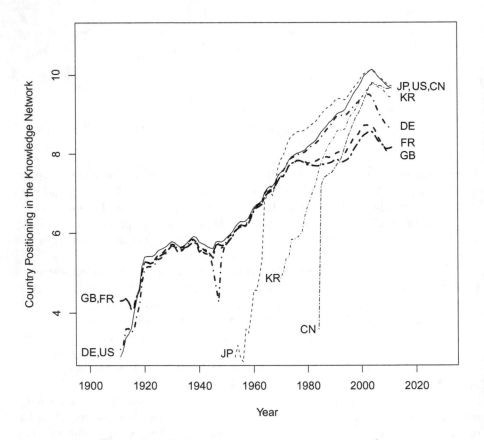

Fig. 4. Trend of representative countries in strength.

After World War Two, Japan, Korea and China entered the global knowledge network respectively in 1952, 1970 and 1984, and rapidly approached to the central position of the network. Japan surpassed the United States in 1970 and maintained the top position until the end of study period. Likewise, Korea and China rapidly approached the centre of the network, respectively surpassing Great Britain in 1984 and 1998. In 2011, their network position is between the United States and Germany. At the end of the study period, Japan, the United States and China were at the center of the global knowledge network. Korea, Germany, France and Great Britain follow them in order.

5   Discussion and Conclusion

Within this paper, we introduced a framework to explore the worldwide knowledge base on the basis of network analysis with patents. In the framework, we defined the global knowledge network through similarities between countries in knowledge constituents, and calculated the network position of selected countries (i.e., U.S.A., Great Britain, France, Germany, Japan, Korea and China) with vertex strength. The global knowledge network involves a cluster consisting mainly of developed countries, surrounded by latecoming countries. The results also show the new leading countries have replaced the former leading countries: Great Britain and France have been replaced with U.S.A. in 1920, and U.S.A. has been replaced with Japan in 1970.

It is anticipated that our framework will contribute to both the academic community and industry. From an academic perspective, our framework provides a methodology that can influence constituents of national knowledge bases. Previous empirical studies considered patents as knowledge bases that affect economic growth. However, they mainly dealt with the quantitative aspect of knowledge bases such as the number of patents [11,18]. According to their analyses, we can anticipate the effect of innovation input and output levels on economic growth. However, they do not refer to what knowledge elements they achieve with economic growth. On the other hand, our framework compares the knowledge components of one country with the other to identify their respective positions in the entire knowledge network. Therefore, our results can identify the knowledge components that supported the economic growth of a country. This new framework also offers political implications. The research model of previous studies considers only innovation input and output, and their effect on economic growth in an isolated system. As we analyze the constituents of knowledge between countries, our results illustrate what a country had learned from whom, and how this is beneficial to economic growth. Therefore, as investing in learning is a key to economic growth, our framework can also identify what an individual country can learn to promote economic growth.

Although our analysis describes the global knowledge network, the framework has currently some limitations that require further studies. First, we need more investigation on the kind of knowledge that is represented by patents, to validate our framework. Currently, we only measured the constituents of the patents applied in a certain year to a certain country. However, since some of applied patents are rejected to be approved in the patent review process, it is therefore arguable that the applied patents describe the knowledge of a country entirely. In addition, a patent is applied for by a foreign company with the aim of earning royalties. Therefore, it is also arguable that the knowledge components which appear in the patent applications of two countries mean that both entail the knowledge; rather, it might mean that one country is subordinated to another one. Second, the results require explanation in the context of historical events. The rise and fall of a country's position in the global knowledge network reflects its economic conditions. For example, the slump of Germany around 1945 is related to World War Two. However, we do not know what made Japan, South Korea and China moved quickly to the center of the global knowledge network, and why Japan was at the center during the last half of 20th century. Third, national entities have also changed while the global knowledge network has continued to evolve. The Soviet Union absorbed some East European countries and many independent countries, while East Germany and West Germany were integrated in the early 1990s. Therefore, it needs to be investigated which country inherited the knowledge of another country. This requires policy analysis of each country, the market environment and all the conditions surrounding their innovation and economic growth.

Acknowledgements. This research was supported by the Basic Science Research Program through the National Research Foundation of Korea (NRF), which is funded by the Ministry of Education (Grant No. 2013R1A1A2058665).

References

1. International Patent Classification (IPC)
2. Strasbourg Agreement Concerning the International Patent Classification: Strasbourg Agreement Concerning the International Patent Classification (as amended on 28 September 1979) (Authentic Text)
3. Autant-Bernard, C., Fadairo, M., Massard, N.: Knowledge diffusion and innovation policies within the European regions: challenges based on recent empirical evidence. Res. Policy **42**(1), 196–210 (2013)
4. Brynjolfsson, E., Saunders, A.: Wired for Innovation: How Information Technology is Reshaping the Economy. The MIT Press, Cambridge (2013)
5. Castellacci, F., Zheng, J.: Technological regimes, schumpeterian patterns of innovation and firm-level productivity growth. Indus. Corp. Change **19**(6), 1829–1865 (2010)
6. Choung, J.-Y., Hameed, T., Ji, I.: Catch-up in ICT standards: policy, implementation and standards-setting in South Korea. Technol. Forecast. Soc. Change **79**(4), 771–788 (2012)
7. Dibiaggio, L., Nasiriyar, M., Nesta, L.: Substitutability and complementarity of technological knowledge and the inventive performance of semiconductor companies. Res. Policy **43**(9), 1582–1593 (2014)
8. Fleming, L.: Recombinant uncertainty in technological search. Manag. Sci. **47**(1), 117–132 (2001)
9. Gibson, D.V., Naquin, H.: Investing in innovation to enable global competitiveness: the case of Portugal. Technol. Forecast. Soc. Change **78**(8), 1299–1309 (2011)

10. Hargadon, A.B.: Brokering knowledge: linking learning and innovation. Res. Organ. Behav. **24**(41–85), 41–85 (2002)
11. Hasan, I., Tucci, C.L.: The innovation economic growth nexus: global evidence. Res. Policy **39**(10), 1264–1276 (2010)
12. Herstad, S.J., Aslesen, H.W., Ebersberger, B.: On industrial knowledge bases, commercial opportunities and global innovation network linkages. Res. Policy **43**(3), 495–504 (2014)
13. Jorgenson, D.W., Ho, M.S., Stiroh, K.J.: A retrospective look at the U.S. productivity growth resurgence. J. Econ. Perspect. **22**(1), 3–24 (2008)
14. Jung, H.-J., Na, K.-Y., Yoon, C.-H.: The role of ICT in Korea's economic growth: productivity changes across industries since the 1990s. Telecommun. Policy **37**(4), 292–310 (2013)
15. Jussawalla, M.: The race for telecommunication technology: The USA v. Japan. Telecommun. Policy **11**(3), 297–307 (1987)
16. Larson, J.F., Park, J.: From developmental to network state: government restructuring and ICT-LED innovation in Korea. Telecommun. Policy **38**(4), 344–359 (2014)
17. Leydesdorff, L.: Patent classifications as indicators of intellectual organization (2009). arXiv: 0911.1439 [physics]
18. Moser, P.: How do patent laws influence innovation? Evidence from nineteenth-century world's fair. Am. Econ. Rev. **95**(4), 1214–1236 (2005)
19. Nakamura, H., Suzuki, S., Sakata, I., Kajikawa, Y.: Knowledge combination modeling: the measurement of knowledge similarity between different technological domains. Technol. Forecast. Soc. Change **94**, 187–201 (2015)
20. Nam, Y., Barnett, G.A.: Globalization of technology: network analysis of global patents and trademarks. Technol. Forecast. Soc. Change **78**(8), 1471–1485 (2011)
21. Nelson, R.R. (ed.): National Innovation Systems: A Comparative Analysis, 1st edn. Oxford University Press, Oxford (1993)
22. Nelson, R.R., Winter, S.G.: An Evolutionary Theory of Economic Change. Belknap Press, Cambridge (1985)
23. European Patent Office: EPO Worldwide Patent Statistical Database (PATSTAT)
24. Oliner, S.D., Sichel, D.E.: The resurgence of growth in the late 1990s: is information technology the story? J. Econ. Perspect. **14**(4), 3–22 (2000)
25. Opsahl, T., Agneessens, F., Skvoretz, J.: Node centrality in weighted networks: generalizing degree and shortest paths. Soc. Netw. **32**(3), 245–251 (2010)
26. Palla, G., Barabsi, A.-L., Vicsek, T.: Quantifying social group evolution. Nature **446**(7136), 664–667 (2007). 00913
27. Ponomariov, B., Toivanen, H.: Knowledgeows and bases in emerging economy innovation systems: Brazilian research 2005–2009. Res. Policy **43**(3), 588–596 (2014)
28. Yayavaram, S., Ahuja, G.: Decomposability in knowledge structures and its impact on the usefulness of inventions and knowledge-base malleability. Adm. Sci. Q. **53**(2), 333–362 (2008)

A Revised Model of the Cloud Computing Ecosystem

Sebastian Floerecke[✉] and Franz Lehner

Chair of Information Systems II, Universität Passau, Passau, Germany
{sebastian.floerecke, franz.lehner}@uni-passau.de

Abstract. Cloud computing breaks up the traditional value chain of IT provisioning and leads to new roles of market players acting in the ecosystem. Although there exist few publications on modeling the cloud computing ecosystem, each contains a different number and various types of roles. The goal of this research paper is, therefore, to perform a comparative analysis of the dominating cloud computing ecosystem models in order to develop a revised, more comprehensive model. After having excluded several roles assessed as being irrelevant and included the findings of eight interviews with experts from cloud computing service providers, the **P**assau **C**loud Computing **E**cosystem Model (PaCE Model) comprises 18 roles. This model serves as a basis to investigate whether each role can actually be covered by real actors and which typical role clusters prevail in practice. Practitioners can gain a deeper understanding of the ecosystem's complexity and recognize where they are situated and how they are related to each other.

Keywords: Cloud computing · Ecosystem · Roles · Actors · Market · Product service system · Comparative analysis · Literature research

1 Introduction

Cloud computing represents an example for the shift from selling products to providing integrated combinations of products and services that deliver value in use [1]. The trend towards these product service systems (PSS) [2, 3] or hybrid products [4, 5] is mainly based on the fact that customers are oftentimes not interested in products or services per se. Instead, they expect a solution to their specific problem or demand [6, 7]. Cloud computing by itself is not a new technology, but rather a new operations model that brings a set of existing technologies such as virtualization, autonomic computing, grid computing and utility-based pricing together [8, 9]. From a business perspective, cloud computing breaks up the traditional value chain of IT provisioning and leads to new roles of players acting in the ecosystem [10, 11]. A role is a *"[...] set of similar services offered by market players to similar customers"* [10]. This abstraction is necessary as companies can offer various services acting in different roles.

Besides the basic vendors of application, platform and infrastructure, additional providers emerge, for instance, building value-added, complex services or offering consulting services upon these three fundamental components [10, 12]. This is enabled by the fact that actors in cloud computing are able to consume other cloud services

© Springer International Publishing Switzerland 2016
J. Altmann et al. (Eds.): GECON 2015, LNCS 9512, pp. 308–321, 2016.
DOI: 10.1007/978-3-319-43177-2_21

enhancing their own service offerings for their customers [13–15]. From the end costumer's viewpoint, the traditional model of a single provider one-stop provision of outsourcing is, hence, replaced by a web of different vendors [11, 16].

Although there exist few publications on modeling the cloud computing ecosystem, each contains a different number and various types of roles. The goal of this contribution is, therefore, to conduct a comparative analysis of the dominating cloud computing ecosystem models with regard to their roles. In order to identify the existing models, a systematic literature study is performed according to the guidelines of Webster and Watson [17]. These models are analyzed, compared and consolidated into a revised, more comprehensive ecosystem model. Subsequently, eight interviews with experts from cloud service providers are conducted to get a deeper understanding of the cloud computing ecosystem and to examine whether there is any further role that has not been integrated in the model so far.

This research paper is structured as follows: Sect. 2 provides an overview of the cloud computing phenomenon in conjunction with the business ecosystem concept. In order to highlight the modifications made in the revised model, the model of Böhm et al. [10] is depicted and explained as initial model in Sect. 3. In Sect. 4, the research design and the findings from the literature research and the expert interviews are presented and analyzed. The Passau Cloud Computing Ecosystem Model (PaCE Model) is introduced and its roles are described according to their main tasks and attributes in Sect. 5. Section 6 discusses the revised model and Sect. 7 provides the practical use of the model, its limitations and an outlook for future work.

2 The Cloud Computing Phenomenon and Its Ecosystem

The paradigm of actors competing against each other in an impersonal marketplace is becoming less and less adequate in a world where enterprises are embedded in networks of professional, social and exchange relationships with other actors [18]. To take this development into account, Moore [19] initiated the terminology of business ecosystem in which "[...] companies coevolve capabilities around a new innovation: they work cooperatively and competitively to support new products, satisfy customer needs, and eventually incorporate the next round of innovations" [19]. Several other researchers advanced this concept subsequently with different focuses and approaches. Their emphasis is generally on the interconnectedness of economic actors and the fact that they depend on each other for their success and survival [20]. A business ecosystem is further located in an environment consisting of legal, political, cultural and social aspects. These aspects have a significant impact on the ecosystem [21]. With the ecosystem concept, it is, thus, possible to consider actors, their roles and their interconnections from a holistic view to find out how different roles affect each other, as well as to analyze how to create or alter strategies that have effect in determining the success and maintenance of actors in the long-run [19, 22].

In this regard, cloud computing is a phenomenon which implies a substantial change of the IT industry's ecosystem. Cloud computing by itself still lacks a generally accepted definition [23, 24]. According to Madhavaiah et al. [25], this stems from the fact that different scientists define cloud computing with respect to its key components and conceptualizations as they perceive it. Based on the widely cited definition of NIST 2009 [26], *"[c]loud computing is a model for enabling ubiquitous, convenient, on-demand network access to a shared pool of configurable computing resources (e.g., networks, servers, storage, applications, and services) that can be rapidly provisioned and released with minimal management effort or service provider interaction"*. Since NIST does not focus on the business aspect of cloud computing, the definition proposed by Marston et al. [27] is used in this research paper. Their definition is considered as the most comprehensive business related definition according to a content analysis study of Madhavaiah et al. [25]:

"Cloud computing is an information technology service model where computing services (both hardware and software) are delivered on-demand to customers over a network in a self-service fashion, independent of device and location. The resources required to provide the requisite quality-of-service levels are shared, dynamically scalable, rapidly provisioned, virtualized and released with minimal service provider interaction. Users pay for the service as an operating expense without incurring any significant initial capital expenditure, with the cloud services employing a metering system that divides the computing resource in appropriate blocks" [27].

Cloud computing in general can be distinguished into three basic services – Infrastructure as a Service (IaaS), Platform as a Service (PaaS) and Software as a Service (SaaS). These three layers are inherently interrelated, each building on the former [8, 26]: IaaS stands for the needs-based provisioning of infrastructural resources, such as storage or computing power. PaaS allows users to build applications by offering operating system support and a development environment with programming languages, libraries and tools. SaaS refers to providing on-demand applications over the Internet.

To meet the requirements of different customers, the cloud computing concept comprises four deployment models. While in public clouds service providers offer their resources to the general public, private clouds are designed for exclusive use by a single organization. Hybrid clouds are a combination of public and private clouds such that part of the service infrastructure is located in private clouds whereas the remaining part runs in public clouds. The community cloud – a particular private cloud – provides an infrastructure that is shared by several organizations, supporting a specific community with common concerns [8, 26].

3   Böhm et al. [10] as Initial Model

For a structured approach and to highlight the modifications to be made in the revised model, it is helpful to choose an existing model as a starting point. In this research paper, the model of Böhm et al. [10] has chosen as initial model since it is one of the first models in the context of cloud computing, represents the most cited one in literature and also serves as a basis for several other studies published later such as [13, 28]. To develop their model, Böhm et al. [10] analyzed literature on market actors in the areas of living systems theory, network organizations, (electronic) business webs, IT outsourcing, grid computing and value networks in traditional industries and initially identified 105 generic roles. After clustering these roles based on their descriptions, the authors assigned actors of the observed cloud computing market to the role clusters and examined which roles are covered. The result set contains the eight roles of *Infrastructure Provider*, *Platform Provider*, *Application Provider*, *Aggregator*, *Integrator*, *Consultant*, *Market Platform* and *Consumer*.

To illustrate their model, they used the e^3-value methodology that is designed to show how economic value is created and exchanged within a network of actors or roles. Besides actors, the method comprises subsequent five main components [29]: Actors exchange *(1) value objects* that are products, services, money or consumer experiences. A *(2) value port* is utilized by actors to demonstrate that they want to provide or request value objects. This concept serves to focus only on how external actors and other components can be plugged in instead of considering the internal business processes. Actors have one or more *(3) value interfaces* grouping individual value ports. A *(4) value exchange* connects two value ports with each other and represents one or more potential trades of value objects between value ports. A *(5) value offering* is a set of value exchanges that shows which value objects are exchanged by value exchanges in return for other value objects. Figure 1 illustrates the cloud computing ecosystem model according to Böhm et al. [10].

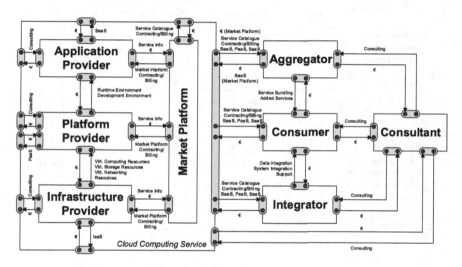

Fig. 1. The Cloud Computing Ecosystem Model according to Böhm et al. [10].

4   Research Design

In order to identify the existing cloud computing ecosystem models – in addition to the initial model – a structured literature research was conducted according to the guidelines of Webster and Watson [17]. Thereby, the literature databases ACM Digital Library, AIS eLibrary, Emerald Insight, Google Scholar, IEEE Xplore and Springer Link were searched for the keywords "Ecosystem", "Value Chain", "Value Creation", "Roles", "Actors", "Market" and "Framework", as well as combinations of them in conjunction with "Cloud Computing". This literature research was restricted to contributions of scientists and professional IT associations, while practical reports were excluded. Firstly, the abstract of each of the 500 most cited publications was screened to examine its relevance for this research paper. After a positive assessment, the publication was read completely. To avoid overlooking relevant literature, the bibliography of the already selected articles were examined (backward search). Simultaneously, a forward search was conducted to identify contributions that were missed by the keyword search as they are newer and, thus, yet still cited less often. Publications on ecosystems from related fields like grid computing (e.g. [30]) have been found to be not close enough to the cloud topic and have, therefore, been skipped. Papers with insufficient descriptions of the roles were also excluded. Finally, thirteen models were selected that form the sample pool for this analysis. These models comprise 29 different roles in total as it is shown in Table 1. In this table, an "x" means that a role is an integral part of the specific model. The main roles already described in the initial model by Böhm et al. [10] are marked in bold.

Table 1. Roles within the cloud computing ecosystem models in literature.

Roles \ Publications	[15]	[11]	[10]	[33]	[13]	[14]	[35]	[37]	[9]	[34]	[28]	[32]	[36]	Σ
Application Provider	x	x	x	x	x	x	x	x	x	x	x	x	x	13
Platform Provider	x		x	x	x		x	x	x	x	x	x	x	11
Infrastructure Provider	x	x	x	x	x	x	x	x	x	x	x	x	x	13
Cloud Infrastructure Provider							x							1
Application Reseller					x									1
Platform Reseller					x									1
Infrastructure Reseller					x									1
Market Platform	x	x	x			x	x		x	x	x		x	9
Application Market Place					x									1
Platform Market Place					x									1
Infrastructure Market Place					x									1
Software Platform							x							1
Consultant	x	x	x			x	x		x	x	x	x		9
Aggregator	x	x	x	x	x	x	x		x	x	x	x		11
Integrator	x	x	x			x	x		x	x	x	x		9
Customer	x	x	x	x	x		x	x	x	x	x	x	x	12
Independent Software Vendor							x		x				x	3
Help Desk	x						x							2
Hybrid Cloud Computing Provider											x			1
Cloud Auditor	x			x								x		3
Service Auditor											x			1
User Auditor											x			1
Hardware Developer	x									x			x	3
Cloud Carrier	x			x					x	x		x	x	6
Terminal Equipment Vendor										x			x	2
Data Provider			x											1
Monitor			x											1
Technique Supporting Vendor										x				1
Virtualization Vendor	x													1
Σ	13	7	10	7	11	6	12	7	11	8	11	9	9	

As Table 1 reveals, out of the 29 identified roles, the main eight roles of Böhm et al. [10] can also be found in most of the other models. But numerous further roles have been identified in literature and could be considered as extensions in the revised model. Therefore, the identified roles were subsequently analyzed and compared in terms of relevance. In this process, eleven roles were excluded. Table 2 provides a detailed justification for the exclusion of the respective roles.

Table 2. Excluded roles of the cloud computing ecosystem models from literature.

Excluded roles	Reason for exclusion
Application, Platform and *Infrastructure Resellers*	These three roles are service providers using an external infrastructure and other pre-products to sell a service bundle for their *Customers* [13]. However, these roles strongly overlap with the *Aggregator* role which for a better understanding was renamed in *Aggregator/Reseller*.
Hybrid Cloud Computing Provider	As [28] explore the topic from a product service system (PSS) viewpoint, they added the *Hybrid Cloud Computing Provider*, from whom *Customers* can buy everything from one source. Even though this is a characteristic of PSS [7], it does not reflect the situation of cloud computing.
Market Platform	According to [13] and in line with the role concept, a market platform should be further differentiated with regard to its type of offering in *Application, Platform* and *Infrastructure Market Place*.
Software Platform	A *Software Platform* is a market platform initiated by enterprises in contrast to open market places [35]. But for this study, it is negligible which type of actor is responsible for a specific role.
Terminal Equipment Vendor	The *Terminal Equipment Vendor* [37] is only a special subset of a *Cloud Carrier* offering communication device maintenance service.
Service and *User Auditor*	The difference between the *Service Auditor* and the *User Auditor* is only that they are commissioned by a service provider respectively by the *Customer* [28].
Monitor	A *Monitor* [10] provides permanent control of data privacy and security, controlling the end-to- end connection. This role is, however, only stated once and has high similarities to *Auditors* as well.
Technique Supporting Vendor	As the *Technique Supporting Vendor* offers technical support including software development, testing, provisioning and operation [37], it strongly overlaps with the *Independent Software Vendor*.

After having deleted these eleven roles, the revised cloud computing ecosystem model comprising 18 remaining roles was developed according to the design science paradigm. The goal of the design science process is the creation of an artifact, which has not existed before [31]. Although several ecosystem models such as [10, 28, 32] use the e^3-value method, in this contribution a more simplified representation with nodes for roles and edges for relationships is applied. Moreover, contrary to other existing models, the relationships contain only the service flows, but no financial flows since they are identical for all interrelations. The reason for the selection of this type of representation is to reach a maximum degree of clarity and simplicity.

In order to get a deeper understanding of the cloud ecosystem and to assign real actors to the roles of the revised model and, therefore, to examine whether there exists any further role that has not been integrated so far, eight interviews with experts from service providers fulfilling various roles were conducted. These semi-structured interviews were performed between November 2014 and February 2015 and each lasted 60 to 90 min. As a result, the role of *Data Provider* which was initially excluded within the analysis due to its status as a possibly emerging role for the future in literature was added to the model since it was identified as one of the currently existing roles in industry by the interviewees. Overall, the interviews confirmed the proposed revised model as a complete description of the cloud computing ecosystem.

5   Revised Model of the Cloud Computing Ecosystem

The Passau Cloud Computing Ecosystem Model (PaCE Model) consists of 18 roles and shows the most likely value paths between the roles according to the literature, even though further relations may exist in practice. As illustrated in Fig. 2, the roles are generally grouped into four categories, namely vendor (provider), client, hybrid role and support. A vendor provides one or more services for his clients. In many situations, the customer's and service vendor's role is combined. This is characterized by split nodes and the role is named hybrid. Thus, the *Customer* is the only role that does not deliver a service to any other unit. The group of supporters stands for 3rd party players that do not offer technological services, but conventional services. The legends of the edges explain which main services are provided by the respective roles.

In the following, an overview of the roles being part of the PaCE Model is given according to the four role categories by describing their main tasks and attributes:

Client. The *Customer* is defined as a person or an organization that actually pays all value adding activities in the ecosystem. As the starting point of the service request and the end point of the service delivery, it is the only role that does not offer any cloud computing service [10]. The *Customer* can either buy services directly from a service provider or through one of the *Market Platforms* [33, 34].

Vendor/Provider. An *Independent Software Vendor* develops, tests and maintains the software which is offered as SaaS. Unlike the *Application Provider*, he does not have any real contact with the cloud computing *Customers* [35, 36].

A *Hardware Provider* develops and sells the hardware needed for providing IaaS, such as servers and processors [9, 15].

A *Cloud Infrastructure Provider* or *Physical Infrastructure Provider* provisions and operates the physical infrastructure and, therefore, acts as predecessor of an *Infrastructure Provider* [35].

A *Cloud Carrier* acts as an intermediary providing connectivity and transport of cloud services between consumers and vendors [37]. *Cloud Carriers* offer access to consumers through network, telecommunication and other access devices. A cloud provider sets up the service level agreements (SLAs) with a *Cloud Carrier* to provide services consistent with the level of SLAs offered to consumers. Hence, he might require the *Cloud Carrier* to provide dedicated and encrypted connections [33].

The *Virtualization Vendor* develops and sells virtualization software. Virtualization is one of the main prerequisites of the cloud computing concept [15].

The *Data Provider* is responsible for generating, aggregating and delivering data and information for other roles in the ecosystem [10].

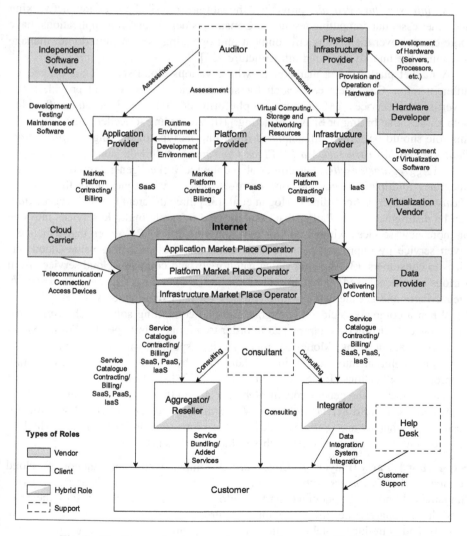

Fig. 2. The Passau cloud computing ecosystem model (PaCE model).

Hybrid Role. An *Application Provider* deploys, configures, maintains and updates the operation of the software applications on its own or outsourced cloud infrastructure. Moreover, this role assumes most of the responsibilities in managing and controlling the applications and the infrastructure, whereas its consumers have limited administrative control of the applications [33, 34]. An *Application Provider* also performs additional tasks, such as monitoring, resource management and failure management [10].

A *Platform Provider* is responsible for managing the cloud infrastructure for the platform, and provisioning tools and executing resources for the consumers to develop, test, deploy and administrate applications [35]. Consumers have control over the applications and possibly the hosting environment settings, but cannot access the infrastructure underlying the platform including network, servers or storage [33].

An *Infrastructure Provider* provisions the storage, physical processing, networking and other essential computing resources. Consumers deploy and run applications, have more control over the hosting environment and operating systems, but do not manage or control the underlying cloud infrastructure [33].

A market platform is a marketplace where various cloud services are offered by different roles. Customers can search for suitable cloud services and providers can advertise their services [28]. On a market platform additional services can be offered to both parties, like billing or SLA contracting [10]. According to Keller and König [13], this role should be further differentiated regarding its type of offering in *Application, Platform* and *Infrastructure Market Place Operator* to fulfill the concept of roles.

An *Aggregator/Reseller*, sometimes also called a Broker, generates, combines and integrates multiple services into one or more new services and offers them to his *Customers* [10, 35]. According to Hogan et al. [33] three different types of *Aggregators* can be distinguished: (1) Parties that combine and integrate multiple services into one or more new services without adding new functionalities. (2) Actors that enhance a given service by improving some specific capability and providing value-added services to consumers. (3) The type which categorizes and compares cloud services from various providers based on certain selection criteria. Therefore, *Customers* can specify their criteria and get the best possible solution for their requirements.

When a company decides to integrate a cloud computing solution, the *Integrator* must convert existing on-premise data in order to migrate it into the cloud or prepare it for certain applications. Moreover, this role is responsible for integrating a cloud computing solution into the existing IT landscape by developing interfaces to other on-premise applications [10]. Some authors [15, 28, 34] synthesize the roles *Integrator* and *Aggregator* to the general role of *Mediator* due to their slightly overlapping tasks. However, the main difference is that an *Integrator* creates an individual solution for customers, whereas an *Aggregator* develops a more standardized solution which is offered to a larger group of users with similar requirements [10].

Support/3rd Party Player. A *Consultant* accompanies the introduction of cloud services at the *Customers* with his knowhow. On the one hand, he is able to provide fundamental knowledge about the market's cloud computing offerings and on the other hand, he can analyze the customer company's processes and prevailing requirements to identify and introduce suitable cloud services. In this context, there are topics like assessment of the cost-benefit ratio, security or billing. However, consulting services are not limited to the *Customer*, providers are also served, for example, to solve technical problems, evaluate the service offering or analyze customers [10, 34].

An *Auditor* conducts independent assessment of cloud services, information system operations, as well as the performance and security of a cloud implementation [33].

The role of *Help Desk* deals with the professional customer support and acts as the primarily contact person for customers [15, 35].

6   Discussion

It is a consensus in all of the examined cloud computing ecosystem models that there are the basic service providers for application and infrastructure. The roles *Platform Provider*, *Market Platforms*, *Consultant*, *Aggregator/Reseller*, *Integrator* and *Customer* are also an integral part of the majority of the models. Less attention is given to *Physical Infrastructure Provider*, *Cloud Carrier*, *Independent Software Vendor*, *Hardware Developer*, *Help Desk*, *Virtualization Vendor*, *Data Provider* and *Auditor* which is surprising due to their huge importance for the value creation process. This clearly shows that several models are focusing on limited aspects and do not reflect the entire complexity of the cloud computing ecosystem.

With its 18 roles, the PaCE Model is the most comprehensive model in literature so far. Nevertheless, there is still room for refinements as some roles of the revised model include a wide range of tasks. It would have been possible, for example, to refine the role of the *Aggregator* further with respect to specific activity types. In order to avoid unnecessary complexity in the model this has not been done. Also the question arises whether the revised model covers all four cloud deployment models (public, private, hybrid and community). It might be that especially for private cloud applications further roles will be found useful. Currently, it is assumed that this area is fully covered by the *Application Market Place Operator*.

The PaCE Model shows the most likely value paths between the roles according to the existing literature. In business practice, however, there might be additional interdependencies. Irrespective of the exact dependencies, each service provider role is generally dependent on its suppliers or partners that they deliver their service in a sufficient way since all roles share a performance outcome responsibility towards the *Customer*. This leads to a high risk situation within the ecosystem as an incident at one role can lead to cascading effects that affect several other participants of the ecosystem. For instance, if the *Infrastructure Provider* fails, then the *Application Provider* and the *Aggregator/Reseller* will not be able to provide their service anymore. Against this background, it is remarkable that there is according to Keller and König [13] only little research regarding the risk management of cloud computing from a network perspective up to now.

An important aspect is the shape of the relationship between real actors and roles: According to the literature, actors oftentimes fulfill more than one role. This circumstance is also confirmed by the conducted expert interviews. However, there is only little research about which typical role clusters exist precisely in practice. One possible combination could comprise for example the roles of *Aggregator/Reseller*, *Integrator*, *Consultant* and *Help Desk* due to their similar range of tasks. An increasing consolidation of roles would lead to a win-win situation as the respective market player could generate greater revenues and *Customers* would only have one contact person in line with the PSS concept. In this way, the selection, procurement and usage of cloud computing services would be facilitated for the *Customers*.

Like other ecosystems, the cloud computing ecosystem is influenced by its environment. But this topic has hardly been addressed in the literature so far. One critical factor among others is that private information can be stored in a country which is different from its owner. Hence, heterogeneous national laws pose a problem [27]. Although some progress has already been made, for instance, through the development of the US-EU Safe Harbor laws, this situation still leads to uncertainties particularly among *Customers* [38]. A further issue is the lack of standards, even though a step towards standardization related to interfaces, protocols or SLAs can be identified. Unfortunately, many different institutions try to define a standard isolated from the other groups [39, 40]. *Costumers* might be, therefore, scared off from a limited portability and interoperability which could lead to a vendor lock-in.

7 Practical Use of the Revised Model, Limitations and Outlook

In this research paper, the existing cloud computing ecosystem models were analyzed and compared with regard to their roles. On the basis of 29 initially identified roles, the PaCE Model comprising 18 roles was developed. In this design process, the findings of eight interviews with experts from cloud service providers were included. The goal of the interviews was to get a deeper understanding of the cloud computing ecosystem and to assign real actors to the roles of the revised model and, therefore, to examine whether there exists any further role that has not been integrated so far. As a result, the role of *Data Provider* which was initially excluded became part of the model. The revised model integrates roles that have been particularly neglected so far, despite their high relevance with respect to the cloud computing value creation. This includes the roles *Physical Infrastructure Provider, Cloud Carrier, Independent Software Vendor, Hardware Developer, Help Desk, Virtualization Vendor, Data Provider* and *Auditor*. Numerous existing models are, thus, focusing on limited aspects of the ecosystem.

The PaCE Model is useful both for researchers and practitioners. Due to the created transparency regarding the cloud ecosystem, researchers can use the revised model as a starting point to guide their research in the cloud computing field. From a provider's perspective, the revised model can serve to recognize where each actor is situated in the market and how they relate to each other. Thereby, they can identify their needs, anticipate potential alliances and create new service provisioning scenarios. This model also supports new market entrants to understand potential markets, to formulate their value model and fully utilize existing services. *Customers* may use the model to gain a deeper understanding of the high complexity of the cloud computing market which can reduce their doubts to move into the cloud.

However, this research is not without limitations. Although some of the examined publications are based on practical observations and the insights from eight expert interviews were included, the revised ecosystem model was mainly developed by means of theoretical literature. In addition, the goal of the conducted interviews was only to investigate whether there exists any further role that has not been integrated so far and not whether all roles being part of the model are covered by real actors. Thus, the validity of the revised model cannot be guaranteed for the practice as "*[t]he dangers of a design science paradigm are an overemphasis on the technological artifacts and a failure to maintain an adequate theory base, potentially resulting in well-designed artifacts that are useless in real organizational settings*" [41]. In order to prove the theoretical foundation and the practical applicability of the model, an evaluation should, therefore, be performed with practitioners of the field. In this context, as the cloud computing market is still a highly dynamic one, the validity of an even originally validated model can also not be assured for the future and is, hence, a topic of continuous adaption and development.

Based on that, an important research topic is to investigate which typical role clusters prevail in practice. Up to now, there exists only the contribution of Pelzl et al. [35] which is limited to service providers in Germany. Furthermore, as the influence of the environment on the cloud computing ecosystem has hardly been addressed by the analyzed models, future research should concentrate more on these external forces as well. Overall, future research needs to explore the cloud computing ecosystem on a broader empirical basis.

References

1. Sultan, N.: Servitization of the IT industry: the cloud phenomenon. Strateg. Change **23**, 375–388 (2014)
2. Baines, T.S., Lightfoot, H.W., Evans, S., Neely, A., Greenough, R., Peppard, J., Roy, R., Shehab, E., Braganza, A., Tiwari, A., Alcock, J.R., Angus, J.P., Bastl, M., Cousens, A., Irving, P., Johnson, M., Kingston, J., Lockett, H., Martinez, V., Michele, P., Tranfield, D., Walton, I.M., Wilson, H.: State-of-the-art in product-service systems. J. Eng. Manuf. **221**, 1543–1552 (2007)
3. Wolfenstetter, T., Floerecke, S., Böhm, M., Krcmar, H.: Analyse der Eignung domänenspezifischer Methoden der Anforderungsverfolgung für Produkt-Service-Systeme. In: 12 Internationale Tagung Wirtschaftsinformatik, Osnabrück, Germany, pp. 210–224 (2015)
4. Floerecke, S., Wolfenstetter, T., Krcmar, H.: Hybride Produkte – Stand der Literatur und Umsetzung in der Praxis. IM+io – Magazin für Innovation Organisation und Management **30**, 61–66 (2015)
5. Velamuri, V.K., Neyer, A.-K., Möslein, K.M.: Hybrid value creation: a systematic review of an evolving research area. Journal für Betriebswirtschaft **61**, 3–35 (2011)
6. Leimeister, J.M., Glauner, C.: Hybride Produkte – Einordnung und Herausforderungen für die Wirtschaftsinformatik. Wirtschaftsinformatik **50**, 248–251 (2008)
7. Sawhney, M.: Going beyond the product: defining, designing and delivering customer solutions. In: Lusch, R.F., Vargo, S.L. (eds.) Toward a Service-Dominant Logic of Marketing: Dialog, Debate, and Directions, pp. 65–80. M. E. Sharpe, Armonk (2006)
8. Zhang, Q., Cheng, L., Boutaba, R.: Cloud computing: state-of-the-art and research challenges. J. Internet Serv. Appl. **1**, 7–18 (2010)

9. Repschläger, J., Pannicke, D., Zarnekow, R.: Cloud Computing: Definitionen, Geschäfts-modelle und Entwicklungspotenziale. HMD – Praxis der Wirtschaftsinformatik **47**, 6–15 (2010)

10. Böhm, M., Koleva, G., Leimeister, S., Riedl, C., Krcmar, H.: Towards a generic value network for cloud computing. In: Altmann, J., Rana, O.F. (eds.) GECON 2010. LNCS, vol. 6296, pp. 129–140. Springer, Heidelberg (2010)

11. Böhm, M., Leimeister, S., Riedl, C., Krcmar, H.: Cloud computing – outsourcing 2.0 or a new business model for IT provisioning? In: Keuper, F., Oecking, C., Degenhardt, A. (eds.) Application Management, pp. 31–56. Gabler, Wiesbaden (2011)

12. Briscoe, G., Marinos, A.: Digital ecosystems in the clouds: towards community cloud computing. In: 3rd IEEE International Conference on Digital Ecosystems and Technologies, Istanbul, Turkey, pp. 103–108 (2009)

13. Keller, R., König, C.: A reference model to support risk identification in cloud networks. In: 35th International Conference on Information Systems, Auckland, New Zealand, pp. 1–19 (2014)

14. Leimeister, S., Böhm, M., Riedl, C., Krcmar, H.: The business perspective of cloud computing: actors, roles and value networks. In: 18th European Conference on Information Systems, Pretoria, South Africa, pp. 1–12 (2010)

15. Bitkom: Cloud Computing – Evolution in der Technik, Revolution im Business. Bitkom (2009)

16. Pelzl, N., Helferich, A., Herzwurm, G.: Systematisierung und Klassifizierung von ASP, Grid- und Utility-Computing Wertschöpfungsketten für Cloud Computing. In: Multikonferenz der Wirtschaftsinformatik, Braunschweig, Germany, pp. 1–13 (2012)

17. Webster, J., Watson, R.T.: Analyzing the past to prepare for the future: writing a literature review. Manag. Inf. Syst. Quart. **26**, 13–23 (2002)

18. Anggraeni, E., Den Hartigh, E., Zegveld, M.: Business ecosystem as a perspective for studying the relations between firms and their business networks. In: Seventh Annual ECCON Meeting, Bergen aan Zee, The Netherlands (2007)

19. Moore, J.F.: Predators and prey: a new ecology of competition. Harvard Bus. Rev. **71**, 75–83 (1993)

20. Peltoniemi, M.V.E.: Business ecosystem as the new approach to complex adaptive business environments. In: E-Business Research Forum, Tampere, Finland, pp. 267–281 (2004)

21. Peltoniemi, M., Vuori, E., Laihonen, H.: Business ecosystem as a tool for the conceptualisation of the external diversity of an organisation. In: Complexity, Science and Society Conference, Liverpool, England, pp. 11–14 (2005)

22. Zahra, S.A., Nambisan, S.: Entrepreneurship and strategic thinking in business ecosystems. Bus. Horiz. **55**, 219–229 (2012)

23. Vaquero, L.M., Rodero-Merino, L., Caceres, J., Lindner, M.: A break in the clouds: towards a cloud definition. ACM SIGCOMM Comput. Commun. Rev. **39**, 50–55 (2008)

24. Weinhardt, C., Anandasivam, D.I.W.A., Blau, B., Borissov, D.I.N., Meinl, D.M.T., Michalk, D.I.W.W., Stößer, J.: Cloud computing – a classification, business models, and research directions. Bus. Inf. Syst. Eng. **1**, 391–399 (2009)

25. Madhavaiah, C., Bashir, I., Shafi, S.I.: Defining cloud computing in business perspective: a review of research. Vis.: J. Bus. Perspect. **16**, 163–173 (2012)

26. Mell, P., Grance, T.: The NIST definition of cloud computing. Nat. Inst. Stand. Technol. **53**, 1–7 (2009)

27. Marston, S., Li, Z., Bandyopadhyay, S., Zhang, J., Ghalsasi, A.: Cloud computing – the business perspective. Decis. Support Syst. **5**, 176–189 (2011)

28. Walterbusch, M., Truh, S., Teuteberg, F.: Hybride Wertschöpfung durch Cloud Computing. In: Thomas, O., Nüttgens, M. (eds.) Dienstleistungsmodellierung 2014, pp. 155–174. Springer, Wiesbaden (2014)
29. Gordijn, J., Akkermans, H.: Designing and evaluating e-business models. IEEE Intell. Syst. **16**, 11–17 (2001)
30. Altmann, J., Ion, M., Bany Mohammed, A.A.: Taxonomy of grid business models. In: Veit, D.J., Altmann, J. (eds.) GECON 2007. LNCS, vol. 4685, pp. 29–43. Springer, Heidelberg (2007)
31. Simon, H.A.: The Sciences of the Artificial. MIT Press, Cambridge (1996)
32. Petkovics, I., Petkovics, A.: ICT ecosystem for advanced higher education. In: 12th International Symposium on Intelligent Systems and Informatics, Subotica, Serbia, pp. 181–185 (2014)
33. Hogan, M., Liu, F., Sokol, A., Tong, J.: Nist Cloud Computing Standards Roadmap, vol. 35. NIST Special Publication, Gaithersburg (2011)
34. Walterbusch, M., Teuteberg, F.: Vertrauen im Cloud Computing. HMD – Praxis der Wirtschaftsinformatik **49**, 50–59 (2012)
35. Pelzl, D.W.I.N., Helferich, A., Herzwurm, G.: Wertschöpfungsnetzwerke deutscher Cloud-Anbieter. HMD – Praxis der Wirtschaftsinformatik **50**, 42–52 (2013)
36. Fang, Z., Chen, J., Yi, M., Wu, Z., Qian, H.: Cloud computing business model based on value net theory. In: 7th IEEE International Conference on E-Business Engineering, Shang-hai, China (2010)
37. Qian, L., Luo, Z., Du, Y., Guo, L.: Cloud computing: an overview. In: Jaatun, M.G., Zhao, G., Rong, C. (eds.) Cloud Computing. LNCS, vol. 5931, pp. 626–631. Springer, Heidelberg (2009)
38. King, N.J., Raja, V.T.: What do they really know about me in the cloud? A comparative law perspective on protecting privacy and security of sensitive consumer data. Am. Bus. Law J. **50**, 413–482 (2013)
39. Fischer, R., Janiesch, C., Strach, J., Bieber, N., Zink, W., Tai, S.: Eine Bestandsaufnahme von Standardisierungspotentialen und -lücken im Cloud Computing. In: 11 Internationale Tagung Wirtschaftsinformatik, Leipzig, Germany, pp. 1359–1373 (2013)
40. Ortiz Jr., S.: The problem with cloud-computing standardization. Computer **44**, 13–16 (2011)
41. von Alan, R.H., March, S.T., Park, J., Ram, S.: Design science in information systems research. MIS Q. **28**, 75–105 (2004)

Author Index

Printed in the United States
by Baker & Taylor Publisher Services

Printed in the United States
By Bookmasters